Out of
Our Minds

Second Edition

Out of Our Minds

*Turning the Tide of Anti-Intellectualism
in American Schools*

Craig B. Howley,
Aimee Howley,
& Edwina D. Pendarvis

PRUFROCK PRESS INC.
WACO, TEXAS

Library of Congress Cataloging-in-Publication Data

Names: Howley, Craig B., author. | Howley, Aimee, author. | Pendarvis, Edwina
  D., author.
Title: Out of our minds : turning the tide of anti-intellectualism in
  American schools / by Craig B. Howley, Aimee Howley, and
  Edwina D. Pendarvis
Description: Second edition, revised edition. | Waco, Texas : Prufrock Press
  Inc., [2016] | Previous edition: 1995. | Includes bibliographical
  references.
Identifiers: LCCN 2016047669| ISBN 9781618216007 (Paperback) | ISBN
  9781618216014 (pdf) | ISBN 9781618216021 (epub)
Subjects: LCSH: Gifted children--Education--United States. | Education--Aims
  and objectives--United States. | Learning, Psychology of.
Classification: LCC LC3993.9 .H69 2016 | DDC 371.95/0973--dc23
LC record available at https://lccn.loc.gov/2016047669

Copyright ©2017, Prufrock Press Inc.

Edited by Lacy Compton

Cover and layout design by Raquel Trevino

ISBN-13: 978-1-61821-600-7

Printed in the United States of America.

At the time of this book's publication, all facts and figures cited are the most current avail-able. All telephone numbers, addresses, and websites URLs are accurate and active. All publications, organizations, websites, and other resources exist as described in the book, and all have been verified. The authors and Prufrock Press Inc. make no warranty or guar-antee concerning the information and materials given out by organizations or content found at websites, and we are not responsible for any changes that occur after this book's publication. If you find an error, please contact Prufrock Press Inc.

Prufrock Press Inc.
P.O. Box 8813
Waco, TX 76714-8813
Phone: (800) 998-2208
Fax: (800) 240-0333
http://www.prufrock.com

Table of Contents

Preface

Initially, the decision to revise *Out of Our Minds* landed us squarely in the middle of the epistemological conundrum of not knowing what we didn't know. That ignorance was a sort of bliss that was soon interrupted by the experience of revising the book.

We thought, in our ignorance, that updating the book would be a matter of reading the most recent research, situating our discussion in relationship to a somewhat changed educational landscape, and, as older people, offering counsel from the perspective of a longer life and career trajectory.

The experience of rewriting the book showed us just how wrong we could be on all counts. The recent research in the field of gifted education offered a limited source of knowledge about intellectual education, and few other fields opened up the topic in a serious way despite intensified rhetoric about "rigor" and "relevance." Furthermore, and notably despite the rhetoric, schooling since 1995 has become a less fruitful place for offering opportunities for intellectual and democratic engagement. In fact, it's now harder even to *imagine* a schooling alternative that would engage ordinary students in meaningful intellectual work on behalf of a common inheritance, experience, or bequest to the future. Twenty-five years of neoliberalism have eroded hope.

We are older and different as well. Since 1995, for instance, our scholarship has led us to understand human variability, especially the variability contributed by cultural and economic circumstances, as both the basis for and an impediment to common purpose and even common decency. Our commitment to the life of the mind is still strong, but also chastened.

Studying rural places has in particular given us insight into why intellectual education might not seem sensible in everyone's view of the world or life plan. At the same time, studying rural places has shown us that making sense of the world is what happens everywhere and for everyone. Our studies have allowed us to admire the Amish, atheist teachers, school principals, mathematics educators, Appalachian children and families, and writers of dissertations in the field of education. One of us published collections of poetry. One of us farmed and retired from farming. One of us became a small business owner.

The world is different and we are different—but making sense of it through writing is the same for all three of us. Over the years we have found the effort difficult. We struggled with this revision in particular to make collective sense of changes in the world from our changing perspectives, and it was especially difficult.

What we believe emerged from the struggle is a nine-chapter book that is both more carefully argued and more thoroughly warranted than its 1995 precursor. It starts with two chapters that define intellect, distinguish it from intelligence, and trace the roots and current trajectory of anti-intellectualism in the United States. Chapter 1 focuses on society at large; Chapter 2 considers schooling more directly. Together they present a collectivist understanding of what intellect contributes to a broadly practical cultural legacy supporting both the self-determination of individuals and cultivation of the common good.

At the heart of the book are four chapters that present evidence of anti-intellectualism in schooling institutions. Chapter 3 discusses the intellectualism (and far more typical anti-intellectualism) of teachers. The impact of credentialism on families' views of schooling systems, opportunities, and outcomes is the topic of Chapter 4, followed by the related discussion of the anti-intellectual university in Chapter 5. A discussion of specific concerns about the anti-intellectual approach to the education of students with evident academic talents concludes the middle section of the book.

Three final chapters offer alternatives, with Chapter 7 providing an ethical warrant for the specific principles and arrangements discussed in the next two. Taken together, the chapters answer the question, "What is a 'true education' and how might schooling contribute to it?" In its broad swath *and* in its specific recommendations, the discussion intends to provoke controversy. The educational and social ills that the earlier sections of the book examine require the kind of deep thinking and conversation that controversy encourages. In recent decades (and perhaps always in the United States), strong vested interests have eclipsed public and professional debate about educational ends and means. Citizens and educators have walked down the primrose path, although not happily in many cases. We think it's time for the debate to heat up—for critique to move to the forefront and then for wisdom to prevail on behalf of ordinary people and a sane planetary future.

The revision of the book coincides with political maneuvers that may officially remove "democracy" as a meaningful aspiration for the country. Rarely has the "banality of evil" (to quote Hannah Arendt) been so evident as a force to be reckoned with on our home shores. Ordinary people can turn the tide; engagement with the life of the mind can help. Perhaps the schools dare not change the social order. We dare intellect to try.

Chapter 1

What Is Intellect and Why Is It Important?

The Origins of Anti-Intellectualism in U.S. Schools

Elementary and secondary schools in the United States apply the term *intellectually gifted* to students who appear to have the greatest academic promise. The practice derives from the conviction that public schooling does not serve able students particularly well, and gifted education is the formal attempt to change that circumstance. The mechanism, in most cases, for determining which students are intellectually gifted is to administer an intelligence test. Although the history of these and similar tests presents a record of misconception and misapplication, other methods of assessing intellectual giftedness are also problematic. The continuing debate about what giftedness really is and how to identify it, however, overlooks the troubling fact that "giftedness" is a social construct and therefore serves particular social, political, and economic interests (e.g., Borland, 2009). It also ignores significant questions about intellectual purpose and worth.

We can bring the substance of intellectual purpose into view by examining the differences between intelligence and intellect, differences that bear on the potential of schooling as a means of developing talent in the United States—talent construed much more broadly than as the actualized performance of students identified as gifted. To consider this issue is to deal more with culture and ideology, however, than with the empirical investigations of the construct of intelligence, the varieties of talent, or the methods proposed for the identification and schooling of gifted students.

The Distinction Between Intelligence and Intellect

Intelligence and intellect represent dramatically different concepts although they are sometimes conflated (e.g., Mussel, 2013). Because *intellect* is a term seldom considered with respect to K–12 schooling, we wish to highlight the differences before interpreting them in greater detail.

Intelligence concerns practical performances; it is quantifiable, often individualistic, and typically instrumental (Borland, 2009). The concept of *intelligence* suggests the presence of inborn qualities of mental superiority or inferiority that can be passed genetically from generation to generation. Certain features of the concept are in the process of change, however, and whether or not the concept itself will survive is not yet clear (e.g., Borland, 2003a). Intellect concerns thoughtful (principally literate) understandings; it is a quality, not a quantity; and it is cultural and expressive. Intellect, in sharp contrast to intelligence, requires intensive nurture, in individuals certainly, but, perhaps more importantly, throughout a culture. It cannot survive otherwise.

Certainly intelligence and intellect are overlapping constructs. We can imagine collectivist understandings of intelligence, as in Daniel Calhoun's (1973) book title, *The Intelligence of a People*, or the ideas presented in *The Wisdom of Crowds* (Surowiecki, 2004), and some psychologists have recently proposed *intellect* as an individual personality trait relating to concern for intellectual matters (e.g., DeYoung, Quilty, Peterson, & Gray, 2014). As the discussion below suggests, however, the contrast between the most individualistic view of the work of the mind and the most collectivist view is what concerns us.

The possibility of an education for a collectivist version of intellect occupies hardly any place in discussions of public policy.[1] Some observers have even claimed that schooling in the United States more widely reflects a strong anti-intellectual current in the culture, suggesting that not talking much about intellect makes sense because, as a culture, we don't value it (e.g., Adler, 1990; Barzun, 1989; Bell, 1976; Cobb, 2015; Hofstadter, 1963; Lasch, 1991; Spann & Davison, 2004).

Even those who advocate for gifted education hardly ever make the case that the purpose of special arrangements for gifted students is to contribute to the collective intellect. Instead, two other arguments typically justify the special accommodations schooling extends to those it identifies as most intellectually able. The first argument asserts that schools must meet the "special educational needs" of gifted students. The second asserts that gifted children are the nation's greatest natural resource in the struggle for global political and economic dominance. Both arguments serve anti-intellectual aims.

In the first argument, "special educational needs" represent the lack of something in students that requires schools to provide unusual services or supports (e.g., Rytivaara & Vehkakoski, 2015). Perhaps the lack refers to sufficient academic progress. Often, though, gifted educators conceptualize the needs of academically capable students in terms of presumed nonacademic deficiencies (e.g., poor social adjustment, uncertainty about career options). The language of "needs" with respect to exceptionally able students parrots the language used to describe the circumstances of students with (exceptional) disabilities, but the usage in both cases portrays a class of students as deficient in competence, agency, or both (Hallahan, 2015). For the exceptionally able, the deficiency is social or emotional, but that deficiency also colors their intellectual "disposition" as worrisome. More importantly, in both cases, the usage—

---

1   By contrast, attention among policy makers in recent decades to critical thinking might be construed as increased concern for the intelligence of individuals—especially when their increased intelligence promotes job readiness or performance on the job (De Fruyt, Wille, & John, 2015). By *collectivist*, we mean to indicate a common human stake in the human mind and its products (cf. Barzun, 1959), and not at all State-dominated control of the mind—as will be obvious in all that follows.

or misusage—obscures schools' responsibility to fill children's time in meaningful ways (White, 2009, 2011).

Because the second argument (i.e., that giftedness is a national resource) compels an even more widespread acceptance than the first, its anti-intellectual basis is perhaps more difficult—and more important—to grasp. The national resource argument reflects human capital theory (see, e.g., Becker, 1964), which maintains that what people know and are able to do helps account for international differences in productivity and "competitiveness" (Tan, 2014). People, in short, exist to serve national security interests, whether construed in economic or military terms.

This argument is dangerous. It runs deep, is accepted widely throughout society, is backed by powerful organizations, and manipulates the patriotic sentiments of the general public. In the United States, the influence of the human capital ideology is pervasive, and it is supported—albeit in different ways—by both ends of the political spectrum, liberals as well as conservatives (Shea, 1989; Tan, 2014). Its powerful supporters, moreover, strive hard to raise their views to the status of common sense. Hence, the human capital argument appears in public service announcements on radio and television (e.g., "Education IS the bottom line!"; "Education pays!") and in official reports by the dozens. Nonetheless, the position that schooling should be a tool for exploiting students—any students—as natural resources rests on questionable ethical and metaphysical assumptions (e.g., Gilead, 2009; Tan, 2014). Indeed, the comparison with natural resources should give us particular pause, since we have a long history of squandering them (Douglas & Walker, 2014).

A curious chain of transformations associated with the development of industrial society and mass schooling has undermined our capacity to care for the intellect. Meyer, Boli, Thomas, and Ramirez (1997) showed that such transformations are occurring worldwide, but they are most firmly established in developed countries, where (1) education is understood to be schooling; (2) literacy is understood as "employability;" (3) employability is understood as the foundation of human capital accumulation; and (4) human capital is understood as the foundation of national economic security (Rose, 2011). This ideological chain preserves for education little "higher" purpose, which now figures as private taste and even as sentimentality (Bell, 1973; Rose, 2011). Across the decades since 1950, this change has been momentous and notably unfriendly to the common good (Blacker, 2013).

As a guide to educational policy and value, human capital arguments about education intend, we believe, to damage intellect—especially intellect in a collectivist sense—so that talent can be directed to instrumental ends. In the long term, educational institutions, under the sway of such instrumentalism, will serve both individuals and society badly (Brown, 1991; Blacker, 2013; Rose, 2011). Our consideration of the origins of anti-intellectualism in U.S. schools and our interpretation of the role of intellect in talent development, therefore, probe this instrumentalism in particular detail.

Intelligence and Intellect

The terms *intelligence* and *intellect* first appeared in written English around the year 1390. Originally synonyms, by 1430 writers had already begun to distinguish usage of the two terms, with intellect referring to the faculty of the mind that knows by reason rather than by intuition (i.e., not by emotion, feeling, or sensing). They used intelligence, then as now, to mean "degree of understanding," and, especially, superior quickness of understanding (Oxford English Dictionary, 1928/1971). The term *intelligence* applied equally to animals and humans, whereas the term *intellect* applied only to humans. No one credits dogs with the possession of intellect, for instance.[2] Intellect represents the complexity of understanding, critique, and imagination of which the human mind is capable. Already in 1430, moreover, intellect had to do with what passes between minds and generations of humans, for reason (unlike intuition) concerns explicit, negotiated meaningfulness.

Centuries of use have made the original distinctions sharper still, especially in response to the widespread acceptance of psychology as

---

2   Certainly dogs and horses (and many other species) have been shown scientifically to possess intelligence, intuition, devotion, and many admirable qualities, but those animals have not produced works that embody such qualities for common apprehension. Their evolution still proceeds biologically. Humans are now evolving culturally, and this fact (Renfrew, 2007) has profound implications for intellect—and its common apprehension.

a science (Adler, 1990). To specify "degree of understanding," educators have, for more than 100 years, measured intelligence as an actual quantity. In this usage, intelligence refers to a student's potential for academic work, even if, in specifying purported educational need, eventual practice sidesteps academics. The observed variation in this quantity is widely, if mistakenly, presumed to be inborn (see, e.g., Kamin, 1977; Mukherjee, 2016; Papierno, Ceci, Makel, & Williams, 2005; Scheffler, 1985). And there has even been much heated debate about the extent to which "degree of understanding" can be passed genetically from parent to child (see, e.g., Kamin, 1977; Mukherjee, 2016). The debate is fueled by the important political and ethical agendas that depend on answers to the question. The rightist position in the debate (see, e.g., Herrnstein & Murray, 1994) seems to desire confirmation of a "natural aristocracy" of merit that would justify the unequal distribution of society's goods. The leftist position is inspired largely by abhorrence of such a determination (see, e.g., Fancher, 1985). Mukherjee (2016), a geneticist, observed that complex traits like intelligence are subject to a variety of environmental mediators: What such traits *are* is socially as well as genetically complex.

As a result of quantifying intelligence, however, psychological expertise originally determined that some students possessed intelligence in very small measure and, also, that most students were not very adept academically. In consequence, we have, according to some commentators, run our schools as if most students could not understand very much (e.g., Barzun, 1959, 1989; Bridgeland, DiIulio, & Balfanz, 2009; Lasch, 1979; Sohasky, 2016), and as if we were not sure what to do with the few who supposedly could.

In comparison to intelligence, intellect—as an idea at least—suffered neglect. The demise, Adler (1990) pointed out, began in the 1600s, as the materialist viewpoint began to exercise dominion ("intellectual dominion," in fact) over the realm of thought.

In the modern era, then, "mind" harbors obscured meanings that we in this book intend to help rehabilitate in the term *intellect*. If you search for contemporary works that discuss intellect, you will most often encounter a discussion of mind. Mind is conceived as an adjunct function of the brain; it represents in that usage the mystery (of thinking and thoughts) that remains when scientific knowledge of brain structure and function is withdrawn. This view has reconstituted mind as a feature, albeit an obscure one, of the brain, particularly of an individual brain—my mind, your mind, but certainly not our mind. The brain, though, attains a collective generality because it is an organ accessible to natural science. We all have one.

The brain, in this view, is an intriguing clockwork that holds the secrets of a constant human nature; to understand the brain is to see clearly what form of education is proper. Hence, even putative knowledge of the brain serves as a warrant for well-intentioned educators (such as those who would construe math instruction differently for girls and boys on the basis of supposed neural differences). According to an increasing number of critics (e.g., Busso & Pollack, 2015; Grant, 2015; Nixon, 2012), however, "brain-based" education (e.g., Wolfe, 2010) is little more than a tool for marketing educational products, perpetuating educational orthodoxies, or both. This book, by the way, is not proposing an intellect-based education, just one that better honors the common intellect and individual minds.

The disappointment in all this fanfare about the brain is that understanding the brain does not help us construct or grasp the meaning of our thoughts at all! The brain has become an object to which its legions of devotees irrationally attribute great power. In the meantime, intellect has nearly vanished from consideration (Robinson, 2010).

Intellect, like intelligence and mind, might in the course of its history have been understood as a personal attribute. But it is, in fact, not taken as inborn, and, though greater or lesser intellects seem to exist, no one troubles too much about measuring the degrees of difference.[3]

Intellect can be distinguished from intelligence in an additional important way. To exist at all, intellect, unlike intelligence, requires nurture. Lots of nurture, and over a long period. Great intelligence, by contrast, is self-disclosing, emerging by virtue of its own force in the behavior of its possessor. This is part of the reason that advocacy of an intellectual education is so difficult in the United States; we have the sense that natural endowment ought to be left alone to flourish or floun-

---

3 Nevertheless, there does seem to be interest in the related project of assessing the relative worth of ideas (e.g., Boynton & Fischer, 2011; Kudrowitz & Wallace, 2013), a project that might well be described as critique (Howley, 2009).

der in its own way. We have no such misconceptions about intellect, even now. It is perhaps too expensive to nurture.

Despite the nurture it requires, intellect is neither "achievement" nor "attainment" as commonly understood. Both achievement (test results) and attainment (credentials) are testimonials. Testimonials of this sort are a proxy for realms of knowledge—skills and meanings—that derive their integrity from the care that a culture accords intellect. One may speak of this care and all that it encompasses as the institution of intellect. When the institution of intellect is weak, inferences about knowledge from mere testimonials become particularly unreliable (Barzun, 1959; Bell, 1973).

Concern about such unreliability has come mainly from conservatives in the 1950s, again in the 1990s, and continuing into the 21st century. They have complained that high school and college diplomas verify little that is useful to sustaining and expanding America's global economic competitiveness—that, in fact, the quality of graduates has been declining. Unreliable testimonials, in this way, appear to threaten the instrumental heart of the human capital scheme (e.g., Barton, 2006). In response to the perceived threat, education reform proposals have called repeatedly for greater "rigor": new kinds of testing, more consistent testing, and diplomas that are more difficult to get (e.g., Lee & Ready, 2009).

But rigor by itself can no more rehabilitate the institution of intellect than cold showers can eliminate drug addiction. It can characterize good pedagogy and bad, it can be applied for the right or wrong reasons, and it can, and often does, enforce thoughtlessness and silence critique (see, e.g., Oxley, 2005; Saltman & Gabbard, 2003; Walters & Lareau, 2009).

Even as the attempt to make schools "accountable" and to "restore" academic rigor moves forward, the most common view remains instrumental: The principal role of academic learning should be to serve economic ends. Official commissions and blue-ribbon panels have seldom taken any other view (Berliner, 1992; Glass, 2007). Schooling aims, as it has for a very long time, to inculcate just those habits, attitudes, and skills that make it legitimate in the eyes of powerful economic interests (e.g., Connell, 2013; Glass, 2007; Lakes, 2008).

In contrast to the instrumental view, an intellectual view of schooling is captured in Frank Moretti's (1993) clever response to his students:

> When forced to put it [i.e., the purpose of education] succinctly to my students, I say that each person under the best circumstances takes up the challenge of learning what he or she has become without having chosen it and in the process sees new worlds and lays claim to a new freedom. (p. 125)

Care of the intellect, in this view, has little to do with rigor—or its lack—in factory schooling. Part of the reason is that serious educational consideration of intellect pertains almost exclusively to higher education. Intellect is considered esoteric: It is not for children and it is certainly not for everyone. We take a far different view.

Literacy and Intellect

Confining intellect to the university, we think, is a large part of the problem. All people possess minds capable of an intellectual turn; more, the intellectual opus of books, music, art, and meaningful creations from all times and places constitutes a world that belongs to all humans by right of inheritance (Arendt, 1958). People can be separated from this world only through intellectual deprivation. Under a regime of schooling fashioned to accumulate human capital, such deprivation can become commonplace, but it also invades universities (Barrow, 1990; Cobb, 2015), even—or especially—the most elite among them (Deresiewicz, 2014).

A true education, by contrast, must base its actions on respect for the intellect. And respect for students, at all levels of their schooling, ultimately derives from respect for the intellect (Weissglass, 2012; What Students Want from Teachers, 2008).

Such respect has several sources. First, it must entail respect for the interests of intellect: contemplation, understanding, meaning, interpretation, inquiry, and critique. Second, it must entail respect for the accumulating artifacts of intellect, especially as embodied in meaningful written expression. These two are prerequisite, and they are often lacking in the institutions of mass education (increasingly including the universities). Finally, respect for the intellectual potential of all students is a pedagogical necessity that arises from the other two. In the typical circumstance, all three forms of respect are lacking (e.g., Blacker, 2013; Deresiewicz, 2014; Saltman, 2014).

In a discussion of literacy and intellect, Winchester (1987), charted the scope of intellect:

> The notion of intellect maps out both a realm of interest and a set of powers or dispositions. . . . It is on disciplines that intellect is properly exercised, since the object of intellection is the increase in knowledge, both personally and collectively, of a certain kind or kinds. (p. 23)

Barzun put it more tersely. For him, intellect is simply "the form intelligence takes in the artificial products we call learning" (Barzun, 1959, p. 216). Although Barzun's misguided confidence in intelligence (i.e., confidence that it is a phenomenon of nature rather than a social construct) is difficult to share, given what we now know about intelligence, these two accounts show a key feature of intellect missing in most accounts of mind and intelligence: Intellect participates in a dialogue among individual minds and the historical community of learning. Intellect covers a domain that the individualistic concepts of "intelligence" and "mind" omit entirely.

A person who participates in the historical community of learning reveals intellect as a turn of mind—a disposition—whether that person is an "intellectual" or not. We would argue that cultivation of such a disposition over the long term is what makes an intellectual, however. Most discussions of intellectuals examine not intellect, but social roles (e.g., Brym, 1980; Gouldner, 1982). Intellectuals are not those with an intellectual disposition, but jobholders whose positions involve mental labor—information specialists, academics, lawyers, and various species of media personalities and opinion manipulators (Misztal, 2012). Some of the people in these roles may exhibit an intellectual turn of mind, but many obviously do not (Moretti, 1993).

What Is Intellect?

Accounts of anti-intellectualism generally focus on intellectuals as the victims. The paragon intellectual, in this view, is the university scholar, and Hofstadter (1963) takes this approach in *Anti-Intellectualism in American Life*. Barzun (1959), by contrast, counted university scholars ("by choice or impressment pedants") among the three greatest enemies of the intellect. The two views overlap, for the state of the intellect in the university—as Barzun (1959) understood—derives from the disregard of intellect prevalent in the culture at large. Intellectuals are part of a larger social apparatus that endorses certain views of the world, discounts others, and legitimizes the deployment of power (Lyotard, 1979/1984; Postman, 1992). Meaningfulness and criticism are not actually functional features of this apparatus, although they may adorn it.

Despite the shortcomings of those who occupy the social role of "intellectual," care for the historical community of learning is most evident in the best work of the mind of one who is truly intellectually disposed. This work might take form in writing, or in the building of houses, the manufacture of machinery, in speech, or even in relationships. The intellect is active even when not in view. Still, the intellect that shapes such works would be most accessible to others, especially in writing, so that it could enter widely into the historical community of learning (Winchester, 1987).

Thus, in terms of formal learning, which must concern us most immediately in this book, literacy is the basis of the historical community of learning. Literacy for this purpose involves the habitual use of, and affection for, text as the chief tool of thought. Literacy is the favorable disposition toward and habit of engaging the mind with text to construct meaning (cf. Brym, 1980; Eisner, 1983; Hofstadter, 1963; Storr, 1988; Winchester, 1987). Literacy of this sort is the handmaiden of intellect (much as mathematics is said to be the handmaiden of science). It is the tool through which human minds most often work, and the institution of intellect becomes stronger or weaker as people maintain it through literacy. Whereas a few individuals may become "intellects," many people must develop intellect as a "turn of mind" if the institution of intellect is to flourish.

Intellect can most certainly operate without literacy, but it does so at great disadvantage. For example, Temple Grandin, an engineer and intellectual with autism whose primary mode of thinking is "in pictures" (Grandin, 2006), nevertheless sees the importance of sharing her ideas in writing. According to Grandin (2006), "[T]he only place on Earth where immortality is provided is in libraries. This is the collective memory of humanity" (p. 173).

Collective memory is a legacy we all need because we all have a limited view of matters that concern heart, mind, and soul. The perspective of our own times has similar limits. But with literacy, intellect has a way to struggle beyond the limits of personal and time-bound association. Literacy offers the mind the chance to extend thought into experience, to render experience as thought, and to represent reality in forms it would not otherwise take. Eisner (1983), for example, wrote of literacy as "the generic process of securing and expressing meaning within patterned forms of expression" (p. 50). The patterns to which Eisner referred are those of the historical community of learning; they represent meaningful traditions. The responsibility of intellect—and of minds that take an intellectual turn—is to develop and extend those traditions.

Literacy and media. Readers may conclude that the forgoing discussion reflects a conservative view of literacy. The meaning of "literacy," though, seems to be changing as media other than text become more pervasive than the written word, even for conveying information. Of course, the arts have always used media in addition to text. But visual, auditory, and film media have come increasingly to augment, and in some cases, replace, written narrative.

And even the written word is changing as a result of computer technology. For instance, reading on-screen may already outpace reading on paper in affluent countries and in the cities of less affluent ones (e.g., Goodwyn, 2014). Although schools are lagging behind this curve, more and more classrooms are presenting instructional material on the screens of desktops, laptops, tablets, and cell phones (Wood & Howley, 2012).

Furthermore, children and youth are using media other than books and periodicals during a great deal of their spare time. A study conducted by the Kaiser Family Foundation (2010), for example, found that during the first 10 years of the 21st century, children and teenagers, 8 to 18 years old, went from spending an average of about 4 1/2 hours a day watching screen media, including television, to about 7 1/2 hours a day.

Interestingly, however, this increase did not appear to affect the amount of time they spent reading. Although the time spent reading decreased slightly, that decrease reflected only the time youngsters spent reading periodicals, such as newspapers and magazines. Time spent reading books actually increased a little, from 21 to 25 minutes a day.

Whether the proliferation of "media" has made students more or less literate is debatable, as is the quality of their intellectual engagement with movies, video games, websites, and social media. For example, some research shows that movie viewing may have a direct and immediate influence on viewers' political attitudes (Adkins & Castle, 2014). Does this finding suggest that popular movies bring political issues to the attention of viewers so they can consider them critically? Or does it provide evidence that popular movies have the power to change attitudes by encouraging adherence to particular perspectives without the bothersome mediation of critique? Furthermore, the extent to which these media enlarge or narrow the perspectives of their users is unclear. It seems premature to herald the usefulness or importance of "media literacy," but certainly much of the world's population is using electronic media, and everyone needs to reflect on what he or she is doing—here as in other realms of life.

Arguably, the proliferation of media has provided unprecedented access to information and ideas. For example, Massive Open Online Courses (MOOCs) offer systematic high school and university level instruction of variable, though often moderate to high, quality to anyone who wishes to enroll (Terras & Ramsay, 2015). And content made available through MOOCs (or other online sources) might benefit students whose learning requires engagement with materials that are more advanced than what is readily available in their local schools (e.g., Thomson, 2010). Whether or not these types of materials (or any types of materials) help cultivate intellect is to a great extent related to how they are used. Literary classics can be used in stultifying ways (e.g., Bartlett, 1995), for instance, and so, too, can online content, even high-quality online content.

Intellect: Inquiry, Critique, and Received Wisdom

As the discussion thus far suggests, the definition of intellect is not as precise as some might wish it to be. For instance, those hoping to make practical decisions about schooling might prefer greater clarity to help them determine which features of schooling (past, present, or future) support the development of intellect and which undermine it or don't support it very well. Answers like "it depends" are not helpful from their perspective.

Nevertheless, the exercise of intellect depends on processes that are difficult to observe, and that circumstance contributes to the difficulty of rendering a precise definition. Furthermore, the substance that provokes intellectual engagement varies from person to person, locale to locale, and time period to time period. Does daily reading of poetry by Emily Dickinson represent intellectual engagement? How about creation of increasingly complex imaginary worlds in Minecraft (currently a popular video game and community)?

These questions point to the difficulty of grounding intellectual engagement in any prescribed content or set of activities. As we will discuss later in the book, intellectual engagement entails efforts to connect to, understand, make sense of, evaluate, criticize, and expand a tradition of work that involves intellect. Each of these types of engagement differs from the others, sometimes in ways that are substantial. For instance, connecting to and seeking meaning from classic works of fiction contributes to sustaining a tradition, without changing it at all. Writing a novel that follows stylistic conventions of novel writing participates in the tradition without radically changing it, but creating a work that expands the novelistic tradition into a new form of literature may radically alter our understandings and use of fiction (e.g., Atkins, 2003). Thomas Kuhn (1962) described these distinctions within the sciences as working within, in contrast to shifting, a prevailing paradigm. And, of course, high culture productions (e.g., poetry) are merely the most elite realm of work that engages intellect. The appreciation of intellect must go very much further: to low culture, domestic culture, and the public realm (see Chapter 8).

A tradition (or a prevailing paradigm within a tradition) has the potential both to enable and constrain intellectual engagement.

Moreover, observers and critics might differ markedly in their assessment of when such constraints and affordances are at play and how they operate. For example, some observers of digital games view them as a new art form (e.g., Atkins, 2003), some see them as a new way to teach reasoning (e.g., Ravenscroft, 2007), and some see them as consumer products that encourage acceptance of and participation in late-capitalist consumerism (e.g., Higgins, 2016). Indeed, inquiry in mathematics and science is subject to a similar range of interpretations (e.g., Skovsmose, 2010).

Because there is no way to resolve such debates, viewing intellectual engagement as varied and potentially dangerous seems to make sense. One of the potential dangers of engaging in intellectual work is that participation in a tradition or paradigm within a tradition can narrow someone's intellectual scope and limit that person's willingness to be self-critical. These dynamics, for instance, turn some scholars into pedants and others into ideologues. Notably, and in spite of individual examples of intellectual ossification and even deceit, such dynamics do not turn scholarship, inquiry, sense making, and critique either into pedantry or into indoctrination (e.g., Grafton, 2015). That intellectual engagement carries the seeds of anti-intellectualism seems fitting—engagement entails commitment, and commitment can (and often does) lead a person to become a believer (and even a true believer, as in Hoffer, 1951). This insight about intellectual engagement helps situate several different interpretations of where an anti-intellectual perspective on life and learning might come from.

The Roots of Anti-Intellectualism

The roots of anti-intellectualism are deep in American culture. For the historian Richard Hofstadter (1963), evangelism and primitivism were the sources of anti-intellectualism; for the cultural critic Jacques Barzun (1959), the sources were art, science, and philanthropy; and for the sociologist Daniel Bell (1973, 1976), the sources were consequences of the cultural contradictions of modernism.

These three thinkers actually have much more in common than their differential diagnoses might suggest. They hold to similar views of culture, and each entertains serious doubts about the beneficent influence of technology. The following section, however, is not a treatment of American culture generally; it is an application of cultural interpretation to schooling.

Barzun, Bell, and Hofstadter—despite differences in their terms—share a disdain for (1) schooling administered in the name of some limited end (e.g., career access) and (2) schooling that regards children as beings whose natural course of development requires only that adults get out of their way. They find such educational perspectives intellectually, culturally, politically, and economically counterproductive. As Barzun (1959, 1989) implied, they actively corrupt the historical community of learning.

Instrumentalism and Sentimentality

As a guiding principle for schooling, instrumentalism so restricts the realm of ideas as to subjugate intellect to the service of particular ends. Much is lost, including reflectiveness, critique, judgment, and ethical action (Weizenbaum, 1976).

Nevertheless, Americans seem to want schools that produce immediate, practical effects "in the real world," which increasingly comes to mean teaching the skills that business leaders and politicians believe to be economically useful (Labaree, 2014). Schooling must at the very least appear to be useful. Hofstadter (1963) long ago asserted that Americans had made "a mystique of practicality" (p. 237) such that the results obtained were a constant disappointment (see p. 305).

The mystique of practicality involves great expectations that practicality alone, as the foundation of schooling, cannot provide. For example, the mystique embeds belief in schooling as the path out of poverty for hard-working individuals from impoverished families—a very great expectation indeed, and supremely practical were the odds not stacked so strongly against it, as they are (Glass, 2007; Leyva, 2009; Sturges, 2015; Tienken, 2012).

Among other things, sentimentality focuses misguidedly on imagined excellence in the past or on great practical breakthroughs by great innovators such as those who, across the generations, judged schooling irrelevant (Brinkley, 2004; Isaacson, 2011). As a standard of judgment for practicality, sentimentality is perhaps the worst possible standard. But the problem lies primarily in instrumentalism, and the sentimentality functions to misrepresent (and even destabilize) the institution of schooling so it remains attentive to corporate purpose (see, e.g., Blacker, 2013; Glass, 2007; Saltman & Gabbard, 2003; Shea, 1989). Eventually the entire enterprise must collapse; recent developments suggest to some observers (e.g., Blacker, 2013), in fact, that collapse is well underway.

Chapter 6 discusses sentimentality—affective education—within gifted education. But, on its own terms, sentimentality also has a long tradition in the rhetoric of American schooling (Arendt, 1954/1968; Barzun, 1959, 1989; Katz, 1968; Lasch, 1979; Zembylas, 2008). For instance, early American school reformers sought to improve the character and attitudes of children at least as much as to reform the organization of schooling (Egan, 2002; Katz, 1968). More recently some have believed that before schools can deal with ideas, they must first shape character (Bennett, 1988; Thanksgiving Statement Group, 1984); that dealing with ideas is a form of character education (Carr, 2014; Orr & Klein, 1991); that schools must either inculcate values (Deaton & McNamara, 1984; Etzioni, 1985) or clarify them (Vann, 1988); that promoting social and emotional well-being takes precedence over or "balances" academics (Wynne, 1988); that spiritual needs merit special emphasis (e.g., Kolander & Chandler, 1990; van der Merwe & Habron, 2015); or that making reading fun takes precedence over teaching significant texts (Warnick, 2015).[4]

The criterion of worth for both instrumentalism and sentimentality, though, is the ordinary operation of the world—competition on (and for) the job, in society, and, in personal circumstances, functional adjustment ("happiness"). Still, until quite recently, the way this

---

4 One must, for real engagement, take pleasure in intellectual pursuits; this sort of "fun," though, is very much an acquired taste, and often one acquires it slowly. Intellectually irrelevant fun works to divert (one meaning of "fun") students from engagement (see Jardine, 1995).

anti-intellectual combination has worked itself out in schooling has been sufficiently effective to satisfy the needs of industrial-era business and the State[5] (Committee for Economic Development, 1985). Recent developments, however, have introduced the neoliberal twist.

The Neoliberal Twist

The post-industrial era, beginning about 1970, called for a new kind of improvement of schooling, not simply for the old quest for the right means to well-worn ends, but for a "radically" new end (Edelstein & Schoeffe, 1989; National Center on Education and the Economy, 1990; Stewart, 2012). From this perspective, the old form of schooling would no longer suffice; assembly-line work, like agricultural work before it, was in rapid decline in Western nations as the global economy supported the allocation of low-wage industrial and service jobs to employees in the developing world (e.g., Foster, McChesney, & Jonna, 2011; Piketty, 2014).

The new end for schooling, however, could be no less instrumental than that supporting mass schooling in the industrial era. Still focused on the needs of corporations, the rhetoric of globalization called for American schools to produce large numbers of employees to whom "more complicated" tasks could be successfully delegated (Bishop & Carter, 1991; Committee for Economic Development, 1985; Secretary's Commission on Achieving Necessary Skills, 1991; Stewart, 2012).

Despite the rhetoric, economies in the United States and in other developed nations would actually be unable to guarantee full employment to well-prepared graduates (e.g., Furman, 2016), in part because of the practice of offshoring technical work (e.g., Craig & Gunn, 2010) and in part because of the benefits to corporations of maintaining an

5   We use the term "State" to indicate the nation constituted as a durable whole, following political theorist James Scott (1998) in this usage. The State in this sense is the durable national entity, and not the 50 states of the United States, for instance, and not the particular national governments that succeed one another as a result of national elections. One might imagine "the American State" as the arrangements that persist absent Republicans and Democrats; or as the federal Constitution, state constitutions, accumulated case law, rules and regulations, and the bureaus and offices that survive changes in administrations. Consult Scott (1998) for additional information.

"industrial reserve army"[6] (e.g., Rigakos & Ergul, 2011). Furthermore, even in face of the gap between the rhetoric (e.g., increased prosperity under globalization) and the reality (e.g., increasing income inequality within nations such as the U.S.), powerful elites were able to impose policies that ostensibly improved the system of schooling while actually undermining it and its public nature (e.g., Giroux, 2014; Waitoller & Kozleski, 2015).

These dynamics, referred to by terms such as *neoliberalism* and the *New Capitalism*, supported a strongly individualistic and instrumental orientation to schooling. Giroux (2014) called this orientation *market-driven illiteracy*, claiming that it "has eviscerated the notion of freedom, turning it largely into the desire to consume and invest exclusively in relationships that serve only one's individual interests" (p. 6).

The new end for schooling—individual success in the marketplace (for some) and total failure (for many others)—is every bit as intellectually narrow as the older aim (i.e., preparation in basic skills and life adjustment), yet far more insidious. According to Giroux (2014), among others (e.g., Blacker, 2013), it destroys not only public schooling, but also the whole conception of the public on which democracy depends. In fact, the neoliberal reframing of the aims of schooling twists the rhetoric of intellectual engagement and accomplishment in ways that obliterate the concept of intellect as a human legacy to which all are entitled. It replaces intellect with the narrowest and most self-serving of all possible constructions of intelligence. Explaining this trend and its elitist implications, Dorling (2010) claimed,

> As inequality becomes ever more deeply entrenched into contemporary everyday life, there has been a creeping return to the idea of innate ability. At the same time, priorities in education have become increasingly determined by a utilitarian concern for the needs of the economy, rather than for developing the thinking of each child. (p. 35)

---

6 This Marxian idea references capitalism's need for unemployed workers—available for employment during periods of expansion within an industry and readily laid off during periods of retrenchment. These are not, of course, the most-skilled, but usually the least-skilled, workers.

Some Consequences of Anti-Intellectualism

What happens when schooling venerates the needs of the economy while simultaneously abandoning all efforts to nurture the thinking of each child? Many answers come to mind. For our purposes, two seem particularly useful to explore. First is the narrowing of life's meaning that comes with the widespread acceptance of the idea that the worth of humans equates to their contribution to "human capital." Second is the restriction of social justice that results from a failure to nurture thinking. In the discussion that follows, we examine these consequences briefly; throughout the rest of the book, we return to these themes to ground our critique and support our consideration of alternatives.

You Are What You Earn

The neoliberal perspective applies Darwinian principles to the analysis of society (Giroux, 2011; Tienken, 2012). It rekindles the claims made by social Darwinists, like Herbert Spencer and William Graham Sumner, who equated social competition (especially competition in a market economy) with the biological processes of natural selection (Darder, 2012; Goodman, 1989; Leyva, 2009; Russett, 1976).

From the perspective of social Darwinists, individualism affirms the individual's "natural right" to participate in life's contest. This view represents a significant reinterpretation of what was originally meant by natural rights (as in "inalienable" natural rights)—for example, the rights to life, liberty, and the pursuit of property. Unlike the views of the Enlightenment philosophers who framed the idea of natural rights, the social Darwinist reinterpretation does not construe these rights as the entitlement of all humans because they are human. Rather, individuals' innate differences determine their rights—their eligibility to participate in life's contest and the contingent outcomes of the contest (thereby alienating the inalienable). According to Russett (1976), social Darwinists believed that "all men were created unequal, for inequality was a law of nature. Man vied with man to win the rewards of nature, and victory went to the fit" (p. 98).

Among strict social Darwinists, the role of public education was to provide a setting for this natural contest, but, if taken too far, schooling could well be socially counterproductive. Spencer, for example, believed that public education, like other social services, would interfere with the natural processes of social selection. Schooling might therefore get in the way of naturally unfolding social progress (DeYoung, 1989; Russett, 1976). Social Darwinism was an ideology that accorded well with the realities of 19th-century laissez-faire capitalism—and also, the return to it in the late 20th century.

Many public educators in the early 20th century did, however, embrace the premises of social Darwinism (Gould, 1981). For them, public schools were a theater in which the struggle among unequal participants could be managed efficiently. Social selection, as a totally natural process, inevitably wasted some talent that might otherwise be profitably redeemed. Schools could do better: by grading, sorting, and tracking the various kinds of talents into programs best suited to them. Society, after all, needed all sorts of talents. Schools could accomplish the task of adapting talents to society's needs more efficiently—that is, more scientifically—than nature. This perspective was common sense among educators of the early decades of the century (Callahan, 1962).

Scientific management of public schools was, in fact, a fad of this era, but it was an influential fad, responsible for laying down the resilient "factory model" of schooling (Callahan, 1962; Tyack, 1974). The scientific managers carved out a new and enduring role for schools, with special reference to students' unequal merits. Schools were henceforth responsible for distributing human capital to the most deserving. According to Spring (1986), "The schools were to create a society based on merit by objectively selecting and preparing students for their ideal places in the social order" (p. 224).

The improved technology of education (e.g., age-grade placement, psychological testing, ability grouping) helped to establish this new "meritocratic" function for schools. At the same time, advocates of scientifically managed schools could argue that technology would make instruction more humane by individualizing it. A very similar perspective, however, underlies the neoliberal claim that science can (and ought to) guide schooling practice. Daza (2013) called this perspective, "neoliberal scientism," which she defined as "the uneven, albeit worldwide, convergence of the discourses of business and pre-Kuhnian views of science, reconfiguring complex ecological and social challenges as apolitical (and often economic) problems in need of technical (nonideological) solutions" (p. 604).

The fundamental problem with these two similar formulations of social Darwinism (i.e., scientific management and neoliberalism), however, is not their misconceptions about science. Instead, it's their answer to the question posed as the title of a collection of essays by Wendell Berry (1990): *What Are People For?* In both formulations, people exist for the use of more powerful others. Whether the contest is a political or economic one and whether it implicates corporations, nations, states or provinces within a nation, or even one community positioned against another—the purpose of the individual is to serve as cannon fodder for the fight. Schooling readies the combatants in part by itself being a site of combat. This interpretation makes sense of the otherwise nonsensical idea of "holding students accountable for their own learning." This too-common phrase has meaning only if every student's learning is thought to be accomplished on behalf of someone other than themselves.

The alternative is to imagine schooling that would enable students to accomplish learning on behalf of what they value most. Of course, this perspective can fit well with social Darwinism, but only in a regime that convinces students that earning a lot of money (or prestige or power) represents the highest value. Other values, in contrast, make better sense of human life (e.g., Berry, 1990): seeking fulfillment, honoring family, sustaining community, keeping the planet alive, improving life for others. These answers address Berry's question in different ways—but all from perspectives that disclose self-determination and attend to higher purpose. They fit well with Eagleton's (2003) answer:

> What are human beings for? The answer is surely: nothing—but this, precisely, is the point. Our function is to be functionless. It is to realize our nature as an end in itself. . . . "Nature" here means something like "the way we are most likely to flourish." (p. 120)

Unthinking, Thoughtlessness, and the Unthinkable

Acting without consideration of consequences is what the word *unthinking* means—a meaning that shows the connection between thought and moral action. The opposite of thoughtful action, on this view, is mere behavior. The contrast is important to the interpretation of evil offered by Hannah Arendt (1963). From her perspective, we manifest thoughtlessness when we fail to distinguish right from wrong, fall prey to ideology, or allow everyday life to lull us into unquestioning acceptance of injustice (Schiff, 2013). The perpetuation of evil belongs on the continuum of thoughtlessness, according to Arendt, and we counteract it by exercising thought routinely through narrative, critique, and public discourse (Schiff, 2013).

Arendt's interpretation treats evil as banal because it depends on the everyday thoughtlessness to which all of us are prone. But we are all also capable of thoughtfulness, even though nothing but our impulse to be virtuous or contribute to a good society compels that we exercise it (Orne & O'Connor, 2012). In fact, compulsion is beside the point: a theory of thoughtfulness positions it as something that by nature must be self-generating and self-sustaining (see, e.g., Orne & O'Connor, 2012; Schiff, 2013). It's the analog to realizing our nature (Eagleton, 2003). Wanting to be thoughtful is, in fact, the end to which an intellectual education leads. Because, unlike learning itself, learning to be thoughtful confronts obstacles in the political world (e.g., neoliberal ideology); adults with a disposition to be thoughtful must be the ones to sponsor an intellectual education for the children and young adults in their care.

Chapter 2

The Impact of Anti-Intellectualism on Schooling

The previous chapter contrasted intellect with intelligence and examined the benefits of engagement with intellect for individuals, communities, and societies. It also considered some of the most serious consequences of an instrumental view of learning—a view that we, among others (e.g., Eigenberger & Sealander, 2001; Elias, 2008; Hook, 2004), term *anti-intellectualism*.

The current chapter builds on ideas presented in Chapter 1 by looking at the implications of anti-intellectualism for schooling in the United States. It argues that anti-intellectualism grounds schooling in a narrow version of practicality that suppresses critique and dissent by suppressing the cultivation of thinking, while at the same time denying students opportunities to make sense of their circumstances either in the present or for the future (see also Aronowitz, 2008; Brown, 1991; Deresiewicz, 2014; Egan, 2001; White, 2011).

The chapter ends with a discussion of a broader view of practicality as the grounding for schooling that would engage intellect well. This discussion implies that rhetoric about a supposed dichotomy between a practical schooling and a theoretical schooling has limited relevance either to the development of thinking or to the development of practical skills (see, e.g., Lewin, 1951). Arguably, as the discussion at the end of the chapter suggests, thinking is a supremely practical skill—practical for making sense of the world and sharing that sense-making with others in our own and future generations. It's evidently what humans were built for (Hrdy, 2009; Renfrew, 2007).

Anti-Intellectualism Takes the Form of Narrow Practicality

We use the word *instrumental* to denote a narrow form of practicality. Educational purposes that are instrumental subordinate self-determined interests and aspirations to the interests and aspirations of a group with power—typically a great deal of power. For example, the production of adequately trained workers—and, more recently, the training of consumers—is an aim that powerful corporations have convinced schools to take seriously (see, e.g., Aronowitz, 2000; Molnar, 2005; Ravitch, 2013). Production of high test scores as the supposed "bottom line" reflecting the worth of schooling is another related aim of powerful corporations (Molnar & Garcia, 2007).[7]

These aims are misguided because they propose corporate well-being as the common project of all Americans. From the corporate vantage, large private firms and their supporting entities (e.g., suppliers, regulatory agencies, politicians, and so forth) provide both jobs and products to all Americans. Despite the questions raised by this rationale, the aim of enlisting everyone to act on behalf of the country's most powerful private companies has played out in a variety of ways: For example, corporations have used their power to gain access through U.S. courts (including the Supreme Court) to the rights of ordinary citizens (e.g., Blair, 2015), and young people have struggled (and continue to struggle) to get ahead so they can gain entry to highly paid positions and live comfortable (even affluent) lives (e.g., Schor, 1991; Whitaker, 2015). Many

---

7 To be clear, test scores and testing are not bad in themselves; as an industry bent to such misguided aims, however, they have proven themselves consistently, and in some cases even dramatically, counterproductive.

families, students, and teachers, moreover, appear captivated by the ideology supporting corporate power—the ideology that defines social and economic relations in terms of competition and positions the market as the arbiter of social good (e.g., Carrington & Zwick, 2016; Demerath, Lynch, & Davidson, 2008).

Arguably, corporations overreach to a worrying degree when they impose their definition of educational purpose on the public at large. By contrast, families, the community, and the State all do have legitimate (although sometimes competing) rights to define educational purpose. Even as legitimate arbiters, however, these groups can overreach ethically if the educational aims and practices they support turn out to limit the self-determination or interfere with the well-being of those in their care (e.g., Aviram & Assor, 2010; Puaca, 2014). Clearly, considerations about how to educate those we care for differ ethically from considerations about how to control them, despite the fact that adults actually need to exert certain kinds of control over children in order to protect and educate them (e.g., McGillivray, 2011). Control that interferes with self-determination or well-being is ethically suspect, however—whether it entails a narrowing of choices, explicit indoctrination, or subtle manipulation (e.g., Arendt, 1958; Higgins, 2010; Webb, 1993).

Corporate self-interest not only produces damaging consequences for the future of schooling in Western nations like the United States, but it also undermines democracy. We will discuss these dynamics throughout the rest of the book, starting here with a discussion of narrow practicality. Our argument about the anti-intellectualism of a narrowly practical approach to schooling raises four concerns, one relating to its basis and three relating to its consequences. We discuss these as (1) ontological limits—a concern about the basis of narrow practicality; (2) sorting students for probable futures; (3) abridging curriculum; and (4) leading to indoctrination—concerns about the consequences of narrow practicality.

Narrow Practicality Has Ontological Limits

Seeking to teach and to preserve only what is most immediately useful, educators must divine precisely which knowledge will be more or less instrumental now or in the future. This task is more problematic than it might at first seem.

As a standard of the worth of knowledge, instrumental utility is a poor criterion because its application depends on the time frame used to encompass judgment. Within any particular time frame, certain ideas gain popularity, not because of their merit but because of their trendiness (e.g., Kuhn, 1962). Santayana (1913), for instance, saw the fashionableness of an idea as a marker of, and even a precursor to, its obsolescence. Conversely, ideas that at first seem useless can, after a time, produce important insights or contribute to significant lines of inquiry. Moreover, not all fashionable ideas actually turn out to be useful, even in an immediately practical way. For example, adherence to the now-popular gluten-free diet offers little medical benefit to most who choose to follow it (e.g., Reilly, 2016). By evaluating knowledge in terms of its immediate applicability to well-delineated situations, problems, or proposed solutions, the instrumental view imposes a standard of worth that is far too narrow.

This view is not new. Echoing Santayana's position in his article, "The Usefulness of Useless Knowledge," Abraham Flexner (1939)— whose progressive ideas on education led to profound changes in universities, particularly in medical schools—pointed out the importance of encouraging the kind of intellectual curiosity and disciplined "fooling around" with difficult ideas that might seem to have no practical application initially. Mentioning the work of James Clerk Maxwell, Carl Friedrich Gauss, and Albert Einstein, among other examples, he argued that apparently useless research can result in theory so original and profound that its implications for advancing understanding and utility are startling. Founder of the Princeton Institute for Advanced Studies, which he conceived as a means of fostering such highly theoretical research, Flexner recognized, too, the existential or "spiritual" value of sustained intellectual pursuit in the interest of purely epistemic curiosity. As he pointed out, whether such theoretical work as he describes will fulfill only that existential human need that transcends generations or will transform our understanding of the world and drastically change how we live in it is not knowable at the time the research is being done (Flexner, 1939).

So encouraging the pursuit of "useless knowledge" usually does prepare humans for what they will encounter in the future. But such preparation does not second-guess the future. When the pursuit of knowledge can cut a wide swath that encompasses the potential to contribute to the future, but does not pretend to know a future it cannot know, the intellectual realm is enriched overall.

By contrast, an instrumental perspective orients to the future in a much more mechanistic way by trying to anticipate what might be needed for corporate prosperity in years to come. In the realm of K–12 and university schooling, this perspective prompts educators to mold the curriculum to conform to predictions of what students are likely to need for success in adult life, especially in the workplace of the future. This view of practicality is so extremely narrow, in part because it assumes that educators and those controlling the work of educators might actually be able to predict what the workplace of the future will be like or what skills future jobs will require.

With respect to predictions of the economic future, including workforce needs and opportunities, historical evidence suggests that they tend to be deeply flawed. Economic research, according to some, can support predictions for the near future (e.g., Toossi, 2012), but even these predictions depend on stability or, at least, consistent patterns. Economic predictions, including those for workforce needs in the more distant future, are highly speculative (Low, 2014), even within particular industries (Stearns, 2009). Workforce predictions assume that current trends (e.g., increasing globalization, increasingly sophisticated mechanization) will persist unchecked. We all know, however, that many types of change—for good or ill—might derail the trends that seem evident today (see, e.g., Thompson, 2013). Furthermore, using such predictions is clearly disastrous for large-scale social planning (Scott, 2012).

Sadly, overreliance on predictions of the future also implies that taking the particularities of students' and families' interests and circumstances into account is wasteful of human capital: Experts (and their corporate sponsors) know better than ordinary people (again, see Scott, 2012). The orientation to corporate needs creates an intellectually ungenerous[8] form of schooling founded on a misunderstanding of practicality itself.

Another problem with a narrowly practical orientation toward the future is that it diminishes the importance of experiences in the present. This way of thinking about education treats students as passive recipients of (or even captives to) schooling, rather than as discerning agents in their own right. Arguments about the degree to which schools ought to be allowed to promote commercial products in trade for corporate support speak of students as a captive audience (McCollum, 2005), but state laws that compel school attendance also hold students captive to the educators who teach them and the curriculum prescribed by the local school board, state, or nation (see, e.g., Gibbs, 2014). Paul Goodman (1962) referred to this practice as *compulsory miseducation*.

Educators are themselves captives as employees of local, state, or national school systems, and are directed to pay most of their attention to exactly those aims previously described. The State doubtless has an appropriate interest in creating an educated citizenry, and students also have a genuine interest in preparation for work. But students' aspirations and concerns also orient to the experiential requirements of the nearer as well as the more remote future, and to curiosity and discovery as well as to narrow practicality.

For example, in the present, students have an interest in experiencing satisfying and meaningful work as well as opportunities for play and socializing. As contributors to the ongoing life of the species, they have an interest in the intellectual legacy their generation passes on to future generations. Di Paolantonio (2016) offered a similar interpretation[9] (although used quite different wording):

---

8   American factory schooling is ungenerous in many ways, chief of which is its denial of intellect. But it is also ungenerous to impoverished as compared to affluent communities, to African American as compared to European American students, and to metropolitan as compared to rural places. It advantages the advantaged and disadvantages the disadvantaged. University participation remains difficult financially, even while participation is hyped beyond reason. These themes will all be addressed in coming chapters.
9   What he called "the endless pursuit of self-improvement and of managing oneself for success through an education" (p. 148) is what we are talking about as a narrowly instrumental orientation to jobs of the future.

Emphasising learning as a transposable mode that can meet any situation promises that education will allow us to adapt to (and survive) an ever volatile and menacing market. The cruel paradox here is that under 'late capitalism' this optimism in education quite literally indebts us to an impossible normative narrative of success. All such optimistic gesticulations and solicitations ultimately wear us down and lock us down, as it were, within the privative sense that it is all up to the individual to inno-vate and improve and to keep innovating and improving herself optimally and persistently through an education. Putting the burden of such optimism on the individual consequently alien-ates and isolates one from what it might mean to hold a world in common. (p. 148)

An orientation to the immediate enjoyableness and meaningfulness of educational experiences does treat children as having autonomy, and also as having the right to decent treatment. But it does not abridge or circumvent adults' responsibility to offer challenging content in intellec-tually honest ways (Sosniak & Gabelko, 2008). Arguably, as Sosniak and Gabelko (2008) suggested in their discussion of the Academic Talent Development Program, inviting children into a conversation with chal-lenging academic content entices them into a form of serious play that offers as much (or more) meaningfulness in the present as it does for the future.

Di Paolantonio's "a world in common" seems a fundamental prin-ciple of generous schooling. The need of adults and schooling to keep children attached to, rather than alienated from, that commonality also seems fundamental. Teaching children inevitably represents the kind of world we want, and preparing them for a decent world held in common is tantamount to the democratic project. Of course, such commonality might be misconstrued as our duty to national survival in a dog-eat-dog corporatized world, and protecting children might be misconstrued as preparing them to survive as adults in such a nasty (mean and brutish) world. But, under that construction, we would no longer be teaching for a world held in common but for a world controlled mostly by a powerful corporate elite (see, e.g., Tam, 1998).

Narrow Practicality Sorts Students for Probable Futures

Besides narrowing the conceptualization of "practicality" to corporate usefulness, instrumentalism has material consequences. Notably, it demands that students be sorted by "probable destinies," as the early champions of the sorting project called it. Harvard's president, Charles Eliot (1908), went to the root of social efficiency as a schooling practice by explaining the purportedly "democratic" rationale for sorting:

> But how shall the decision be made that certain children will go into industrial schools, others into the ordinary high schools, and others again into the mechanic arts high schools? Where is that decision to be made? It must be a choice or a selection. Here we come upon a new function for the teachers in our elementary schools, and in my judgment they have no function more important. The teachers of the elementary schools ought to sort the pupils and sort them by their evident or probable destinies. . . . If democracy means to try and make all children equal, it means to fight nature, and in that fight, democracy is sure to be defeated. (p. 35)

Wirth (1970) contrasted that conception of democracy with Dewey's proposals for more generous schooling, especially the insistence on greater intellectual scope in preparation for industrial-era employment (Dewey, 1913/1979). Whereas the National Association of Manufacturers agitated for job-specific training for young students, Dewey argued for publicly supported community learning centers where adults could explore and prepare for other jobs and lines of work (Dewey, 1913/1979).

At any rate, the construct of "probable destinies" was widely used, as if students' futures were easily knowable—even as the future itself, as stockbrokers know best, remains unshakably dubious. The contemporary usage, then, was entirely too precious. It meant, simply, sorting students by social class and skin color—a mass of ordinary people holding aloft a small elite, with elementary teachers doing the dirty work. The elite enjoyed power and wealth; the former—including teachers— enjoyed modest means or penury, and good jobs, poor jobs, or no jobs at all—if that were their probable destiny. Dewey, predictably, was aghast (Wirth, 1970).

And within a few years of 1908, scientific ("standardized") testing could guide the choices that anyone, not just elementary-school teachers, might make. The development of standardized testing, it's worth noting, removed the seeming arbitrariness from the outcomes of sorting (e.g., Lemann, 1995; Mukherjee, 2016). Tests made students' "needs" palpable and even objective. Under corporate leadership, specialist educators and psychologists would determine "needs" thus defined—the familiar "guidance" industry of factory schooling.[10]

On this model, of course, education-as-schooling could hardly serve as the route to upward social mobility imagined by such disparate heroes of American education as Horace Mann, David Snedden, James Bryant Conant, and (even) Charles Eliot. Alas, we now know exactly how students are sorted because of research that was almost entirely unavailable to the generation that invented factory schooling: by sex (e.g., Corbett, Hill, & St. Rose, 2008); skin color (e.g., Rury & Hill, 2011); social class (e.g., Anyon, 1980; Yoon, 2015); family occupational status (e.g., Lareau, 1989); regional and ethnic culture (e.g., Biggers, 2006; Lemann, 1995); and adherence to so-called "middle-class" norms, including personal appearance and grooming (e.g., DeCastro-Ambrosetti & Cho, 2011)— and all of it still validated by test scores (e.g., Burris & Allison, 2013).

The inappropriateness of the sorting machine and its terrible inertia ought now to seem incredible (see, e.g., Anyon, 2005; White, 2011). Instead, the sorting machine feels normal. It is meant to feel normal.[11]

---

10 Lemann's (1995) history of the Scholastic Aptitude Test (SAT) recounted the use of that "intelligence test" during the Korean War to provide draft deferments to the students supposedly with the greatest potential for contributing to the nation's scientific advancement. According to the authors, about two-thirds of the college students who took the SAT turned out to be eligible for the deferment. This history shows that testing sorted students not only by their "need" for particular kinds of training but also for their "need" to remain alive during wartime.

11 Teaching a class of academically talented undergraduates in recent years, one of us mentioned the "invention" of the middle school in a conversation. One of the students burst into laughter at the word: "Invention??" To the student, the middle school, left by the student not so long ago, simply was a natural phenomenon. Someone invented it? How could that be possible? Normal reality is a lot like that, most of the time. Intellect helps us get over it.

The sorting, though, is still dirty work, whether assigned to teachers or to tests.

Narrow Practicality Abridges Curriculum

What ought students to actually study in schools? It depends on the student, and the student's needs. Who determines the need? Professional educators. Indeed, once schooling sorts students by probable destinies—assembly-line worker, motorcycle mechanic, lawyer—the curriculum accessible to different sorts of students is quite handily determined and dispensed.

In 1934, Ernest Butterfield, at one time Connecticut's state super-intendent, announced the curricular template that would prevail into the 21st century. High schools would ready about 25% for "professional specialization," 25% for "skilled trades," and 50% "for the life of one who holds a job" (Butterfield, 1934, p. 266). What were they like, these 50% who were to dominate high school? In Butterfield's experience they were not very bright, with an average IQ as low as 70 in some schools. Overall, then, high school would be designed to serve dullards, with half of all people considered as such.

The worst consequence of abridgement is that it removes agency from students and families: Educational experts are better positioned to represent the "best interests" of the child, the adolescent, or for that matter, the adult. As Egan (1978) noted, when schooling positions itself to determine the needs of all others, it reserves to itself any account for how it makes the determination. Needs belong to the system. The evidence is not difficult to find: In impoverished neighborhoods, schooling is often inattentive and hostile to parents and families, and schools there are poorly provisioned (see, e.g., Kozol, 1996; Lareau, 1989; Ong-Dean, 2009). It's not an oversight, and it's not accidental. Society and its schooling institution willfully ignore the real shortcomings, and their causes, in such places.

Not only does the abridgement of the curriculum follow from sorting practices, but it also reflects other political trends and professional preferences (e.g., Tanner, 2000). For example, research on the effects of high-stakes testing showed that, at least in some districts (often districts serving large numbers of students in poverty), the explicit content of tests became the de facto curriculum (e.g., David, 2011; Valli & Buese, 2007).

Other research has demonstrated how professional specialization contributes to abridgment of the curriculum. For example, in the 1970s, one popular curriculum for students with learning disabilities focused heavily on remediation of perceptual motor skills. This curriculum, however, had no impact on the development of cognitive, affective, or even perceptual motor skills (Kavale & Mattson, 1983), but time spent on it kept students from learning how to read, work with numbers, and write. Numerous examples can also be found in the field of gifted education: affective curriculum, creativity curriculum, leadership curriculum, career curriculum, and so on (see Chapter 6).

Narrow Practicality Leads to Indoctrination

Abridged curricula provide training in increasingly narrow fields, toward increasingly narrow ends. What might one call this sort of instruction overall? Indoctrination seems the right word: to teach someone to accept a set of beliefs without question (Mish, 2002).

It may seem a surprising word to apply to the whole sequence of American K–24 schooling, but it is apt in our experience. This sort of indoctrination, though, fuses the curriculum both evident and hidden, to the human resource needs of corporations and sometimes to the purported national need for visible signs of patriotism (e.g., Slekar, 2009; Westheimer, 2006).

In both cases, the curriculum shuts down possibilities for thinking and action. Success with "academic knowledge" ceases to provide pathways to comprehension, joy, and insight into content worth studying, but instead cultivates allegiance to the system that delivers the coveted rewards earned by such allegiance (Deresiewicz, 2014; Egan, 2001). The excellent sheep (like those in Deresiewicz's title) focus on academic success as the basis for being sorted to benefit from those rewards: somewhat better jobs, admittance to elite universities, and, if really successful, access to the very best employment. The overarching lesson is the inapplicability of "academics" except for the narrowly practical purposes prescribed (see, e.g., Butterfield, 1934, on "professional specialization")—

precisely what being in bed with corporate America requires (Molnar, 2005). The quixotic Gatto (1995) asserted:

> Schools can be restructured to teach children to develop intellect, resourcefulness and independence, but that would lead, in short order, to structural changes in the old economy so profound it is not likely to be allowed to happen because the social effects are impossible to clearly foretell. (p. 27)

The more restrained Egan (2001) linked the state of intellect in society with the ordinary experience of children in the institution of schooling like this:

> A complaint of aboriginal people on the west coast of Canada who had been compelled to send their children to schools has been that "they taught them to read and made them stupid." The schools disrupted and significantly destroyed the children's native oral culture and in its place were able to put only a crude and debased literacy. This is analogous to what we do to most children in schools. (pp. 929–930)

Indoctrination in the sense implied by both Egan and Gatto might mean something more like "hegemony" than like "official knowledge." But both mechanisms contribute to a narrowing of intellectual vistas, as the work of such educational theorists as Apple (e.g., 2000) and Giroux (e.g., 1981) argued.

Broad Practicality: The Utility of Care for the Intellect

Despite corporate rhetoric to the contrary, the metaphor of industrial efficiency hardly applies to actual education. Children are not assembled from parts, families are not suppliers, and teachers still, after at least 50 years of attempts to deskill them, believe their work is complicated and subtle (see, e.g., Cameron, 2015). Because of the persistent reality of humanity—people are different, they all think, they are all innately curious, meanings occur to them all, they talk to one another—all of the sorting regimes of factory schooling elicit resistance. Even when sorted, humans remain endowed with native agency, and probable destiny (inequality) sits badly with such agency—an idea captured well in Foucault's distinction between "power" and "domination" (Dreyfus & Rabinow, 1982).

In contrast to narrow practicality as grounding for the aims and practices of education (and schooling), we offer a view of intellectual engagement that implicates a different, broader version of practicality. What we offer in place of the narrowly practical motive reflects a commitment to nurturing the life of the mind among ordinary students. Based on the conviction that constructing meaning (i.e., engaging with intellect) and taking wise action in the world are central aims of human existence, we argue that intellectual nurture entails the pursuit and application of reason (see Chapter 7).

Reason depends, though, on breadth and depth of knowledge (e.g., Egan & Madej, 2009): It emerges, develops, and acquires agency in relationship to intellectual content (Egan, 2002; Sosniak & Gabelko, 2008). Moreover, for cultivating the life of the mind, reason demands openness as a necessary disposition toward knowledge, even (or perhaps especially) toward knowledge that challenges our assumptions or has limited applicability to economic life or socialization (see, e.g., Egan, 2001). Reason of this sort means something different from technical rationality: It concerns the capacity to test the limits of ideas—a capacity that is sometimes equated with critique (see, e.g., Kompridis, 2000). Reason of this sort is notably practical.

Throughout the remaining chapters of this book, we explore these bases for education and schooling in considerable depth. Here we set the stage for those discussions by offering four arguments about practicality, construed broadly: (1) why the life of the mind defines the meaning of life, (2) why reason supports the life of the mind, (3) why knowledge supports reason, and (4) how openness contributes to intellect.

Why the Life of the Mind Defines the Meaning of Life

What it means to be a thinking human being is the subject of considerable debate within and across disciplines (e.g., Brennan, 2006). Some characterizations focus on the use of language or the presence of linguistic structures, others on self-awareness of consciousness, still others on social processes and intersubjectivity. Settling the debate is not necessary, however, to a common sense and naturalist interpretation of meaning as a product of thought or of thought as a product of neurological processes. Arguments arise about various mechanisms and causes, such as the extent to which thought is conscious and the role language and emotions play in the linkage between intuition and reasoning (e.g., Jackendoff, 2012).[12] But no one theory or set of evidence seems yet to prevail.

In the absence of widespread agreement about what's really going on either ontologically or neurologically when humans think and make sense of experience, we can nevertheless use our own subjective experience of sentience as the basis for speculation. That experience—the first-hand susceptibility to sensation, the experience of sensing and "knowing"—suggests that when we make meaning of our lives or think about what our lives mean we are already working on ideas, which reside in an incorporeal site we might call "the mind." Furthermore, in consideration of what we experience and what neuroscience confirms, we are probably not too far off base to say that what appears to take place in our minds does have something to do with what is taking place in our brains (e.g., Thagard, 2010).

This cavalier gloss of what thinking is skirts a great deal of careful scholarship in philosophy, psychology, linguistics, neuroscience, and evolutionary biology. We take this liberty with such a substantial body of theory and knowledge because we end up not needing most of it for our argument. Rather than trying to situate individual thought and meaning-making precisely (as a feature of language or a consequence of chemical reactions), we situate meaning outside the individual altogether—in the collective works of the mind, formal and informal, pre-

---

12   Religious traditions, of course, offer quite different ways of thinking about these issues.

served and ephemeral, shared and suppressed (see, e.g., Tartaglia, 2016). In other words, the mind is out there. This approach offers a way to account for the opportunities and limits placed on individuals' thinking by their culture, intellectual assumptions, errors in perception and judgment, and dispositional preferences (e.g., to trust reason first or to trust intuition first).

We suspect that the works of the mind in which meaning resides are explicit efforts to make sense of the things human beings encounter.[13] Sharing those meanings somehow across generations, or at least some of them, might have originally conferred an evolutionary advantage and thereby contributed to the connection between sense perception, thoughts about sense perceptions, emotions, thoughts about emotions, and language (see, e.g., Renfrew, 2007). The process of codifying meaning, through whatever "language" an individual prefers (e.g., oral, written, digital, musical, mathematical, and so forth), allows it to become a thing in itself, accessible to others to use as part of their own sense-making and contributions to collective meaning.

A fundamental assumption in our argument is that individuals, cultures, and the species itself benefit more from a broader set of available meanings than from a more restricted set (e.g., Metz, 2016). Expanding intellect depends, in fact, on the expansion of available meanings. And despite the strong pull of specific cultural and epistemological sources of shared meanings, human beings are remarkably able to understand contradictions, tolerate ambiguity, and even to operate across incompatible systems of ideas and beliefs. Consider what seeing oneself as both a religious fundamentalist and a chemist (or as an atheist and a singer of religious music) might entail. Arguably, the individual capacity to embrace such differences is the basis on which a more encompassing social and cultural plurality might be constructed. It requires intellect and also helps to construct intellect.

Navigating across differences (in perspectives, preferences, values, and even fundamental assumptions) requires a particular kind of thought process and a particular kind of openness. We discuss such a thought process as a broad view of "reason." On such a view, reason is the intentional search for understanding. This kind of reason is made

---

13   Calhoun (2015) referred to this type of meaningfulness as agent-dependent.

possible (and also constrained) by certain logical requirements (such as noncontradiction). But reason of this sort is made interesting through the products of the imagination and it is made moral through force of will (as in the commitment to treat others as valuable in their own right and not as a means to one's own ends). Defined in this way, reason supports understanding, which gives meaning to life by enabling human beings to make sense of what they encounter without having to destroy themselves or others in the process (Metz, 2016).

Why Reason Supports the Life of the Mind

Using this definition, we position reason as both generative and humble. We intentionally contrast this conception of reason with one coming from a critique that casts reason as the inevitable servant of power (e.g., Horkheimer & Adorno, 1972; Popkewitz, 1997; Skovsmose, 2010). Reason works best, in our view, when moral commitments require it to attend to ideas and efforts that inform and enlarge the common good (e.g., Hancock, 2013).[14]

There are, of course, other ways to conceptualize sources of meaning and goads to action (e.g., Richards, 1942). Many answers might be possible: established religious groups, civil authority, existing social institutions, or the license of the marketplace. These alternatives can, indeed, serve the purpose of sense-making. But the meanings they most commonly serve order the world through and on behalf of existing power arrangements, which often entail relations of domination. In fact, they either treat the "common good" cynically (i.e., as self-interest), or limit its applicability to a particular group (i.e., whatever in-group exerts priority). Lacking engagement with a generative approach to reason, such vested interests are more likely to control and define our world than they might otherwise be.

Escape from self-interested applications of reason relies principally on intellect, through active engagement of the mind, and that is why its nurture is so important (Adler, 1990; Arendt, 1981; Richards, 1942). Without it, curriculum and instruction readily corrupt individuals, democratic institutions, and the very learning in whose service good teachers

---

14   We discuss reason more fully along these lines in Chapter 7, where we argue its inherent connection, via ethical reasoning, to the common good.

attempt to act. We alluded to the related dynamics of factory schooling, just above, in the discussions of sorting, narrowing of the curriculum, and indoctrination.

Reason supports the life of the mind by requiring processes of thought that entail work with the existing products of intellect (e.g., ideas, literature, works of art, scientific findings), as well as supporting the creation and sharing of new products of intellect. Whether or not reason (or intellect) viewed in this way will produce objective "truth" is certainly debatable and, for our purposes, beside the point. Reasoning reflects certain cultural and linguistic conventions, and the criterion of objectivity (as "truthiness") therefore seems too limiting, especially for what we mean by reason in recognition of plurality and in service of the common good (see, e.g., Evers, 2007; Kompridis, 2000). Rather, applying reason to important matters and regulating it in consideration of certain values (e.g., honesty, authenticity, integrity, coherence, precision) fits with a generous view of what intellect is and might contribute. Authentic participation in intellectual work, logical argument, internally consistent expression, and clear language are the standards of the kind of reason we have in mind.

Perhaps schooling fails to address intellect adequately because intellect and the reasoning that engages it are so dangerous. Reason has just cause to ignore vested interests, to form questions that may yield inconvenient answers, and to give offense to unfounded advantage. Reason in its proper form is fearless, and that is its strength; the life of the mind is the perilous struggle to realize that strength in the world. Through reason, intellect considers the world and strives to judge it coherently and honestly.

Why Knowledge Supports Reason

Although one can certainly apply reason to everyday practical problems (and arguably, should), applying reason to knowledge (its production, evaluation, revision, and expansion) is particularly relevant to the cultivation of intellect. As Scott (2014) proposed in his discussion of principles for determining what should be included in the school curriculum, "Any knowledge claim has to be placed within the space of reasons, which means that this claim is discourse-specific and positioned within conceptual frameworks that precede it in time and place and have implications for future use" (p. 26). This principle suggests that knowledge is provisional and always situated within a tradition (see, e.g., Burrell & Morgan, 1979). Knowledge within a tradition (and the paradigms produced by the tradition) is important, but, as Kuhn (1962) demonstrated, expansion of knowledge (for Kuhn, it was scientific knowledge in particular) requires the critique of dominant paradigms and the establishment of new ones.

One role for reasoning in the formulation of knowledge is to offer critique. In some cases, such as with paradigm shifts, the critique is foundational. In others it contributes to revisions within a paradigm. Efforts to foster understanding and even conversations across paradigms are a difficult but important part of the intellectual work of critique and interpretation (Barris, 2015; cf. Jackson & Carter, 1991).

Taking a collectivist rather than individualist view of intellect,[15] we position knowledge as contingent (e.g., situated within a paradigm), evocative (e.g., productive of disconfirmation and contradiction), and pluralistic (e.g., capable of incorporating diverse and even conflicting paradigms). It encompasses ideas and ways to conceptualize them that help us work on the world—in the here and now and in the future—and it contributes to a broad understanding of the world (including an appreciation for its complexities and contradictions). Knowledge—on this basis—contributes to broad practicality by helping the human species move forward through its daily routines (e.g., Patriotta, 2003), as well as by supporting its transcendent accomplishments (e.g., Kvanvig, 2003).

How Openness Contributes to Intellect

The discussion thus far might prompt readers to conclude that intellect exists apart from other domains of human experience—particularly

---

15 Intellect as common, not private, property. We remind readers that the conservative cultural critic Jacques Barzun also believed in intellect as common property: "Intellect is the capitalized and communal form of live intelligence . . . stored up and made into habits of discipline, signs and symbols of meaning, chains of reasoning and spurs to emotion" (1959, p. 4). Our definition is a bit different, unless "live intelligence" is understood simply as *thinking*.

emotion, physical work, all sorts of play, and camaraderie. This is not the case. Intellect augments all experience, giving it meaning and sharing that meaning across time and place. Hofstadter (1963), for example, suggested that intellect contributes to important experiences and accomplishments (what he called *excellences*) by enabling their "full consummation":

> Intellect needs to be understood not as some kind of a claim against the other human excellences for which a fatally high price must be paid, but rather as a complement to them without which they cannot be fully consummated. (p. 46)

Another way to look at the role of intellect in relation to other human virtues—such as those of the heart, body, and spirit—is to think about how they are limited by stunted intellect. For Hofstadter, failing to nurture intellect inevitably diminishes the power of all human faculties. Adler (1990) had a similar perspective. For him, intellect encompasses spiritual and emotional qualities that technical rationality has denied the world, for centuries, and to the detriment of humankind.

Intellect and emotion. As Hofstadter (1963) indicated, intellect and emotion—or at least intellectualism and emotionalism—seem incompatible to many people. How can thinking and feeling be related? One might think about falling in love, which is certainly an overwhelming emotional experience that benefits from intellectual openness.

On the one hand, it is *un coup de foudre*, as the French have it: a lightning strike, love at first sight. Seemingly, the emotional fall is so violent as to banish intellect completely. On the other hand, love of this sort wants to but often fails to last. So falling in love comes inscribed with a longing that is too often disappointed. Something is missing. What?

Making a relationship work so that it flourishes requires thoughtfulness toward the other, revision of one's own opinions, and, indeed, inquiry and critique. It requires thinking, and thinking implicates intellect. These practices are in fact features of much that is on offer in that out-there intellect, but they also represent the living spirit and tradition of practice that produces such works of intellect. They are relevant, too, to the hard work of sustaining romantic relationships. The work of romance, then, benefits substantially from intellectual openness. If many people are not up to this work, one might well blame their education.

Do the emotions regulate the intellect or does the intellect regulate the emotions? Which is superior? Or are the emotions and intellect incompatible parts of human experience (see, e.g., Corner, 2016)? The questions are debated, but miss the point, which is the importance of the connection between them (e.g., Stark, 2005).

In fiction, fine exemplars of this outlook lie in the works of Jane Austen. Here is Fitzwilliam Darcy's ("Mr. Darcy") account of his own *coup de foudre*:

> My object then . . . was to show you, by every civility in my power, that I was not so mean as to resent the past; and I hoped to obtain your forgiveness, to lessen your ill opinion, by letting you see that your reproofs had been attended to. How soon any other wishes introduced themselves I can hardly tell, but I believe in about half an hour after I had seen you. (Austen, 1813, Chapter 16)

At this juncture in the story, Darcy has borne protagonist Elizabeth Bennet's distaste and suspicion of him for a considerable time. His "fall," though, was neither unreasonable nor irrational, even if it took just half an hour. In that half hour, in Austen's omniscient mind, he was observant; thereafter he was even more so. Darcy was, in our terms, open to a great deal at the outset. He was, somehow (i.e., by Ms. Austen), well prepared.

As humans we have both intellect and emotion; we experience both, use both, and seem to need both in order to flourish (e.g., Best, 2000b). Severing the connection denies us what we need. No wonder so many relationships founder, and no wonder so many technical innovations fail to take human consequences into account.

The interplay between emotion and intellect, however, is critical to the difficult work of understanding differences in cultures, beliefs, and assumptions (Fried, 1993). Notice, for instance, how Fried (1993) positioned the two in her description of learning about cultures different from one's own:

The processes by which a person from one culture learns to understand and respect a person from another culture are complex and difficult. They require self-respect, self-awareness, and the ability to articulate both one's logic and one's cultural and personal perspectives on issues of common concern. Understanding also requires the discipline of respectful listening and self-control and the presumption that mutual understanding is valuable. (para. 33)

Interestingly, the word *understanding* captures both the emotional openness to new or different ideas or ways of being and the product of that openness in the form of increased knowledge. Recent psychological work on mindfulness and on growth versus fixed mindsets illustrates the complex way that ideas mediate emotions (e.g., Dweck, 2008), as does the relatively long intellectual tradition of arts criticism. Direct engagement with the arts also encourages efforts to meld emotion and intellect or to read one in terms of the other (Best, 2000b; García Mancilla, 2012). As García Mancilla (2012) argued,

The world becomes understandable to us when it transforms from nature into something proximate to us, when it is humanized and reflected in human handiwork, when it awakens a vestige of humanity. The so-called objectivity of positive sciences builds its views on prejudgments which imply the ontological distance; art dissolves this distance. . . . In art we recognize our finiteness and our passions without living them through. (p. 135)

The arts. The philosopher Herbert Marcuse (1978) adopted the construct of "the aesthetic dimension" to characterize the intellectual realm of "the arts." Many sorts of work are visible on this dimension: novels, poems, dramas; all sorts of music from concerto grosso to rap songs; all sorts of fine art from frescos to conceptual art; and ordinary productions, too, such as cooking, gardening, and knitting.

One may object that the arts are not an intellectual realm at all, but rather a more peculiar technology that manipulates the emotions (see, e.g., Best, 2000a; Krueger, 2014). The position is consistent with Plato's view that fiction was a pack of lies (*The Republic*, 370 BC/1871, Book 10). So the alleged opposition of reason to fiction is ancient. And anciently wrong. In his *Poetics*, Plato's student, Aristotle (335 BC/1812), took the contribution of fiction seriously. With less care and insight, one may dismiss the arts as merely diverting or entertaining: a debased form of Plato's approach, but with frivolity tolerated as a profit center (see, e.g., Postman, 2006). Dismissing the arts as either false or frivolous fails to recognize their role in intellect. Good works of art are varied, stunning, and moving, and excellent ones can be culturally and personally transformative (Descollonges & Eisner, 2003; Read, 1967). Works of art provide commentaries on the world that none other can, because they have something in common that powers this contribution: the aesthetic dimension (Marcuse, 1978).

The aesthetic dimension is officially concerned with "the beautiful," but works of art do include, in proportions ranging from nothing to all, representations strange, disturbing, and ugly. Those features of works that project on the aesthetic dimension typically reframe ideas, events, characters, conventions, traditions, and cultural aspirations (see, e.g., Descollonges & Eisner, 2003; Híjar, 2014; Marcuse, 1978). In this way, such works regularly decenter viewers, readers, and listeners. The works may seem ambiguous; they may provoke uncertainty, discomfort, confusion, and even disgust; they often aim to present normal phenomena in decidedly nonnormal light; or they may present abnormal phenomena sympathetically (see, e.g., Read, 1967). In other words, works that situate themselves squarely on the aesthetic dimension treat conceptions of possibility and impossibility, suffering and ecstasy, assent and dissent, and the extremes of life and death.[16] To engage works of art, then, requires openness not only to odd ideas and forms of expression, but also to the full range of human experience (the good, bad, and ugly), but as re-presented in the light of imagination (Read, 1967).

---

16 Twentieth-century classical music, for instance, is dissonant: incomprehensible and painful to many listeners. One can view the music, though, as reactions to the cataclysms of that century. Tens of millions died and hundreds of millions suffered. Works of art inevitably must take account of such a world.

Treatment, and mistreatment, of the aesthetic dimension is profoundly cultural. As compared to Western European culture, the aesthetic dimension receives much shorter shrift in America. For instance, in France, the national constitution gives citizens the positive right not just to education (the U.S. Constitution is silent about education), but to culture. Museums are free to students, and students have free entry or substantial discounts to the full range of cultural events (Nicolau & Lupu, 2013). So it is humanly (and institutionally) possible to provision citizens with experiences that cultivate access to, interest in, and engagement with the aesthetic dimension (Descollonges & Eisner, 2003).

Intellectual dispositions (especially openness). By "intellectual dispositions" we mean two things. First, and quite idiosyncratically, we mean inclination to consult intellect as we have defined it. And second, more relevant to everyday living, we mean the typical ways of engaging intellect in the flesh. Egan (2001) understood the fleshiness issue:

> The really bad news is that there isn't any knowledge stored in our libraries and databases. What we can store are symbols that are a cue to knowledge. . . . The problem here is that knowledge exists only in living human tissue . . . [the] cues . . . need . . . transformation before they can be brought to life again in another mind. (p. 930)

The cumulation of works (a key phase of intellect in our formulation) requires not only the decoding of cues, not only the eventual apprehension of information or knowledge, and not only the inference of meaning, but also the inclination to undertake the whole complex transformation. No wonder formal education is so difficult, and factory schooling so completely inadequate to the task.

The available research on related constructs (e.g., mindfulness, thinking dispositions, disposition toward unbiased thinking) is extensive (see, e.g., Facione, Sanchez, Facione, & Gainen, 1995; Langer, 1989; Stanovich & West, 1997) but not much help to educators (Perkins, Tishman, Ritchhart, Donis, & Andrade, 2000). Its main thrust is to separate such dispositional constructs from intelligence, which it does, but which for us is beside the point. We are more interested in the distinction between intellect as sedimented in works versus the habitual dispositions related to taking the meanings and the motives in the works into everyday life—in the flesh. Perkins and colleagues (2000) particularly noted openness as a new entry among the qualities nominated to characterize these varied sorts of dispositions.[17]

We find that the Perkins team is onto something with openness. As in the case of the arts, engagement of the meanings cued-up in intellect does not merely benefit from emotion (desire, will, feeling), but requires it. Our minds and bodies live and die, breathe and suffocate, and these bodies do the work of intellect under sometimes propitious but more often challenging and too often, for too many of us, dire conditions. These conditions arise in the narrowness of the situations into which all of us are born. Breaking through that narrowness is the project of intellect-in-the-flesh: "intelligence-in-the-wild" for Perkins and colleagues (2000) and "live intelligence" *chez* Barzun (1959).

There is so much knowledge, so much meaning (stored works, but also meanings in our minds and bodies), and so much of it that is strange, peculiar, offensive, and incredible when judged from our little corner of a nation, in a wide world, in a stupendous galaxy, one of billions. How might one deal with the oddness of it all? One becomes dispositionally and habitually open to it. Such a disposition is and must be an acquired taste. Who is to cultivate it?

---

17 For instance, open-mindedness, curiosity, and "desire for deep-level understanding" (Perkins et al., 2000, p. 286).

Chapter 3

The Anti-Intellectualism of Teachers and the Context Sustaining It

In the past, educators sometimes articulated anti-intellectual perspectives overtly (Callahan, 1962; Katz, 1968). Now anti-intellectualism, which on the surface seems incongruous with the prevailing rhetoric of "educational rigor," is a covert aim of schooling. It is accomplished largely through socialization, which occurs through the actions of the people who are most deeply involved in the school enterprise: teachers and students. In making this claim, however, we are not blaming teachers, just as we do not blame the poor for poverty.

Although the specific features of a school's culture respond to local context, the general character of schooling is shaped by the ethos that links teaching and learning to political and economic ends. This ethos underwrites educational practices that emphasize the instrumental rather than the intellectual worth of academic learning (Apple, 2004; Ferrero, 2011; Labaree, 1999). In recent years, the rhetoric of accountability has been insistent in its claim that the most important purpose of schooling is to promote economic competitiveness across individuals, states, and nations (Covaleskie, 2014; Sahlberg, 2006). Symptomatic of this growing insistence is the increased voice of business leaders in the rhetoric on and operation of educational institutions (e.g., Gates, 2008).

Earlier in the book we examined the ideological sources and ramifications of anti-intellectualism. In this chapter, we consider the specific ways in which an anti-intellectual school culture is built. To do so, we look at the anti-intellectualism of teachers, particularly in terms of the forces that limit the scope of their work, such as the number and complexity of their responsibilities, the overselling of commercially produced curriculum materials, and the narrow construction of accountability testing. But we also examine the controversial literature on teachers that faults them for indifference to intellectual concerns and portrays them as weak academically.

The Intellectualism of Teachers and the Schools Where They Work

Can teachers act as intellectuals as some commentators (e.g., Collinson, 2012; Giroux, 1988; Yogev & Michaeli, 2011) suggest they ought? What evidence bears on such a determination? The first body of relevant evidence examines how the role of teaching is conceptualized. A second body of evidence concerns the context in which teachers perform their work, and a third concerns the characteristics of teachers themselves.

The Role of the Teacher

One important determinant of the intellectualism of teachers is the nature of their work. Do they perform intellectual work? Or are they doing something else? The evidence is by no means clear-cut. For example, intellectual work would entail independent thinking and action, work to solve complex problems, and public disclosure of informed perspectives about matters relating to education. Are these the activities with which most teachers engage?

Notably, literature on teachers' work reveals rather dramatic variations across schools and districts in the degree to which teachers, independently or collectively, do these things. In fact, recent trends have tended to produce two quite different approaches aimed at the improvement of instruction.

From the perspective of the first approach, good teaching involves strict fidelity to prescribed instructional routines and typically the use of commercially produced materials—strategies that purportedly lead to higher student achievement on accountability tests. This approach encompasses a range of practices—from curriculum alignment to scripted lessons—that limit teachers' ability to select or design the content of the curriculum, methods of teaching the content, and techniques for assessing students' learning (e.g., Ehren & Hatch, 2013).

A second approach to the work of teaching, by contrast, treats teachers' intellectual engagement in instructional decision making as central. This approach emphasizes the capacity of teachers, typically in collaboration with one another, to engage in systematic, reflective inquiry about their work and to make wise instructional decisions in consideration of evidence from their inquiries. Hardly new, this approach embeds the kind of experimentalism that progressive educators like John Dewey (1938/1997) advocated.

Teachers as automatons. As some research shows, the view of teaching that focuses on prescribed content and methods gives teachers little room for inventiveness or any other form of intellectual engagement (e.g., Dresser, 2012; Parks & Bridges-Rhoads, 2012). This research suggests that overly prescribed instructional programs limit teachers' ability to provide instruction that engages students in meaningful intellectual work. This routinized approach to teaching "deskills" the work, subordinating the intellectual and inventive contributions of teachers to the purported precision of research-based practice. As Dresser (2012) commented, "This move from teacher led to scripted instruction has left teachers feeling powerless and overwhelmed. They are often caught between what they are asked to do and what they know is right for their students" (p. 71). Under highly prescriptive regimes, teachers must do something, of course, and Eisenbach (2012) characterized the possibilities as accommodation, negotiation, or rebellion.

Even when teachers are not required to follow scripted curricula, they often interpret the need to treat accountability testing as a requirement to narrow their instructional focus. Not only do they tend to limit content to what they believe will be on the test, but they also direct more attention to the students whose marginal improvement will bolster overall classroom or school performance (e.g., Booher-Jennings, 2005; Cullen & Reback, 2006; Volante, 2004).

This response on the part of teachers occurs because some schools consider learning and teaching in a constrained and technical way—with learning viewed as the acquisition of information and teaching viewed as the delivery of information using "evidence-based" methods (Hostetler, 2002; Watanabe, 2007). Depicting a limited prospect for both learning and teaching, this approach narrowly circumscribes the teacher's role. Teachers meet the expectations of this role by using the most widely touted techniques for delivering the information that makes up the curriculum. Under the constraints of a "deskilled" role, teachers do not have a voice in choosing the curriculum, developing instructional materials, or selecting teaching methods (Prawat, 1991). Rather, they treat the state standards and the adopted textbooks as their curriculum and rely on teachers' manuals and instructional scripts to offer guidance about how to teach. In addition, they devote a considerable amount of instructional time to explicit preparation for state tests (e.g., Crookes, 1997; Watanabe, 2007).

Several persistent features of schooling and the context in which it operates contribute to a narrow construction of the teacher's role. First, the rhetoric about teaching and its reform is dominated by a politically and economically (rather than empirically) grounded belief that teachers are the source of a variety of social ills (Glass & Berliner, 2014). Judging teachers as incompetent, reformers explicitly seek to control both their sphere of influence and their daily practice. The salvation that such reformers offer comes in the form of products that are marketed to improve upon what teachers would do if left to their own devices (Glass & Berliner, 2014).[18] Haberman (2010a) alluded to these dynamics in the following synoptic statement:

---

18   Glass and Berliner (2014) pointed out that many of these reformers have a vested interest in portraying schools and teachers as incompetent.

It is a source of consternation that I am able to state without equivocation that the overly directive, mind-numbing, mundane, useless, anti-intellectual acts that constitute teaching not only remain the coin of the realm but have become the gold standard. (p. 45)

Second, the structural conditions of factory schooling make the role of teaching so difficult that teachers often find no alternative than to look for shortcuts. In 1988, Devaney and Sykes identified several conditions as posing serious threats to high-quality teaching: (1) the large numbers of students with whom teachers must work, (2) the need for teachers to maintain order, (3) the requirement that teachers use adopted textbooks, (4) the prevalence of accountability systems that rely on standardized tests, and (5) the overarching concern that students learn basic skills. These conditions persist (and, arguably, have worsened in some places). Several other conditions now can be added to the list of threats: high turnover of teachers in many, especially high-needs, schools and districts; inconsistent leadership; and an increasingly complex set of competing demands on schools and educators (Lederhouse, 2008; Tye, 2000). Finally, in response to deteriorating economic circumstances for many Americans, the emotional demands of teaching may be increasing (Byrd-Blake, Afolayan, Hunt, Fabunmi, Pryor, & Leander, 2010).

A description of the consequences of these conditions—a description that we quoted in the 1995 edition of our book—still characterizes what takes place in many schools and districts:

Most teachers who begin with a sense of intellectual mission lose it after several years of teaching, and either continue to teach in an uninspired routinized way or leave the profession to avoid intellectual stultification and emotional despair. (Guttmann, 1987, p. 77)

Teachers as inquirers. A second perspective on teaching treats intellectual engagement, especially engagement with structured processes of collaborative inquiry, as crucial to the work of teaching. Whereas this approach has long been advocated in teacher preparation programs (e.g., Cochran-Smith, 1991), its appearance at the heart of mainstream recommendations for school and district-level reform is relatively new (e.g., Correa, Martínez-Arbelaiz, & Gutierrez, 2014; Lewis, Perry, & Murata, 2006; McNulty & Besser, 2011). Educational reformers who advocate this approach draw on insights from organizational theorists such as Peter Senge (1994) and cognitive anthropologists such as Jean Lave and Etienne Wenger (1991) as a basis for efforts to engage teachers in collaborative processes aimed at improving teaching and learning (e.g., DuFour, 2004). Of particular concern, from this perspective, is the need to bring teachers' expertise to bear on local instructional decision making (Levine & Marcus, 2007).

For example, a recent book by Costa, Garmston, and Zimmerman (2013) built on their earlier work on cognitive coaching to propose a model for improving teaching in which the collective professional capacity of the teaching staff at a school becomes that school's "cognitive capital." The intellectual work of making sense of curriculum; selecting, designing, and evaluating instructional and assessment strategies; and developing and deploying effective interventions represent the core of teaching on this view. Moreover, extending intellectual engagement to children is what these authors see as the central mission of the school, which they characterize as "the home for the mind" (p. 46).

For these authors, as for others, the intellectual engagement of teachers requires particular capabilities and dispositions, most of which fare badly in schools in which a narrow approach to standards-based instruction and school accountability prevails (Costa et al., 2013). Towers (2012) offered a list of these skills and dispositions:

- knowing how to "teach for understanding";
- the ability to understand and draw out the deep structure of the discipline so that learners learn to reason and connect ideas;
- responsiveness to students;
- a commitment to exploring student thinking as well as skill in probing and making sense of students' ideas;
- being comfortable with ambiguity and uncertainty;
- understanding the provisional nature of knowledge and the complexity of the teaching/learning relationship;

> ➤ a commitment to building a community of inquiry in the class-room; as well as
> ➤ a host of social and personal capacities such as care and concern for others. (Towers, 2012, pp. 261–262)

Furthermore, some recent research demonstrates the impact on students' learning that this type of teacher involvement promotes (e.g., Cosner, 2011; Wayman, Cho, Jimerson, & Spikes, 2012). These research-ers and others (e.g., Datnow, Park, & Kennedy, 2008; Robinson, 2011), however, acknowledge that to expect this type of involvement to emerge on its own without a great deal of guidance and ongoing support from school leaders, or to sustain itself without stewardship, is unreasonable.

Teachers as intellectual crusaders. In reading education literature for our 1995 edition of the book, we found few illustrations of main-stream rhetoric that positioned teaching as complex intellectual work (but cf. Duckworth, 1986; Glickman, 1990; Schaefer, 1967). For that reason, we presented critical pedagogy as the only significant alternative to the dominant standpoint about teaching, which treated teachers as deficient, and teaching—even when it was competent—as a necessarily regulated and regimented type of work.

Since that time, critical pedagogy has persisted as a rhetorical per-spective on schooling and its processes (e.g., teaching, assessing, creden-tialing). But it has, from our perspective, moved mostly to the sidelines. Its major adherents speak primarily about a hypothetical realm, reflect-ing what they hope will happen. Critical pedagogy does, of course, con-tinue to provide a fertile basis for critique (e.g., Tarlau, 2014). But despite its concern with praxis, it actually does not engage what is going on in most schools and communities well enough to serve as a basis either for praxis or for the less elevated domain, practice (see Gutstein, 2003, for one of the notable exceptions).

The Characteristics of Teachers

In this section, we take a look at how the characteristics of teach-ers themselves might predispose them to seek out or avoid intellectual pursuits. This consideration of teachers' characteristics is not meant as "teacher bashing" simply because it concludes that teachers' propensities limit their prospects for deep intellectual engagement. We are not suggesting, for instance, that teachers in general share some character flaw that restrains their intellectual engagement, but rather that cultural and ideological influences operate on teachers to repress such engagement. Teaching is among the most difficult types of work that anyone can undertake. Yet schooling in the United States and in many other nations has been designed for purposes other than to support good teaching and meaningful learning of academic content (e.g., Hoadley, 2007). We conclude that the culture of schooling—the gestalt of the enterprise—militates against intellectualism, even among those teachers who most clearly understand the significance of an intellectual mission.

The cognitive aptitudes of teachers. Even though, as we discussed above, one version of educational reform asks teachers to engage in active processes of inquiry, many teachers do not undertake challenging intellectual work for its own sake. One indication of this characteristic of teachers is their relatively low performance on measures of academic aptitude and achievement (in comparison to other college graduates). Another indication is their limited interest in scholarly activities.

Several studies (e.g., Corcoran, Evans, & Schwab, 2004; Podgursky, Monroe, & Watson, 2004) document the comparatively lower standardized test scores of prospective teachers. These studies suggest that high school seniors and college students who intend to major in education show less academic promise than those who intend to major in other subjects. Some studies also suggest that there is a negative correlation between teachers' academic ability and their tenure as teachers (e.g., Schlechty & Vance, 1981; Vance & Schlecty, 1982). Furthermore, according to some research (Podgursky et al., 2004), many academically capable educators, especially those in fields such as math and science, give up teaching in order to pursue careers that more generously reward their talents.

The evidence about teachers' academic competence is murky, however, in part because the issue has become so highly politicized (Pecheone & Vasudeva, 2006). Notably, conservative think tanks have publicized evidence about teachers' allegedly low levels of academic competence (e.g., Gryphon, 2006; Walsh, 2001) in their efforts to support policies that promote school choice and undercut public education. These efforts, moreover, seek to denigrate university-based teacher preparation programs, perhaps because these programs harbor the strongest and most vocal critics of the conservative (a.k.a. neoliberal) agenda for education (e.g., Sleeter, 2008).

For example, a researcher for the Cato Institute claimed,

> Although many of the attributes that make great teachers are elusive, school administrators seldom hire teachers possessing the qualities that are known to boost student achievement. In fact, high-ability teaching candidates may fare worse than their lower-ability counterparts because of biases in the hiring and compensation system, and they are more likely to leave the profession after a few years for other careers. (Gryphon, 2006, p. 1)

Even though its claims are framed to appear definitive, the Cato report draws limited support from the research evidence, which tends to show a relatively low association between teachers' academic ability and student achievement (Aloe & Becker, 2009). But the liberal countermove is equally troubling. It often appears as a claim that the modest but statistically significant association between teachers' verbal ability and students' academic achievement means that teachers' verbal ability is not at all important (e.g., Good, 2014).

Neither perspective, however, makes sense of the evidence, which is, at best, contradictory. Efforts to synthesize it (e.g., Aloe & Becker, 2009) reveal, for instance, that different studies measure teachers' verbal ability and students' achievement in different ways—they are hardly comparable to one another. Furthermore, the range of verbal ability is necessarily restricted in studies of teachers, almost all of whom have succeeded in college—a circumstance suggesting that teachers are likely to have verbal abilities that are at least average, and likely above. Correlations, of course, are attenuated under such conditions. Many measures of student achievement, moreover, target grade-level content deemed to represent the minimum level of acceptable performance. So range restriction applies with respect to this variable as well. Considering that correlational studies of this relationship will inevitably underestimate the association, the fact that teachers' verbal ability continues to show any association with their students' achievement suggests that it is indeed something, but hardly the only thing, to think about in discussions of teacher quality.

Although findings about teachers' verbal ability indicate that it *does* belong on the list of relevant criteria of teacher quality, we need to be cautious in equating it with intellectual engagement. Academic aptitude is, after all, not the only condition for the exercise of intellect. We know, for example, that many academically capable individuals use their talents to pursue practical rather than scholarly occupations (see, e.g., Crawford, 2009; Rose, 2004). It might then be the case that somewhat less talented individuals choose to pursue scholarship rather than other sorts of work. Public school teaching might, according to this logic, provide such individuals with the opportunity to follow their academic interests.

The academic interests of teachers. Considering this possibility, it makes sense to examine research that describes the academic interests of teachers. We could find no body of research that directly addresses this question, however. But related research of two types allows us to make some reasonable inferences. One type of related research considers teachers' reading habits and preferences; another considers their use of action research and other forms of systematic classroom inquiry.

For several reasons, measures of teachers' reading habits and preferences are appropriate (if proximate) ways to gauge their scholarly interests. First, reading is, by its nature, an intellectual act, requiring the reader to reflect on what is written and construct meaning from it (e.g., Freire & Macedo, 1987; Perfetti, 1986). Readers tend, in general, to be more reflective and more critical than nonreaders (e.g., Chambliss, 1995). Second, reading provides access to content that is available nowhere else because text is a means of recording ideas in great detail. People who are concerned with ideas (i.e., those with an interest in academic subject matter) must frequently encounter text in order to compare and contrast their ideas with those of others who make use of the literate tradition (e.g. Kalpakgian, 2013). In short, reading provides entry to the intellectual forum in which scholarly dialogue takes place (e.g., Applegate et al., 2014). As a consequence, those who read widely in a field are more likely than others to make a significant contribution to that field. According to one recent study, moreover, teachers who reported doing more reading tended to use instructional strategies with more research support than did teachers who reported doing less reading (McKool & Gespass, 2009; but cf. Burgess, Sargent, Smith, Hill, & Morrison, 2011 for a less definitive set of related findings).

Taking these benefits of reading into account, we believe we are justified in considering the frequent reading of literature in an academic field as a necessary (if not sufficient) condition for scholarship. Moreover, we find that the types of books and periodicals that a person reads provide evidence of the nature and intensity of that person's academic interests. With these premises in mind, we turn to the research on teachers' reading habits and preferences.

Studies of teachers' reading show two consistent patterns. First, they show that many prospective and practicing teachers do not see reading as a pleasurable leisure-time activity and therefore do not read very much (e.g., Applegate & Applegate, 2004; Applegate et al., 2014; Nathanson, Pruslow, & Levitt, 2008). For example in Nathanson and associates' study, only 48% of teachers and prospective teachers who were completing a graduate program reported reading two or more books of any type during one summer. In contrast to other undergraduates, moreover, education majors reported being less enthusiastic as readers than humanities majors, although they reported being somewhat more enthusiastic as readers than undergraduates in math, science, and professional fields such as business (Applegate et al., 2014).

The second pattern that this research reveals is teachers' preference for popular rather than scholarly or professional literature. According to Duffey (1974), nearly 69% of the teachers in his sample who were reading a book at the time of the survey were reading a popular book. Of those who were reading about education, most were reading books intended for the general public. Even award-winning teachers tend to confine their professional reading to magazines and journals that offer ideas about how to teach their subject rather than reading scholarly literature from their academic disciplines or from the growing body of educational research (Barrow, 1989). Of course, findings from Duffey's and Barrow's studies might be dated, but a relatively recent study conducted in Canada suggested similar preferences (Benevides & Stagg Peterson, 2010).

Research on teachers' journal reading also reveals a preference for popular rather than scholarly writing, although the relevant studies are now out of date. Cogan and Anderson (1977), for example, concluded that teachers spent very little time reading professional journals. A survey conducted by Koballa (1987) showed that middle school teachers of life science most often selected practical rather than theoretical journals about science or science teaching. Nevertheless, as part of some recent reform initiatives, the involvement of teachers in study groups may have increased their engagement with professional literature, a circumstance that seems to have positive effects on their own reading abilities and those of their students (e.g., Gersten, Dimino, Jayanthi, Kim, & Santoro, 2010).

The research about teachers' reading is illustrative, certainly not definitive. But it does seem to suggest that, on average, teachers do not have well-developed academic interests that they pursue through avid reading of theoretical and empirical texts (either in their teaching fields or in the field of pedagogy). This general picture contrasts sharply with some descriptions of outstanding teachers, for whom the compulsion to engage in scholarship in a field appears to precede their choice to teach it (e.g., Cohen, 1990).

Another way to evaluate teachers' intellectual interests is to consider their level of engagement with teacher-directed inquiry: action research projects, professional writing and publication, and production of masters' and doctoral dissertations. Limited empirical evidence addresses questions about the proportions of teachers who do conduct action research or write professional articles. Flawed as the literature is, however, we review it briefly in order to offer some summary, if inconclusive, statements about teachers' engagement with systematic inquiry.

Many teacher education programs and some professional development programs involve prospective and practicing teachers in inquiry projects as a way to cultivate their reflectivity and professionalism as well as their ability to distinguish more from less effective instructional practices (e.g., Dana, Yendol-Hoppey, & Snow-Gerono, 2006; Schultz & Mandzuk, 2005). The reported success of these efforts shows that prospective and practicing teachers can learn how to conduct systematic studies pertinent to their practice and can benefit from designing and conducting such studies (e.g., Truxaw, Casa, & Adelson, 2011).

Whether or not increasing numbers of teachers do use systematic types of inquiry to investigate the impact of instruction or examine conditions in their schools and communities is not known. What we do know, however, is that existing school cultures—shaped and sustained by the majority of teachers or by a toxic, but powerful few—exert a potent influence on the beliefs and practices of new teachers who become members (e.g., Achinstein, Ogawa, & Speiglman, 2004; Cherubini, 2009; Zeichner & Gore, 1990). The likelihood that beginning teachers' use of inquiry will persist in a culture that discourages such efforts is probably small. Troubling research findings suggest, moreover, that schools serving students from low-income families and from other marginalized groups tend to actively suppress teacher inquiry, not to simply ignore it (Achinstein et al., 2004).

The Anti-Intellectual Context for Teaching

In most school districts, including those that rely on teachers, individually and in teams, to use inquiry and self-reflection as the basis for improvement, structural and procedural conditions keep teachers from becoming deeply engaged in the kind of intellectual work that characterizes teaching at its best. As the discussion thus far implies, these constraints can be more or less delimiting of teachers' intellectual engagement with their work. Rarely, though, do conditions in contemporary schools permit teachers fully to experience the intellectual work of teaching. As Oral (2013) reported,

> Most of us (teachers) do not experience teaching in a fulfilling manner most of the time. There is no significant heightened sense of meaning in what we are doing. More often than not, teaching becomes a routinized activity and turns into a deadening experience, not only for us but for our students as well. (pp. 133–134)

In addition to constraints we have mentioned previously—the punitive use of accountability testing and the typical requirement that commercially produced materials constitute the curriculum—other conditions undoubtedly also contribute to this circumstance. Of particular concern are the many (and progressively increasing) demands placed on teachers. Furthermore, the ostensible ratcheting up of the curriculum through the adoption of one generation of new standards followed by another has had at best a contradictory influence on the intellectual mission of schools and the teachers who work there. A critical examination of the standards movement, therefore, is an important basis for understanding the dynamics that enable and constrain teaching as intellectual work (e.g., Au, 2009; Müller & Hernández, 2009).

The demands placed on teachers. Several recent studies document the burdens that teaching brings to the lives of teachers (e.g., Day, 2012; Richards, 2012). Not only have teachers been required to take on more responsibilities without being given more time, but in many communities they have also experienced the difficulties of a deteriorating political economy. Economic downturns, immigration, and changes in social mores have contributed to conditions (e.g., impoverization, discrimination, family instability) that extenuate the already vulnerable place of children in U.S. society (e.g., Anthony, King, & Austin, 2011; Fass & Grossberg, 2012; Moro, 2014; Thompson & Haskins, 2014). And the State has increased pressure on schools (and by extension, on teachers) to respond to worsening conditions by assuming responsibility for more and more social services (e.g., Dryfoos & McGuire, 2002).

According to some research, teaching in certain fields is more likely than teaching in other fields to lead to stress and burnout (e.g., Brunsting, Sreckovic, & Lane, 2014). Brunsting and colleagues (2014) reported literature showing that special education teachers are especially susceptible to burnout because their jobs require them to complete large amounts of paperwork, offer them limited resources and administrative support, and entail ongoing interaction with children who exhibit challenging behaviors. Teachers who assume other school responsibilities during afterschool hours (e.g., coaching) also experience greater stress and burnout than other teachers (Brown & Roloff, 2011).

Furthermore, whereas role overload affects teachers in general, it has the potential to affect most deeply those teachers who already are the most committed (Brown & Roloff, 2011). As a result of role overload, teachers report that they lack time for some of the most intellectually engaging parts of their work: teaching students for whom learning seems to be a struggle, preparing rich and engaging lessons, and finding ways to encourage high levels of student involvement (Richards, 2012). Recent research from Belgium, however, suggests that high levels of trust in a school can mediate burnout—findings that seem especially relevant to teaching contexts in the United States where trust levels in schools seem to be declining (Van Maele & Van Houtte, 2015).

What standards add and what they take away. The standards movement in the United States, which began to gain prominence and to acquire an identity sometime in the 1980s, started with work in professional organizations and in state education agencies (e.g., Pipho, 1986; Ravitch, 1993). By the 2000s, however, the State (i.e., especially the federal Department of Education) was taking an increasingly directive role in promoting common standards nationwide (e.g., Kornhaber, Griffith, & Tyler, 2014).

The primary motive for federal interest in standards was concern about global economic competitiveness—a concern that gained force with the release of the 1983 report *A Nation at Risk* (National Commission on Excellence in Education, 1983). It was fueled, moreover, by international comparisons made possible through cross-national testing programs such as the Trends in International Mathematics and Science Study (TIMSS), which first reported results in 1995, and the Program for International Student Assessment (PISA), which first reported results in 2000. In part to manufacture consent for national standards and accountability mechanisms, proponents of standards in service of global competitiveness sought bipartisan endorsement by claiming that equity was an important secondary motive for these policy initiatives (e.g., Hursh, 2005; Ravitch, 2010).

Nevertheless, because global competitiveness was their primary aim, the standards that came from organizations, states, and most recently the consortium of the National Governors Association and members of the Council for Chief State School Officers—which produced the Common

Core State Standards (CCSS)—all claimed to increase "rigor." Over time, states and professional organizations disseminated one supposedly rigorous set of standards after another, with each quickly replaced by a subsequent set purporting to be even more rigorous. According to contemporary proponents like Ravitch (1993)[19], the standards and the tests connected to them would benefit the nation because they would promote a richer kind of standardization than what textbook-based curricula had thus far been able to promote. Moreover, standardization of this sort would, from their perspective, reduce inequities in the quality of education by making clear to teachers the content they should be teaching and the levels of performance their students should be attaining (Kornhaber et al., 2014). This logic construed the equity provisions of the standards as a sort of wake-up call to teachers in the schools serving low-income students and those from other underprivileged groups.

Nonetheless, an increasing body of research now shows that standards, standards-based accountability testing, and subsequent privatization efforts have done little to close achievement gaps or rectify the inequitable distribution of teaching competence across the United States—a source of inequity that partially explains different levels of student performance "by zip code" (Clotfelter, Ladd, & Vigdor, 2005; Clotfelter, Ladd, Vigdor, & Wheeler, 2007; Houck, 2010; Knoeppel, 2007; Kornhaber et al., 2014). Some studies, moreover, suggest that recent standards are less rigorous than what teachers with high levels of content expertise would be likely to create on their own (e.g., Esprivalo Harrell & Eddy, 2012).

However ineffectual they have been to date, standards might at least hold the potential to extend high-quality curriculum across the nation. Nevertheless, as even strong proponents admit (e.g., Chingos & Whitehurst, 2012), standards do not constitute curriculum. Teachers must either invent curriculum based on standards or rely on textbook companies to produce it (Leifer & Udall, 2014). Arguably, however, the ability to invent rigorous curriculum is requisite to teaching it well, and the teachers with content expertise sufficient to invent it are too few overall and, as studies of the distribution of teaching talent show (e.g., Clotfelter et al., 2005; Clotfelter et al., 2007), inequitably distributed

19   Ravitch eventually recanted her perspective on market-driven reform of the U.S. educational system (see Ravich, 2010).

across schools and districts. Furthermore, one might question why teachers who do have the ability to invent rigorous curriculum are not doing so already.

With these considerations in mind, we might expect to see a number of research studies that examine the intellectual import of the standards. But only a few studies have addressed the issue, and their primary aims were not explicitly to characterize the standards in terms of their comparative level of rigor. For example, Wolf, Yuan, Blood, and Huang (2014) compared the linguistic demands for English language learners of the CCSS in English language arts (ELA) with earlier ELA standards from several states. Their analyses showed that the CCSS provided more focus than some sets of state standards and also required the use of more complicated cognitive and linguistic processes. Another relevant example was a study of how teachers made sense of the Common Core standards—a research focus that implicated teachers' views about the degree of difference between the CCSS and earlier standards (e.g., Porter, Fusarelli, & Fusarelli, 2015). Porter and associates' findings suggested that, from the vantage of the teachers in the study, the Common Core standards were not so different from the standards that preceded them.

Most of the discussion in the education literature about the CCSS, however, is not empirical. The creation of the standards took place within a charged political context, and states' deliberations about adopting them have continued to polarize professional and public opinion (McDonnell & Weatherford, 2013; VanTassel-Baska-2015).

For several reasons, researchers and policy analysts find it difficult to investigate the merits and drawbacks of the standards in and of themselves. First, the adoption of the standards has failed to trigger increases in the resources needed by many of the schools implementing them—resources enabling the purchase of instructional materials, provision of relevant training, and allocation of time for teachers to plan collaboratively (Heibert & Mesmer, 2013; VanTassel-Baska, 2015). Because the standards may have exacerbated the stressful conditions under which some schools were already operating, the impact of the standards per se cannot be differentiated from the impact of increasing levels of stress. Second, their adoption has been accompanied by a set of contentious arrangements: punitive testing regimes, extensive blaming of public schools, and the reallocation of educational funding to for-profit and charter schools—arrangements that some argue have been put in place purposely to undermine public education (e.g., Dorn, 2014; Koyama & Kania, 2014; Ravitch, 2013). As a result, research analyzing the impact of the CCSS cannot exist without being subject to serious validity threats from confounding conditions. Finally, because the meaning of the CCSS differs across constituencies and is highly politicized (e.g., McDonnell & Weatherford, 2013; VanTassel-Baska, 2015), questions about the political intent of the standards eclipse questions about how the standards support or undermine an intellectual mission and for whom.

Does the current context for teaching support intellectual growth? Intellectual growth takes place in a context that supports meaningful engagement with difficult work. As Dweck (2010) commented in speaking about the importance of providing challenging content to students, "I believe that meaningful work can also teach students to love challenges, to enjoy effort, to be resilient, and to value their own improvement" (p. 16). Arguably, however, difficult work becomes a meaningful challenge when people assume responsibility for it and see its accomplishment as something they can actually do (e.g., Lauermann & Karabenick, 2013).

The political, social, and economic context of schooling in the United States appears, however, to offer fewer and fewer opportunities for teachers to engage meaningfully in challenging but feasible work. The work of teaching continually gets harder, while at the same time politicians and the media denigrate it to an increasing degree. The sphere of teachers' control has become limited in many places, and the intense politicization of educational issues crowds out opportunities for thoughtful reasoning in consideration of valid and reliable evidence. Whereas these conditions might produce just the sort of challenge that motivates the engagement of some teachers, they hardly constitute a conducive environment overall for sustained intellectual work across the profession.

Summary

The discussion in this chapter shows how the characteristics of teachers and the conditions of their work conspire to perpetuate an anti-intellectual culture of schooling. This culture reproduces itself, as veteran teachers socialize beginners to adapt to what appear to be the inevitable conditions of classroom teaching. Furthermore, the socialization that takes place in teachers' early years of service tends to offset the efforts of teacher education programs that advocate and sometimes model a more reflective or critical stance (but cf. Urban, 2013). We suspect, however, that teachers with strong commitments to inquiry and other forms of academic engagement often do exert influence on the cultures of the schools employing them. They may be too few to lead significant change, in part because their work sits in an even wider context than the school or district where they are employed.

Chapter 4

Families and Credentialism

Schooling as a Commodity

There is no help for it—we must teach and we must learn, each
for himself and herself, using words and working at the perennial difficulties. That is the condition of living and surviving at
least tolerably well.—Jacques Barzun, *Teacher in America*, preface to the 1983 edition

In this chapter, we devote attention to the rise of credentialism, link-
ing it to the even more widespread cultural mandate in the U.S. for
consumption (of products, educational degrees, status markers, and so
on). Discussion starts with a review of pertinent scholarship on credentialism and its connection to broader cultural manifestations, including the even more curious idea of "commodification." Next comes a
consideration of how political rhetoric promotes the commodification
of education in particular, first through its design in support of global
economic competitiveness and later through its claims about the benefits
of market-based schooling. The chapter concludes with an interpretation
of these developments for families as the educational center of human
existence—and for the long-neglected intellectual significance of families *per se*, an interpretation that may strike educators as strange or even
reactionary (it is neither, as the chapter explains).

Commoditization and Commodification

To explain credentialism, we begin by considering the idea of the commodity. The commodity is a defining feature of the modern world. In the usual usage, *commodity* refers to an object commodiously for sale (i.e., in great abundance).[20] When determining commodiousness of this sort, the applicable standards are larger scale and lower price per unit (see, e.g., the discussion of consumer ease and convenience in Jacobs, 1994).

Our two key terms related to commodities are *commoditization* and *commodification*. The distinction is important because it helps us get a clearer perspective on how education might be rendered as something easily and conveniently for sale. The puzzlement over this strange possibility would be sharp if we recalled that John Dewey viewed education as life itself. How does one turn life itself into a commodity without enslaving those who live it? So let us start to explore the issue by briefly explaining commoditization and commodification.

Commoditization is the process of making something already marketable cheaper and more abundant—turning a thing for sale into a veritable commodity. The Industrial Revolution expanded the scale and ease of both production and marketing, creating national markets that eventually supplanted local ones, and it brought to the new national markets much lower-priced, mass-produced versions of formerly expensive handcrafted items (e.g., saucepans). The Industrial Revolution, moreover, vastly enlarged the array of industrially produced objects that might henceforth be treated as commodities—not only saucepans, but also entirely new, expensive, and culturally transformative objects such as automobiles (Brinkley, 2004; Kunstler, 1993).

Commodification adds the notion that some *phenomenon* (an actual thing, a service, or a process) not offered previously for sale can be repurposed as an object useful in trade (see the OED entry).[21] An example

---

20   See the OED entry for the interesting etymology that leads from 1436 (a thing commodious) to 1985 (bulk goods for sale) per the dictionary's quotations.

21   The applicable OED entry (online) reads: "The action of turning something into, or treating something as, a (mere) commodity; commercialization of an activity, etc., *that is not by nature commercial*." [emphasis added].

that should be familiar to contemporary readers is Facebook. Such social networking organizations have *commodified* humans' natural tendency to socialize. That sort of sociability was once an entirely private or social matter, obscure, either way, to those not involved. Facebook offers people ways to interact with family and friends via a palette of digital media (messages, videos, photos, audio files, hyperlinks). The company renders the interaction easy and convenient, and seemingly free. But, in fact, the time we spend on such Internet-based computer applications generates both capital investment and corporate profit. Our time is commodified, and we barely notice.

In short, one can generally understand the Industrial Revolution (and its organization of capital: equipment, money, labor, skills, and knowledge, and now even individuals' use of leisure time) as an overall process of commodification. When individual crafts workers (as in medieval guilds) produced items one at a time and sold them locally (often for barter), such objects did not yet constitute commodities as we have understood them after the Industrial Revolution. They were more like works of art from our post-industrial vantage; in fact, because they were produced individually with inherent variations, they are now, perhaps, regarded as "charming" (e.g., hand-hammered saucepans).

Pre-industrial production was labor- and time-intensive. Until mechanization and industrial organization were able to produce a flood of saucepans, no one could have thought of them as a commodity.[22] By supplanting handicraft with machine craft, the Industrial Revolution commoditized one realm of production after another. It also "commodified" previously unmarketable phenomena, sometimes by inventing them (e.g., stocks and bonds) and sometimes by appropriating them (as with the Facebook example). The point here is not the detail of that history, but its sweep and the historical process of rendering *profitable* as many phenomena as possible, and in the digital age, those phenomena include relationships, values, and privacy itself (see, e.g., Etzioni, 2012).

---

22 The great 18th-century political economist Adam Smith (1776) famously used the manufacture of pins to illustrate a point. The pin factory was not "industrial" as we understand it—using fossil energy to power elaborate machines of iron and steel—but it was organized and rationalized and it did yield a commodity. It was a step up in pin production from village handicraft.

Perhaps most remarkable, if least remarked, is the clear fact that the industrial system—the industrialized workplace—both commoditized and commodified *workers*. First, the mechanized factory system slowly dissolved traditional life ways (e.g., weaver, peasant) and, second, it reconstituted people set adrift in this way into something new—a labor market (Thompson, 1963). Employing large numbers of children, women, and men in factories did something more than commoditize their labor, however—it essentially commoditized their *existence*, which is to say, their persons. No longer attached to a place, to villages, to craft or farming knowledge, successive generations adjusted to the system represented by the factory and to the factory wage as the defining feature of their existence. Most of us live still on exactly those terms, whether we work in factories, call centers, offices, schools, or universities: One needs a wage-paying job to survive.

Although seemingly ridiculous that life might ever have been otherwise, it *was* otherwise until quite recently in human history. Initially, the fate of workers—the mass of industrialized people—seemed grim. Political economists of the 19th century devoted considerable effort to understanding this change (see, e.g., Marx, 1867; Ricardo, 1817; Sismondi, 1819). Marx, for instance, had predicted that workers would be pushed to starvation and revolt by the falling rate of industrial profit; the economic system, he believed, was bound to self-destruct on this basis. The meek, he felt certain, would inherit the Earth.

His prediction did not materialize. The capitalist system proved more resilient, and eventually the stewards of the system, and the system itself, learned that its massive productive power required that wage slaves also be consumers. Their consumption of the fabulous output of industrial production was required for the continued survival of the system that gave them their jobs.

Furthermore, relatively recent changes to an economy grounded in consumption deepened the commodification of the lives of workers and their families. Acquisition now figures importantly in all lives. Signs of (paltry) "success" include the latest technology, the flashiest car, housing that announces affluence. Possessing such things signals one's adequacy, psychologically speaking, and one's success economically (and thus personally). We are now, in short, born to hold jobs *and* to shop.

We learned well. Just as a good life without a job seems ridiculous, the prospect of life without access to extensive consumer choice seems meager to most of us. The connection between commoditizing workers (for a labor market) and commodifying their existence (as addicted consumers) should now be clear. The economic system depends on commodifying ever more realms of existence.

Within the familiar reality of everyday American existence, everything presents itself for commodification—and so, therefore, must education also. The commodification of education has taken time, but it *is* well in progress, perhaps best manifested as *credentialism* (Collins, 1979; Deresiewicz, 2014; Labaree, 1999), the topic of the next section.

Credentialism: Higher Education Degrees as Commodities

Higher education has been a high-status experience since its inception. We cannot present that history here, but it is a long one—at least a thousand years in the West, evolving from cathedral schools in medieval Europe (see, e.g., Barrow, 1990; Karabell, 1998; Story, 1980). Only those families with sufficient leisure and funds for tuition and influence (circa 1000–1600) could send their sons to far-off cities to attend lectures and take degrees. The vast majority of people (peasants, merchants, craftspeople, and most clerics) remained locally fixed and oblivious to the student experience in, for instance, Bologna, Paris, or Oxford.

In the American colonies, after 1600, the pattern was, of course, similar: A few children of the more leisured classes could participate, largely as preparation for the clergy, but the experience gradually embraced a more secular mission during the 18th century (Morison, 1935). But even by 1900, American higher education was *still* the province of a small minority, and *still* much entwined with religious purpose (Hofstadter, 1961). Indeed, only a small minority even attended the emergent "high school" (Cremin, 1980).

Early 20th-century scholars (e.g., Adams, 1918/1931) saw that attendance at an elite college was increasingly regarded as providing access to useful social connections (Story, 1980). As Adams (1918/1931) observed, "Any other education would have required a serious effort, but no one took Harvard College seriously. All went there because their friends went there, and the College was their ideal of social self-respect" (para. 1).[23]

As the American Industrial Revolution matured sufficiently to offer manufactured goods at commodity scale (to a national market, as with the Model T), higher education, too, was brought to commodity scale. More and more people were led to want what the elite thought they already had. This tendency, more particularly to our purpose, tended toward commodification: For nearly everyone, possession of the bachelor's credential (in particular) began to outweigh the opportunity it presented for personal growth and even to trump the development of skills and knowledge. Social self-respect demanded the degree.

This emergence of the credential as a genuinely valuable personal possession (apart from any educative purpose at all, as Henry Adams claimed) is the feature of credentialism that most concerns us. To be clear: The separation of the credential from the traditional higher purpose associated with it (e.g., preparation of a clergy to serve God and community, engagement with the ancient and modern classics, the high purposes of skeptical—or scientific—inquiry) was already evident to the astute Henry Adams by 1910 or so. The commodification of the credential has actually *depended* on that separation of sham from real value. We next set credentialism in its intellectual and social context.

Three Theories of Instrumental Schooling

Credentialism is one of three outlooks that theorize the role of education in preparing students for the workplace (Brown, 2001; Labaree, 1999). The first—an economic theory—assumes that schooling conveys the skills and dispositions needed for job performance, thereby preparing students for the work they will do once they are employed. This first outlook reflects "human capital theory" (Becker, 1964), which asserts that skills and knowledge (however learned, but notably practiced out of school, and often acquired out of school) function in the process of production much like the traditional forms of capital—land, equipment, and labor. Individuals make rational decisions about the kind and

---

23   Adams, one may note, graduated from Harvard at the age of 20 in 1858.

amount of training to get, on this view, investing their time and effort to enhance their future marketability. Once in the market, they use the skills and knowledge in practical ways.

In making rational decisions about training, of course, individuals also invest money in tuition and living expenses while going to school. Depending on circumstances (personal affluence) and on the kind of training chosen (4-year lockstep or a slower pace at night or online), they may forgo current employment as well—another aspect of this kind of investment. In the end, all such "rational" investment is predicted to yield positive returns on investment as employers purchase the improved person's labor, with the highly valued skills and knowledge bringing returns to both employer and employee.

A second, quite different, perspective—from sociology—assumes that schooling keeps the existing social structure, with its existing power differentials, in place primarily by preparing working-class students for working-class jobs and upper middle class students for professional jobs (Bowles & Gintis, 1976). This outlook offers the construct "social reproduction" as a way to explain the durable, differential allocation of educational experiences (and the opportunities subsequently made available by those experiences) based on the social class position of students. Social reproduction theory helps explain why so many students in programs for the gifted turn out to come from advantaged backgrounds and seem headed toward affluence themselves.

One notable difference from human capital theory is that social reproduction theory does not assume that schooling processes are individually rational. Such processes are instead seen to involve the exploitation of many sorts of existing privilege (Bourdieu, 1997) in order to secure privilege for the rising generation: a perhaps intentional arrangement, but one that is part of the system rather than one recognized and directed by any individual. Another notable difference is that human capital theory assumes that schooling confers actual, marketable skills whereas social reproduction theory is silent on the question. For social reproduction theorists, schooling would be capable of reproducing the social structure by differentiating graduates either on the basis of the status of their degrees or on the marketability of their skills. Whatever schooling outcomes function to enable privileged families to confer privilege to their children is what counts for social reproduction theorists.

The third outlook—credentialism—is related to both human capital theory and to social reproduction theory, but it conceptualizes schooling as a market for credentials *themselves* (see Collins, 1979, for the original formulation). Credentialism theory proposes that credentials *per se* bestow status, and that high-status institutions (e.g., those in the storied Ivy League) bestow very high status indeed. Obviously, there is a hierarchy of *institutional status* that makes the degrees awarded more or less highly sought, and a hierarchy of degrees from associate to bachelor's to professional and doctoral degrees. The credentials secured by individuals become the "possession" of those on whom a higher education entity bestows them.

The possession, per se, is far more significant in credentialism theory than the experience of acquiring it, and more significant than the skills and knowledge supposedly derived from such experience (Deresiewicz, 2014; Labaree, 1999). The credential is a kind of ticket purchased for a mostly boring trip that must be endured. In this trip, though, one presents the ticket to an employment market (and to actual employers) once the destination is reached. And more significantly, one retains possession of the ticket, which is reusable. If the ticket is a bachelor's degree, a third-class ticket, it can be used to purchase a second-class (master's) or first-class (doctoral) ticket.

Credentialism: Degrees as Status Possessions

Credentialism theory predicts that the press to secure the higher status conferred by higher degrees (a sought-after commodity) will produce a kind of inflation such that lower order credentials (high school diplomas, bachelor's degrees) will lose status—and become less economically valuable overall (Collins, 2002). For instance, the high school diploma, a rare and valued credential in 1900, has been rendered by credential inflation worthless as a token of status (it no longer yields entry to any but menial jobs). Thus, in order to match the employment advantages one's grandparents achieved even without a high school diploma, and one's parents achieved with a high school diploma or bachelor's degree, today's young adults need a master's, professional, or doctoral degree (see Servage, 2009, p. 773).

Theorists of credentialism (e.g., Collins, 1979, Labaree, 1999) suggest that narrow focus on higher education degrees as possessions or even entitlements (that is, pay tuition, attend classes: automatically receive a degree) renders "going to college" an increasingly ritualistic exercise. Deresiewicz (2014) claimed that ritualistic performance and fixation on subsequent employment frustrates the intellectual engagement even of the reputedly most successful students. These scholars argue that the marketplace in credentials not only compounds the difficulty of commending the inherent value of substantive engagement (with works of intellect) in higher education, but that it also undermines concern for the use-value of knowledge and skills for job performance.

This circumstance ought to trouble those who appreciate human capital theory, as well as those concerned for higher meaning and purpose, because the skills and knowledge at the center of human capital theory must proceed from a substantive experience and not a pro forma or ritualistic one. One might say that the higher education "consumer" purchases credentials via an elaborate, but largely pointless, ritual. Skills and knowledge are not irrelevant even within the ritual, but they are shunted to the periphery of the college experience.

Now, if the primary goal of the elaborate ritual were to acquire status needed to secure economic privilege, then existing privilege (e.g., an upper-middle-class background) would be predicted to exercise a large influence on the range of feasible choices and, in fact, on the choices eventually made. In this view, one can see that credentialism works to reinforce a class-based social reproduction, but rather in the complex way suggested in particular by the late Pierre Bourdieu (1997), whose work, arising from the French context, is especially attentive to the cultural symbolism of such degrees. This association of class background and adult status is well-established in sociological research even though the contribution of more and less valuable college degrees to social reproduction is discussed less frequently (see, e.g., Bickel, 2013; Jencks, 1979; Lareau, 1989; Pascarella, Pierson, Wolniak, & Terenzini, 2004).

Indeed, acting on a belief in the efficacy of credentials as status goods, anyone should "choose" an Ivy League pathway into adulthood, but Ivy

League admissions are now several times more selective than even 30 years ago, sometimes by a full order of magnitude (Deresiewicz, 2014). And gaining entry at Ivy League schools and their equally elite cousins in the South, Midwest, and West will involve a rather more expensive financial "investment" than the other higher education options. Tuition is at a historically high level. Even with ample financial aid, the average debt burden for middle-class students will be high (Pascarella et al., 2004). Most people, then, cannot do at all what the logic-model for the marketplace of credentials suggests: attend an elite school. But are Ivy League graduates really more valuable—more worthy—than community college graduates, say, of equally enviable IQs? Maybe not. Consider the testimony of William Deresiewicz (2014; a former English professor at Yale); he describes in this passage an *elitist variety* of miseducation:

> Growing up elite means learning to value yourself in terms of the measures of success that mark your progress into and through the elite: the grades, the scores, the trophies. That is what you're praised for; that is what you are rewarded for. Your parents brag; your teachers glow; your rivals grit their teeth . . . The result is what we might refer to as credentialism. The purpose of life becomes the accumulation of gold stars. Hence the relentless extracurricular busyness, the neglect of learning as an end in itself, the inability to imagine doing something that you can't put on your resume. (pp. 15–16)

Credentialism theory seems compelling, and it is applicable even in the case of the most seemingly successful students, but what evidence supports the theory?

Consider that students' "rational" action when purchasing credentials would resemble their rational action as consumers of *any other* commodity or service: They would seek to maximize the cost-benefit ratio, obtaining the product recognized as best for the least cost. Indeed, one can see such behavior as a timeworn part of the rational action assumed in the field of economics: buy low, sell high. So from the vantage of students who seek the best bargain, buying low entails the least possible expenditure of both time and money. If the increasingly expensive credential itself is the most important goal, then *technically rational action* dictates that students obtain as many schooling credentials as possible with the least amount of effort (Labaree, 1999).

Some empirical evidence suggests that students behave in this way. Related first-person accounts include those of Deresiewicz (2014) for higher education and Gatto (2002) for K–12 schooling, but two lines of empirical inquiry harbor findings that are more generalizable, namely those on: (1) social class and the dynamics of educational aspirations (see, e.g., McGhee Hassrick, 2005) and (2) the implicit bargains students strike with their teachers (e.g., Cusick, 1983; Fulmer & Turner, 2014; Sedlak, Wheeler, Pullin, & Cusick, 1986).

Readers need to keep in mind, however, that most students and families function within this system believing it to be "normal." They lack the capacity or motive to imagine or generate alternatives very often. Resistance may not be futile, but it is not—by definition—effective in the ordinary experience of students and families. We explore the related evidence next.

Empirical studies confirm the increasing competitiveness of affluent parents for coveted credentials on their children's behalf. For example, a study conducted by McGhee Hassrick (2005) showed that middle-class parents in an urban school serving students from mixed SES backgrounds used various strategies to intervene on behalf of their children, even when their efforts threatened educational opportunities for less affluent students. Kohn (1998) characterized several similar (but earlier) studies as showing:

> It isn't just that these parents are ignoring everyone else's children, focusing their efforts solely on giving their own children the most desirable education. Rather, they are in effect sacrificing other children to their own. It's not about success but victory, not about responding to a competitive environment but creating one. (para. 22)

For other than advantaged students, the dynamics are different, however. These students (and their families) may give up on schooling altogether because they believe it is already rigged against them (e.g.,

Ogbu, 2003) or they may bargain for the best credentials they can obtain with the least effort they must expend, as credentialism theory would predict. We refer to the latter dynamics as an "implicit bargain."

The second line of evidence describes the tacit agreement that prevails in many classrooms (even sometimes in schools for children of the elite), where teachers assign *pro forma* exercises in return for compliant behavior. Children are not born cynics, of course, and decades of research (e.g., Anderson-Levitt, 2005; Hudson-Ross, 1989) support the commonplace observation that young children are natural learners. Schooling, though, seems to intervene systematically to alter the natural endowment (Leafgren, 2009; Nystrand & Gamoran, 1989). Perhaps, as Sedlak and associates (1986) suggested, this change results from students' experiences in the elementary grades. At any rate, most children seem to acquire, often by middle childhood, a jaded attitude toward schooling and the "learning" expected of them at school: completing seatwork that often has little academic merit, seldom encountering unstructured problems or thought-provoking questions, and having "discussion" that is more like recitation (Anderson, 1981; Anderson-Levitt, 2005; Gall, 1984; National Institute of Child Health and Human Development, 2005; Nystrand & Gamoran, 1989). As might be predicted, the most repressive expectations prevail in schools for working-class students (Anyon, 1980; Leafgren, 2009).

With a steady diet of this type of schooling, all but the lucky few enter high school primed to exercise the cynic's option, that is, to use the threat of noncompliance and disruptiveness to bargain down the expectations that teachers hold for academic engagement and performance (Cusick, 1983; DePalma, Matusov, & Smith, 2009; Sedlak et al., 1986). That not all high school students actually respond to schooling in this way is evident in the fact that, across schools and classrooms, teachers observe (and often take responsibility for cultivating) some students from low- and moderate-SES backgrounds who exhibit high levels of achievement motivation (see, e.g., Burney & Beilke, 2008; Gatto, 2002; Gutstein, 2003; Nieto, 2007; Shernoff & Schmidt, 2008).

Recapitulation

Credentialism seems to exact a needless toll on the intellectual potential of Americans in several ways. First, it commodifies learning, an activity that cannot actually be bought or sold. The frenzy for credentials renders poverty and the fear of poverty as a profit center for higher education, exploiting families' fears and hopes. The effects are dire in fact for impoverished students and families (Howley & Howley, 2015). Second, it reframes robust intellectual engagement as inefficient and possibly distracting (Labaree, 1999). Third, by substituting the end for the means, it actually lessens the usefulness of skills and knowledge once admired for what they could *do* (Crawford, 2009). Fourth, and worse than all the rest, credentialism as a cultural development makes the university an increasingly unhappy home for the human legacy of meaningful inquiry and interpretation, disabling an important center for intellect (Giroux, 2007).

Although credentialism is principally manifest in higher education, the institution that bestows the high-status credentials, preparation for students' competition in that marketplace is increasingly an official goal of K–12 schooling; for instance, the Common Core's focus on "college and career" (Common Core State Standards Initiative, 2015, para. 1). In large measure, this unfortunate circumstance has relatively recent political origins, explained next.

The Political Economy of Credentialism

The aspirations of students and families aside, American political rhetoric since the 1980s has emphasized the instrumental functions of schooling for both the national economy and individuals' participation in it (Bickel, 2013; Emery, 2002; Magrini, 2014; Theobald, 2009). Where does this political rhetoric, which now seems like common sense, come from?

A logical connection seems to exist with human capital theory, but the original formulation of human capital theory had much less to do with schooling and more to do with the general cultural stock of skills and knowledge actually in play economically (see, e.g., Becker, 1964).

The nature of American economic activity, however, has shifted from industrial manufacturing (moved offshore to developing nations) to a so-called "service" base, with finance and digital inventiveness as the most elite services and the most elite employment. So the logical connection for the revised purposing of the economy concerns the sort of preparation prescribed for the new high-status careers. The fact that most people will be employed, however, in far different services—retail, home health care, teaching, for instance—is irrelevant. What the nation purportedly needs is the sort of schooling program prescribed for future financiers and software developers. In other words, schools should embed knowledge and skills appropriate to the economic needs of the future *as imagined and articulated by business leaders* (Emery, 2002).

According to some critics (Gabbard, 2000; Saltman & Gabbard, 2003), the combination of purpose and those espousing it indicates that continued American global economic dominance has become the primary official purpose of State schooling. We took this position, in fact, in the first edition of this book, where we characterized as anti-intellectual such *instrumental purposes* as (later) articulated by Gates (2008). The applicable business rhetoric has, however, exerted continuing and ever-greater influence on American schooling (Emery, 2002).

Narrow and manipulative as this logic of State schooling appears, privatization has extended the rhetorical reach to large swaths of school operations, according to many critics (e.g., Blacker, 2013; Bowers, 2004; Labaree, 1999; Magrini, 2014; Sturges, 2015). The instrumental rhetoric argues, implies, and assumes that the American common good is identical with global corporate interests and that aspirations for continued American global economic dominance are worthy and feasible. But, according to such critics as just mentioned, privatization replaces allusion to any common good with another virtue: consumer choice. Of course, more than 30 years of school reform that deploys such rhetoric itself "educates" a broad and deep portion of American teachers and the American public, so that a sizable proportion of families and educators now tolerates the corporate view of schooling (Blacker, 2013; Molnar, 1996).[24] The idea that education is a private rather than a public ben-

---

24   Principals and superintendents might be more inclined to accept the rhetoric, as a study from Australia (Cranston, Mulford, & Keating, 2010) suggested.

efit has been made to seem natural, but one needs to recognize that the idea is carefully orchestrated and of recent construction. Moreover, many teachers and families chafe under the value-added accountability schemes, an offensive scientism, testing regimes designed more to unsettle than to assist schools and families, and the change from public to corporate oversight (Blacker, 2013; Howley & Howley, 2015; Woodrum, 2004).

Educational aims have seldom been defined so meagerly, nor their enforcement conducted so systemically. The elimination of ordinary citizens' voices (i.e., the public's voice) in schooling helps ensure the dominance of the corporate voice as well. Across the decades of the postwar years, surveys of ordinary citizens had identified four categories of purpose: (1) intellectual or academic, (2) instrumental or productive, (3) social or political, and (4) spiritual or aesthetic (Howley, Pickett, Brown, & Kay, 2011). After 1980, however, hardly any State authority has turned to ordinary citizens to inform new definitions of the aims of education (Blacker, 2013; Emery, 2002; Theobald, 2009). Gone from contemporary rhetoric are purposes such as the formation of an active citizenry, of a rising generation of excellent teachers, and, notably in our concern, independent-minded scholars and public intellectuals. Why?

Active citizens take to the streets, excellent teachers help students ask dangerous questions, and independent-minded scholars and public intellectuals lead vigorous public debate. These sorts of activities can stymie corporate plans. Excellent sheep (Deresciewicz, 2014) are indeed what the meager purpose and viciously enforced "rigor" demand. Instead of our hearing from our varied neighbors, we all hear from such world-class leaders as Bill Gates (cf. Gates, 2008; Glass, 2016; Sturges, 2015). We in the profession find ourselves uniquely dismissed as unpatriotic complainers (see, e.g., Labaree, 2005), a status hardly more enviable than that of the silenced citizen (Blacker, 2013).

So the actual commodification of public schooling is well underway, proceeding forward on the terms of a narrow instrumentalism and increasing privatization. Howley and Howley (2015) illustrated the processes of privatization with a discussion of "farming the poor." Their argument maintained that privatization renders profitable the schooling of impoverished students, however unlikely such a financial opportunity might seem. Recall, however, that commodification renders profitable phenomena not previously relevant to economic activity. The related profit centers for the schooling of the poor include teacher-proof curricula branded as effective, the chartering system and its private Education Management Organizations, State-funded private tutoring, the indebtedness of impoverished students seeking higher education credentials, and the grading of schools and districts as a reference point for real estate values. Decades of privatization have accomplished nothing to improve schooling for the poor (see, e.g., Betts & Tang, 2011), but this predictable result makes the profit stream sustainable. Public schooling has not served the poor very well, perhaps, but privatization commodifies the participation of the poor in the meager service that has traditionally been their lot. Privatization impoverishes the poor more effectively and with clear corporate benefit.

Whereas differential allocation of schools on the basis of quality is commonplace in an ostensibly public system, fairness nonetheless remains an issue. It remains an issue precisely *because*, as a public system, the common good remains an advertised purpose. So misrepresenting an unfair State system as fair is quite difficult (e.g., Kozol, 1991). But when free-market choice is invoked, the difficulties of fairness begin to vanish, partly as a result of choice, but also because the free market is assumed to be properly self-regulating and even "smart" (Surowiecki, 2004). The political rhetoric, however, goes further to assert that whatever happens can normally be regarded as fair (see, e.g., Tomasi, 2012). Choice itself is the major educational improvement, on such a view. For the affluent, of course, reputedly excellent choices exist even in the nonprivatized public system. One simply purchases housing in an affluent neighborhood, perhaps where the district's grade is an A+ (Howley & Howley, 2015).

The free-market assumption, though, fuels a very long-standing political debate outside education, and the assumption does not represent a definitive truth (DeYoung, 1989). Markets may indeed be argued as smart and efficient, but one must observe that securing reputed quality in the marketplace, short of outright cheating and theft, depends on one's ability to pay the price asked. One gets what one pays for, in education as at the supermarket.

So parents without the resources to augment the minimal funding provided by the State find that they must send their children to cheaper, lower quality schools, while those with more resources can afford to send their children to expensive, better quality schools (Ravitch, 2013). The State might fully subsidize the poor, but the prospect seems very unlikely in America, especially as equitable funding has been such a long struggle under the historical public system (Cremin, 1980; DeYoung, 1989). If the poor want better schooling, they should, on this view, exercise more initiative and expand their realm of choice. If they do not, they display their lack of virtue and character, proving that they deserve what they get (a peculiarly American view; see Bénabou & Tirole, 2006).

As schooling privatizes, and commodification more completely establishes itself within schooling, a predictable and already visible phenomenon begins to mark the choices available to the consumers who were once citizens: branding. According to Healy (2007), loyalty to brand itself tends to undermine loyalty to the common good. Some brands, though, attract suspicion, as a recent Ohio episode illustrates. In White Hat Management's Ohio charter schools just 2% of students reportedly demonstrated adequate yearly progress (Coutts, 2011). The firm was sued by public school districts in collaboration with the Ohio Department of Education. At issue was the allocation of funds: A recent study with relevance to the Ohio case (Arsen & Ni, 2012) had found that on average, charter operations spend, per pupil, $800 more on administration and $1,100 less on instruction. What proportion of the public funds that White Hat had received went to instructional expenses and what proportion to administration and profit? White Hat's lawyer resisted disclosure of financial records with a remarkably offensive logic:

> If I'm Coca-Cola, and you're a Coca-Cola distributor or a Coca-Cola purchaser, that doesn't entitle you to know the Coke formula or find any financial information you'd be interested in learning from the Coca-Cola company. And that's kind of what they're demanding. (quoted by Coutts, 2011, para. 11)

In other words, once the public funds get onto the private corporate ledger of a "public school" operator, the public is not entitled to any financial accounting—let alone a discussion of fairness. This corporate logic, which might not be argued so fatuously by every corporate lawyer, nonetheless pertains even to brands that attract less suspicion or even admiration: The offensiveness of this logic is evident only by comparison to a public schooling norm. If that norm eroded completely, corporate accounting norms would instead seem natural. They are indeed beginning to seem as such to many casual observers (see Bushaw & Calderon, 2014, about the high level of support Americans give the charter movement).

As the evidence shows, credentialism works quite broadly to reinforce class-based social reproduction. But its mechanisms function in the complex way suggested in particular by Bourdieu, 1997: The status adornment of an advanced degree from an elite school passes on the advantaged status of those to whom it is most accessible—children of the upper middle classes. For the many families who lack upper-middle-class status, the acceptance of degrees as essential status adornments remains a terrible but largely unremarked challenge. Ensuring that their children get the best degrees possible irrespective of cost jeopardizes the economic security of these families, as evidence of debilitating debt attests (Deresiewicz, 2014; Pascarella et al., 2004). Nevertheless, conventional wisdom, as we have seen, is constructed to disguise the challenge as a virtue.

To mitigate the miseducative influence of credentialism or to disengage from it entirely, teachers and families need, or would need, to realize *uncommon* perspectives and take *unusual* action. To illustrate such perspectives and actions, the final section of the chapter discusses the relationship of families to "schooling goods," the relevance of the American neglect of family well-being, the idea of living well as central to a higher purpose for education at all levels, and the implications of such considerations for teachers working with talented students. Throughout this discussion, we highlight the unfamiliar principle, surprising as it may seem to most readers, that the best cultural work takes place at the professional, cultural, and economic *margins*. These are precisely where, as compared to the mainstream, unusual arrangements stand better odds of flourishing.

Families and Schooling Goods

Schooling with a mission made more meager by the policies previously described has been positioned to subvert the active and informed participation of ordinary people (*many* of whom are unusually talented), both in the realities that confront them and in their minds. In this light, policies and practices that inequitably allocate opportunities for the exercise of intellect, and for contributing to the intellectual legacy, erode both democratic engagement *and* the ability of intellect to enrich the common good.

That the commodification of education is anti-democratic may thus be much easier to argue than that it is anti-intellectual (e.g., Garcia, 2004), but the anti-intellectual character of commodified schooling becomes clearer once intellect is construed not as an individual attainment but as a collective creation and a collective source of meaning (as it is in this book). On this view, credentialism arguably damages the cultivation of intellect (i.e., the intellectual portion of the common good), compounding future ecological disasters with a cultural one.

Greater participation in intellectual meaning-making represents the promise of a decent public education. Although educative schooling sponsors abundant forms of thoughtfulness, instrumental schooling and credentialism, operating under market conditions, not only make a mockery of such thoughtfulness, but also reposition educative experiences as useless (see, e.g., Magrini, 2014).

This fate is what has *already* become of the public endeavor that founders of 18th-century republics (the United States, France, Haiti) had hoped would prepare citizens to govern. Today, large corporations govern in place of citizens, and they have refashioned former citizens mostly as consumers (e.g., Blacker, 2013). Schooling, too, is an object of consumption, and some public school districts refer to their families as "customers." And so, most families are unlikely—as a result of both the political "schooling" and the schooling guided by corporate intent—to question the lack of better purpose (Magrini, 2014). The schooling system as it has been reshaped simply confronts them, and they must deal with it on the terms they can muster. Miseducation is not just normal, but valuable. It, too, has been commoditized and commodified.

This misconstruction of purpose and diminishment of aspiration, of course, coincides with the "fracture" of the American Dream (H. B. Johnson, 2014, p. 1). The fracture, though, seems to us more like a collapse—and the desperation of credentialism is an arguable sign of the collapse, as other authors chillingly suggested:

> A viable, sustainable and authentic understanding of the learner can only emerge in concert with a viable, sustainable, and authentic world for that learner to inhabit, adore, question and care for and about. That is, the deepest cut of instrumentalism and social efficiency is not simply that the agency and authenticity of the original learner has been rendered into the instrumental and standardized follower of rules. The world which teachers and students inhabit has become uninhabitable, unlovable. (Gilham & Jardine, 2015, p. 2)

Instead of hard work leading to success (the American Dream), we have instead a dodgy trade in symbols of status and in misguided hope, tied to a rigged lottery of life chances. The rigged lottery is left in place because free-market thinking assumes that a freer market (e.g., customer choice and privatization) will correct all improprieties. Teachers in K–12 schooling and in universities who operate from this vantage ("serving our customers") are indeed merely acting thoughtlessly, and in exactly the way intended for them to act in their uninhabitable and unlovable world. As Magrini (2014) suggested, this eventuality has been long in the making. Under such a regime, as we explain next, the deep structure of schooling (Tye, 2000) is bound to mistreat families and children—to view them, systemically, as *the enemy*—even as, and because, it constructs them as "the customer."

Sociologist Edgar Friedenberg (1979) offered an interesting, perhaps prescient, view of State schooling's mistreatment of children—and by implication—its outlook on their families. In a discussion of how State schooling renders children as objects of fear and loathing, Friedenberg observed that it was a "metaphysical absurdity" (p. 70) that State schooling should assume

> the right and power to group people together and tell them what they may pay attention to and what meanings to draw from the sights, sounds, and symbols they are bombarded with. This is exactly the way you *don't* teach anyone you care for anything that is to be really important to them for their own purposes, anything they are to master and make their own. (p. 70)

Sending children to corporate-oriented State schooling, observed Friedenberg, thus renders a family's smallest and most beloved members as "objects of fear and loathing," the title of the cited essay. First, it does so by alienating children from those who would naturally care for them, and second, by imposing the State's national-corporate curriculum on children and parents alike. At this late remove from Friedenberg's days, the imposition has become far more insistent (e.g., Bickel, 2013; Blacker, 2013; Labaree, 1999; Magrini, 2014; Molnar, 1996; Saltman & Gabbard, 2003).

Of course, Friedenberg was looking with rare objectivity at the early, but already evolving, manifestation of the phenomenon—objective, that is, in the sense of observing it as if he were an outsider to the culture of schooling. This capacity is an intellectual move rarely accessed by those within a culture—simply because cultures are founded on assumptions that must normally remain tacit so that the cultural arrangements they support remain functional (Bicchieri, 2006). Friedenberg's sort of thinking, however, is an essential manifestation of intellect known as critique (see, e.g., Gee, 2011). So we want to press on with the perspective Friedenberg opened two generations ago.

In this line of critique, children are not, in fact, "students." The State, rather, calls them by that moniker, and normalizes the usage, to help legitimize its intervention with the family. Children "study" in some fashion, of course, on the model prescribed in State schooling (e.g., as per Friedenberg's first sentence, above). But that model casts families out of an educational role (Arendt, 1954/1968; Magrini, 2014). Parents have instead become "laymen," so far as the schooling of their own children is concerned. No longer do many people regard the home as either economically *or* educationally productive. Parents still educate, but the formalized profession hardly cares.[25]

The officially approved parental role in this dysfunctional scheme is for parents to make themselves available for direction by the State school and its sponsored professionals (as "parent involvement"). The imagined role of cooperative helper, though, has proven an entirely fictive one: Working-class parents usually feel alienated from schools because of their own miserable experiences there (Horvat, Weininger, & Lareau, 2003; Woodrum, 2004) and affluent parents are often seen as bullying the educators (Horvat et al., 2003; Lareau, 1989). In this way, and at both ends of the status continuum, families, too, become objects of professional fear and loathing (Hoffman [2009] offered a related assessment).

So in the main, as Friedenberg seems to imply, State-schooled children *do not* study; rather, they receive assignments that they complete reluctantly (often inattentively), they experience forms of drudgery and boredom that normalize drudgery and boredom as "work" (Oral, 2013), and all the while they also absorb an abundantly unjust hidden curriculum about their own assigned current and future place in the world (Anyon, 1980; Brown, 1991; Deresiewicz, 2014; Leafgren, 2009; Willis, 1977). To dignify *any* of this familiar misery with the term *study*, or to call a child incumbent in this misery a *student* is a mistake, even though it is a mistake accepted by almost everyone (again, as it must be for the culture to function). It is indeed a world uninhabitable and unlovable (Gilham & Jardine, 2015). And yet we all (readers and authors) hold jobs within this world and subscribe to it as we can or must.

The implications for teachers and for teaching seem clear to us. On one hand, coping is the default option. We complain, we grumble, we simply persist and survive. Most teachers try to cope—feigning acceptance, suffering through deceptive "professional development," generally soldiering on, accommodating or negotiating but seldom resisting in an intellectual mode. The effort is exhausting and debilitating (Olsen &

---

25 Pamela Druckerman (2012), a journalist, developed an interesting contrast between miseducative American and educative French parenting styles. The French understand their parenting as education, in Druckerman's account.

Sexton, 2009). But it makes sense to behave in this way: The culture of schooling—its deep structure (Tye, 2000)—relies on such behavior.

Another option, though, is to take the side of both families and the higher purposes of intellectual engagement. This path is extremely difficult, given norms of compliance and passive-aggressive resistance, yet we know personally teachers and principals who do follow this path. "Taking their side" does not render challenged families less challenged, or children facing severe threats less traumatized. The American political economy has, after all, become an increasingly rough place (see, e.g., Blacker, 2013; H. B. Johnson, 2014; Katz, 1989; Labaree, 1999): a less habitable and certainly less lovable world in its own right. But it is liberating for teachers to see the problem not as reluctant learners and uncaring families, but as the politics and economics that surround and infest schooling at both the K–12 and university levels (see Cameron, 2015 for the description of one such teacher's experience).

As for higher purpose, actual learning—as Friedenberg (1979) intimated and as Magrini (2014) detailed—is necessarily a more legitimate activity and a more heartily engaged one (Jardine et al., 2006). After all, which of us thinks much or well in a context of fear and loathing? Dignity escapes one, and mere emotional survival (coping) becomes more important.[26] This circumstance is as familiar among gifted children as others, and probably more so in view of the anti-intellectual tenor of American schooling overall (see, e.g., Gray, 2013).

So we now turn the discussion to the plight of families. Understanding this plight can help teachers nuance what it means to "take the side" of families. But we also want to suggest that appreciating the position of the family in education (and not just schooling) harbors momentous possibilities for creating a form of schooling that is ultimately much kinder to intellect. This is important work at the cultural margins.

Of course, we have in mind not so much the professional families interested to use schooling to pass on their own high status, but far less advantaged ones. At the same time, though, we remind readers that *all*

---

26 Within schooling itself teachers, too, experience the fear and loathing of the State as they cope with accountability pressures. A number of recent studies demonstrate the counterproductive "threat rigidity" induced by accountability measures (Daly, Der-Martirosian, Ong-Dean, Park, & Wishard-Guerra, 2011; Olsen & Sexton, 2009).

families are positioned to be objects of fear and loathing. And one does well to remember that affluent families are as subject to the prevalent intellectually dysfunctional norms as are many others. Indeed, such affluent families may well confront much greater difficulty than working-class families in this respect, even though it may seem otherwise.

Schooling and the Good of Families

The unfortunate reality of the State's conversion of children and families into consumers and commodities might be less widely crippling than one would reasonably imagine, because of a simple and durable part of the human condition. Parents *make the babies* that cultures everywhere understand as *their* children (Ross, 1994).

This circumstance is ontological: *Making babies* is a key part of the human condition itself. The world is simply made in this fashion, by necessity privileging—although more and more reluctantly—the role of families in the upbringing of the young (Ross, 1994). So despite the "absurd" (Friedenberg, 1979) depredations of State schooling, it remains for now the case that children (humans aged 0–18) *must* receive much, perhaps *most*, of their authentic educational help from their families. This feature of the human condition persists even if the role of parents is widely disparaged and undermined to the utmost (Hoffman, 2009; Ross, 1994). But perhaps a far more durable reality remains: Only families (however constituted) can really care for children. Parental latitude thus remains wide. Philosopher Jacob Ross observed that this latitude must encompass choices

> so crucial for the child's future as whether he is to be brought up as an Old Order Amish adolescent or provided with a high-school education so that he can be free to decide to be an astronaut when he grows up. If such decisions are granted to parents, then it can only be because parents are no mere caretakers; they are designers of the child's future, and builders of his self-image and his identity. So the view that they are mere caretakers must be amended or replaced by one that is more adequate. (Ross, 1994, p. 154).

Americans seem to acknowledge the reality noted by Ross (1994) less and less, however, and they rely more and more on State schooling to fill a void created by a diminished family parenting enterprise.[27] In fact, a long line of evidence in sociology shows that affluent families *use* schooling in contemporary America simply to pass along existing class privilege (Bickel, 2013; Collins, 2002; deMarrais & LeCompte, 1999; Jencks, 1979; Lareau, 1989). This startling conclusion also suggests that State schooling is mostly useless not only for actual educational purpose, but also for the traditional American purposes (Kliebard, 1995) of preparation for citizenship and social improvement. Schooling is clearly not the avenue to social mobility once legitimately hoped for.

What about the gifted? One might assert that the evolution of American State schooling toward a militarized (Lagotte & Wheeler-Bell, 2015; Saltman & Gabbard, 2003), corporatized, and anti-intellectual mission damages the gifted precisely because it damages everyone intellectually. Deresiewicz's fine account (2014) shows this damage among the supposed *beneficiaries* attending America's elite colleges. Proof of his thesis is difficult largely because those with exceptional talents are presumed to be successful—a high degree of talent seems virtuous by definition. More importantly, though, attainment of a lucrative career by one who is exceptionally talented and hardworking is regarded as the very definition in America of "success."

Such unquestioned views, however, set the value of both the common good and the common intellectual legacy quite low. Thus we direct the skeptical reader to the many critical works cited in this chapter and the others that also point in this direction (e.g., Aronowitz, 2000; Blacker, 2013; Gatto, 2002; Giroux, 2007; Glass, 2007; Magrini, 2014; Molnar, 1996; Saltman & Gabbard, 2003; Scott, 1998; Theobald, 2009). The

---

27 Schooling has a critical childcare function, which effectively puts the State in charge of daytime supervision of children. But the disappearance of the family role in production (small-scale retailing, manufacture, and farming) is perhaps the more important diminution of the family role in education. Again, when factories and a fully monetized economy came into being, a logical consequence was factory schooling with a monetized purpose (e.g., careerism over intellectual purpose and commodification over higher purpose). Alternative transitions (see Howley, Howley, Burgess, & Pusateri, 2008, for one largely ignored alternative) could not be considered in the rush to industrialize and commodify everything possible.

evidence may still not add up to proof, but we find the related outlooks and interpretations compelling.

If the current direction of State schooling diminishes intellect while simultaneously eroding community well-being and social justice, what alternative educative purpose seems worthy? Living life well and fully seems to us a much more worthy project on which to spend one's days in and out of school—more worthy than feigning preparation for lucrative employment or seeking a symbol that one hopes is worthy of such employment: as in the K–12 story told by Gatto (2002) or the higher-education one told by Deresiewicz (2014). Perhaps surprisingly, many, maybe all, of the families we have known well have prized this sort of alternative project (living well and fully) for their children and themselves. Maybe this is a feature of the comparatively more rural, smaller scaled places we have lived? But living well seems to remain a familial sort of project quite widely, even as the corporate culture has pushed such purposes well out of schooling both "lower" and "higher." We turn next to this quintessential educational project, set in a context of admiration for the family.

Living the Good Life as the Educational Project

In *Howards End*, the great novelist E. M. Forster (1910/1921) provides two remarkable passages about the importance of human scale for intellect. The first, from early in the novel, we quote at length:

> "Do you imply that we Germans are stupid, Uncle Ernst?" exclaimed a haughty and magnificent nephew. Uncle Ernst replied, "To my mind. You use the intellect, but you no longer care about it. That I call stupidity." As the haughty nephew did not follow, he continued, "You only care about the things that you can use, and therefore arrange them in the following order: Money, supremely useful; intellect, rather useful; imagination, of no use at all. No"—for the other had protested—"your Pan-Germanism is no more imaginative than is our Imperialism over here. It is the vice of a vulgar mind to be thrilled by bigness, to think that a thousand square miles are a thousand times more wonderful than one square mile, and that a million square miles

are almost the same as heaven. That is not imagination. No, it kills it. When their poets over here try to celebrate bigness they are dead at once, and naturally. Your poets too are dying, your philosophers, your musicians, to whom Europe has listened for two hundred years. Gone. Gone with the little courts that nurtured them—gone with Esterhaz and Weimar. What? What's that? Your universities? Oh, yes, you have learned men, who collect more facts than do the learned men of England. They collect facts, and facts, and empires of facts. But which of them will rekindle the light within?" (Forster, 1910/1921, pp. 35–36)

Forster also grasped the connection with industrial bigness, which is implied above, but which he makes explicit in the following passage, near the middle of the novel:

London was but a foretaste of this nomadic civilization which is altering human nature so profoundly, and throws upon personal relations a stress greater than they have ever borne before. Under cosmopolitanism, if it comes, we shall receive no help from the earth. Trees and meadows and mountains will only be a spectacle, and the binding force that they once exercised on character must be entrusted to Love alone. May Love be equal to the task! (Forster, 1910/1921, p. 298)

Love, beauty, truth, curiosity, care and attention, passion, compassion, imagination: These qualities are surely essential, even intellectual, features of "the good life" and, indeed, of high educational purpose. Living life well surely requires the engagement of these qualities, and forming, fostering, and cultivating them must sound like proper education to those who are teachers and to all who wonder what education (and schooling) might legitimately do and aspire to do.

Aristotle offered one classic view of living well (Aristotle, 350 BC/1954), and although the ancient philosopher might not have approved entirely of "passion," he was a reportedly devoted and even passionate father and husband, and his idea of the good life articulated a surprisingly nuanced version of happiness (see, e.g., Rubenstein, 2003).

2005; Blacker, 2013; Bowles & Gintis, 1976; Deresiewicz, 2014; Orr, 1995, 2009) conclude that nearly everyone is oppressed by the uninhabitable and unlovable factory schooling.

Teachers working the margins. General education teachers in many K–12 schools struggle with the compunction to produce higher test scores by cleaving to a hopeless routine: honoring the letter of whatever official "standards" prevail, administering "evidence-based"—often teacher-proofed—materials, and spending large blocks of time on test preparation (e.g., Baez & Boyles, 2009; Blacker, 2013; Howley & Howley, 2015). Gifted education teachers are typically not subject to this inversion of means and ends, but many are nonetheless embedded in school organizations dominated by such oppressive routines.

In some fashion, then, all teachers confront the dysfunctions of factory schooling. In schools for the poor, the oppressive routines are visible and well documented (see, e.g., Blacker, 2013; Saltman & Gabbard, 2003), as is the related outrage of a vocal minority. In factory schooling for the affluent, it's the oppressive routines of credentialism and greed that go with privilege (Deresiewicz, 2014; Kozol, 1990)—which are more difficult to see and quite unlikely to be found objectionable.

In schools serving affluent areas, however, as many as 50% of students might be formally identified as gifted. Especially in such schools, all teachers—including teachers of the gifted—confront the frenzy of credentialism and the State's official (mis)conception of the low purposes of education, characterized so well by Deresiewicz (2014) for higher education. Teachers in such circumstances have a far greater struggle to make the leap of imagination that reconstructs themselves and their work as occupying any sort of culturally productive margin. Why? Such schools are those at the very center of the contemporary arrangements of power. Teachers in such "fortunate" schools would have to repudiate much that nearly everyone there approves and values.

Sadly, the measure of success for teachers and schools elsewhere is informed by the frenzied credentialism and instrumentalism common in the small, favored, affluent group of schools mistakenly thought to be "excellent." The implication is that everyone should embrace the vices of the affluent. By contrast, occupying a margin generatively would point one—even in affluent schools and communities—in *very* different directions; for instance, toward the project of engaging the intellect as a common legacy of everyone.

Exploring the common legacy of formal culture—great works of all sorts—might be one project of such teaching. The exact curriculum (which authors, which works, which student projects) is rather less important, in our view, than the big ideas one's teaching might implement via the substantive works that it helps students enjoy. This is not new work, and some (few) teachers have done it since antiquity. In the contemporary world, though, such alternative teaching—in both sorts of schools just characterized—necessarily enacts outlooks and discloses commitments nearly the opposite of those proposed by corporations and enacted in the State's version of schooling. This book suggests the nature of those outlooks and commitments, but does not precisely propose any of them as "standard" or "best" (for similar outlooks, see also Arons, 1997; Deresiewicz, 2014; Gatto, 2002; Orr, 1995; Scott, 2012; White, 2011).

Such outlooks and commitments, such big ideas (see, e.g., Williams, 1976), establish the positive features of the margin to be occupied but also suggest many sorts of educative projects and "alternative traditions"—and these can be deployed, we find, in many different schools and communities by anyone who understands and develops them. Just as it is human to create culture, it seems also that humans aspire naturally to purposes higher than possession of a high-status credential or securing membership in a high-status career. Observe, too, that we are not advising some sort of wholesale conversion from merely coping to critical pedagogy. Change can, and usually should be, far more incremental, but a teacher on this path would surely find more and more opportunities as time passes. Later chapters will have more to say about alternatives for teachers and administrators concerned with developing exceptional talent (their own and that of those with whom they work).

Families working the margins. Some families may find talk of the higher purposes of intellectual engagement, meaning-making, and critique impractical and strange. As well they should. The system of State schooling will provide little help with this purpose. Families, as well as teachers *must*, we think, operate marginally.[28]

Instruction that addresses living well, for reasons given previously, ought to appeal to families. Such instruction would by definition or logic provide mostly authentic (habitable and lovable) experiences, and these sorts of experiences always, as we have often seen, demonstrate to parents—to families—the practicality and importance of the work being done. "What did you do in school today?" The usual answer—*nothing*—is acceptable to no one at all: not teachers, not children, not parents. When children come home with something different and more articulate to say, parents are predictably impressed.

So whatever the discipline or school subject, instruction in this margin supports the intellectual growth of children in ways that parents can see—what Hattie (2008), for instance, called "visible learning." But almost nothing like it is possible in the context of fear and loathing. So, in fact, it is rather easier to convince parents of the value of the margin than it might seem: Nearly all of them are there already.

28　*Marginalization* is always considered a curse. But when mainstream purposes and aspirations prove themselves dubious, it makes sense to occupy the margins that present themselves.

Chapter 5

The Anti-Intellectual University

If I don't go to a top-ranked college, I'll have to go to a public university. I'll be stupid.—Student quoted by Thacker (2008)

The previous chapter described the credentialism in American culture in general and its consequences for families. That discussion implicated universities in the construction of anti-intellectualism, an implication that might seem shocking or unfair if news stories about chicanery in higher education were less common. So in this chapter we want to do something other than examine chicanery. Instead we want to develop a much broader argument that interprets the relevant dilemmas and tensions of an anti-intellectual higher education in American culture—with particular relevance for talent development.

First, the chapter interrogates the phenomenon of higher learning in America. This part reviews the history of the university in America, paying most attention to developments in the latter 19th century and in the 20th century. It discusses evidence of major shifts in universities' aims and strategies, arguing that, in the 21st century, universities have developed as large businesses. In fact, universities now operate on the presumption that free trade is the arrangement that best ensures public well-being (Bok, 2004). True, universities also harbor some intellectual and political contrarians. After all, academic freedom—established by American case law as a right of university faculty—permits it.

Second, the chapter describes the prospects among the gifted for higher learning in contemporary American universities as they exist now. It recommends alternative pathways through higher education, with discussion to be provided in Chapter 9, where we present our overall proposals for schooling that better accommodates intellect. Having seen Deresiewicz's (2014) work cited so often in the previous chapter, however, readers may well imagine the tenor of the discussion in this one.

Finally, although many talented students will too predictably look to medicine and the law for suitable careers, the third section of the chapter unusually (perhaps surprisingly) commends scholarship as a career. It does so, however, in view of its assessment of the distractions and toxicities of contemporary universities. The discussion contrasts commitment to an intellectual project with commitment to an academic career—commitments with some overlap, but not so much an overlap as one might suspect. The *intellectual project*, we find, is far more important than the university career. Alternative homes for scholarship can also advance the work if universities prove unhappy homes.

Interrogating Higher Learning in America

A society, like the American one, that does not particularly value intellectual work would be unlikely to sponsor, on a large scale, organizations (such as universities) with the expressed goal of nurturing such work. It may seem odd or even outrageous to make this charge—America has some of the vaunted "best" universities in the world. And the goal of nurturing intellectual work is also espoused in two of the three conventional representations of any university's mission (i.e., teaching, research, service). First, the teaching mission purports to engage students in the work of becoming erudite, and, second, the research mission engages scholars in the process of extending knowledge. In recent decades, moreover, the resources devoted to university teaching and research have increased substantially (Willie, 2012). What, therefore, can we possibly mean?

Despite their espoused goals, universities by no means give free reign to intellectual endeavor. Barzun (1991), for example, claimed,

> The college—and the university around it—have been transformed into a motley social organism dedicated to the full life. It does include the mental life, but certainly makes no fetish of it. Rather, intellect weaves in and out of the main business, which is socialization, entertainment, political activism, and the struggle to get high grades so as to qualify for future employment. (p. 151)

And, more recently, Moir (2012) provided a similar critique:

> This new vocationalist emphasis has been conceptualized as part of a neoliberal discourse in which "the market" has come to dictate how we view the "outputs" of higher education. This new rhetoric represents fundamental change in how higher education is legitimated; one in which knowledge content is relegated to that of the possession of attributes that equip graduates to respond to the changing nature of the labor market. Given the impact of the current global economic situation there is an imperative on higher education to "deliver" on employability. However, as with the role of academics, the intellectual nature of higher education has arguably been devalued. (p. 19)

As these critiques—the first conservative and the second liberal—suggest, the intellectual work of the university, both the transmission and production of knowledge, has become narrowly construed so as to coincide with its economic and political interests (Atwell, 1993; see Ransome, 2011, for a similar argument). We use the term *instrumentalism* to describe this narrow construction.

Narrow instrumentalism has not always characterized higher education in America, however. When colleges and universities served a small, elite clientele, their concern for utility was restricted to the general notion that good education would help citizens—especially those earmarked as future leaders—take action in the world (e.g., Barzun, 1991; Rothblatt,

2003; but cf. Adams, 1918/1931). This view of higher education supported a "traditional" curriculum, rooted in the liberal arts. As industrialization progressed throughout the late 19th and across most of the 20th century, however, this rationale for higher education diminished in importance (see Veblen, 1918/2015, for a trenchant critique from the early days of this development). A brief review of the history of colleges and universities in America elaborates these changes.

The Useless College

Beginning in the colonial period in the United States, colleges prepared an elite group of young men for service in the institutionalized church. To the extent possible, such colleges resembled their European counterparts, cultivating a guild of scholars who nurtured, extended, and promulgated the ecclesiastical tradition (Cremin, 1970; Nisbet, 1971). According to Hofstadter (1961), however, these colleges differed from those in Europe in their emphasis on sectarian dogma to the detriment of intellectual inquiry. Nevertheless, the colleges provided a certain sort of intellectual nurture, producing a cadre of clerics, educators, and landowners, including some who (e.g., Veysey, 1965) became vocal advocates of serious scholarship. Colleges promoted the view that liberal studies would condition both mental and moral discipline.

For the early college teachers, however, scholarship and inquiry were not fully compatible; neither were they completely incompatible (Nieli, 2007). Whereas these educators considered scholarship as a means to foster the reasoning skills of students and thereby strengthen students' understanding of religious truths, they viewed inquiry, particularly scientific inquiry, as a threat to these truths—in line with the tenor of the times:[29]

> Science . . . was to be mistrusted on a variety of levels. It conveyed a tone which these men did not like, one which the older phrase "natural philosophy" had comfortably muffled. Science paraded nakedly, seemed vulgar; it appeared to denigrate the

[29] Veysey held this view, but his perspective is not shared by all historians of the academy (see, e.g., Nieli, 2007).

position of man in the universe. Its subject matter was also believed too easy and undemanding [sic] to deserve a major place in the classroom. In theory, science might reluctantly be given a realm of its own, comparable to that of religion in providing an understanding of the universe. In practice, science was chastised for abandoning its humble subservience. (Veysey, 1965, p. 41)

Despite the efforts of those educators holding such an outlook to preserve tradition, scientific and practical studies became prominent features of colleges just prior to the Civil War, in part because the Enlightenment offered an alternative kind of education that fit well with the ethos of the emergent industrial nation (Grubb & Lazerson, 2005; Owens, 2011; Rothblatt, 2003). Interest in the German model of higher education furthered this trend, resulting in the transformation of some of the nation's elite liberal arts colleges into major, multipurpose universities (Kerr, 1963). Science harbored a profitable practicality.

The Useful University

The multipurpose institution that developed after the Civil War attempted to accomplish a variety of possibly conflicting aims: cultivation of intellect, production of new and useful knowledge, preparation of bureaucrats and statesmen, and training in professional and vocational skills (Cohen, 2012; Grubb & Lazerson, 2005; Veblen, 1918/2015; Veysey, 1965). This institution combined elements of the British, German, and American traditions into an amalgam that some educators and social critics found workable but others did not. Kerr (1963, p. 18), for example, saw considerable value in the emerging institution, which he termed the "multiversity":

The . . . combination does not seem plausible but it has given America a remarkably effective educational institution. A university anywhere can aim no higher than to be as British as possible for the sake of the undergraduates, as German as possible for the sake of the graduates and the research personnel, as

American as possible for the sake of the public at large—and as confused as possible for the sake of the preservation of the whole uneasy balance. (p. 18)

Dungan (1970), though, questioned the extent to which universities actually managed to perform the different, seemingly incompatible ("confused") functions expected of them:

> The university in the United States has long been described as multi-functional, but a candid examination of the distribution of resources within the collectivity of institutions would show that there is a concentration in activities of interest to relatively few. Despite our protestations about pluralism and multi-functionality, we tend on the whole in higher education to do essentially the same thing with quite divergent degrees of quality. (p. 143)

According to Sigurdson (2013), moreover, that "same thing" that universities increasingly tended to focus on was research:

> The new institutional form that was emerging, although diverse and flexible, was heavily influenced by its research mission. The formation of graduate schools, the agricultural and engineering research bases of the land-grant universities and also the growth of medical education provided fertile ground for the research agenda to grow. (para. 19)

Although some critics (e.g., Kurtz, 1974; Readings, 1996; Veblen, 1918/2015) questioned the direction in which higher education in the U.S. (and other developed nations) was headed, universities in the United States became increasingly dependent on (and therefore responsive to) the interests of their funders—tuition-paying students, private donors, the State, and large corporations. In fact, some universities attempted to be so responsive that they developed academic programs constructed solely of elective courses.

Charles Eliot, president of Harvard from 1869 to 1909, was perhaps the most notable advocate of this system. Eliot believed that an elective system would allow students to enroll in the courses that were most likely to prepare them for their chosen occupations. Furthermore, he believed that individual choice would advance the interests of society by sponsoring progress of all sorts—social, economic, and scientific (Miller, 1988; Smilie, 2012).

Many faculty and administrators in higher education subsequently argued against this system, but most did not disagree with its intent (e.g., Cohen, 2012). Only a small group of these dissenters insisted that the purpose of the university was to preserve and expand the Western intellectual heritage, rather than to prepare *useful* citizens (Nieli, 2007). Many dissenters, by contrast, condemned the elective system, not for its ultimate goal of social utility, but rather for its inefficiency in meeting that goal, as evidenced by what it lacked: coherence, moral focus, and common cultural grounding (Nieli, 2007).

At Columbia, for example, President Nicholas Murray Butler argued that a *required* core curriculum grounded in the liberal arts would be the type of program most likely to cultivate in students a willingness to align personal interests with the interests of the larger society (Howley & Hartnett, 1994). Butler and many other educators of the time believed that this outcome was particularly important because increasing numbers of students from diverse backgrounds—and with different aspirations from those previously seen in the American elite—had begun to be (somewhat reluctantly) admitted to elite colleges and universities.

These students saw higher education as the route to specialized and lucrative jobs in an economy in which social progress seemed contingent on economic growth (e.g., Grubb & Lazerson, 2005). Furthermore, such students and their families began to see the college degree as a symbol of status (Deresiewicz, 2014; Levine, 1986; Veblen, 1918/2015). As a consequence, educators responded to the market demand and founded new colleges to accommodate the vocational interests and socioeconomic aspirations of an increasingly large minority of young people (Bankston, 2011). Indeed, well-established colleges expanded and modified their offerings to address the needs of this more diverse clientele (Levine,

1986). According to Levine (see also Grubb & Lazerson, 2005), these changes resulted in stratification among institutions of higher education:

> The culture of aspiration stimulated an unprecedented demand for higher education of any kind as a symbol of economic and social mobility; it also created the demand for status that enabled some colleges to select their students for the first time. Ethnic and poor students often surpassed their more affluent peers in academic ability and drive, but more often than not they were channeled into less acclaimed schools and less prestigious occupations. (Levine, 1986, p. 21)

Levine's analysis, however, simplified what seems to have been a more complicated response on the part of institutions of higher education, and considerable evidence suggests that changes took place even at elite schools like Harvard and Columbia (e.g., Howley & Hartnett, 1994; Miller, 1988; Rudolph, 1977). These institutions made significant efforts to broaden their curricula and to establish mechanisms for working with promising students from diverse backgrounds. For example, such schools began to offer essential types of courses, such as English and mathematics, at varying levels of difficulty (e.g., Arendale, 2011). They set up advising systems to help students match their aptitudes to their vocational goals, they established articulated sequences of courses in particular subject areas to correspond to the presumed needs of students at various stages in their academic careers, and they adopted tests to determine students' initial placement in these curricular sequences (Arendale, 2011).

To institutionalize these changes, universities saw the value of organizing their faculties into specialized divisions and departments (Lee, 2007). This organizational structure, in turn, encouraged further specialization of faculty and also promoted competition among departments (Rudolph, 1977).

In addition, the new organizational structure supported the development of graduate programs—many to educate aspiring professionals and some to nurture new generations of scholars (Miller, 1988). In the 1900s, institutions of higher education became increasingly vocational, in both their undergraduate and graduate programs (Grubb & Lazerson, 2005).

Interestingly, from today's vantage, their vocationalism *did not* appear to result from the concern of business for a technically educated work force. Rather, it derived from educators' interest in demonstrating the *practicality* of higher education. Whereas many business leaders[30] of that era doubted the association between academic and real-world success (Callahan, 1962), educators anticipated the benefits—both humanitarian and material—of promoting such an association (Cole, 2009; Miller, 1988). As they saw it, an expanded system of higher education, while providing business with necessary expertise, would also, and probably more importantly, provide the nation with the human resources required to solve technical and social problems. In an era characterized by its infatuation with progress, the university seemed like the logical place to bridge the gap between theoretical knowledge in the sciences and practical utility (Cole, 2009).

U.S. involvement in World War I provided colleges and universities with the opportunity to follow through on the claim that their principal role was to serve the nation. Not only did they incorporate military training into their curricula, but many colleges and universities—also at the behest of the federal government—adopted courses in history and economics that illuminated "war issues" in particular ways (Howley & Hartnett, 1994). The Army appointed a faculty member from the Massachusetts Institute of Technology as the national director of the course, who framed the purpose of the war issues course this way:

> This is a war of ideas, and . . . the course should give to the members of the Corps some understanding of the view of life and of society which they are called upon to defend and of that view against which we are fighting. (Aydelotte, 1919, cited in Allardyce, 1982, p. 706)

The course consisted of propaganda disseminated by the National Historical Service Board (NHSB), whose task, according to Barrow

---

30   See Brinkley (2004) for the view of Henry Ford, arguably the key 20th-century industrialist, who prevented his cultured and able son Edsel from attending university.

(1990), involved "rewriting social science and humanities curricula and . . . developing interdisciplinary 'war issues' courses at colleges to help institutions meet their responsibility for interpreting the war correctly" (p. 128).

The chauvinism that prompted such efforts did not end, however, once the war was over. Many colleges and universities, for example, incorporated the ideological tenets of the war issues courses into new curricular offerings (Howley & Hartnett, 1994). These courses, which were required of all students at some colleges, reconfigured the history curriculum to address political, social, and economic problems of the day. At Columbia, for instance, social science and humanities professors worked collaboratively to develop a "peace issues" course, which, soon after, became the cornerstone of an interdisciplinary core curriculum (Allardyce, 1982).

Another consequence of the global wars in the 20th century was the expansion of the research mission of American universities. Institutions of higher education responded to the State's call for scientific research to advance the nation's military and industrial aims (Ledbetter, 2011; Scott, 2006). The National Academy of Sciences (NAS), for example, passed a preparedness resolution in 1916 that advocated increased cooperation among "governmental, educational, industrial, and other research organizations to facilitate national preparedness" (Barrow, 1990, p. 131). Moreover, the NAS, in league with the federal government, established the National Research Council, whose goals were to formulate national research priorities, to assign teams of researchers to carry out high-priority research projects, and to funnel money to the organizations that employed these researchers (Barrow, 1990). The power elite began to buy university research, in other words: a new development.

Applied natural science had an obvious military utility, but social science also had a place. The Army, for example, hired university psychologists to design mental tests of various sorts to assist in the assignment of personnel (e.g., Holmes, 2014). Social science offered the promise of controlling social problems at home, a promise particularly encouraging to dispirited progressives who encountered with some alarm the social and cultural dislocations resulting from the war (Miller, 1988).

In a number of ways, the world wars attuned university administrators and faculty to the needs of the nation (Scott, 2006). Attention to such needs was not, however, incompatible with the aims that such institutions had already started to formulate for themselves: (1) the education of technical experts, (2) the production of knowledge with immediate social utility, and (3) the direct application of such knowledge in service to society (Scott, 2006). Following the world wars, however, these practical aims came increasingly to form the character of the contemporary university across the remainder of the century (Rhoads, 2011). Furthermore, they permanently altered the university's conception of intellectual work, rendering academic scholarship valuable primarily by virtue of its commercial and military usefulness (e.g., Krimsky, 2003; Rhoads, 2011).

This is the sort of transformation we have in mind, in fact, when we characterize the university as anti-intellectual. In the transformed university, research has come to be valued not only for its usefulness in the world, but notably also for its usefulness within the university as a funding stream. The best research has, in effect, become the best-funded research.

Educating technical experts. As the 20th century progressed, more and more Americans acquired respectability and a modicum of prosperity by moving into the middle class (Samuel, 2014). Their upward mobility was supported by structural changes in the economy that shifted the focus from agrarian to industrial production (Howley, Howley, & Eppley, 2013; Samuel, 2014). These changes resulted in the unprecedented growth of cities, with a consequent increase in social and political challenges (Denton, 2014). Further, the expansion of factories and their potential to generate profit led industrialists to seek ways to rationalize the production process through the application of more and more sophisticated technologies (e.g., Frontini & Kennedy, 2003). Thus, the expansion and continuing rationalization of factory work and the amelioration of social problems became important new roles for aspiring professionals (e.g., Downey, 2007). The modern university, with its authority to confer credentials, provided legitimacy to a new class of social and managerial "engineers" (Bledstein, 1976). Many observers (e.g., Adams, 1918/1931; Barzun, 1991; Crawford, 2009; Veblen, 1918/2015) have noted that to qualify for this sort of employment, socialization and attitude are far more important than knowledge or skill.

The increasing vocationalism of the university manifested itself differently in elite institutions in contrast to more accessible ones (Rudolph, 1977; Shavit, Arum, & Gamoran, 2004). According to Rudolph (1977), "specialization and a professional orientation . . . came to dominate the undergraduate experience at the very colleges and universities that had been the most trustworthy guardians of the humanist tradition" (p. 247). The land-grant colleges and state universities, which had always had a more vocational focus, abandoned the B.A. in favor of more practically named degrees (e.g., "bachelor of science"). Although elite schools tended to preserve the traditional B.A. degree, they henceforth conferred it on students regardless of whether their studies were academic or vocational. Both types of institutions, however, began to expand the duration of professional training beyond the baccalaureate level.

Moreover, vocational education, such as the training of teachers and nurses, which had previously taken place outside of higher education, gained in stature by finding a place within higher education institutions (Blank, 2010; Goodlad, 1991; Tobbell, 2014). Teacher preparation, for example, moved from 2-year programs at normal schools to 4-year programs at teachers' colleges (Goodlad, 1991). In fact, as the programs became longer, the institutions renamed themselves to signal their elevation in status: first as normal schools, then as teachers' colleges, then as state colleges, and finally as state universities (Goodlad, 1991).

Whether the university's motive was primarily institutional self-interest or primarily a response to the economic self-interest in society (i.e., corporations and individual consumers) is debatable. According to some authors (e.g., Goyette & Mullen, 2006; Reisman, 1981), for instance, the vocationalism of higher education has been a response to the consumer demands of students and their families. On this view, competition for student enrollment has caused colleges and universities to become increasingly sensitive to students' demands for practical programs leading to employment or for elite programs conferring high status (e.g., Goyette & Mullen, 2006; Veysey, 1965). Another perspective, however, suggests that colleges and universities actively shaped public demand for vocational programs and services:

The university and its sources of livelihood reflect the structural organization of our society itself. This has generated the entrepreneurial system of the American university, in which the policy-initiating bodies—both administrations and faculties—acting in the manner of capitalist entrepreneurs have become actively and competitively involved in seeking out what kinds of intellectual pursuits society could use (and therefore be willing to support) and in developing the corresponding programs of research, education, and service. (Luria & Luria, 1970, p. 76)

Regardless of which view is correct, contemporary colleges and universities, even the most elite, place greater emphasis on the training of technical experts than on the cultivation of liberal learning or the elaboration of reflective thought or critique (Baker, Baldwin, & Makker, 2012; Deresiewicz, 2014; Wilshire, 1990). Students, too, seem to be more interested than ever before in the immediate use value of what they learn, measured in dollars (e.g., Barzun, 1991; Covaleskie, 2014).

At the same time, the expertise of a widening cadre of professionals altered the conventional understanding of what knowledge is and what purposes it accomplishes (e.g., Foucault, 1975). According to Wilshire (1990), a technical view of "knowledge" (as in the knowledge of experts) discredits personal experience and alienates individuals from a sense of community. As a consequence, people come to substitute their narrowly circumscribed technical roles for more legitimate forms of self-definition, and they accept the seeming necessity of the linkage between expertise and power (Koppl, 2010). This view of social reality compels people, overall, to cede considerable power to experts—a default position that advances the economic and political interests of a ruling elite (e.g., Habermas, 1987; Koppl, 2010; Lasch, 1995; Lyotard, 1979/1984; Orr, 1995).

Such transfer of power to specialists obviously implicates the university, whose role in the production of expertise is twofold (Bledstein, 1976). As noted above, the university takes a primary role in training each new cadre of experts. Its other role in promoting expertise, however, is more direct and, as a consequence, even more significant. This role involves the employment and protection of professors who build small, but potent and durable, empires for soliciting, conducting, and marketing research (Barzun, 1991; Larsen, 2011).

Producing useful knowledge. An essential focus of the contemporary university—one derived from the German model—is the production of scientific knowledge, a mission that has come to be known as *research*. As we mentioned earlier, the work of research and the products of research became important to business, the State, and the military during World War I. Research increased in volume considerably during World War II, moreover, and, by the 1950s, had eclipsed teaching as the major function at many prominent universities (Barzun, 1968). Research also altered power relationships in institutions of higher education in ways that tended to degrade the authority of academic scholarship. Nisbet (1971) described this process:

> No one who was on the American university campus when the large research institutes began to flourish is likely to forget the shifts which took place in authority, in influence, in wealth, and in status. Overnight, it seemed, two nations came into being: the haves and the have nots; the first possessed of a form of wealth and power that owed little if anything to the university; the second identified increasingly by their lack of research money, their dependence upon the university, their largely local identities, and their ever-diminishing status in the eyes of not only administration and faculty but, in due time, of the students. (pp. 99–100)

The university's shift in focus from academic scholarship to marketable research not only altered its relationship to the larger society, but it also, and more importantly, changed the way the university viewed knowledge and how Americans, in general, came to view knowledge (Kerr, 1991; Koppl, 2010).

In the earlier view, knowledge consisted of the collective wisdom of past and present thinkers. *Any person* could decipher such wisdom through rigorous study and could contribute to it by following systematic procedures of inquiry. In the revised and now prevailing view, knowledge is specialized, impersonal, and both timely and transitory. It is available only to those who have *privileged access*, and only some people can contribute to it, namely those with certain experiences and prerogatives (Stehr & Grundmann, 2011). Knowledge has become the province of expertise, on this view. The usefulness of such knowledge, moreover, is temporary rather than durable. Its production requires continual updating by experts.

This revised view of knowledge has made it easy to *commercialize* (Koppl, 2010; Larsen, 2011). Whereas some knowledge is, of necessity, accessible to everyone, the most current and arguably significant knowledge now belongs to a select few (Konig, 2013; cf. Stehr & Mast, 2011), functioning as insider information that enlarges the dominion (a.k.a. "intellectual property rights") of particular corporate interests (Howley, 1993; Page, Bartels, & Seawright, 2013).[31] As some critics argue, however, such developments suppress the intellectual commons—that is, knowledge available to everyone and from which the human species might, as a whole, derive benefit (e.g., Lemley, 2004).

Can Knowledge Be Anti-Intellectual?

The three-pronged mission of higher education clearly concerns work that involves knowledge, and common sense holds that work with knowledge is, almost by definition, intellectual. Furthermore, for the thinkers of the Enlightenment, intellectual work *necessarily* contributed to the common good (Barzun, 2000). As our interpretation suggests, however, the extent to which work with anything called *knowledge* might contribute to the development of intellect, much less the common good, depends largely on the way knowing and knowledge are construed. There is no reason, in short, to believe that everything that today might be called *knowledge* would necessarily be healthy to the intellect—much less contribute to the common good. In fact, there is every reason to think otherwise.

When knowledge is atomized as information with a particular temporary utility and commercial value, its role in cultivating intellect (as

---

31   The field of "intellectual property rights" has expanded to include all sorts of digital code, including the addition of DNA to natural organisms, which addition, courts have sometimes ruled, renders the entire organism the intellectual property of corporations.

defined in this book, at any rate) becomes suspect. Under such circumstances, knowledge functions as a commodity rather than as an important aspect of reason or fodder for reasoning (e.g., Oreskes & Conway, 2010; Teixeira & Rotta, 2012; Vermeir, 2013). Both professors and students come to appreciate it for the price it fetches rather than for the insights it permits (Labaree, 1999). And the logic of knowledge production and knowledge use becomes the logic of the marketplace rather than the logic of internally consistent warrant or ethical reflection about intentions and consequences (Lemley, 2004; Oreskes & Conway, 2010). The gulf between these outlooks is enormous—the difference is not a subtle one.

In our view, the dynamics of teaching, research, and service in the contemporary American university contribute to making what passes as "knowledge" anti-intellectual in just these ways (cf. Barzun, 1991; Deresiewicz, 2014; Hofstadter, 1963; Urban, 2013). For the 1995 edition of this book, we drew on evidence of these developments. More recent scholarship suggests that the situation is worsening—in some cases, even to the point of threatening global stability (e.g., Blacker, 2013; Deresiewicz, 2014; Engelen et al., 2012; Oreskes & Conway, 2010). Much of what the university now teaches appears problematic to the cited observers, among many others.

This analysis offers little that is sanguine for gifted students. And yet, in niches and margins in nearly every institution of higher education, including community colleges, opportunities exist for able students seeking more than status and power. So we turn next to such prospects as do exist for a genuine education for able students in higher education: those looking to engage and honor higher intellectual purposes.

Prospects Among the Gifted for Higher Learning in America Under Neoliberal Direction

Abundantly talented students are not simply manifestations of nature, but also and importantly manifestations of nurture, that is, of culture, especially if we consider education itself as the working of culture on the young, a process lodged principally in families and communities (Arendt, 1954/1968; Eliot, 1948; Mukherjee, 2016; Ross, 1994). Abundant talent comes from culture, and arguably needs to give back to culture. For this reason, provisions for the schooling of abundantly talented students (from preschool to university) are by no means a neutral technology of best practices or the actions of a set of familial and culturally derived entitlements. Any argument that proceeds from the principle that students (including abundantly talented ones) should attend the "best college" that admits them misconstrues education, culture, and intellect. Our perspective pushes against conventional wisdom, so let us explain it.

Gifted Students and Higher Learning in the University

In America at least, a wide profusion of institutions of higher education exists. They cannot really be ordered from best to worst, though of course, a great many schemes purport to provide such rankings, and nearly everyone—from students and their families, to university administrators and professors, to higher education policymakers—pays attention (Sponsler, 2009). The rankings exhibit varying commitments and purposes, but their methods remain ad hoc, and, worse, the many steps from design to data collection to interpretation to consequences in use (Sponsler, 2009) are dubious at best. One might well, as some suggest, regard the whole business as a sort of game played to propagate envy and pretension (Thacker, 2008). Sponsler (2009) imagined helpful uses for rankings but tellingly observed, "Rankings have the potential to shift institutional behaviors in ways that may negatively affect policy goals"

(p. 2). It seems reasonable to entertain the corollary observation with respect to the goals held by families and students: Rankings may mislead and confuse them. We suspect that many are indeed misled and confused.

Thacker (2008) quoted a student and a parent to illustrate the corollary, which serves as the epigraph for this chapter. The student believed that "if I do not get into a top ranked college, I'll have to go to a public university. I'll be stupid" (p. 15). The parent remarked on the rating of her child's college, "So you're only a 14!" The admissions officer at a "highly ranked" university summed up the main proposition: "We are all lying to improve our rank" (Thacker, 2008, p. 15). Deresiewicz (2014) would doubtless agree, but his critique is more foundational, plumbing the cultural depths of what education means at elite American schools under such a regime of envy and pretension. The foolish rankings are but a symptom of a more general dysfunction, in his view, and ours.

That view, we argue, is neither rightist nor leftist, but human. In human terms, families are exercising proper interest when they consider what their children will (and should) study in college, why they should study it, and how they plan to use it. This circumstance remains true even as institutional and familial thought and action are deformed by the powerful messages of corporate and government spokespersons who conflate higher education with career preparation in service of national or narrowly instrumental personal agendas. Corporations (and the corporate university) use families' concern for their children's well-being to market college degrees as a protection against all manner of future miseries, both personal and social (e.g., Deresiewicz, 2014). After all, the predominant view of human welfare is that free trade will best secure the benefits that all desire. Such marketing of degrees predictably directs many families and students toward a narrow view of personal gains and away from intellectual sense-making and critique.

By contrast—some few families and some talented students within some of them—find reason to evade the envy and the pretension and to value educational experiences for their contribution to self-realization and sense-making. Rural parents, for instance, often treat family and community relationships as more important than the career advancement of their children (Howley, Howley, & Showalter, 2015); for a discussion of able rural high school *students* who think and act this way, see Burnell (2003). Outside rural places, though, it has seemed to us that many families accept the conventional view of higher education, perhaps because they see few alternatives. But according to some accounts both past and present, the upper middle class routinely embraces schooling as a route to status and affluence (e.g., Adams, 1918/1931; Bickel, 2013; Collins, 2002; deMarrais & LeCompte, 1999; Deresiewicz, 2014; Jencks, 1979).

So we find that the project of helping gifted students sort out their intellectual projects and intellectual mission in life is an improvisation for both families and students. The improvisation may benefit from highly unconventional thinking about all of schooling, and from a clear perspective on education as a deeply cultural process (e.g., Bruner, 1996). Precisely because it is deeply cultural, it is also a process that is completely ordinary and ordinarily humble (Williams, 1958/2001). Rural families, occupying a cultural margin, are understandably better positioned to contradict conventional wisdom.

The sort of thinking called for is quite out of step with the conventional view that education, first, coincides quite well with schooling, and, second, that investments in higher education secure success in America. The investments to be made, however, are increasingly personal ones from family resources: Even the states are abandoning public support of higher education. Mortenson (2012) tellingly asserted, "Based on the trends since 1980, average state fiscal support for higher education will reach *zero* by 2059" (p. 26, emphasis added). The prediction may be inaccurate, but the trend is clear. One needs to think more deeply about culture and education, and plan much more circumspectly. What is to be done? We make suggestions next for gifted students in particular.

Higher Schooling and Lower Aspirations

As described in detail above and in the previous chapter, university schooling in contemporary America is advertised nearly everywhere as the surest pathway to economic security for everyone (Rosenbaum, Stephan, & Rosenbaum, 2010). Our speculations, below, proceed from a sense of the mismatch between the capacities and dispositions of gifted students and what universities now typically have on offer.

Our best guess is that the *mismatch* will be discomfiting: Expectations for privileged employment, even or especially among the gifted, are unlikely to materialize widely (see, e.g., Piketty, 2014). Many will be left—as indeed they already are—to improvise using whatever financial, intellectual, and personal resources they possess. This unfortunate circumstance, however, is still the one that confronts humans *de rigueur*: It is the human condition. One therefore needs more than much-admired degrees and devoted careerism for the inevitable confrontation (Green, 2000). One traditional option is religion. Still another—increasingly less accessible—is a strong family. Another is intellectual engagement with philosophy, science, literature, art, and music. Rapid-school learners would seem well positioned to access these latter intellectual options, but whatever choices one makes benefit from the sense one can make of life as a result of education far beyond schooling. Knowledge of electrical engineering or the derivatives market may prove quite useful but will not usually suffice to make sense of life.

But what exactly does "mismatch" mean in this context? For the minority who develop an intellectual mission, employment is typically a more subsidiary—but not irrelevant—concern. For such as these, Dorothy Parker's (1928) famous line applies: "Salary is no object; I want only enough to keep body and soul apart. The one thing I ask is that I have a bit of time to myself" (p. 77). Of course, a bit of time to oneself is *precisely* what nearly all employers cannot give: One has already sold one's time to them. Finding employment where one can do a job while simultaneously conducting one's own work is—jesting quite aside—the secret behind Parker's jest. One ought to take employment seriously, but not too seriously.

Like Parker (whose work was wit), *one needs a work*. Work is not synonymous with a job: It's only that one *does* need enough to keep body and soul apart—or together, if that is more important. Of course (and sadly), most people hate their jobs (e.g., Gallup, 2013). With a job that proves compatible with one's work, the job and the work support one another. The Gallup (2013) survey suggested that about 20% of workers experience this happy congruence to some extent. A high degree of congruence must be rarer still.

Remember, however, that high-school dropout William Faulkner is said to have written *As I Lay Dying* while employed as a security guard (Spillman, 2012). One can hold a job and carry out one's own project, completely unauthorized and unappreciated by, and even contrary to the real purposes of, one's employer. One must, like Faulkner (and many others, including Parker), extemporize and not calculate success, American-style, in dollars and status. The common good in America needs many more such people than it gets.

Those able students who can extemporize in this way, though, will be the lucky few: Whatever their resources, meager or sufficient, they will understand the necessity and value of improvisation to their intellectual project. Many with budding intellectual projects will be less lucky, and too few others will ever claim a project of their own, as a result of both miseducation and luck—including even the conventional good luck of college in the Ivy League (see Deresiewicz, 2014). Lower aspirations as conventionally understood (that is, lower aspirations for status and wealth), we find, are definitely in order for able students. Much higher aspirations (that is, aspirations to a much higher purpose), though, are needed for discovering and pursuing intellectual projects in America. This sobriety about aspirations is wanting, in gifted education as well as in American education in general. Indeed, lower salary and status aspirations coupled with aspirations to higher purpose will push talented students to the margins where they can do their best cultural work (see Chapter 4 for the extended presentation about why cultural margins are so important).

Making lower salary and status aspirations work. The greatest foolishness in the field of gifted education has been the expectation—the fatuous aspiration—that those identified "scientifically" and schooled "appropriately" would succeed brilliantly by producing wondrous works and influencing culture profoundly (e.g., Terman, 1925). We now recognize such expectations as part of the hubris of 20th-century scientism (Scott, 1998; cf. Terman & Oden, 1959; Terzian, 2008). What were we thinking?

Ordinary people have always known—and will say so—that being good at school is not much of a predictor at being good in work or in life.[32] The aspirations of the field were, in essence, a hope for its own justification, and they have proven far less sound than once hoped. Terman's gifted students who became "successful" succeeded in the ordinary American way. But many from this famed sample did not even become professionals (Terman & Oden, 1959). And those who did so exhibited, for instance, the modal "achievement" of completing medical or law school. Studies of more recent cohorts, not surprisingly, show much the same results (e.g., Freeman, 2006). This sort of outcome is clearly tied more to family background and cultural capital than to high IQ (Bourdieu & Passeron, 1977; Bowles & Gintis, 1976; Hauser, Warren, Huang, & Carter, 2000).

Being good at school knowledge surely helps one gain access to professional training, but *giftedness* is not necessarily an advantage in this respect. *Many* students are quite good at school knowledge, do not require instruction more "advanced" than usual, and can earn grades that demonstrate sufficient mastery of school knowledge. Many of these students will (and do) thrive better in high school than many gifted students do. Indeed, whatever the level of schooling, the more *normal* and generally *compliant* they are—given a baseline of academic aptitude— the more acceptable they will be as students in the eyes of conventional educators (Clinkenbeard, 2012; Gatto, 2002; Schlechty, 2002; Speirs Neumeister, Adams, Pierce, Cassady, & Dixon, 2007). They, too, can go to law school and medical school; they, too, can secure a Ph.D. Thus, no good reason exists to conclude that *the gifted* should aspire more than a great many others to eventual professional status—and such success is decidedly not tantamount to realizing great expectations. A long line of empirical research supports this conclusion (well-reviewed and extended, for instance, by R. Hauser and colleagues, 2000).

Service-related jobs, including professional as well as working-class services, comprise a larger proportion of jobs at present than in the past,

---

32   They are only partly right. Correlations between intelligence and income are moderate—for all the predictable reasons, including unfair privilege. Bowles and Gintis (1976) showed that once the privilege is accounted for (e.g., educational attainment), IQ does not actually correlate so strongly with earnings.

but competition for the proportion that *is* professional (about one-third) is inevitably intense. This competition, though, is governed by the same norms of inequity and disregard of solidarity (e.g., Walker & Mehr, 1992) that not coincidentally characterize so much of schooling and of American society in general (e.g., Autor, Katz, & Kearney, 2006; deMarrais & LeCompte, 1999; Tye, 2000).

Both agriculture and manufacturing now offer vastly diminished employment (Wyatt & Hecker, 2006), the result of corporate and governmental decisions across the second half of the 20th century. In the stead of agriculture and manufacturing, Americans confront nonunionized, largely part-time jobs, in the "service industry," largely in big-box stores, in fast-food restaurants, and in paraprofessional health care work. This work is *not* inherently demeaning, but the related *jobs* are almost always constructed that way socially and economically: Hourly wages are inadequate to support a family, weekly hours are short, and benefits meager. The prospect of living in such circumstances is enough to engender the sort of desperation required to convince everyone of the need to attend college. It's the dreadful war of each against each, famously described as the state of nature by philosopher Thomas Hobbes (1651).

"College for all" seems positioned as a maneuver more desperate than hopeful, especially in view of declining state support for public universities (Mortenson, 2012) and rising tuitions for families. Our objection here is practical: *Because* predictions about the rather distant future (10 years hence, for instance) are famously inaccurate, and *because* employment is inherently insecure, we see two very different options—under prevailing circumstances—for pursuit of university education by gifted students, armed with suitably unconventional aspirations (see Chapter 9 for the discussion of the pathways we call "rotated" and "accelerated").

Life In and Out of the Anti-Intellectual University

This chapter concludes with an assessment of the anti-intellectual university as a home for active intellect. We know that beyond becoming lawyers and physicians, academically talented students will also think of becoming university faculty members. This is something we know about from having exercised this aspiration ourselves—after real-world experience in K–12 schooling. But the university is now very different from the one our parents experienced in the 1930s and 1940s, and the one we experienced in the 1960s.

We should use the plural, *universities*, because they differ in many ways: size, location, tuition, structure, curriculum, and, of course, prestige. But they are also much alike in that nearly all, like K–12 schools, have become ever more like businesses (Bok, 2004). Certainly the most prominent universities in every state, even the least populous, have become large businesses in their own right, and their own profitability takes precedence over other purposes (Bok, 2004).

Why would anyone with an intellectual project work in such places? The answer is that teaching, research, and "service" still *do* exist within this corporatized university context. So with respect to gifted students maturing to work in faculty roles, we advise that some good work *is* possible in a university. What follows next, then, is a rare account of the intellectual purposes and strategies for maintaining intellectual focus as a faculty member. We provide it for students and families thinking about the other well-trodden pathway (aside from doctor and lawyer) for exceptionally talented youngsters: *professor.*

In the midst of the higher education gloom, some scholars thrive with intellectual projects rightly at odds with the tenor of the commercialized and commodified university. Such scholars cannot, of course, constitute the norm, nor have they ever, to judge from the history of human inquiry (Rubenstein, 2003). The difference in the contemporary world is that universities have only now become fully integrated, intellectually speaking, into the ideology of free trade and globalization represented as best securing the common good (Aronowitz, 2000; Barrow,

1990; Blacker, 2013; Bok, 2004; Deresiewicz, 2014; Labaree, 1999; Oreskes & Conway, 2010).[33] And so—in view of the challenges—we turn to the opportunities for students interested to work (nonetheless) in the compromised university.

Marginality. There are still excellent reasons to work in universities, although they are not the old reasons or the conventionally imagined ones. Scholars are typically caricatured as absent-minded, isolated, and ineffectual, of course. We know some such colleagues, but the caricature is inapt because it is such an exception. The caricature at least points in the direction of cultural marginality, a construct we explored in the previous chapter, as the likely place to do good work.

If the tenor of the university is inimical to intellectual work, then intellectual projects carried on within it are best positioned at its margins. Let us explain what we mean in this case. Four sorts of margins apply: (1) of focus on "the work," (2) of intellectual independence, (3) of doubt and skepticism, and (4) of critique. We treat each form of marginality next. These margins, moreover, apply across faculty roles (i.e., teaching, research, service).

Focus on "the work" trumps all else in the faculty role.[34] We refer to the specific intellectual work of being a faculty member. Why? The purpose of the role is to help others engage the work (teaching), to do it oneself (research), and to help struggle for arrangements that facilitate the work (service). What is "the work" exactly? It's an intellectual project or mission, and we describe its features shortly, but first we point out the alternative foci that distract so many faculty members from the work. These include worry about tenure; academic and intellectual fearfulness; a routine approach to teaching; and wasting time on organizational pet-

---

33   The original European universities were invented by the Roman church. But they soon troubled and changed the Church by incorporating pagan (i.e., classical and Muslim) sources into Catholic scholarship, developments that led to the rise of empiricism and to the Reformation (Barzun, 2000; Rubenstein, 2003). Observe that, like neoliberalism, the ideology of the Church claimed to represent and secure the common good. It is the project of intellect (as we define it) to examine and to critique such momentous positions. Indeed, that project seems to us the core of a scholar's vocation.
34   Schlechty (2002) recognized that focus on the work ought to prevail in K–12 schooling, as well. Working on the work is apparently difficult to sustain in most organizations. When profitability takes charge of the decision making, however, some sorts of work—good teaching, for instance—will be rendered unsustainable.

tiness. The distractions are so compelling that they seem to overwhelm most junior faculty members and quite a few senior colleagues. Resisting the distractions—being resilient to them—is needed to sustain "the work." There is no other legitimate purpose for working as a university faculty member. *Keeping to the work* therefore is an actual margin because so many colleagues prove susceptible to the distractions. If one acts otherwise, one therefore occupies a generative margin within the institution.

Intellectual independence depends on having a mission (the work) that one defines for oneself. It will surely connect with others' intellectual projects, but discovering those others is in fact part of how one positions the work. Piggybacking one's career on the work of others can indeed be worthy effort, but it hardly constitutes intellectual independence. What *does* make one intellectually independent? In our experience, the essential preparation is wide reading, especially wide reading well beyond one's specialization. We find that one's specialization needs context, whatever the field. Scientists should read history and novels and historians should read science (see, e.g., Snow, 1959/1993).

But this sort of reading is very rare—in our experience—even, and perhaps especially, among faculty members. As explained in the first section of the chapter, university faculty members are, after all, more and more constructed by their schooling and by American culture as specialists and grant-seekers (e.g., Barrow, 1990; Bok, 2004; Vermeir, 2013). Intellectual independence is not practical—in that craven sense. So intellectual independence is another margin—one that reinforces the marginality of "the work."

Doubt and skepticism may be the hallmarks of science, but they are also, we find, essential to genuine thinking of any sort. Thinking—at the high levels we are considering here—requires one to examine claims, positions, and arguments, and not just to bring analysis to bear on an issue or hypothesis. Unfortunately, received wisdom accrues in academic fields, as in other walks of life, to the point where opposition to it requires unusual fortitude—and the capacity to endure the abuse that opposition to it provokes. But few students prepare themselves for this eventuality, and most, in our experience, fear it.

In the field of education, for instance, received wisdom is actually purveyed as "best practice." Doubting established best educational practice threatens established interests and invites condemnation. But every field has its set of best practices not easily subjected to doubt because its worth is considered indubitable. So doubt and skepticism normally involve one in an oppositional stance that puts one's original ideas firmly in a field's margins. Honest inquiry, as well as intellectual independence, clearly requires a scholar to occupy this margin. It's excellent work if one can get it, and "getting it" requires hard work.

Critique defines the fourth, and perhaps most difficult, margin. The critique that the intellectual work known as *scholarship* requires is to explore the limits of ideas (Howley, 2009). This margin remains unappreciated, we find, in many corners of academe. In our own field of education research, for instance, the standards of the American Educational Research Association (see AERA, 2006) fail completely to grasp the concept or the practice of critique (Howley, 2009). Thus, in our own field (and that of most readers of this book) the margin has been solidly—and ignorantly—established by those charged with creating "best practices" for research! Some fields (e.g., philosophy, arts criticism) are better informed, perhaps. But critique as systematic testing of the limits of ideas will remain difficult and contentious work everywhere. Such is its nature.

How does one test the limits of ideas? In all research efforts, scholars need to assess concepts, constructs, dilemmas, contentions—as well as bald controversies—as applicable to defining research questions; developing and adopting methods; accessing sources (e.g., gathering data); carrying out all sorts of analyses; interpreting results; and making recommendations. Such considerations are those most momentous in scholarship, particularly for discovering or inventing one's scholarly project, and all its bits and pieces. The want of critique in scholarship ensures poor science, poor thinking, and poor writing. Much academic work is meager, even poor (Barzun, 2001; Howley, Howley, & Yahn, 2014; Kneller, 1957/1994).

The kind of marginality under these four rubrics (focus on "the work," intellectual independence, doubt and skepticism, critique) concerns what other sources fatuously imagine to be "excellence" (cf.

Ericsson, 1996). In particular, we are not referring to work assessed *later on* in its existence as excellent by those supposedly qualified to judge it (Ericsson's concern). We are instead referring to *work-in-progress* that would *not* be welcomed as excellent when the worker is actually producing it. This in-progress situation is where "the work" actually transpires.

Thus, any intellectual worker seeking recognition as a producer of excellent work *later on* has entirely missed the point of "the work." In short, a proper focus actually *requires* the marginality that prevents conventional wisdom from seeing its value early on. So the conventional wisdom that both values and awards honors, ribbons, and medals must remain perpetually clueless about serious work in progress. It's an ontological condition, a condition of reality. To embrace the work, one must grasp this reality.

It should be easy to see that seeking excellence tends to confine intellectual effort to best practice, fearfulness, and intellectual subservience in place of intellectual independence. The focus turns from "the work" to the distractions explained previously. Later on, the work-in-progress may be found excellent, but just as often it will not. Its justification is simply that we do it—trying our damnedest. These margins tend to be lonely places.

This point is difficult for anyone not doing such work to grasp, but it is crucially important. Ericsson's famous claim that expertise requires 10 years (10,000 hours) of practice strikes us apt, but his view is retrospective, and the place where one does "the work" (and one always hopes it may be one's best work) is in an actual moment—in the now, and right here in front of one. Worry, then, about eventual accolades is not just distracting, but intellectually, and perhaps emotionally, crippling. In fact, any such worry seems to us to be *always* unfortunate. Many in academe seem afflicted by it, however!

A university vocation. A university home cannot supply a vocation: This is our principal message in this final section. One must bring the vocation to the university, whose appreciation of it will be predictably limited. Nonetheless, universities are one of the few organizations that claim to provide such a home, and the claim itself is some encouragement to attempt a faculty role.

If the university is not a happy home, other good ones exist. One's own home, for instance, could prove a better one for "the work." Mandelbrot (2012), for example, although sometimes courted by universities for his mathematical brilliance, spent most of his career at IBM, whose research department reportedly gave him that "bit of time for myself" for which Dorothy Parker (1928) longed.

One can, it seems, pursue an intellectual project in adulthood in the same spirit of improvisation previously commended for dealing with undergraduate schooling. Many advisors to government and industry also have behaved in this way, and one suspects that the movement in and out of academe is good for their intellectual projects. But over everything the importance of "the work" must loom large.

Prospects for the University

Derek Bok (2004), former president of Harvard, warned that universities are losing their intellectual focus, and *his* account focuses on elite universities. Bok is a moderate who argued, in fact, for the relevance of free trade to the improvement of teaching (yet another claim that free trade underwrites the common good). Despite such a position, even he believes that universities suffer from commercialization (his term) and that time is short for action to save *any* higher purpose for higher education. This conclusion from an insider of such stature is remarkable, and remarkably disturbing.

Our perspective, though, is rather different from Bok's—we find that universities are not simply commercialized, but instead that their entire ideological base has changed. They have become adherents to the free-trade ideology that we characterize with others as neoliberalism: the ideology of globalized capital (e.g., Harvey, 2005; Labaree, 1999; Slaughter & Rhoades, 2000). When knowledge becomes intellectual property instead of being a gift to all humankind (Walsh, 2015), it seems that an educational collapse has already begun. Public K–12 schooling, too, is collapsing under the related assault of privatization (Blacker, 2013; Glass, 2016; Ravitch, 2013).

Schooling, however—both lower (K–12) and higher (university)—is simply one historical provision to educate, although it certainly was a stunning provision. It's useful to remember, in this context, that mass schooling—schooling as we know it—is itself a feature of mass society created by industrialization (Cremin, 1988; Katz, 1968; Meyer et al., 1997). Mass society shows no sign of disappearing, and one must suspect that K–12 schooling, in some massive form, will also persist. So it seems that those with an intellectual mission who choose the professorial path in the future will find a still vigorous higher education machine. Finding a minimally suitable context in which to do one's work will remain much the challenge that it has always actually been across the centuries (Barzun, 1945, 1968, 1991, 2000). The details and devils of 2050 will differ in kind and degree from those characterized by Veblen (1918/2015), but they will probably be familiar in outline to academics past and present as well as the future ones.

Predictions aside, whatever ensues in the future, two related prospects for the university will be addressed in reality, and perhaps soon. First, tuition that outstrips inflation will have families—goaded to action by fear of a dicey future—taking on ever greater debt. It will not prove a sustainable arrangement. Even worse, desperate action to secure degrees will probably not suffice—indebted graduates would not find employment. Or, possibly, the market will simply price itself out of customers. Eventually, a better system to manage postsecondary enrollments and cost will have to emerge—logic seems to require it. Bok (2004) and his allies suspected the "invisible hand" of the market will arrange things well. It will certainly arrange something, eventually.

Second, though, is the strange imperative that everyone attend a 4-year program. No other nation, to our knowledge, insists on such an arrangement. Many other arrangements seem wiser, including robust apprenticeship programs for skilled trades, and even competitive examinations to apportion places in universities, which is a provision that progressive-minded educators find distasteful. Comparatively few of us are temperamentally suited to *intellectual engagement as an academic experience*. One does not, after all, need the university for intellectual engagement, and even the supposed best universities are inauspicious places for the intellectual engagement of most students (Deresiewicz,

2014). So the notion of college-for-all seems unsustainable both on its own merits, as well as on its practicalities (i.e., debt, universal degree completion).

Even from a market perspective (i.e., citizens as consumers of the higher education product), pushback to the prevailing circumstances seems probable. More public financial support for college attendance is clearly in order. But providing better options than college-for-all also makes logical and practical sense. Chapter 9 presents our own proposals for a revamped system of public schooling positioned to honor intellectual development very broadly.

In any case, the sweep of history is vast and the possibilities for the future, to read them from the past, must be equally vast. In this frame of reference we are certain, in fact, that something like the university will continue, some place where those concerned with "the work" will somehow carry on doing it. The human artifact, and humanity along with its artifact, need the work to continue on their behalf—even as corporations attempt to extract maximum profit from it. We suspect that the spirit of skepticism, critique, and intellectual independence will continue to do what it must, and not only, or in the most productive way, in whatever might persist as "the university."

Chapter 6

Gifted Education Opposing Intellect

Schooling practice over the many decades since about 1940 has found acceleration widely repugnant (see, e.g., Cox, Daniel, & Boston, 1985; Gallagher, 2004; Olthouse, 2015; Stanley, 1978, 1986),[35] even though grade skipping is said to have been common practice before the consolidation of factory schooling during the first half of the 20th century (see, e.g., Henry, 1920; Matthews, 2010). Acceleration makes sense empirically: fiscally (Assouline, Colangelo, VanTassel-Baska, & Lupkowski-Shoplik, 2015; Christopherson, 1981; Colangelo, Assouline, & Gross, 2004), intellectually (Colangelo et al., 2004; Gallagher, 2004; Kulik & Kulik, 1984; Stanley, 1978), and emotionally (Cross, Andersen, & Mammadov, 2015; Gronostaj, Werner, Bochow, & Vrock, 2016; Steenbergen-Hu & Moon, 2011). And it remains seldom practiced, especially in its most prominent, whole-grade forms (Assouline et al., 2015; Kanevsky, 2011). What happened? This chapter tries to explain the phenomenon in the context of anti-intellectualism in American schooling and culture, rather than as a failure of policy (Gallagher, 2004) or common sense (Stanley, 1986)—although both failures are implicated by the discussion in this chapter.

Removal of bright children from the mainstream has, in our opinion, been a fateful turn, possibly a fatal one for gifted education. Common

35 Gallagher (2004) characterized educator reaction as "strongly negative" (p. 43). The term *repugnance* seems more appropriate than *reluctance*.

use of "radical acceleration" (Gross & van Vliet, 2004; Stanley, 1978) for exceptionally talented students would have helped both the children and the field thrive, and perhaps helped even schooling itself to do a bit better.[36] Acceleration is the strategy that usually keeps gifted students in the mainstream, though not, of course, in the lockstep of age-grade placement.

The numerous accelerative tactics are not and cannot be made ideal, but they offer proven efficiency and effectiveness; yet their deployment remains uncommon (Assouline et al., 2015; Olthouse, 2015). As Stanley (2004) noted, there are "at least twenty different ways in which this can be done well" (p. 5). Southern and Jones (2015) discussed all 20 of them. Sorting out, facilitating, sustaining, and modifying the arrangements would be good and steady work for an instructional team in *any* school or district (Assouline et al., 2015; Colangelo, Assouline, & Lupkowski-Shoplik, 2004). But it's not happening often.

What happens instead of what makes proven sense? The overall strategy of gifted education *practice* within factory schooling might be characterized as "bait-and-switch." Here's how it works. Schooling first identifies some students as academically or intellectually superior, then separates them part-time from other students in enrichment pull-out classes, and there cultivates the selected students to regard themselves as especially deserving of privilege (Howley, 1986; Margolin, 1996): bait-and-switch. The "bait" is academic talent with the implied obligation to develop it through hard work, and the "switch" is to easy entitlement, gifted processes, and feeling (instead of thinking). The evasion of thinking, as the previous chapters explained, is a hallmark of American schooling. Why should the principle not apply to gifted education? Clearly, it does apply.

Gifted education might have challenged the age-grade lockstep by insisting and arranging acceleration as a routine accommodation, but it has very seldom managed this simple provision. Olthouse (2015) is on the right track: "Teachers are too often caught in the crossfire between

---

36 We believe that pacing equivalent to a reduction of 3 years in the K–12 sequence is needed by most exceptionally talented students, and not only the "highly gifted." So, in our reading of it, Stanley's "radical" modifier indicates more the strength of the resistance to this modest variance, not some extremely bold proposal reserved for rare precocity.

the real learning needs of students and district policies or traditions" (p. 160). The local manifestations that deflect interest in acceleration are not rarities. And the local policies and traditions are not accidental or ignorant mistakes. They are, to the contrary, intentional and remarkably effective. And they come from deeply structured cultural, political, and economic norms (see, e.g., Tye, 2000).

Gifted education practice is, we find, anti-intellectual on purpose. To explain, the chapter unpacks three relevant displacements (phases of the bait-and-switch gambit): (1) displacement of effort by entitlement, (2) displacement of content by process, and (3) displacement of thought by feeling. The chapter concludes with a few suggestions for advocating better arrangements for gifted students in schooling as it now exists. Chapter 9 will extend the discussion considerably.

Entitlement Displaces Effort

The view that ability bestows an unearned entitlement seems to be peculiarly American (see, e.g., Bianchi & Lancianese, 2005; Holloway, 1988), but it may seem astonishing that gifted programs often adopt goals that are irrelevant to students' abilities. Nonetheless, many or most programs emphasize affective counseling, creativity, problem solving, and leadership. This curriculum is a regime of socialization that is, at best, irrelevant to intellectual substance. In this first subsection we unpack two things: (1) the debate about qualitatively different gifted education and (2) leadership training in gifted education.

Gifted Children Are Not Qualitatively Different Children

Circumstances are so structured as to silence curiosity in the classroom about special programming given to children called gifted.[37]

---

37   Children not selected as gifted nonetheless learn via the hidden curriculum that their own shortcomings keep them from the privileges the "gifted" enjoy (see, e.g., Margolin, 1994; Weiler, 1978).

Sapon-Shevin (1994) found that teachers discourage discussions about why some children are selected for gifted programs while others are not:

> Some teachers said that the children simply "never ask," and many of the teachers seemed quite relieved that there was limited discussion about the issue and added parenthetic comments such as "They're good about it, they don't ask," or "I don't have any problems with them—they don't ask." (p. 37)

What are the different experiences reserved for the "gifted" classmates? Why do they get them? For those not selected, as Sapon-Shevin's evidence suggested, *it's none of their business.* The discourse of the classroom and the profession put discussion not only off-limits, but also quite literally "out of mind."

So, how *do* gifted and regular programs differ? The answer is easily given, and wrong: Gifted programs are different because gifted children are themselves qualitatively different from all others (see Borland, 1997, and Dai, 2010, for extended discussions). The gifted child is a different kind of child.

To illustrate the supposed qualitative difference, some writers ascribe to giftedness qualities such as creativity, a sense of humor, independence, and the ability to transfer or generalize concepts readily (see Tuttle & Brecker, 1980, pp. 11–17 for examples). Alas, such qualities are universally human, and by no means restricted to the class of individuals singled out by virtue of a superior ability to do schoolwork (Borland, 1997; Dai, 2010).

If the argument that the gifted are a different kind of child sounds familiar, it may be because a very similar argument was used to justify separate schooling for African Americans (supposed to be a different kind of person from European Americans). The comparison is apt and the reality equally odious; let us explain.

As Gould (1981) suggested, such misconceptions as the qualitative difference of the gifted preposterously misrepresent both nature and society. No empirical support at all exists for the widely accepted misconception that gifted children are different in kind from other children (Dai, 2010). The misconception also exhibits a convenient, and profoundly unsettling, consistency with virulent forms of 19th-century racism (Fancher, 1985; Gould, 1981). Terman, of course, is a principal originator of gifted education, and his own sloppy misconceptions, marred by the racism of his day (e.g., the eugenics movement in America), have had preponderant influence in the field (Fancher, 1985; Gould, 1981; Margolin, 1994, 1996).

No wonder gifted programs have been institutionalized as qualitatively different. And no wonder most such programs are elitist. They were designed that way (Margolin, 1996): "The gifted curriculum was not and never became focused on core academic subjects (e.g., math, science, or language arts) but instead became focused on giftedness itself" (p. 164).

Pull-out enrichment exemplifies programs designed to reflect "qualitative differences." Class sizes are generally smaller than in general education and instructional formats are more varied. Instructional objectives usually focus on cognitive processes (such as inquiry, divergent thinking, and problem solving) and on metacognitive processes (such as planning and organizing complex tasks). Many enrichment programs include the development of social and leadership skills among their objectives. Academic content is unnecessary—responsibility for that phase of instruction falls to general education.[38]

Propagating the myth of qualitative difference entails a host of evils, the worst of which are the embedded lessons. We teach children that something called *giftedness* is an entitlement to a privileged life, and we teach children not selected for the gifted program that this allocation of privilege is perfectly natural and fair.

But schoolchildren identified as gifted (e.g., those selected for high test scores) are *not* different in kind from other children, and they do not require instruction in different sorts of things (e.g., leadership, creative problem solving, and "enrichment" generally). The unfairness is mistaken by some educators as indicating that all children must be gifted

---

38   Kim (2016) found a positive effect of enrichment on achievement in a recent meta-analysis. The achievement measures, though, were not restricted to actual academics but included interest levels, metacognition, thinking skills, attitudes, career aspirations, and creative abilities. The confounding of achievement with enrichment curriculum itself renders results of this study moot.

(e.g., Myers & Ridl, 1981). But that claim is false, too: By definition, only a few children demonstrate *exceptional* academic ability.

What do these students require? They require faster progress through the usual academic curriculum, advanced courses, and early matriculation in higher education (or entry into other postsecondary options). *Most* gifted children require these arrangements, but *few* receive it—and this bait-and-switch routine has been institutionalized for decades (Assouline et al., 2015; Colangelo et al., 2004).

Acceleration and advanced classes can be understood as *quantitatively* different programs for gifted students. The rationale reflects the defining characteristic of exceptionally talented students: They learn verbal and mathematical concepts more rapidly than other children and should have instruction to match. The reality is quite simple—vexingly simple. Absent a momentous and unlikely cultural sea change, opposition to acceleration will remain strong in both gifted and general education, even if none of the claims against it has much merit (see, e.g., Kulik & Kulik, 1984; Margolin, 1996; Steenbergen-Hu & Moon, 2011).

Nonetheless, a few families and teachers convinced by common sense and research will (and must) conduct rear-guard actions to arrange acceleration; we have ourselves done so. This is the reality that leads many observers (e.g., Gallagher, 2004) to note the importance of excellent parenting in arranging the education of exceptionally able students. Neither the profession, nor the polity, nor the anti-intellectual culture supports schooling that is appropriate for their children. They must take it on themselves. Children from impoverished backgrounds suffer disproportionately as a result: Their families' attention is absorbed by threats more dire than inappropriate schooling.

Make no mistake: The age-grade-level instruction of factory schooling is imposed as best for everyone. Exceptionally talented students are those achieving substantially above that level already. The only way to slow such students down is to bore them to tears and misbehavior. Gross (1992) quoted a letter from a dismayed parent whose bright child was confined to the "regular" age-grade placement in this way:

> He has lost, or rather is no longer able to display, the "spark" that he always had. This was the sharpness; the quick, often

humorous, comment; the sudden bubbling over of enthusiasm when he starts following through a series of ideas. It is rather like a stone with many sharp edges; they have knocked these edges off and as a result he is rolling more smoothly in class and they are happy about that . . . They believe they have had great success, but I know they are depressing some vital spark. (p. 96)

Archambault, Westberg, Brown, Hallmark, Emmons, and Zhang (1993) reported that 70% of American school districts had official policies that barred teachers from advancing students one grade level. As of 2015, only 13 states reported having adopted policies "permitting" acceleration (National Association for Gifted Children [NAGC] & Council of State Directors of Programs for the Gifted [CSDPG], 2015). Opposition to acceleration, so strong and so durable, obviously comes from many quarters, notably including gifted education itself (Margolin, 1996). Some gifted education leaders and many general education teachers (Cross et al., 2015; Siegle, Wilson, & Little, 2013) argue that acceleration is not appropriate for very many students, that moving faster through an inadequate curriculum (i.e., one that is not qualitatively different) is a mistake, and especially that social and emotional threats make acceleration dangerous.[39] Again, none of the claims has sufficient merit to explain the prevalent *repugnance* (Cross et al., 2015; Hertberg-Davis, 2009; Kulik & Kulik, 1984; Rogers, 2007; Siegle et al., 2013). The unfair allocation of entitlement does seem a partially sufficient explanation. The role of leadership training deepens the argument.

Leadership Training and the Reproduction of the Managerial Class

The elitist character of gifted programs is usually justified by the rationale that such programs offer specialized instruction to students who will probably become leaders in whatever fields they occupy later in

---

39 Interestingly, Kanevsky (2011) reported that although the Canadian situation overall resembles the American one, Québec districts report far greater support for early entry to Kindergarten and first grade and for grade-skipping. The difference illustrates the effect of culture, in this case anglophone versus francophone Canadian cultures.

life (Bull, 1985; Howley, 1986; Kitano & Kirby, 1986; Margolin, 1996; Terman, 1925). In this view, gifted children as a group are presumed to be more essential than other children to the national interest. It's a false, but convenient, presumption (Howley, 1986; Margolin, 1994; Sapon-Shevin, 1994, 2003).[40]

The work of a principal believer in the misconception proved it to be just that. Terman believed the misconception and followed his students for decades to discover what became of them. It turned out that many were successful, but in ordinary ways, and that many were not so successful, again in ordinary ways (Terman & Oden, 1959). Hardly any became "eminent." Destiny has undisclosed plans for all of humanity, including all those that schooling calls *gifted*. The upshot of this insight is that leadership training *for exceptionally able students* must be up to something else than its advertised ends. What might that be?

The prevalence of leadership training for able students absent adequate empirical support for the practice (for a recent study see Muammar, 2015) stems, in our opinion, from the imperative to create a professional and managerial stratum that advances the material interests of the wealthy and powerful, as Margolin (1996) and Sapon-Shevin (1994) suggested. Of course, such identification and training, albeit indirectly, advance the material interests of the majority of the "graduates" of gifted programs (Margolin, 1996). Why? For the most part, these graduates come from affluent families, and schooling is so arranged as to bestow additional economic advantages on affluent families (deMarrais & LeCompte, 1999; Jencks, 1979; Lareau, 1989). Being in the gifted program is, on this view, rather like another extracurricular activity to brag about on college applications. This arrangement is bad enough, if predictable, but doing so at the expense of intellectual development adds intellectual insult to economic injury (see, e.g., Deresiewicz, 2014; Labaree, 1999; Trumpbour, 1989; Wilder, 2013).

Perhaps leadership potential is a neglected kind of giftedness? We don't think so (see also, Jarrell & Borland, 1990; Renzulli, 1978). Because of the circumstantial nature of leadership (see, e.g., Bass, 2008; House,

---

40 Margolin (1996, citing Pollner, 1987) suggested, alternatively, that we are all "ontological dopes," especially those of us concerned with gifted education (p. 164). Her trope is exactly what we have in mind when we refer to bait-and-switch.

1971), reliable identification of leadership potential *in adults* is dubious (see, e.g., Silzer, 2010). Reliable instruments for use with children do not exist, and identification efforts for gifted programs rely on routines of self- and teacher-rating that have no validity whatsoever (Shaunessy & Karnes, 2004). Certainly, leadership training may be warranted for some adults who occupy or are being chosen and prepared for particular organizational positions, but schoolchildren don't need it (see, e.g., Matthews, 2004) because they are so remote from that prospect, class and cultural bias notwithstanding.

Identifying Gifted Students: Entitling the Elite

Who ought to receive instruction in "the gifted program"? It's a local issue of some concern. The question is whether selection ought to be for whatever program happens to exist locally, or for something else. The typical answer is *something else*: a high intelligence quotient (IQ).[41] Having a lot of it (e.g., at least two standard deviations above the mean) is considered sufficient to render a child gifted. This relationship between testing and being a qualitatively different "gifted child" needs unpacking.

Testing and qualitative difference. Individually administered intelligence tests, which Terman popularized in America, remain a very common identification tool (e.g., Terman's Stanford-Binet test or the Wechsler Intelligence Scale for Children) down the years. Alfred Binet, the author of the original IQ test, simply wanted to identify children for whom the (French) curriculum at the end of the 19th century was problematic—the pacing seemed notably out of step with the accomplishments of some children (slower or faster). He measured the difference and suggested that schools alter the pacing appropriately (Gould, 1981). So intelligence in Binet's seemingly original formulation was related to a faster pace for exceptionally talented students and a slower pace for those for whom that might make sense.

Terman, though, had a different conception: The gifted were so different in degree that they were different *kinds* of children. Terman

---

41   What is this "quotient"? It's mental age divided by chronological age (Stern, 1912).

(1925) broadened the meaning of intelligence (fast or slow learner) and the domain it covered (school curriculum) toward a general, genetically based fitness for life. He succeeded in building a substantial empire on this basis (Fancher, 1985). Privileged families could see the advantage of imperial alliance: Their children might turn out to be judged the best fit for the struggle for existence in the modern world and could then be held up—and helped up—as such. A high IQ would henceforth be the badge that might (if they were lucky) mark their children as destined for imperial greatness. Giftedness would be a kind of adornment—the sign of a family's rightful superiority (see, e.g., Margolin, 1994; Sapon-Shevin, 1994, 2003). The varied procedures and cut-off scores entailed in selection have ensured that gifted programs serve a largely privileged clientele.

The underlying social reality, remote from Binet's modest intention, is privilege. The badge earned by a high IQ permits children of the privileged classes to enjoy a slightly liberalized and humanistic curriculum, largely divorced from academic content. The gifted learn to enjoy unearned privilege—their qualitative difference entitles them to it. Most children, surely, would prefer respite in the gifted program to the relentless custodial routines of factory schooling?

The cause of injustice, though, lies neither with IQ tests per se (which are a kind of generalized achievement test) nor with the terrible bargain (described previously) that gifted programs have so often made in order to exist (less focus on academic content at all levels and more focus on thinking skills and process; see next section). The cause, rather, is the level of privilege and injustice tolerated in America, one that factory schooling helps to sustain.

America's most notable and difficult injustice, some have argued (e.g., Gould, 1981; Kamin, 1977; Wilkerson, 2010), is its enduring racism. Racism leads to the belief that if African Americans (for instance) score lower as a group on intelligence tests, then they must be genetically inferior to European Americans (and Asians, or the upper middle class, and so forth). The proposition is another, and particularly egregious, example of claimed qualitative difference.

The influence of living conditions on academic engagement, however, is momentous. Families living near and below the poverty level, whatever their skin color, confront threats (i.e., day-to-day survival, shortfall on the rent, inadequate healthcare, and staying sane throughout the struggle) that demand their full attention. Under such threats, the struggle for survival is much more important than intellectual or academic engagement. The severe nature of the threats they and their children confront mean that impoverished children (see Chapter 7) seldom experience opportunities to learn that resemble those regularly enjoyed by children from affluent families and prized by schools and educators (Lareau, 1989). Lower test scores are to be predicted in impoverished circumstances.

Good schools can go a long way to supply the want for impoverished children, but schools *that good* are much rarer in impoverished neighborhoods and communities and entire states than in affluent ones (e.g., Goldhaber, Lavery, & Theobald, 2015; Kozol, 2013). That is, resources are, as a matter of practice and tacit policy, directed away from them and toward schools that serve advantaged families (see, e.g., Albjerg-Graham, 2005; Johnson, 2007; Johnson, Kraft, & Papay, 2012). In this game of resource misallocation, advantaged neighborhoods are further advantaged, and disadvantaged ones are likewise further disadvantaged.[42] And this tendency pertains not only in schooling, but also across many key American social institutions (housing, law, medicine, employment). In America, racism helps ensure the privation of those with dark skins. The decision to impoverish African Americans was, and remains, political, economic, and systemic. The offensive history begins in the dispossession of the freedom of Africans whom Americans enslaved and whose descendants the political economy continues to oppress and abuse.

A high IQ score is clearly less important than many think it must be. What it really means is "speed up the pace of schooling." Instead, as the discussion argues, it serves, in schooling practice, as yet another provision to help secure disproportionate privileges to the already privileged.

Using tests fairly. We conclude—quite out of step with trendy opinion and practice—that (1) comprehensive *individually administered* intelligence tests and (2) *individually administered* achievement tests that have high ceilings *can still* serve selection procedures fairly (see also Howley & Howley, 1988; Ortiz & Gonzalez, 1989; Pendarvis & Wood, 2009). There's one important caveat, difficult because of the misconcep-

---

42   See Merton (1968) for the classic formulation of "the Matthew effect" (p. 2).

tions ("ontological dopiness") and the rigged game of life chances and resource allocation in the American political economy.

This is the caveat: Educators must interpret test scores to reflect the inequitable arrangements that structure life chances and resource allocation in the American political economy.

Why? It's empirical and simple. A preponderance of research shows that the IQ- and achievement-test penalty imposed as a result of membership in disparaged groups (African American race or Appalachian culture, for instance) is about one standard deviation (Haney, 1993; Roth, Bevier, Bobko, Switzer, & Tyler, 2001). This penalty is a massive artifact of injustice, not only in America (Chiu & Khoo, 2005; Condron, 2011; Williams, 2005). In America, though, children from disparaged social groups experience *sharply* reduced opportunities to learn what tests measure, undermining test validity (Salvia, Ysseldyke, & Witmer, 2012). Allowances must be made. Nations, in fact, vary in how they manage the gradients of economic inequality on educational outcomes (Chiu & Khoo, 2005; Condron, 2011; Williams, 2005), so the arrangement prevailing in America is neither natural nor inevitable. One can see the difficulty: The ontological dopiness, the bait-and-switch, is institutionalized.

By establishing local norms, by using tests normed on disparaged groups, and by implementing quotas, schools can ensure selection of children from disparaged groups (Howley & Howley, 1988). Quotas will be necessary. Although affirmative action policies have been eliminated in eight states, federal policy allows their use as a way to achieve diversity in programs and to avoid racial isolation in elementary and secondary schools (Office for Civil Rights, 2011). Being dubbed gifted, however, produces benefits only if decent, intellectually appropriate instruction follows—which is rarely the case, as we explain next.

Process Replaces Content

The displacement of effort by entitlement, logically enough, involves the displacement of legitimate instructional content (real knowledge, real thinking, real writing) with instruction in abstract procedures argued as especially needful for those with exceptional academic talents (Margolin, 1996): the curriculum of giftedness itself. Instructional arrangements for able students ought, instead, to consist of advanced academic curriculum, taught well; without such provision, exceptionally talented students fail to progress commensurate with their capacities for intellectual work (Stanley, 1986).

The industrial lockstep was not designed for them, and it does not work for them (nor does it work well for many others). Nonetheless, gifted programs continue to "teach" cognitive and affective processes disconnected from intellectual substance (Gallagher, 2004; Margolin, 1996; Matthews, 2004). The entire enrichment regimen displaces sustainable and intellectually critical content in favor of ephemeral processes—ephemeral because they are unmoored *from* substance and not verifiably transferable *to* it. One astute education philosopher (Egan, 2002), applying this critique to factory schooling wholesale, calls the displacement *Getting It Wrong From the Beginning*. Gifted education is, in Egan's logic, simply following a prevalent pattern. As Margolin (1996) asserted, "giftedness" is the curriculum.

One cannot be an accomplished physicist without knowing a lot about physics, without being able to read difficult scientific material, and without mastering appropriate mathematical concepts. The point applies in similar ways to the humanities, and indeed to automobile mechanics and gardening (e.g., Rose, 2004). Although one can master many things later on, informally (e.g., on the job), instruction in school is supposed to be timely, and diplomas and degrees carry authority in the real world, albeit an odd sort of authority. So factory schooling misses the mark by a wide margin in the case of many students (Egan, 2002; Hattie, 2008; White, 2011), notably those with exceptional academic talent.

Next we consider the prominent displacements of content by process: (1) higher order thinking, (2) problem solving, and (3) child development itself (the core of Egan's and Margolin's critiques). Leadership training, dealt with previously, is also among the displacements, but will not be discussed again.

Higher Order Thinking: Deskilling Knowledge

As used routinely in gifted programs, this process-oriented approach is intended to develop students' higher level thinking: as if thinking might really be segmented in this way (i.e., shorn of content as well as from thinking of "lower" sorts). Curriculum and materials for this approach in gifted education are usually unrelated to academic content, and mere facts, such as historical dates, names, and events, are treated with contempt. Indeed, programs of this sort have been developed with gifted students particularly in mind (see Margolin, 1996, for especially "precious" examples).

Psychologist Jerome Bruner, one of the earliest advocates of process-oriented instruction (Bruner, 1960), considered factual knowledge *necessary* for the development of problem-solving skills (see Taba, 1963, for a similar discussion). McPeck (1986) described the relationship between factual knowledge and higher order thinking:

> Facts are complex things which have connections and logical implications which reach beyond themselves. And the mental weaving of these connections is what education and critical thinking is fundamentally about. Indeed, so-called "higher order" learning is itself predicated on having this broad understanding of how certain facts and information are connected or related to something else. (p. 8)

Note the sentence about *weaving connections*: Cultivating *with disciplinary substance* the capacity to make such connections should be high on the task list of educators. Thinking is one core purpose in education and life, but by definition thinking must work on something, not on nothing, and not too self-consciously on itself ("metacognition").[43] Despite the sensible view of these educators, and of such educators of gifted students as Julian Stanley (e.g., Cohn, George, & Stanley, 1979) and Joyce VanTassel-Baska (e.g., VanTassel-Baska & Little, 2017), other advocates continue to find instructional value in generic cognitive and

---

43 Humans can think about their thinking, and clearly benefit from doing so. This sort of thinking, though, is useful for everyone who thinks.

affective processes (e.g., Reis, Gentry, & Sunghee, 1995; Renzulli & Richards, 2000).

As Bloom's (1956) taxonomy came into widespread use (with its hierarchy of cognitive functions), many educators began to emphasize the verbs associated with different levels of the hierarchy over the nouns to which the verbs should clearly apply. For example, in gifted education, *analysis* is often considered as pedagogically valuable when it is directed toward solving jejune (naive and superficial) problems—for instance, determining what one might need to take on an imaginary trip to the Australian outback or whether gnomes or elves might make better assistants for Santa Claus (Margolin, 1996, see p. 174)—as it is when it is directed toward understanding the problem of a character's behavior in a literary work or plotting a strategy to deal with a mathematical problem.

The prevalent assumption *has* been more generally questioned in the past two decades, as Egan's *Getting It Wrong From the Beginning* (2002) may suggest. Analyzing a literary work or understanding a mathematical relationship requires an array of skills and cultivates insights and habits of mind quite different from the skills, insights, and habits of mind that come from trivial activities such as "analyzing" the "reasons" that elves make better assistants for Santa (see also Jardine, 1995).

Putting aside for the moment the question of value, the influence of the subject on the thinking process should seem evident to anyone with relevant disciplinary knowledge. Among the many differences, analyzing a work of literature or a mathematical relationship or problem requires comprehension of ideas and propositions with a bearing on real issues—simply because of the sorts of distinctions literary or mathematical analysis must make. It also usually requires reasoning with ideas embodied in a vocabulary used with considerable nuance by an author or a field. Beghetto, Kaufman, and Baer (2015) questioned the validity of the concept of content-free thinking skills, as did Keating (1988), who summarized the status of research about the effectiveness of programs that purport to teach critical thinking skills:

> Convincing evidence . . . has not been forthcoming. In many cases, there is little formal evaluation of any sort. Where careful evaluations have been done, the criteria of success are typically

the students' performance on materials exactly the same as, or very much like, the training materials. Though this may be a necessary first step in the evaluation process, it is weak evidence of a strong claim (the general enhancement of thinking). The next and crucial step of transfer to quite different kinds of content has apparently not been undertaken in any systematic way. Of course, the criteria may be hard to specify, but without this information the issue is reduced to how effectively particular programs "teach to their own test." (p. 15)

Even Guilford's (1959) Structure of Intellect model recognizes these distinctions by defining broad categories of content among its 120 independent factors.[44]

Problem Solving: Applications of Deskilled Knowledge

"Yankee ingenuity"—ingenious approaches to getting things done—is a traditional American virtue. In the early years of the nation, this peculiarly American sense of practicality was not an object of special training. It was an approach accessible, to some degree, to every citizen regardless of station in life, but it was also a new spirit of inquiry and freshness; it was simply part of the American outlook (Curti, 1943). Americans were eager to discard the old ways of viewing the world and doing its work, and to see and do things differently.

So "Yankee ingenuity" was more an attitude than a technique. And, as an everyday practice, it was more a myth and an aspiration than a reality. Being an American, though, indicated that one had adopted the American attitude (Spring, 1994). And the freshness of this attitude would permit an American (or an immigrant who was seeking to become an American) to refashion traditional ways of doing things in virtually any field of activity, but most particularly in agriculture and manufacture—production of food and goods. The ingenuity was a famed, per-

---

44   Guilford (1959) proposed the relatedness of process and content. For instance, his model classified (a) divergent productive operations on semantic material as relatively independent from (b) divergent productive operations on symbolic, figural, or behavioral content.

haps silly, abstraction from a little bit of inspiration and a great deal of hard work: 99% hard work (see, e.g., McCullough, 2015, for one account of the phenomenon in practice at the turn of the 20th century).

Although some Americans did prove to be wildly and productively inventive, the heroes of the 19th- and early 20th-century industrial and agricultural ingenuity—Cyrus McCormick, Thomas Edison, Henry Ford, and the brothers Wright—owed remarkably little to their formal training (Brinkley, 2004; McCullough, 2015; Zinn, 2003). The sort of schooling practiced on the frontier and in the wards of young cities might have aimed to propagate American allegiance among immigrants (Spring, 2013), but it did not ever aim to teach "problem-solving skills" to anyone.

Culturally and historically, the importance of problem solving, abstracted from any discipline, is thus reactionary—a sort of nostalgia for a lost educational heyday that, like all reactionary fantasies, never existed. But, pedagogically, the move also misunderstands instruction, substituting an enhancement of instruction (e.g., synthesis, analysis, evaluation) for the instruction itself. As noted previously, process-oriented instruction, advocated by Bruner (1960), was *intended* to improve the teaching of academic content. Development of the intellect and its habits was his aim. The new math, the new biology, and the new physics—developed partially under Bruner's influence—integrated intellectual processes with substantial academic content. Bruner's social studies program, *Man: A Course of Study* (MACOS), for example, used movies, readings, and artifacts to help students understand basic anthropological concepts. It was difficult and provocative work, as the historical record suggests (see, e.g., Barlage, 1982, on the new math).

The sort of instruction Bruner imagined and helped to design has not been widely practiced since the 1960s, although it has been better represented in recent iterations of influential standards (e.g., Common Core State Standards). Inductive lessons (like the innovative curricula of the 1960s) are difficult to teach. But reassessments of the 1960s' curricula do indicate the general superiority of those conceptions over conventional instruction of the late 20th and early 21st centuries, particularly in terms of achievement gains for a gamut of bright students (e.g., Gallagher & Gallagher, 1994). The contemporary consensus about "constructivist" learning regimes, indeed, recommends such enhancements to factory schooling as appropriate for all students, and not just the gifted (see, e.g., DeVries, Zan, Hildebrandt, Edmiaston, & Sales, 2002). Higher order processes cannot take place in an intellectual vacuum.

Child Development as the Curriculum

Partly a legacy of the whole-child movement and partly a legacy of the process-education method, the curriculum of many special education programs derives almost as much from child development as from a conception of pertinent academic goals. In essence, views of child development, rather than knowledge or learning, constitute the curriculum (Egan, 2002; Margolin, 1996).

As a form of special education—schooling for students who do not appear to fit well into the factory system designed for most children— gifted education has always been gripped by this view of the nature of curriculum. For instance, goals for individual gifted children often come from the children's performance on measures of cognitive or affective domains such as visual-motor perception, vocabulary, reasoning, divergent thinking, and interest in abstract ideas and aesthetic activities. On this view, it is no wonder that efforts to cultivate these supposed capacities are prioritized over knowledge and ideas as the focus of special programs. In this way, giftedness itself becomes the curriculum. Gifted programs that subordinate the academic curriculum for a "curriculum" that implements content-free process skills or multiple intelligences— such as Gardner's (1983) interpersonal intelligence or Sternberg's (1995) metacognitive or executive processes—serve more to stunt development than to promote it.

Certainly, the value of an academic curriculum can be disputed (e.g., when not animated by good teaching or when delivered perversely to control student misbehavior); certainly, complaints against the nature of instruction in the liberal arts (e.g., that it relies too much on lecture; that it is too remote from experience to interest students; that it is merely elitist) are common and even justified; and certainly scholarship *can* be carried on as pointless quibbling (cf. Barzun, 1959). But the intellectual tradition, no matter how poorly taught, still contains substantial value to which students might connect, once they manage to see beyond the dysfunctional features of classroom life. Too few students (certainly) get this chance, whether dubbed "gifted" or not. The trivialized process curriculum harbors no such chance, no matter how humanistic and student-centered the intent.

So the value of good books persists, and the community of intellect that such books, in all fields, represent reaches into the past and into the future. To move it from past to future, though, requires connections in the present. Displacement in schooling itself of intellectual substance by psychologized processes must be an institutional blow against intellect (see, e.g., Egan, 2002).

Feeling Replaces Thought

Affective education, like process-oriented instruction, avoids dealing with intellectual development. For the most part, it aims to teach gifted children how to get along with others (e.g., Johnson, 2001). Given the limited resources available, the emphasis on affective education for gifted students is offered at considerable cost to the development of students' intellect. The mistaken justification for this sacrifice is, in essence, that exceptional intellectual potential constitutes an exceptional threat to the emotional well-being of the gifted. Never mind that teachers of the gifted are ill-prepared to serve as counselors and therapists: filling the gifted curriculum with "giftedness content" takes priority.

Emotional Risks of Exceptional Talent

Whereas concern over emotional difficulties is appropriate for children who are emotionally disturbed, such concern seems at best misplaced with respect to gifted children. Substantial evidence over the years confirms Terman's (1925) findings that gifted children are generally better off emotionally and socially than other children (e.g., Lubinski & Benbow, 2006): They should be, since they generally come from better-resourced families. Douthitt (1992) found a significant positive relationship between children's IQ scores and their adaptive behavior scores, and Zeidner and Shani-Zinovich (2011), in a study of gifted high school students in Israel, found the students to exhibit greater openness to experience and less neuroticism and anxiety than other students. On the basis of fact, then, affective education for gifted children is unjustified.

In American factory schooling, gifted programs are, understandably, valued as emotionally "safe harbors" for gifted children (Fetterman, 1988). If these programs must eschew real (intellectual) work in favor of entertainment and emotional respite care (respite from boredom and pointless academic instruction), then an affective component to the curriculum makes a perverse sort of sense. So it appears to many involved with gifted programs (Colangelo et al., 2004; Johnson, 2001).

There are, however, particular emotional risks thought to afflict the gifted: those supposedly associated with the challenges of rigorous academic work. Hard work is apparently stressful. Parental, teacher, and peer pressure for academic performance are seen as threatening to the well-being of gifted students, who may respond with a debilitating need for perfection (e.g., Speirs Neumeister, Williams, & Cross, 2009). This view deserves a deeper look.

A distinction exists between *debilitating* and *challenging* expectations. Challenging expectations can be met because meeting them is abundantly supported. If the expectations are not fully met, the attempt still has value: lessons are learned that pose new challenges; everyone involved learns something. The effort of making the attempt provides satisfaction and, usually, academic and intellectual benefit, even if unintended; instruction in factory schools is planned in straight lines, but students' minds follow their own paths (see, e.g., White, 2011).

But debilitating expectations are *designed* for failure. Worse still, the failures are intended as *conclusive* and even intended to reinforce *repetition*. Support to engage the challenge and to meet it are not on offer. In other words, some cohorts of children (e.g., impoverished rural African American males) are set up by schooling for failure (see Chapter 7). If a debilitating expectation is not met, the result is *necessarily* damaging; the habit of failure, after all, is the *de facto* expectation and aim. The deep structure of schooling (Tye, 2000), moreover, ensures the legacy of this sort of expectation. But certainly, as well, the logic of debilitating expectations can be used on those with exceptional academic talents (Carper, 2002; Delisle & Galbraith, 2002; Whitmore, 1980).

The distinction between challenging and debilitating expectations may seem subtle, but it is the sort of distinction that the development of talent and the nurture of intellect (among all students) require. From the pedagogical perspective that constructs debilitating expectations, authenticity is anathema, ambiguity is wrong, and interaction inappropriate (Anyon, 1980). The point, tacit or explicit, is to foil intellectual engagement, to make it impermissible. The most debilitating expectation of all, of course, is that a predictable population of students will fail repeatedly, until such time as they finally realize that their accumulating failures are permanent (Anyon, 2005).

Far too many students are doomed by schooling in this way. In one sense, then, the concerns of parents and gifted-program teachers are reasonable. The proper course of action, though, is not to shield a privileged few from this theater of humiliating trial and error, but to implement an intellectual program in which challenging expectations shape curriculum and instruction for all students, including the gifted. Factory schooling cannot manage it very often, although some heroic efforts are noteworthy exceptions (see, e.g., Meier, 1995).

Unfortunately, much of the instruction experienced by gifted students arrives with expectations for perfection that do, indeed, teach bad emotional lessons (e.g., "If you are so smart, why don't you get A's on every assignment?"). Indeed, as many writers (e.g., Delucci & Korgen, 2002; Deresiewicz, 2014; Harland, McLean, Wass, & Sim, 2015; Orr, 1995) have noted, grade-grubbing (the highest grade for the least effort) is anti-intellectual. The quest for high grades as a socially approved regimen not only cultivates able students' dependence on teacher approval, but also systematically foils authentic engagement with intellectual substance (Deresiewicz, 2014). In a great many American schools, in both K–12 and university settings, academic routines are misused as a form of classroom discipline (see, e.g., Anyon, 1980; Harland et al., 2015; Labaree, 1999; Sedlak et al., 1986; Wilcox, 1982). So *everyone* is emotionally at risk, as well as intellectually at risk, in American schooling, though some are routinely subjected to more risk than others.

The pedagogy of challenging expectations requires authenticity, tolerance of ambiguity, and authentic intellectual interaction with students: It is a high bar for teacher performance. In this pedagogy, instructional events are an opportunity to elicit intellectual engagement from students in a variety of ways, some of which will be delightful and surprising, and others provocative and "interesting."

In our experience, educators and parents of gifted students often err by confusing debilitating expectations and challenging expectations. Relatively few seem to understand the distinction, which is not in any case evident in how schooling is usually practiced (i.e., so as to obscure the distinction). Research about the social and emotional development of gifted students ought nonetheless to reassure parents and educators. The preponderance of studies shows that, in general, children identified as gifted are at least as well-adjusted and mature as other students. Those identified on the basis of high scores on IQ tests or tests of academic aptitude usually view themselves positively (Pufal-Struzik, 1999; Shore, Cornell, Robinson, & Ward, 1991).

Despite the research, however, concerns about gifted children's mental health and socialization persist widely. Some parents do not share such concerns, however, and these parents tend to encourage their children to accept academic challenges (Assouline et al., 2015; Gallagher, 2003; Gross, 1992; Stanley, 2004). Such parents typically encounter resistance and criticism from educators (Assouline et al., 2015; Colangelo et al., 2004). Educators often presume that such parents, in demanding acceleration, for instance, are reckless—sacrificing childhood happiness to intellectual vanity (Gross, 1992; Howley & Howley, 2002). The way factory schooling is organized—and the way gifted programs have bargained to exist within factory schooling—forces parents concerned with intellectual development into this bind. They have few allies (Colangelo et al., 2004) inside the profession or out.

Gifted underachievers, of course, do harbor less positive images of themselves than other gifted children (Speirs Neumeister, Williams, & Cross 2007). Schooling itself, however, contributes to the problem in a number of ways, as Whitmore's (1980) landmark study showed. In addition to failing to provide a stimulating, challenging curriculum to gifted students, the schools' conventional association of academic achievement with relative personal merit (and perfection) may actually *cause* some gifted students to perform poorly (see, e.g., Whitmore, 1980). Indeed, gifted dropouts regard as offensive the competitive, impersonal climate so typical of schooling (Carper, 2002).

The social climate of the classroom, lodged in the competitive climate of schooling, may well distract such students from the academic issues at hand, which can, in the midst of this destructive climate, seem intellectually and practically irrelevant. As Delisle and Galbraith (2002) and Kanevsky and Keighley (2003) suggested, some underachievers make considered judgments as to the value, for them, of different elements of their schooling and elect to engage with some elements of the experience and to reject others. It seems to us right to regard the trivialization of content and the routinization of instruction, combined with an emphasis on good grades, as pointless, counterproductive, and possibly immoral.

The Threat of Normative Emotional Balance

The way American society enforces normative emotional balance, according to some observers, is by placing a higher value on social amenities than on intellectual endeavors (Barzun, 1959; Hofstadter, 1963; Orr, 1995; Veblen, 1918/2015). In this view, devotion to intellectual pursuits over material comfort is unhealthy. The story of child prodigy William Sidis, perhaps the most infamous case in the literature on gifted education, is sometimes used as a cautionary tale (e.g., Montour, 1977). Margolin (1994), for instance, repeated the Sidis story to suggest the questionable validity of efforts to identify giftedness in children. Sidis, because not conventionally successful, is portrayed as a miserable failure: isolated, impoverished, and unhappy. Few commentators consider that his refusal of "success" was a principled refusal to employ his talents for ends he considered unworthy (see Wallace, 1986, for this interpretation). Buckminister Fuller seemed to have thought so, at any rate:

> Imagine my excitement and joy on being handed this xerox of Sidis's 1925 book, in which he clearly predicts the black hole. In

fact, I find the book to be a fine cosmological piece. . . . I hope you will become as excited as I am at this discovery that Sidis did go on after college to do the most magnificent thinking and writing. (Cited in Wallace, 1986, p. 157)

The American fixation on conventional success does a great deal of mischief in schooling and in gifted education.

Concern for ensuring the "normalness" of bright students also inspires educators' persistent and zealous warnings about the dangers of exposing such students to extranormal (i.e., appropriate) academic challenges. The practices of acceleration and retention constitute a telling example. On the one hand, schooling employs acceleration very seldom, despite the consistently positive research (which ought logically to dispel resistance but doesn't). On the other hand, schooling routinely employs retention in grade, even though research shows that the practice results in little academic benefit with some risk for emotional harm (see, e.g., Hong & Raudenbush, 2005; Huddleston, 2014). The contrast between these two well-researched school practices, deployed differently, both of them known to harm children, is real. It seems incredible, but good research establishes the reality beyond reasonable doubt—beyond even the shadow of doubt.

Schooling, Talent Development, and Provisions for Students With Talents

Some critical works about gifted education (e.g., Borland, 2003b; Margolin, 1996; Sapon-Shevin, 2003) question, as do we, the ethical and pedagogical assumptions on which contemporary arrangements for exceptionally able students rest. We agree with much of the criticism, but possessing demonstrable talent is no more the fault of children than the phenomenon of poverty is the fault of the poor. So neither justice nor good sense warrants provisions that ignore, much less subvert, the learning of demonstrably able students, even if privilege has enabled such a demonstration. Furthermore, a schooling focused on intellect has a better chance of helping children from privileged families think their way to higher purpose than one focused on careers (i.e., high-status careers) and college (i.e., admission to elite universities).

Sapon-Shevin (1994, 2003) seemed to believe that gifted children should remain in the regular program for all of their academic instruction. The enrichment philosophy and pull-out programs are elitist and they harm everyone. In addition, ability-grouping practices—including high school tracking—that characterize the provision of general education in many schools harm many students and benefit academically talented students comparatively little intellectually (Gamoran, 1992; Lleras & Rangel, 2009; Lucas & Gamoran, 1993; Peters, Matthews, McBee, & McCoach, 2014; Wuthrick, 1990; Young, 1990; Young & McCullough, 1992).

So, of all the methods of meeting gifted students' needs, only acceleration appears to leave other students relatively unharmed, while giving a better approximation of the rate at which able students learn. Through whatever means it is accomplished in the general education classroom, *for most gifted students* an acceleration of 3 or 4 years in K–12 schooling seems to us about right (see, e.g., Stanley, 1986).[45] More is often sensible, but very seldom secured (Jung & Gross, 2015).

Among the benefits for schooling as a whole, acceleration is comparatively cheap because it does not require so many special teachers (very expensive) or special materials (an additional cost everywhere). It does require that knowledgeable teachers and administrators manage the arrangement and provide assistance and intervention as needed; so there are some costs—but nothing resembling the cost of the prevalent system of pull-out enrichment programming.[46]

---

45   Unfortunately, acceleration to this "radical" degree, when it is used, is assumed to be appropriate only for the highly gifted (e.g., those with IQs 3 or 4 standard deviations above average); these are the only students with which it is used; and they are the only students to appear in this light in the empirical literature! Little research, in other words, directly supports our claim. We advance it partly on the basis of personal experience (e.g., Howley & Howley, 2002), professional judgment (e.g., Pendarvis, Howley, & Howley, 1990), and a systematic critique of American schooling (e.g., Howley & Howley, 2007).

46   Research on these claims awaits a reality that might be investigated, but the status quo does not accommodate the needed inquiry.

After all, industrial-style K–12 schooling is a system of efficiently delivering an amalgam of education and childcare. Children are kept safe while parents work: fed, housed, supervised, and instructed en masse in basic skills. This odd combination of custodial and training services, offered so efficiently, has become an uncomfortable compromise. The system is maintained at the cost of an inflexibility that accommodates well neither childhood nor learning, much less intellect. The system has clear virtues, though, and the quality of life in American society would be worse without free publicly supported schooling for all.

One crucial feature that factory schooling lacks—a feature that affects all students—is the capacity to attend closely to the educational and intellectual circumstances of the individual children who present themselves: a feature that might be called *responsiveness*. This shortcoming is why Meier (2003) suggested that provisions for schooling need to be generous.

Factory schooling is unresponsive, in fact, by definition. Students are products. Quality control seems indifferent though, perhaps because American society is planned so as to use the products badly. But, of course, the production metaphor is all wrong. Students and families are people with an agency that determines education, with or without schooling, and which agency educators need to respect and engage (Cohen, 1988), but which industrial schooling systemically frustrates (Horvat, Weininger, & Lareau, 2003; Lareau, 1989; Tye, 2000).

Many schools and many teachers try to notice individual students, but the requirements of scale, cost efficiency, and the rigid procedures of industrial-scale schooling ensure that such efforts remain exceptions (see, e.g., Brasington, 2003; Callahan, 1962; Johnson et al., 2012; Kuziemko, 2006; Purdy, 1997). It's difficult to believe that anyone would really harbor the expectation that "individualization" and responsively "differentiated" instruction (see, e.g., Robinson, Maldonado, & Whaley, 2014; Tomlinson, 1999) could become widely possible under current arrangements for schooling: bringing to scale what the system is designed to avoid. As Bloom and Sosniak (1981) noted of schooling: "The teacher's explanations are expected to be equally good for all students in the class, and the types of rewards and reinforcements offered by the teacher tend to be similar for all" (p. 89). Indeed, changing this model as a whole, and for everyone (attempted and advocated by so many), has proved not just difficult but impossible. Factory schooling (Bloom and Sosniak [1981] withheld the modifier, but this is the schooling they describe with such restraint) is efficient and actually sufficient for an anti-intellectual culture. Not surprisingly, some commentators complain that, as efficient as it is, it is still too costly for what it delivers (e.g., Farkas & Duffett, 2012).

Gifted children deal intellectually with this inattentive system about as well as other children do—that is, with surprising resilience from day to day, but not so well overall. Schooling, in fact, victimizes talent development among *all* the children it is supposed to serve; in this project no child is left behind. Hattie (2008) estimated the effect size on achievement exerted by the average teacher as es=+.20. The estimate is imprecise for many reasons, but it is not a cause for hope, in particular because it is the system, and not individual teachers per se, that structure this meager effect.

But because gifted children usually negotiate the basics with comparative ease, and because many eventually do secure comfortable jobs, people assume that schooling has succeeded, at least, in developing the talent of able students. On such a view, able students would require nothing different from what they already get during the course of their schooling (Gallagher & Gallagher, 1994): Talented children will succeed, and *should* succeed if they are not somehow morally lax or genetically flawed, despite all obstacles.

In reality, this widespread view means that whenever an uncommon talent presents itself in school it *should* be ignored; or, at least, it should not be permitted to disturb the smooth operation of the system. The system of schooling is thus positioned to discount the value of developing talent, incredible as that conclusion will seem to many people.

To posit excellence as the goal of schooling (e.g., Subotnik, Olszewski-Kubilius, & Worrell, 2011) is sharply unrealistic. Further, as those in gifted education surely ought to realize, one can never demand something *be* excellent, as Jacques Barzun (2001) quipped, although one can *find* something excellent.

Some observers, moreover, argue that equality is the prerequisite of quality (e.g., Condron, 2011; Ravitch, 2013). A modicum of school improvement over a wide swath is thus, we find, the hostage of American inequity and the lack of political will to address it (Ravitch, 2013).

What Are Teachers and Administrators in Factory Schooling To Do?

In the meantime, some of the educators lodged in the beast's belly can promote acceleration in their schools and districts. One of us (Howley, 2002) has reported the success of one such effort. It produced changes in policy and practice that have persisted in one rural district in an impoverished state.

Additionally, acceleration can easily be used with children who present themselves (in tested achievement) as somewhat less than "gifted." Indeed, whenever the achievement level of an elementary child substantially exceeds grade-level norms, grade skipping should be discussed, and often used ("substantial" is a matter of judgment). Strong leadership (see Howley, 2002) can, in a few years, accomplish changes that prove locally sustainable (even if they remain exceptional across the institution of industrial schooling). A sustained program will influence other educators and other districts. None of this good work, though, can bring the impossible to scale. Acceleration—particularly as the abridgement of the K–12 sequence—is not going to "catch on" as things are; this chapter and the others argue why not.

How does one get acceleration going in some corner of a hostile land? One makes allies, first by sharing evidence (acceleration is effective and dangers are manageable, as argued in Assouline et al., 2015), and second, by acting together as an alliance to confront the presenting difficulties. Of course, alliances must be based on principles and shared values. The realization that equity is the precursor of quality is such a principle, and applying it to academically focused arrangements for acceleration is a clear difficulty to be confronted. Professional development can surely help (Croft & Wood, 2015), but at least one person who can think straight about the challenges that acceleration poses to the typical school culture must organize and steward the effort.

Because equality is the precursor of quality, schools need to monitor the provision of accelerative options among both sexes, locally represented ethnic groups, and underprivileged students. Local norms and quotas are useful for this purpose (see previous discussion). Once school personnel realize that many students—and not only those officially dubbed "gifted"—can benefit from acceleration and advanced courses, they may envision even wider provisions to cultivate equity and intellectual engagement *simultaneously*.

This effort will always remain a struggle, within and outside of factory schooling. But better approximations could be a lot more widespread than they are, even within factory schooling. The literature on inclusive leadership practice (e.g., Theoharis, 2009) could be helpful; any team working on inclusive leadership would need an advocate for acceleration—pushback against the prevailing misconceptions would likely be necessary in most schools and districts (see Assouline et al., 2015; Gallagher, 2004). So talent development, as contrasted with mere schooling, requires careful and responsive nurture (Bloom & Sosniak, 1981; Sosniak, 2006). Indeed, the quest for practices that elaborate intellectual options for all students has the potential to change the organizational climate of many schools, even now.

Chapter 7

Social Justice

Ethical Implications for Intellect and Talent Development

> By reducing learning to purely instrumental and vocational ends, instrumentally inclined policymakers undermine the very nature of learning and elevate its pale imitation—rote learning and the fear of failure. —Peter Cookson (2015)

Many who become teachers enter the field not only because they like children, but also because they want to change children's lives for the better (see, e.g., Tye, 2000). These motives do not necessarily indicate concern for social justice or equality. These motives, though, *do* address the common good. They are decidedly more generous than the age-old desire to become rich—and, since justice itself is a major dimension of the common good (e.g., Counts, 1932; Kozol, 1991; Labaree, 2005; Ravitch, 2010), such motives implicate social justice at least obliquely.

In America, concern for social justice does not necessarily, or even usually, imply support for equality, but rather for some species of "fairness" (e.g., Rawls, 1999). *Inequality*, in other words, is readily misconstructed (as in the American Constitution of 1789) as socially just.[47] Equality is a *stringent* species of social justice. Indeed, in America generally, a strong concern for simple social justice (fairness) marks one as a liberal. Support for equality would perhaps (on this view) mark one as a radical.[48]

It is nonetheless true—so far as "radicalism" goes—that social justice relates to *traditional* revolutionary values, as in the slogan "Liberty, Equality, and Fraternity." All three commitments are stock values espoused in the French Revolution of 1789, and inscribed everywhere to this day on public buildings in France. But the American founders, too, at least argued about equality.[49] The framing of the U.S. Constitution unfortunately entailed compromises that elevated liberty above equality and far above solidarity, which was actually never mentioned. Extending the conversation about social justice in America required the Civil War (equality) and the trade union movement (fraternity given a practical meaning as *solidarity*).

Perhaps predictably, given the history, the American conversation about social justice has again faltered. Instead, free (global) trade[50] is now advertised and widely accepted as a guarantor (e.g., Hayek, 1988) not only of a properly low level of equality (justified by competition), but also of a weak solidarity—based on the claim that free trade floats all

47   That is, largely by its silence on key issues: the three-fifths rule (Article 1, section 2, paragraph 3) applied to "all other Persons"—its euphemism for enslaved African Americans, and the Constitution reserved the actual determination of the franchise to states, which in practice defaulted to property-owning White males; neither African Americans, nor women, nor Indians, nor landless men (a large proportion of the population in 1789) could vote, nor would they, for a long time. And to this day the Electoral College places the *actual election* in the hands of political operatives.

48   The term *class warfare* is no longer much used by the Left, but the Right now uses it frequently to castigate those more actively concerned to promote social justice (Nunberg, 2011). Indeed, Nunberg notes that the *New Left Review* uses the term about 1/4 as frequently as it did in 1970, but that the *Wall Street Journal* now uses the term 5 times more frequently than it did in 1970!

49   Equality—but not solidarity—is commemorated on a series of American stamps issued at this writing; a series in which, however, "liberty" gets double billing (i.e., as itself but also as "freedom"). In this same series, "justice" appears—but decidedly *not* "social justice." The American form of justice is perhaps best understand as devotion to the rule of law. Actual access to the law is strongly mediated in America by economic standing (see, e.g., Isenberg, 2016).

50   See the discussion elsewhere of neoliberalism as the world capitalist system.

boats—and even common decency, in that functional markets require trust among participants (see, e.g., Jacobs, 1994, on the "trader moral code").

No wonder educators concerned with social justice, equality, and solidarity are doubly marginalized in America—first because they are educators and second because they dare to harbor such concerns. The cultural margin, though, as we have previously suggested, is an excellent place for doing authentic cultural and intellectual work (see Chapter 4). Even so, it hardly seems right to qualify the concern for social justice, or even for equality and solidarity, as radical! It seems to us, indeed, more a set of concerns that *ought* to represent, and to enlarge, common decency.

In this chapter, we are occupied with issues other than plans for the reconstruction and enlargement of common decency (see the final chapter for such a plan). Here we consider the origins of concern for social justice and the paths to such concern in a society where even concern for common decency falters. And, of course, we are interested in exploring what a manifest concern for social justice has to do with intellect (as this book defines it).

We have not been convinced by arguments suggesting that free trade either requires or obviates a concern for social justice, so in this chapter, we consider the role of *ethical reasoning* in necessitating a concern for social justice (and for some of us, both equality and solidarity, too). We then apply this necessary concern as a critical vantage on how American schooling fails to cultivate the fuller participation of certain groups (e.g., the poor, those with darker skin, women) in formal manifestations of intellect. These cultural circumstances, of course, influence programming, and particular programs, for gifted students—and we consider those influences as well. In this telling, social justice, equality, and solidarity are essential to care of the intellect and to forms of education that take intellect seriously. Social justice, education, and intellect are mutually dependent—even mutually constitutive—and thus they jointly enable the common good more fully. No wonder, on this view, that American culture would denigrate intellect.

Social Justice and the Culture of Thoughtfulness

Where might concern for social justice originate if not from common decency? The question is crucial because it concerns the "common good," which is an aim to which "common schooling" ought properly to be committed. Moreover, "decency" represents a lower bar than advocates of liberty, equality, and fraternity might prefer.

Competing Explanations

Karl Marx believed that concern for social justice (his own demonstrable commitment included) originated in a kind of science (e.g., Heilbroner, 1980), a law of history under which the meek (the proletariat) would inherit the Earth (i.e., oversee construction of a just and classless society in which the State itself would wither away). What people thought—the ideologies that commonly prescribed all sorts of virtues in Marx's time—were (to Marx) quite irrelevant. Concern? Irrelevant! History made the justice of the proletariat a necessity, almost an inevitability. Concern was beside the point: Even *understanding* the laws of history was less relevant to Marx. The natural processes (of history) would ensure the triumph of the working class, and social justice would follow.

The evolution of capitalism (and of world history itself) has rendered Marx's answer far less satisfying than it once seemed to many people worldwide. Stalin's massive brutality ushered in a wave of revulsion toward Marxian certainties (e.g., Heilbroner, 1980). If fixed laws of history exist, then, they have remained obscure to most historians and political theorists since the time of Stalin (however, cf. Fukuyama, 1992). So, neither common decency nor the Marxian "science" of history provides acceptable accounts of the need for social justice, let alone the need for equality or solidarity.

The other traditionally credited origins of concern for social justice include God (Norenzayan, 2013); certain views of evolution (e.g., Hrdy, 2009); politics (e.g., Easton, 1953); and logic (e.g., Rawls, 1999). All of these perspectives offer interesting alternates, and they all have inspired considerable elaboration and debate, most of which is well beyond the scope of our discussion here.

What else is there? Our purpose in this discussion, of course, is to trace, if possible, the connection between intellect and concern for social justice. The connection is closer than it might at first seem. Recall that we have already defined intellect as the common intellectual heritage and as all humanity's continuing work on it. Intellect is not, in our telling, an individual characteristic or attribute. We are not discussing mightier or more inferior "intellects," but the common cultural project of the human mind itself. This outlook inscribes concern for the common good in a common project of understanding.

It seems to us, then, that among the possibilities, a consideration of the arguably most relevant branch of philosophy—ethics—is worth the reader's effort and ours. Why? Ethics is in part an intellectual exercise (in its philosophical manifestation), but it is also a realm of everyday practice—an ethic of caring (e.g., Noddings, 2013), for instance, or a land ethic (Leopold, 1949). Such particular, everyday ethics also engage and constitute intellect, as do everyday instances of thoughtfulness, kindness, reflection, curiosity, and imagination. In some fashion, ethical reasoning would seem to support a range of views and outcomes relevant to action on behalf of the common good and possibly on behalf of social justice (and even equality and solidarity).

The Role of Ethical Reasoning

As we mentioned above, one perspective on ethical action treats God as the source of concern for the just treatment of others. And studies show that many Americans believe moral behavior primarily involves adherence to the word of God (e.g., as codified in the Ten Commandments; Aikin & Talisse, 2011; Norenzayan, 2013). Ethical action, on this view, requires application of the word of God. But the codified word of God does not (and cannot) prescribe all actions under all circumstances. Action in the real world requires, at the very least, interpretation of the word of God. Arguably, though, the act of interpretation itself shows that human beings are capable of far more than simple adherence to rules. In fact, the interpretative bent of human beings offers a competing explanation of where ethical action might come from.

But whatever one's beliefs about the *origins* of ethical action, all people must nonetheless make ethical judgments—and many of them—in the course of day-to-day life. Whether or not ethical reasoning is the *ultimate* source of such judgments has limited bearing on questions about how humans make those judgments and where those judgments lead.

What Is Ethical Reasoning?

The long history of philosophical thinking (as well as self-reflection on the matter) shows that ethical reasoning supports ethical action. Without it evil becomes more probable. The connection between ethical reasoning and action is particularly important to some philosophers— for instance, Hannah Arendt's observation of "the banality of evil" at the trial of an infamous war criminal (Arendt, 1963).[51]

But what is ethics? What is reason? And what, then, is ethical reasoning? We give our simple answers, which represent a distinctive position well articulated in philosophy (for an extended discussion see, e.g., Kompridis, 2000).

Ethics is the branch of philosophy dealing abstractly with questions of the good and also, less abstractly, the varied ways of genuinely thinking about such matters and undertaking action. It is an ongoing reflexive *cycle of genuine thinking* involved in continuous attempts to define, refine, and enact action on behalf of "the good." Clearly, the good is not only what it might be for oneself and one's family in the private realm, but notably also what might be good in the public sphere (Arendt, 1958; Kompridis, 2000; Rorty, 1997). In this sense—a definitional one— social justice is inherent in ethics because it encompasses concerns about what actions in the public sphere promote the good.

---

51   The famous phrase is the subtitle of the cited work. Arendt covered the trial of Adolf Eichmann, elusive Nazi war criminal, and watched how he presented himself as a reasonable technician who just didn't think too much about the industrial slaughter he actually facilitated (principally by organizing it). In his own view, apparently, he was just another careerist—another good manager—unluckily placed in a war machine.

Coming up with a definition of "ethics" might appear easy, although the thousands of years of debate about the origins and requirements of ethics suggest that it actually is not. For our purposes, however, treating "ethics" as concern for the good gives us a simple basis for exploring how ethics might relate to intellect. We might call the mediating concept *reason* (e.g., Kompridis, 2000): Reason is what makes ethics intellectual.

But the definition of "reason" is difficult too. The difficulty is largely a 20th-century one, the legacy of reason narrowed by natural scientists to the sort of technical rationality characteristic of, and even modeled by, rocket science (Forester, 1993; Saul, 1993). Sending humans to the moon or a rocket to photograph Pluto exemplifies that sort of "reason." Reason along these lines entails the application of a set of well-validated criteria to obtain a predictable result. This narrow approach to reason gets things done, but it does not support the important intellectual practices of valuing, imagining, speculating, interpreting, or offering critique.

If one treats the narrow construction of reason as applicable to ethics, one falls quickly out of the domain of reasoning properly understood. That is, a well-laid-out and predictable procedure for resolving ethical questions does not, in fact, rely on thinking, but rather on following a formula. A much broader, and much more robust treatment of reason is needed to allow for what ethics actually asks of us: the determination of value, the imagination of possibilities, speculation about consequences, interpretation of events and their larger meanings, and critique of the human enterprise as it currently exists.

This broader work of reasoning reflects a long tradition—much longer than that supporting technical rationality—and it functions not primarily to get things done, but instead to push the boundaries of who we are and to help us imagine who we might want to become. In other words, it is a use of thought and language to expand human agency and aspiration (see, e.g., Kompridis, 2000).

Reason of this more expansive type is fully compatible with the project of developing conceptions, judgments, and practices on behalf of the good. To distinguish this approach to reason from a narrow, instrumental one, we will use the term *critical reason*. On this view, a modern, deflated version of reason can lead only to ethical devolution (Kompridis, 2000), and it contributes thereby also to political and cultural devolution. Critical reason, then, has immense import for the development of intellect, as it always has (Barzun, 2000). Critical reason opens up a variety of ways of looking at the good, in more and less global terms. This perspective is compatible with the political theories of Norberto Bobbio as described by Vitale (2010):

> It is impossible to spell out the philosophical foundation of human rights—in the sense of an ultimate metaphysical foundation—but this does not imply that philosophical thought, in the sense of critical reason, cannot make a useful contribution or provide valuable arguments in support of human rights. (p. 386)

Used to interpret ethical action, critical reasoning is not primarily a process of discernment. Discernment, in fact, *requires* a metaphysical foundation because it asks that we make distinctions on the basis of criteria, that is, that we read events and possibilities in light of principles or rules that are already given. With critical reasoning, by contrast, we invent the good based on our interpretation of the world. The broader our understanding of the world and its possibilities, the better able are we to interpret what's going on so that we can alter ourselves and human society for the better (e.g., Kompridis, 2000; Putnam, 1990). Ethical reasoning cultivates a thoughtful practice that supports the agency to change oneself and one's world. Because broad understanding can lead both to more productive self-reflection and a more thoughtful understanding of solidarity (Rorty, 1989), cultivation of critical reasoning often leads to greater concern for social justice.

Observe, as well, that, with this aim, ethical reasoning ought to enjoy a place in everyday thoughtfulness, and not primarily belong to the province of academic philosophers. Education, then, plays an important role in nurturing critical reasoning.

First, to make a wise judgment about "the good," an individual benefits from the ability to situate the judgment within a larger frame of reference. Second, to extend care beyond oneself, a person needs to assess existential possibilities and limits—in short the scope, indeterminacies, frailties, and constraints of the human condition (Martí, 1999).

What are the relevant sources? Understandings derived from reading history, philosophy, and religion seem particularly relevant for supplying a frame of reference, but we have no particular program in mind for what we are calling *critical reason* beyond cultivating an open mind eager to engage relevant sources.

In an everyday sense, to deploy critical reason one must develop at least the habit of reading widely—not as a specialist but as a very curious generalist. It seems clear that schooling rarely facilitates even such a modest level of accomplishment. But it certainly might do so far better than it has.

We turn next to connections between ethical reasoning and the American cultural context in which schooling is embedded. That discussion will conclude the question of how intellect informs an understanding of and commitment to social justice, and it will also introduce issues to be dealt with in the second major section of the chapter: the implications of American social *injustice* for intellectual development within the institution of schooling.

The American Cultural Surround: The Ethical Connection

A European observer (Lévy, 2007) recently cited as peculiarly *American* the State's disregard of its poor. Indeed, rather than ethical reasoning, as just argued, marketing determines the nature of "the good" in America (for a classic application of the logic to schooling, see Chubb & Moe, 1990). The cornucopia of consumer goods (much of which are not accessible to the poor) translates in America into political, social, and personal well-being—precisely "the good" that might be elaborated quite differently by critical reason in service of ethical action. The misery of the poor in one of the world's richest nations thus appears intentional: as de facto national policy (see, e.g., Gans, 1994; Katz, 1989; Lévy, 2007; Piketty, 2014).

More than 30 years ago, in fact, and well before this national policy was fully realized, Robert Bellah and colleagues summed up the ethical situation depressingly well:

The extent to which many Americans can understand the workings of our economic and social organization is limited by the capacity of their chief moral language to make sense of human interaction. The limit set by individualism is clear: events that escape the control of individual choice and will cannot coherently be encompassed in a moral calculation. But that means that much, if not most, of the workings of the interdependent American political economy, through which individuals achieve or are assigned their places and relative power in this society, cannot be understood in terms that make coherent moral sense. (Bellah, Madsen, Sullivan, Swidler, & Tipton, 1985, p. 204)

Bellah's team advised that citizens reclaim shared understandings about the relationship between self-identity and the common good as embedded in religious and secular American traditions. In our view, however, that well-intended counsel was naive intellectually and politically (see also Lévy, 2007). Whereas tradition has the potential to support transformative thought and action, in practice it frequently provides the rationale and the mechanism for repressing both (Friedrich, 1972). Such repression occurs most often when the authority that legitimates a tradition comes from beliefs that have no reasonable support (Friedrich, 1972). Bellah's "habits of the heart" argument seems to us an emotivist approach to ethics: sentimental, nostalgic, and perhaps even reactionary, because it looks to an American golden age that did not really exist (cf. Williams, 1973, for the British case).

We conclude, by contrast, that the traditions with the greatest potential for fostering social justice require a more substantive public forum and therefore do not reside primarily in the observances, however altruistic, of established civic and religious groups. A public forum requires discussion and debate—careful use of language, multiple interpretations, and relentless comparison of interpretations. Actions considered deeply in a public forum have a greater chance of producing solidarity on behalf of social justice than those improvised in other ways (Habermas, 1984, 1987). We view the accumulated legacy of the human mind's wondrous works as grounding for the *critical reasoning* that might, under the best of circumstances, enable a public forum to remain focused on and support action on behalf of a shared understanding of the common good. This view represents a high standard, of course, but observe that cultivating the relevant capacity is an educational project that would seem essential to public schooling in a claimed democracy.

Social Injustice, Schooling, and Intellect

Having connected social justice to ethical reasoning, the chapter now turns to a discussion of social *in*justice present in and cultivated so widely by American schooling. The story is a difficult one, but familiar enough. Here, though, we work to link the familiar story to a concern for cultivating intellect. In this context, thinking *produces* concern for social justice, and so a schooling that cultivated thinking well would be one that *necessarily* took the enlargement of social justice—and even, perhaps, equality and solidarity—*seriously*. Thus, the following account of how schooling really works to disable intellect and thoughtfulness should be especially disturbing. We segment the discussion according to (1) social class and (2) cultural location (e.g., ethnicity and sex: notably "people of color" and women). The categories represent the distinction between less and more visible markers (e.g., social class versus skin pigmentation or sex characteristics) around which elites organize and reorganize the rationalization and practices of injustice.

Schooling to Control the Working Class and Underprivileged

According to Navarro (1991), "How people live and die depends largely on their class" (p. 3). His claim runs counter to the popular American belief in individuals' ability to succeed no matter how adverse their circumstances, but strong empirical evidence supports the claim. The U.S. ranks lower in class mobility than many industrialized nations (Beller & Hout, 2006), and much of the recent mobility is downward

(Urahn, Currier, Elliott, Wechsler, Wilson, & Colbert, 2012). As Urahn and colleagues[52] (2012) noted:

> Across the distribution, 20 percent of Americans are "falling despite the rising tide"—they make more money than their parents did, but have actually fallen to a lower rung of the income ladder. Another 29 percent have higher family incomes but are at the same place on the income ladder as their parents were. (p. 9)

Furthermore, wealth (i.e., accumulated resources or "net worth") has become more polarized, with overall wealth controlled by fewer and fewer people. One reason for the increasing polarization of wealth is that wealth is no longer closely connected to workers' income: profits rise, but salaries do not. In 2013, corporate profits were newsworthy, the highest (in constant dollars) on record since 1929, according to *The New York Times* (Schwartz, 2013), and yet wages and salaries were at a record low—41.9% of the gross domestic product (Federal Reserve Bank of St. Louis, 2014). The current trend of paying workers less and less for their contribution of skills and talent threatens the national economy (Piketty, 2014) and, as this section will argue, undermines the development of intellect (and giftedness) to an ever greater extent.

Observe that in this chapter we categorize "class" in fairly unconventional terms: the underprivileged, the working class, and the privileged. We use these rather idiosyncratic categories in an attempt to call attention to the effects of class segmentation. The terms *lower*, *middle*, and *upper class* do not, in themselves, denote characteristics of class membership; worse, they gratuitously stigmatize the poor as "below" the other classes.[53] So we have chosen our terms specifically to counter the misconception that people who live in poverty are less worthy than others. We do believe, for instance, that all humans are inherently equal by virtue

---

52 For its analysis this source adjusts family income for family size, which declined over the time-frame of the analysis (1968–2008), giving the average family a "raise" disconnected from the operation of the economy per se. Real wages per worker have in fact fallen (see, e.g., Kristal, 2013).

53 For a history of the stigmatization of the poor across 400 years of American history, see Isenberg (2016).

of their common humanity, but this time-worn and hard-won principle of democracy is being carefully undermined in America (e.g., Dorrien, 2012; Gilens & Page, 2014; Orlov, 2011).

Conventional designations (low, middle, upper) are obviously inappropriate. But structural categories, which do distinguish among discrete classes based on their relationship to the production process (e.g., Wright, 1985, 1997), seem inadequate here as well, even though they clearly explain the dialectical relationship of working and owning. Considering this prevalent view, does our alternative perspective constitute a prejudicial treatment of the privileged? Readers, again, can decide for themselves. We think, however, that a concern for social justice entails an important corollary: Impoverished people are *not* inferior because they are poor, nor are the wealthy or advantaged superior because of their wealth. Such an outlook seems objective: All humans are human.

Being cast into the underprivileged class, of course, relates to the other circumstances of life. After all, much of what determines the class to which people in the U.S. belong is their ethnic or racial membership, gender, and geography. A much larger percentage of African Americans, Hispanics, and Native Americans than members of northern European ethnic groups are assigned membership in the working and underprivileged classes. More women than men live at the poverty level or below it. Among descendants of northern Europe, a larger percentage of rural than urban descendants find themselves confined to low wages or poverty.

Schooling helps allocate poverty. Real wages and income (i.e., income adjusted for inflation) have declined in the past half-century (e.g., Kristal, 2013). And while some families have become wealthy, many more have experienced impoverishment. Increasing poverty has been *allocated* primarily to vulnerable working-class families, especially families of ethnic descent and families headed by women (e.g., Pettit & Ewert, 2009). Poverty has increased dramatically for a number of reasons, chief among them the globalization of corporate interests and action; industrialization abroad; accelerated computerization and automation in the workplace; and increased corporate influence on economic policies at international, federal, and state levels (Aronowitz & DiFazio, 2010; Gilens & Page, 2014; Giroux, 2013). In 2008 and 2009, more than eight million jobs were lost—the greatest loss of jobs since the Great Depression in the early 1930s.

This expansion of poverty clarifies the function of the working class in the economic system: Its labor-power is productive when employed, but its unemployment when not needed is equally important, because it helps preserve corporate well-being in times of trouble (e.g., Tsuru, 1991). Working-class impoverishment, in a sense, thus funds corporate survival. Furthermore, because corporations need the working class to play this role (what Marx thought of as service in the "industrial reserve army"), they have a vested interest in not considering the human costs of such an arrangement. Arguably, corporations *abandon* their workers when they no longer need them (e.g., Schor, 1991).

Because corporations exert preponderant influence on the State (Gilens & Page, 2014; Sachs, 2011), moreover, government, too, abandons unemployed workers and their families. That abandonment entails neglect for the country's social safety net (e.g., Parish, 2013), and it also includes the persistent neglect of schooling for large segments of the working and underprivileged classes. Schooling thus plays its part in allocating poverty (see, e.g., Carr, Gray, & Holley, 2007; Chiu & Khoo, 2005).

As Jonathan Kozol (1991, 2005) has suggested in his critique of U.S. schools, working-class and underprivileged children receive significantly fewer educational benefits than the children of wealthy parents. His critique is supported by numerous studies showing that students from low-income families are not afforded equitable educational opportunities (see, e.g., Goldhaber et al., 2015, on systematic bias in the allocation of teacher quality). Kozol noted that parents who can secure educational advantages for their children do so even when securing these benefits comes at great expense to other children (see also Glass, 2007). Depriving other children of a "good education" gives the children of the privileged a competitive advantage and conveniently ensures a cheap labor pool for the future. Kozol (1991) quoted a school superintendent in San Antonio, TX:

> If all of these poor kids in Cassiano get to go to real good schools—I mean, so they're educated well and so they're smart

enough to go to colleges and universities—you have got to ask who there will be to trim the lawns and scrub the kitchen floors in Alamo Heights. (p. 228)

Of course, many of the children now in school will not be needed in the near future even for menial labor, much less for skilled or professional work (Aronowitz & DiFazio, 2010; Krymkowski & Krauze, 1992). And if current employment trends continue, the labor force will shrink, the quality of schooling for the poor will deteriorate, and educational pathways for rich and poor will diverge even more (e.g., Del Val & Normore, 2008; Howley & Howley, 2015). So the superintendent's pessimism of 25 years ago appears even more justified now than then.

Confronted with increasing levels of inequity, many Americans nevertheless conveniently choose to regard wealth as the just reward for superior merit (Bénabou & Tirole, 2006; Rank, Yoon, & Hirschl, 2003). In this way, the increasingly unequal distribution of resources among the populace seems to many Americans to reflect a form of social justice: Wealth comes to people because of their talents and hard work; poverty comes to people because of their deficiencies of intelligence or character (Bénabou & Tirole, 2006; Rank et al., 2003).

In other words, the cause of poverty is poor people themselves (Rank, 2005). Even well-meaning educators—educators who dedicate themselves to helping the children of the poor—endorse this perspective when they voice popular, though unwarranted, beliefs about so-called "generational" poverty (Gorski, 2008; see Lewis, 1966, for a classic original work on the culture of poverty). Substantial international research, however, shows that States that provide better resources to families and schools elicit higher tested performance from students (see, e.g., Chiu & Khoo, 2005; Condron, 2011; Williams, 2005).

Much evidence shows that, despite educators' intentions, school policies and practices actually make use of *putatively equal* opportunities to enforce *inequality* (Bowles, Gintis, & Groves, 2008; Lukes, 1974; Tye, 2000). Indeed, the routines of instruction very effectively teach inequality: dumb kids and smart kids, C students and A students, college material and likely dropouts, and so forth. Students learn readily to accept such invidious distinctions as justifiable and ordinary instead of rejecting them as spurious, demeaning, and, in fact, outrageous (e.g., Anyon, 1980; Oakes, Ormseth, Bell, & Camp, 1990; Tye, 2000).

The messages about where students fall along a continuum of merit and how that positioning ought to impact their performance and aspirations constitute what some have called the "hidden curriculum" (e.g., Martin, 1976). The hidden curriculum differs in schools serving children from different types of families. At schools for the privileged, the hidden curriculum teaches internalized responsibility and self-control in the expectation that graduates will assume their place among the nation's leaders (Anyon, 1980; Khan, 2011). At schools for the working and underprivileged classes, by contrast, the hidden curriculum stresses obedience to external sources of authority—even to arbitrary authority—in the expectation that graduates will, at best, assume subservient positions in the workplace (e.g., Anyon, 1980; Brown, 1991; Nespor, 1997; Wilcox, 1982; Willis, 1977). The two sorts of schools apparently pursue the cultivation of different sorts of outcomes: one to assume agency and leadership, the other to submit to subordination and manipulation.

Furthermore, schooling also inhibits the intellectual development of working-class students and represses their social mobility (Bowles et al., 2008; Haberman, 1991, 2010b). These circumstances are disturbing because the most fundamental power of public schooling is its power to force children to attend: Parents who fail to send their children to school can be fined or sentenced to jail. Students who drop out of school before the allowable age are truant, and those who miss school can be penalized, in some states, by having their driver's licenses revoked or being declared ineligible to apply for one (see, e.g., Florida Drivers Association, 2015).

Harsh disciplinary policies (e.g., the infamous "zero-tolerance" policies), including the schools' increased use of the police and the courts to address minor infractions of rules, have affected working-class and underprivileged students to a greater degree than other students, and with greater risk for harm (e.g., Irwin, Davidson, & Hall-Sanchez, 2013). Even the school organizations that such students often attend are subject to harsh discipline (e.g., Duncan & Murnane, 2014). In recent decades, that is, states have imposed accountability regimes that extend punishments to professional educators (e.g. Olsen & Sexton, 2009). The dislocations engendered in these schools (e.g., low morale, high turnover) further penalize working-class and underprivileged students (e.g., Daly et al., 2011; Olsen & Sexton, 2009).

School practices for the working class and underprivileged. Schooling's role in the allocation of poverty seems clear to those who can read the evidence (e.g., Haberman, 1991, 2010b), but more diffuse trends in schooling combine to restrain the *intellectual development* of working-class and underprivileged students. These trends include inadequate resources, underprepared and transient teachers, inappropriate curriculum and instruction, alienating classroom environments, and lack of access to college—conditions that have long contributed to the underachievement of working-class and underprivileged students. We consider each, briefly, next.

We begin with resource issues. Although many state constitutions explicitly require *thorough and efficient systems* of schooling for all students, states fall short, particularly in schools for underprivileged and working-class students (Kozol, 2005). This shortfall is perhaps most obvious in the squalid buildings and grounds, dilapidated equipment, and inadequate supplies provided in schools for working-class and underprivileged children.

But facilities are just one indicator of inadequate (and inequitably distributed) resources. In fact, vast discrepancies exist in the resources available to schools (Biddle & Berliner, 2002; Lynam & Fix, 2012). The pattern of discrepant resource allocation begins with differences across states and continues to filter down within state school systems to the level of the school. In 2012, the poorest state, Mississippi, spent $8,164 per pupil, whereas New York, the highest spending state, spent an average of $19,552 per pupil in the same year (Lynam & Fix, 2012). There are also great disparities *within* states and even within districts: In the Long Island, NY, school district the figure in Montauk is $36,400—equal to tuition at an expensive private preparatory school—while in Floral Park, in the same district, it is just $13,950 (Lynam & Fix, 2012). The history of lawsuits brought in order to correct such obvious inequities is a long one and includes suits in 47 states (National Education Access Network, 2015). Litigation has sometimes resulted in decisions requiring action, but the court decrees are seldom carried out in full, largely because influential resistance to the rulings persists (see, e.g., J. Johnson, 2014, for the Mississippi case).

Gifted programs, which predominantly serve children of the privileged, sometimes have better facilities than other programs in the schools. But resources for gifted programs vary greatly, as might be predicted. For instance, although 32 states mandate programs, just 4 of these fully fund their mandates, and 8 provide no funding at all (NAGC/CSDPG, 2015).

Curriculum and instruction for working-class and underprivileged students are often haphazard and inadequate. Their teachers are less well prepared than those who serve more affluent students (Goldhaber et al., 2015), and their teachers receive less support than their counterparts in other districts (Johnson, Kardos, Kauffman, Liu, & Donaldson, 2004). School leadership is often less consistent (Clotfelter et al., 2007). Under pressure to improve quickly, moreover, their schools or districts often try one "quick fix" after another, rendering curriculum and instruction incoherent and faddish (e.g., Cuban, 2008), and the frenzy guarantees ineffectiveness.

Furthermore, whatever their achievement level, students in schools in working-class and underprivileged communities seldom have the opportunities offered to children in schools in affluent communities. Working-class and underprivileged students are, for example, given fewer chances to design experiments or projects, to analyze ideas, or to express themselves in creative work (Brown, 1991; Haberman, 2010b; Thadani, Cook, Griffis, Wise, & Blakey, 2010). They are also more likely than others to be retained in grade or placed in remedial classes (Hauser, Pager, & Simmons, 2000; Jimerson, 2001; Oakes, 1985): proven methods of delaying academic progress (e.g., Jimerson, 2004; Martin, 2011).

Despite reformist literature on failing schools, there is little evidence that things are improving for working-class and underprivileged students (Reardon, 2013). Indeed, the responses to high-stakes testing have made pedagogy more mechanical than in the past, often involving rote memorization, practice of routines for demonstrating compliance, and very little decision-making opportunity for students (Shepard, 2003; Wiliam, 2010). Nationwide, schools' responses to high-stakes testing are associated with a larger probability of dropping out for low-achieving students and for students from low-income families (Reardon & Galindo, 2002).

School and classroom environments for children of the underprivileged and working classes are often constructed to frustrate learning: They are crowded, impersonal, and alienating—what some call *hostile* (Lleras, 2008). Hostile environments confront and breed disorder, even violence, and the punitive responses of educators to students' adjustment difficulties often exacerbate the problem (Chen & Weikart, 2008). In such schools, punishments are meted out to poor children with *more* severity and *greater* certainty than to other children (Skiba, 2000). Furthermore, although punishments such as detention, suspension, and expulsion have been found to be ineffective in changing students' behavior, schools for these children often use these practices rather than interventions such as PBIS (positive behavior interventions and supports), which are more likely to be effective (Kauffman, 1993; Noltemeyer & McLoughlin, 2010). By contrast, schools and classrooms for privileged students are more likely than those for working-class or underprivileged students to foster internalized responsibility and self-control by offering more instructional and motivational support (Khan, 2011).

Nevertheless, despite comparatively adverse circumstances, most working-class students are well-behaved (Atkins et al., 2002). Thus, the inappropriate emphasis on school security and heavy punishment proliferates a custodial climate, which in turn tends to perpetuate social inequalities (Kupchik, 2010). Indeed, schools serving underprivileged and working-class students often turn disciplinary measures over to legal authorities, introducing their students early to the world of courts and prisons (Hirschfield, 2008).

Schooling for underprivileged and working class students also prepares them inadequately for meaningful postsecondary options, including college. In part, this outcome reflects the fact that such students have less time than their affluent counterparts to study and complete assignments (e.g., DeAngelo, Franke, Hurtado, Pryor, & Tran, 2011). In part, it reflects their greater likelihood of becoming frustrated with school and dropping out. Tough (2014) summed up the situation bluntly as follows:

> Rich kids graduate; poor and working-class kids don't. Or to put it more statistically: About a quarter of college freshmen born into the bottom half of the income distribution will manage to

collect a bachelor's degree by age 24, while almost 90 percent of freshmen born into families in the top income quartile will go on to finish their degree. . . . If you compare college students with the same standardized-test scores who come from different family backgrounds, you find that their educational outcomes reflect their parents' income. (para. 10–11)

As this quote indicates and as a great deal of empirical research confirms, working-class and underprivileged students, no matter how capable, are much less likely than their privileged counterparts to attend college and to attain a bachelor's degree.

Systematic Discrimination as a Threat to Intellect

In this section of the chapter, we briefly talk about systematic discrimination based on social markers such as race, ethnicity, gender, culture, and locale. In general, these types of social markers influence the life chances of people from different groups. For example, proportionally more women than men, more Blacks than Whites, more Hispanics than Anglos, and more Native Americans than others are poor (e.g., Clark, 2014). How do social markers differ from and how do they interact with class?

The related concepts of *social class* and *cultural location* help illuminate this interaction. In addition to social class, one's cultural location influences the likelihood of success in school and the labor market (Willis, 1977). Whereas social class (based on economic markers) primarily concerns someone's location within the economy, cultural location (based on cultural markers) takes more than the economy into account: race, gender, age, and geography, for example. Each cultural location, moreover, gives people who occupy it access to certain cultural legacies and ongoing traditions.

These cultural traditions and their products embed symbolic meanings and confer certain status distinctions, which are viewed in different ways by others depending on the social and cultural locations those people occupy. For example, consider classical music. In general, most of us imagine that people who appreciate classical music are of European descent and are older and more affluent than average. Symbolically, appreciation for classical music also connotes an elite education and perhaps a higher status in social hierarchies. A preference for jazz, bluegrass, or rap each carries a different set of connotations, but is equally likely to elicit particular characterizations about the person who prefers that type of music.

Such symbols—and the social world is populated and even *made* by them—are in fact social markers, just as economic conditions and physical characteristics are markers. They go along with class membership, but offer a richer and far more subtle characterization of what it means to be underprivileged, working class, or privileged. For instance, they help characterize (in a stereotypical way) what it might mean to be a working-class male aged 30 living in a small town in the Great Plains or (again in a stereotypical way) what it might mean to be a middle-class African American woman living in a suburb of a major Eastern city.

Because social and cultural locations suggest, and even provide, rich characterizations of particular people and subgroups of people, they point to social practices that systematically undermine or elevate the life chances of those people and subgroups. In other words, the prejudices directed toward people who occupy certain social and cultural locations (e.g., hillbillies are stupid, Blacks are lazy, the French are immoral) function in conjunction with social class to the particular detriment of certain individuals and families (notably, working-class and underprivileged families) and to the benefit of the privileged—*even though* individuals from privileged backgrounds may feel little personal prejudice or animosity toward the victims of such unfair prejudice. Under this arrangement, moreover, those who benefit most from the advantages of their social and cultural locations typically determine what locations are most desirable by using their privilege to impress upon everyone the superiority of their own characteristics and preferences.

The privilege to determine what is desirable and acceptable on such a basis is institutionalized. It is diffused throughout government and throughout both civic and private institutions. The most prominent of these institutionalized prejudices, of course, is institutionalized racism, which is more insidious than the bigotry of individuals (e.g., Kamali, 2009). The insidiousness of institutionalized racism slows the pace of social change to one acceptable to American elites. For example, despite serious attempts to change discriminatory practices in the U.S. (e.g., the Civil Rights Movement, the women's movement), American society and the American political economy *still* favor Whites—and urban White males in particular—allocating to them higher status and higher incomes than others enjoy (e.g., Gradin, 2014).

Clearly, institutional prejudice poses a threat to social justice, but does it also pose a threat to intellect? The evidence suggests that it does and in three ways. First, members of groups that are the victims of institutional prejudice and discrimination (a short-hand term is "marginalized" groups) are less well prepared than their privileged counterparts to contribute to the intellectual legacy of the nation—a circumstance that in part results from their inadequate schooling. Second, the admirable works (e.g., novels, scientific discoveries) of people from these groups are less likely to be represented in the official curriculum of schools than the works of members of dominant groups, and, through this mechanism, tend to be silenced or relegated to a lesser status. Third, misrepresentations of marginalized groups in intellectual works (e.g., novels, movies) contribute to widespread characterizations of them as one-dimensional, deficient, weak, or dangerous.

For the sake of simplicity, we might call these three threats, respectively, (1) limiting access, (2) silencing, and (3) essentializing. We will illustrate how these threats operate by looking first at mechanisms that limit women's educational attainment (limiting access), then at ways that the intellectual works of African Americans are diminished (silencing), and finally at unflattering media portrayals of rural Appalachians (essentializing).

Sexism and limitations on women's intellectual development. Despite the fact that women outstrip men in degree attainment at the high school, bachelor's, and master's levels (National Center for Education Statistics, 2014), their opportunities for highly skilled, intellectually challenging work lag behind those of men (Burgess, 2013). This circumstance results from the fact that employers tend to view women as less competent than men (Correll, Bernard, & Paik, 2007) and to penalize them for trying to combine motherhood with work (Burgess, 2013). Evidence of these dynamics reveals that women *of all social classes, races,* *and ethnicities* predominate in relatively low paying jobs, and even when they have high-paying jobs, they are paid less than their male counterparts (Hegewisch & Ellis, 2015).

Limitations on women's opportunities for meaningful and well-paid work persist *despite* women's improved academic success. With very few exceptions, females outperform males in school. For example, there are more girls than boys represented in gifted programs, girls make better grades and score higher on most reading and math achievement tests, and more females than males enroll in college and attain college degrees (Office for Civil Rights, 2012). The few exceptions relate to performance in science and math. On Advanced Placement and Scholastic Aptitude Tests, male students perform higher in math (calculus and statistics) than female students (Hedges & Nowell, 1995). These exceptions may reflect female students' continuing underenrollment in advanced science and mathematics classes at the secondary and postsecondary level or their tendency to be less competitive than males (Niederle & Vesterlund, 2010).

Although researchers seldom attribute the superior academic performance of female students to superior innate intelligence, some research has attributed gaps in performance at the advanced level to male's superior innate intelligence (e.g., Benbow & Stanley, 1980). A more recent study attempting to replicate Benbow and Stanley's findings, however, did not support their conclusions (Wiley & Goldstein, 1991). Current meta-analyses, however, reveal no differences in math performance by gender (Lindberg, Hyde, & Petersen, 2010). The Benbow and Stanley study and related research illustrate the complexity of issues relevant to attributing causation. Family income, race, and ethnicity appear to affect academic achievement test scores more than does gender. With few exceptions, girls in each income, racial, and ethnic category score closer to boys in that same category than to other girls in the same age cohort (Corbett et al., 2008).

Where they exist, declines in gender-based achievement at the secondary school level result from girls' socialization via the "hidden curriculum." In mathematics, for instance, schooling has in effect suppressed the achievement of females (see, e.g., Lindberg et al., 2010; Niederle & Vesterlund, 2010). Without thinking, teachers convey messages that reinforce and reproduce behaviors associated with gender stereotypes. Indeed, historically, girls—even gifted girls—have expressed less confidence in their abilities than boys (e.g., Eccles, Barber, Josefowicz, Malanchuk, & Vida, 1999; Fox, 1976; Meredith, 2009). They still generally remain skeptical of their abilities to excel in science and mathematics. Consequently, girls—especially working-class and underprivileged girls—are less likely than boys to pursue advanced studies even when they have the ability to succeed in these fields (e.g., Archer et al., 2013; Fox, 1976; Lindberg et al., 2010). Although increasing numbers of women *are* studying mathematics and science at the college level, earning about 50% of degrees since 1990 (National Science Foundation, 2015), stereotypes can still affect their test performance even in high-level college mathematics and science (Good, Aronson, & Harder, 2008), and women are *still* sharply underrepresented among math and science doctorates: about 25% in mathematics and 20% in physics (National Science Foundation, 2015).

Historical data certainly show that women now have far greater access to meaningful schooling and employment than they did in past centuries and even past decades. But their access to a full range of intellectually challenging school and work experiences is still limited in comparison to the access afforded their male counterparts. For example, fewer female than male artists are sufficiently successful to achieve acclaim (Vigneault, 2012). And, within colleges and universities, women find it harder than men to obtain full-time academic positions and to retain those positions by earning tenure (e.g., Tierney & Bensimon, 1996). Although women are making "progress" in gaining access to meaningful education and careers, their struggles to do so illustrate the influence of social markers on social, economic, political, and intellectual outcomes.

Silencing of African American voices. Prejudice creates another consequence for intellect through the mechanism of silencing (e.g., Gates, 1992; Traore, 2007). Silencing occurs when the production of curriculum (both for K–12 schools and universities) privileges the experiences and works of some groups of people (e.g., European Americans) over those of others (e.g., African Americans; Kharem, 2006; Pollock, 2004). It also takes place when schools limit the opportunities of African American students (and other students of color) to participate in meaningful intellectual conversations about the content they are studying in school (e.g., Cammarota & Romero, 2006). A similar dynamic occurs in institutions of higher education when entrenched faculty members from dominant groups keep African American faculty members (and other faculty members of color)—often in subordinate, untenured positions—from participating in significant intellectual debates (Dade, Tartakov, Hargave, & Leigh, 2015).

As Kharem (2006) argued, the school curriculum does not serve the interests of African American students, and, in fact, works against their interests by communicating a "white supremacist" message and enacting a "white supremacist" agenda:

> Schools and other cultural institutions select, preserve, and distribute ideas of the dominant white elite as seen in their quest to control knowledge and true transformation in our society. . . . The dominant white society constructs opinions that make nonwhite people feel there is something wrong with them. (p. 4)

The curriculum undermines the interests of African American students, according to Kharem, in several ways: (1) by diminishing the contributions of African Americans, (2) by emphasizing narratives that stereotype and belittle African Americans, and (3) by curtailing discussion of the country's history of racial repression.

Some ethnographic research also characterizes African American students' experiences of being silenced by illustrating various dynamics, such as shutting down contributions to classroom discourse and limiting discussion to safe topics (e.g., Fine, 1991). Arguably, in an effort to maintain control, teachers *often* use discourse in classrooms that skims the surface and curtails, rather than encourages, inquiry and debate. Rexford Brown (1991) called this strategy *talkinbout*:

> In most schools, the language of the classroom is primarily a language about the process of teaching something, it is not itself a language of learning. "Talkinbout" is . . . an adult reconstruction after the fact of an experience that the student is not allowed to have firsthand. It is a rumor about learning. (p. 234)

As our earlier discussion suggests, this strategy is used more often in schools with a custodial culture, such as those that serve African American students and other students of color, than in schools with a more nurturing one, such as those that serve affluent White students (Rocques & Paternoster, 2011; Warikoo & Carter, 2009).

Essentializing rural Appalachians. Intellect also suffers when schools and other institutions that communicate information reinforce inaccurate and negative attributions by "essentializing" people from particular cultural locations. Although stereotyping and essentializing are similar, stereotypes tend to be more permeable. Essentializing identifies an essence or defining characteristic or set of characteristics of a group and, through that process, limits consideration of possible (and even evident) variability within that group (e.g., Fuss, 1989). When people encounter an exception to a *stereotypical* characterization, they tend to see it as part of the within-group variability they would expect. When they encounter an individual who appears to be an exception because he or she lacks an *essentialized* characteristic, they tend to believe that the individual is not really a member of the group.

So if someone sees churchgoing as an essential characteristic of rural Appalachians, he or she would be likely to view a non-churchgoer as not being a "real" rural Appalachian. Treating essential characteristics as fixed not only promulgates an inaccurate view of the essentialized group or member of the group, it makes it easier for members of dominant groups to denigrate and discriminate against members of a smaller, less powerful group. Furthermore, inaptly treating complex patterns of commonality and difference as a set of fixed characteristics narrows the scope of the imagination of the person who thinks about people in terms of such characteristics. In this way, essentializing limits openness to intellectual exploration more generally.

As a group, rural Appalachians have been essentialized in the visual media (e.g., Harkins, 2004), textbooks (Howley, Eppley, & Dudek, 2016), newspapers (e.g., Wood & Hendricks, 2009), and fiction (e.g., Algeo, 2003). Although these characterizations have changed over time (Isenberg, 2016), the portrait of Appalachians across the years has been negative. They have variously been essentialized as backward, inbred, violent, excessively independent-minded, and clannish (Biggers, 2006;

Isenberg, 2016). Occasionally, however, more objective or even celebratory accounts do appear. For instance, Biggers (2006) described the nationally significant contributions of Appalachians to the culture and politics of the U.S., and to social justice in particular; and Isenberg (2016) recently explained the marginalization of the rural poor as a historic American economic and cultural principle, as opposed to an accidental bias.

The misuse of schooling to allocate poverty and enforce the advantages of the privileged class and those in favored social and cultural locations has, we have tried to show, been remarkably consistent. The consistency is remarkable, moreover, in a nation formed as a manifestation of democratic principles. The consistency is not perfect, not continuous and unbroken, but persistent and continual—a punctuated equilibrium, to adopt a term from evolutionary biology. We mean that the unfair system is punctuated with attempts to blunt its consistent prejudices. So to conclude the chapter, we now turn to some notable punctuation.

Efforts to Promote Social Justice in Education

Before the industrial revolution, Americans established public schools rapidly not only in cities and towns, but especially on the expanding rural frontier (Cremin, 1980). Indeed, nearly all White children were attending elementary schools before the turn of the 20th century, and literacy was commonplace according to Cremin (1980). Schooling for Blacks, Hispanics, and Indians was a different matter (see, e.g., Anderson, 1988; Bullock, 1967; Rodriguez, 1999; Swisher & Deyhle, 1987). True, attendance was irregular for many White students—although home-based and church-based literacy instruction often filled the gap (Cremin, 1980). African Americans also had ways to fill their much larger gap (Anderson, 1988; Bullock, 1967).

So the first efforts for school improvement *per se* (i.e., as distinct from literacy efforts outside formal schooling) were designed to make the school term longer and, simultaneously, with the adoption of child labor laws, to release working-class White children from labor in farms, mines, and factories so they could attend the longer terms (Katz, 1968). The social justice intent was clear, although as Katz (1968) demonstrated, concern for public order was paramount—getting the urchins of the poor off the streets. Whatever their exact class and cultural locations, however, children from impoverished families were seen as the chief beneficiaries of early school improvement: The new laws made the hiring of children illegal, even though their families usually *needed* the children's wages (Hall, 1989). The application of the set of related laws was initially problematic, but it was problematic far longer for non-White children (Anderson, 1988; Bullock, 1967; Rury & Hill, 2011).

Longer terms were a beginning for improvement efforts, but what was needed next? The popular answer in the early 20th century was a state system of schooling organized for efficiency (for an early example, see Rice, 1913) from elementary through tertiary levels (Callahan, 1962; Cremin, 1962, 1980; Spring, 2013). To improve schools, education leaders allied themselves with interested business leaders to define the improvement agenda as better inputs to schooling, used more efficiently: buildings, transportation, instructional materials, teaching expertise, and professional administration (Callahan, 1962; Robertson, 2007; Tyack, 1974; Tyack & Cuban, 1995).

States variously systematized and regularized, and also kept schools segregated especially by social class and cultural location ("race" and "ethnicity"). Even the university system was kept segregated (Wilder, 2013). The very rich often sent their children to well-esteemed private schools, where the children could make durable and useful social connections (cf. Adams, 1918/1931, about this function at Harvard). The emergence of the high school as a publicly funded institution, however, initially served the needs of local elites (Cremin, 1980; Katz, 1968); very few students attended high school at the turn of the 20th century (Cremin, 1980). Improvement was clearly entangled with society's prevalent discrimination by class and cultural location; improvement did not apply to everyone, and only some notions of what was "better" applied.

Children in the systematized and regularized public schools were also segregated by chronological age—and not only by skin color and social class—as the scientific ideal (Cremin, 1980). Everyone was increasingly required to use the same textbook, which had not been common previously (Kliebard, 2000). Smaller schools and districts, as well, were closed to create larger ones (Strang, 1987). The official argument was always that consolidation would save money, although it hardly ever did (Howley, Johnson, & Petrie, 2010).

So the new inputs and the greater attention to efficiencies did not redress the widespread inequities very well (Rury & Hill, 2011), they did not reliably or obviously improve the learning process (Cuban, 1982; Tyack & Cuban, 1995), and they sometimes institutionalized systemic barriers to improvement (see Bruce & Calhoun, 1996; Jobrack, 2011; and Tyson-Bernstein, 1988, for the case against textbooks), including the surprising creation of substantial economic *inefficiencies* (see, e.g., Howley et al., 2010; and Robertson, 2007, for the case against massively larger schools and districts). Some contemporary observers have concluded that the overall improvements to about 1940 served more to magnify existing social injustices in schooling than to redress them (e.g., Blacker, 2013; Spring, 2013).

In any case, by early mid-20th century, many things that certainly seemed like improvements to many contemporaries were clearly visible: larger, better buildings; motorized transportation; larger districts; teachers with more schooling; pedagogical specialization; and professional administration. But sharp inequities persisted, and as the Great Depression unfolded across the 1930s, those inequities became more visible and concern about them suddenly had much more political salience than it had ever had in the past.

As now (following the Great Recession of 2008–2009), rising inequity then prompted popular outcry. At that point, one critic asked a durable question, as we explain next. Instead of elusive "improvement" and the devotion to "efficiency," a focus on social justice within schooling could be heard clearly to apply even to students from disparaged cultural locations (e.g., African Americans).

Progressive Education and Daring the School to Build a New Social Order

"Progressive education" began much longer ago than the life of John Dewey (Hayes, 2006), but it was Dewey who formulated the progressive ideas for the industrial era (see, e.g., Dewey, 1897). Dewey (born in 1859) saw the 19th-century school as a species of child abuse: memorization in place of thinking, silence and stillness instead of language and activity, and beatings—not invitations—to "motivate" students. He emphasized methods of teaching that attended carefully to the nature and interests of the child (Egan, 2002). Dewey clearly advocated a more humane approach to schooling than he had personally known. His approach was philosophical rather than scientific because the discipline of child psychology barely existed when Dewey began his campaign for a more humane schooling. Dewey's focus, and that of many progressive educators, was on the individual child.

But in the 1930s, one progressive educator took exception to the individualistic focus of the movement as a whole: George Counts (1932). Counts, a politically active colleague of Dewey's and later a founder of the American Federation of Teachers, asked a durable question about American schooling: "Dare the School Build a New Social Order?"

His dare to American educators was based on an assessment of who takes charge of designing and conducting schooling:

> [They] pride themselves on their open-mindedness and tolerance . . . [but] rarely move outside the pleasant circles of the class to which they belong. . . . These people have shown themselves entirely incapable of dealing with any of the great crises of our time—war, prosperity, and depression. At bottom they are romantic sentimentalists, but with a sharp eye on the main chance. That they can be trusted to write our educational theories and shape our educational programs is highly improbable. (Counts, 1932, pp. 7–8)

Where did Counts look for better leadership of schools? He looked to teachers. And he advised them to organize politically, to refashion schooling so as to refashion American society itself, namely to refashion it to promote social justice. It's a long causal chain, from schooling to political liberation, and it is prone to much slippage even under ideal conditions. Furthermore, despite some efforts to keep Counts' injunction at the forefront (e.g., critical pedagogy), much change since 1932 has instead recreated American schooling as an infamous "sorting machine" (e.g., Oakes, 1985; Spring, 1988; Tye, 2000).

Counts (1932) himself understood the immense challenges involved, and so his famous dare was circumspect: "If America should lose her honest devotion to democracy, she will no longer be America; she will be known merely as the richest and most powerful of nations" (p. 40). By "democracy," Counts meant the struggle to create an egalitarian society—not a form of government (see p. 41). But 90 years on, even America's sorry reputation as the richest and most powerful nation seems unlikely to endure much longer (see, e.g., Jacques, 2009). Worse still, the American sentiment favoring equality as an official concern of the State (a legacy of the New Deal) has been thoroughly undermined since 1980 (Bickel, 2013).

More to the point, the struggle for an enlarging and active—or simply *humane*—pedagogy (a.k.a. "progressive") languishes particularly in schools for working-class and underprivileged students and for students from disparaged social and cultural locations (see, e.g., Anyon, 1980, 2005; Atkins et al., 2002; Blacker, 2013; Brown, 1991; Gutstein, 2003; Kharem, 2006; Labaree, 2005; Moses & Cobb, 2001; Wilcox, 1982; Willis, 1977). Today, impoverished communities cannot compete with affluent ones in the "educational marketplace" to secure the services of reputedly good to excellent teachers (Clotfelter et al., 2007), and they struggle to offer an organizational climate in which excellent teaching can flourish (Atkins et al., 2002).

Clearly, the famous question from 1932 ("Dare the School?") was not intended to be *answered*. It was intended as a *provocation* to continue a struggle. Counts knew he was addressing a political and economic issue—social justice—and not a technical feature of schooling (e.g., not "What pedagogy is best?", "What is the best reading program?", "What makes a good principal?"). His focus on social justice went far beyond concern for the individual's experience of schooling. Like some later progressive reformers (especially those promoting critical pedagogy), he imagined that schools could nurture democratic, egalitarian engagement while simultaneously preparing students for a changing world.

The Civil Rights Movement

Many Americans, like Counts, had hoped the State would take over key industries on a socialist model in order to redress inequities and forestall future collapses (see, e.g., Cochran, 1978). It didn't happen, of course, and today socialism has limited currency in the U.S. Although the Roosevelt administration sponsored a number of helpful social-welfare programs, the New Deal addressed only superficially the fundamental American inequities based on cultural location and social class. Notably, the schools remained segregated (Orfield, 2001; Orfield, Kuscera, & Siegel-Hawley, 2012), and income and wealth inequality are still as extreme as before the Depression (Kristal, 2013; Piketty, 2014).

In particular, the foundational racism of the nation (foundational in that this gross inequity was built into the federal Constitution) continued to be ignored into the 1950s precisely because it *was* constitutional. But all the while, during Reconstruction and following (Reconstruction ended in 1877), African Americans built and operated schools as harbingers of their own self-determination and liberation—regardless of the State's neglect and White oppression of them (Anderson, 1988; Foner, 1991; Rury & Hill, 2011). Being kept from reading and calculating is tantamount to being kept from the capacity to reason—always the capacity most dangerous to enslavers, oppressors, and the manipulators of privilege (see, e.g., Barzun, 2000; Blacker, 2013; Bullock, 1967; Labaree, 2005).

Wars, of course, had always disclosed to White Americans how much the national interest required the labor of its second- and third-class citizens. In this context, each war since the Civil War (1861–1865) sharpened the demands of African American veterans and their families for a wider scope in postwar civilian life (Bullock, 1967; Rury & Hill, 2011). But it was ultimately the generative legacy of African American struggle and resistance that finally weakened the nation's foundational racism. That weakening, though, is most often associated with the accomplishments of the Civil Rights Movement (Rury & Hill, 2011).

With the rise of an identifiable movement in the mid-1950s and across the turbulent 1960s, the national cultural and political dynamics shifted decidedly toward greater acknowledgement and somewhat fuller participation of African Americans in American life. Resentment of

African American agitation among the White establishment was intense in those years, and demonstrates how deep-seated, how *normalized*, the oppression of African Americans was (see, e.g., Bullock, 1967; Garrow, 1986). For instance, Martin Luther King was routinely vilified (Garrow, 1986), and White society was terrified of Malcolm X (Cone, 1992).

Only in the late 1960s did positive media images of African Americans begin, quite tentatively, to appear in mainstream television, radio, publishing, and advertising (U.S. Commission on Civil Rights, 1977). Much resentment and mistreatment persists, of course; this chapter documents some of what that dynamic is like now in schooling at all levels. But the Civil Rights Movement, beneficiary of hundreds of years of struggle, durably advanced the agenda that African Americans still press against the nation's (somewhat weakened) foundational (if no longer Constitutional) racism.

The Civil Rights Movement, however, is not typically represented as an educational movement, although it was that, too. Rury and Hill (2011) argued that African American schooling created the generation of Civil Rights leaders, and hence in some sense the movement itself. But the roots of the movement in the provision of schooling extend back at least to Reconstruction (the postbellum South; see, e.g., Foner, 1991). The Jim Crow regime cut short the gains of Reconstruction, but the African American press for more schooling persisted and grew (Anderson, 1988; Bullock, 1967). Indeed, some have argued that the Jim Crow outrage had the effect of redoubling African Americans' concern with schooling (Anderson, 1988; Rury & Hill, 2011).

And of course, for a milestone for society and for schooling proceeding from the Movement, there is 1954's *Brown v. Board of Education* decision. The decision produced appallingly little desegregation, but it nonetheless set a momentous precedent. It overthrew the doctrine of "separate but equal" that a previous Supreme Court had institutionalized in *Plessy v. Ferguson* (1896). Until 1954, any form of segregation by "race" (skin color) was smiled upon by the State—by the federal government and its highest and most prestigious court. Afterward, it was frowned upon. The participation in that work by the nation's first African American Supreme Court Justice (1967–1991, Thurgood Marshall) attests to the reach of the movement's influence.

Looking back from 2017, the America of 1877 to 1960 seems as outrageous as it actually was. But in 1954, few White Americans complained or cared (see, e.g., Pascoe, 1996); when it came to African Americans in particular, injustice was viewed as normal and proper across the nation as a whole. Thus the achievement of a simple ruling in *Brown*—focused on schooling—swept away the legal and constitutional basis of a long era of outrage. The *Brown* litigation was a direct action of one of the Movement's organizations (the National Association for the Advancement of Colored People or NAACP), and the reach of the decision, argued by Thurgood Marshall, but representing a deep grassroots preparation, went far beyond schooling.

Still, much else remains outrageous today for African Americans— "ordinary" inequities that remain invisible only because they are misunderstood as ordinary, and therefore acceptable—just as was the doctrine of "separate but equal." At this writing, the Black Lives Matter movement has taken on the "ordinary" police violence that includes murder. African Americans, of course, always understood the White double-talk and the privileged White double-think inherent in American society and its prevalent forms of injustice and mistreatment (see, e.g., Bullock, 1967; Garrow, 1986; Rury & Hill, 2011).

Once one understands that racism is foundational to the American State, however, all the double-talk and double-think comes into focus as necessary (foundational) self-delusion. Notably in his account of African American schooling from 1860–1935, Anderson (1988) made a telling argument: Schooling to cultivate the free hand of elites and schooling to cultivate the confinement of African Americans (and the working class and underprivileged) comprise a single system. Injustice is not accidental: It is intentional. In such a system, moreover, the miseducation practiced in schools is a broadly tolerated phenomenon (see Wilder, 2013, on the role of racism in elite universities). And this observation brings the discussion to the next intervention for social justice.

Deschooling, Unschooling, and Alternative Schooling

If *public* schooling is systematically rigged to defend and secure injustice, as some have argued (e.g., Anderson, 1988; Spring, 1988; Tye,

2000), and to hobble both reason and thoughtfulness, as others have argued (e.g., Gatto, 2002; Goodman, 1962), then justice-minded citizens might pursue other options for a family's or even an entire community's children. On such views, that action, for those motives, might well serve a social justice interest: to avoid a system that propagates injustice, and to avoid the systemic miseducation that keeps one's children ignorant of the implications of such injustice.

Almost at the height of the Civil Rights Movement, and not coincidentally, a related tendency of school critique emerged to explore alternatives. In the early 1960s, Herbert Kohl and Jonathan Kozol were privileged White men (Harvard graduates) teaching African American children in segregated schools. Both, however, received their most genuine education in league with their African American students (Kohl, 1967; Kozol, 1967). Their stories fed the views of other Whites who were dissatisfied with the injustice, indoctrination, and intellectual meagerness of American schooling: The schooling context in those years, of course, was the return-to-normality conformism of the 1950s (Friedenberg, 1979; Goodman, 1962). Indeed, a "free school" movement was already underway, as a liberal- or radical-minded mostly White alternative sort of schooling (see, e.g., Neill, 1960).

Among the apostates of schooling as an institution, however, the most notable was Ivan Illich, a multilingual polymath who worked for a time in New York in impoverished Puerto Rican neighborhoods. Illich's *Deschooling Society* (1971) argued that schooling *per se* helped render society socially and intellectually stagnant. Illich was one of the very few observers to offer a sweeping alternative to modernist schooling around the world, but America was by 1970 on the verge of starting a now long-standing alternative to schooling both public and private. That alternative was homeschooling.

Although the 1950s and 1960s ethos suggested that the best education was to be had in schools staffed by state-approved teachers in public schools or by teachers selected for intelligence and competence by elite private schools, homeschooling proponents undercut that public-private agreement with the assertion that any parent could educate children at home (see, e.g., Holt, 1981). The fledgling movement had clear roots in the 19th century, when school terms had been short and the curricula usually meager (Cremin, 1980). As Angus (2001) observed, the 19th-century view was indeed that any adult could teach children, although some were more apt than others. The 20th century had preferred expertise, but many citizens understood that the prevailing public school arrangements actually deformed "common schooling" into a sorting machine whose beneficiaries were primarily the rich and powerful.

John Holt (1972, 1981) was perhaps the most visible proponent of the emergent alternative: He had enjoyed considerable popularity as a proponent of school improvement. When he formally "deschooled" himself, his decision probably helped establish the legitimacy of the homeschooling movement among those with intellectual and social justice aspirations for their children, since he had written bestsellers about learning that were critical of institutionalized schooling. In the years 1977 to 2001, Holt published a homeschooling newsletter, "Growing Without Schools" (Farenga, 2015). The movement grew substantially in those decades, and it is still growing—although certainly the main practitioners are unlike the early ones (Bielick, 2008).

Today, homeschooling is widespread: About two million children were reportedly homeschooled in 2007 (Bielick, 2008). Although the phenomenon is now often characterized as a separatist move of religious fundamentalists,[54] homeschooling parents are diverse in other ways: 25% are non-White and 10% are African American (Mazama & Lundy, 2013), and they span the socioeconomic spectrum (Rudner, 1999). Some African American parents in fact report that they exercise the option because of the poor schooling available in a racist society (Fields-Smith & Williams, 2009). Some homeschooling White parents, however, also understand that their children learn prejudice via schooling's hidden curriculum, and nonreligious ideological reasons have long been cited as the motivation to homeschool (e.g., Fields-Smith & Williams, 2009; Ray, 1992). Indeed, even in 2007, 20% of parents reported they were

---

54   About 83% of homeschooling parents give "a desire to provide religious or moral instruction" as a motive for the decision to homeschool (Bielick, 2008). This reason covers wide ground, but the American belief that morality comes from religion suggests that most of those responding in this fashion would be motivated by religious reasons, and most of those by a fundamentalist, or literalist, view of Biblical text. Fundamentalists, of course, come from a variety of ethnic backgrounds.

homeschooling because of their "nontraditional" views about education (Bielick, 2008).

Plunging Toward Dystopia

Two keen observers of the American schooling system (Tyack & Cuban, 1995) described, some time ago, the long history of American school reform efforts as *Tinkering Toward Utopia*. It now seems better to characterize recent "reform" efforts as *plunging toward dystopia*, or even leaping with abandon into it. Why?

Unlike earlier reform efforts, such as progressive education and the Civil Rights Movement, recent reforms position schooling primarily as a private good rather than as a public good. Arguably, of course, because of its role in perpetuating an inequitable distribution of benefits—the sorting function discussed previously—schooling has not lived up to its potential as a public good.

Rather than helping the system of public schooling become more equitable and more inclusive, however, recent reforms seek to undermine it. Why and in what ways? Before we can answer these questions, we need to explain what we see as the potential of *public* schooling as a *public* good.

What is the potential of public education? Although not well and certainly not fully realized, public schooling—as a project of the people, by the people, and for the people—has the potential to prepare literate and thoughtful citizens to live meaningful lives and contribute meaningfully to their communities and other democratic institutions (see, e.g., Ravitch, 2010, 2013; Tye, 2000). Such potential, most importantly to the perspective of this book, aims to educate and not just to school: to help cultivate fulfilling lives and an enlarged view of living among everyone in successive generations.

In fact, with its legacy of increasing inclusiveness throughout the 20th and early 21st centuries, public schooling *has* demonstrated that this potential can be realized at least to a certain extent. The nation's public schools now enroll a more diverse population of students than they did 50 years ago, and the academic performance of students, overall, has increased (Berliner & Glass, 2014). In some public schools, moreover, resources are adequate to the task of educating, and students routinely benefit from curricula and teaching methods that both enrich and enlarge their experiences of the world (see, e.g., Gutstein, 2003; Howley & Harmon, 2000; Howley, Howley, Burgess, & Pusateri, 2008; Lawrence et al., 2005).

Why do recent reforms undercut the potential of public education? According to Glass (2016), the same corporate and political forces that are conspiring to make American society more inequitable in general are also conspiring to undermine the public purposes of schooling. In brief, schooling that is educative is both expensive and dangerous, and the interests of a White oligarchy are best served by limiting an educative sort of schooling to an already affluent few (Berliner & Glass, 2014; Ravitch, 2013). At the same time, the history of taxation to support schooling has generated large sums of money—and corporations stand to realize substantial benefits from siphoning off a profitable share of those dollars (Glass, 2016; Howley & Howley, 2015).

Within this context, reforms combining high standards, high-stakes tests, and punishments to struggling school districts while at the same time failing to provide equitable staffing, adequate resources, and high-quality support serve one purpose only—to undermine schooling for working-class and underprivileged students (see, e.g., Blacker, 2013; Glass, 2016; Ravitch, 2013). Along with many others, we come to this conclusion because (1) punishing accountability regimes do not produce improvements (Daly et al., 2011; Olsen & Sexton, 2009), (2) punishing accountability regimes strip intellectual purpose from academic curricula (Anyon, 2005; Shepard, 2003; White, 2011; Wiliam, 2010), and (3) the transfer of public funds to private corporations has substantially reduced the resources available to the schools that most need those resources (Glass, 2016; Howley & Howley, 2015; Miron & Urschel, 2010; Ravitch, 2013).

To implement these "reforms"—regimes and practices that actually function to undermine public schooling—a powerful elite has worked for years to erode confidence in schooling as a public trust. Its arguments prey on parents' fears for and vanities about their children—fears of exposure to an increasingly diverse student body (Blacker, 2013; Glass,

2007), fears of school violence (Blacker, 2013; Glass, 2016), and vanities about special talents and needs (Sapon-Shevin, 1994; White, 2011).

Why might citizens and educators want to reclaim public schooling? Despite the fact that some of the working class and the poor in the United States support politicians with interests inimical to their own (Blacker, 2013; Foner, 1984; Frank, 2004; Goad, 1997), many of these same people value their communities and want to take actions to enable their communities to flourish (Frank, 2004; Goad, 1997). Furthermore, many see their local public schools as central to community well-being (Lawrence et al., 2005; Lyson, 2002). In fact, strategists working to undermine public trust in public schools have exploited communities' care for their schools by courting the involvement of certain grassroots citizen groups in urban communities and using those groups' concerns to cultivate a sense of urgency (Gordon, 2016).

Clearly families and communities have an interest in schools that value their children, care for their children, and offer hope to their children (Kozol, 1996; White, 2011). If sustained, public schooling that accomplished these aims would help to create a more just, more flourishing society (Counts, 1932; Blacker, 2013; White, 2011). In fact, it dare not try to create a new social order as Counts (1932) hoped it might, but it seems that it could help create a better one as political conditions permitted—and they would permit it from time to time. But that potential exists only if education endures as a public trust and is not replaced by for-profit schooling.

Lessons

This chapter has described factually how the American system of schooling sustains injustice. We have also argued philosophically that concern for social justice is implicit in ethical reasoning and that ethical reasoning leads, across individual biographies and even the sweep of history, to concern with social justice and equality. An education that makes much of reading, writing, and reasoning (we mean disciplinary reasoning—historical, sociological, political, mathematical, and empirical) creates in people the disposition to think, to question, to doubt, to dialogue, and to debate. That disposition and those practices inevitably lead individuals, the political economy, and the culture toward engagement with ideas and judgments about what is good, what is just, and what is equitable.

There is not one best answer to such considerations, of course. But the failure to pose the questions and to grapple with them limits the scope of the dialogue the questions inevitably sponsor as well as the variety and power of the answers offered in response. Worse still, if few people are grappling with the questions, power increasingly falls into the hands of a few—notably the few who benefit when questions about social justice and the common good remain unspoken.

At this juncture in the book, the discussion begins to take a more prescriptive turn. We have done our best thus far to make arguments and to support them with evidence. Ultimately, however, when contrasting "anti-intellectualism" with an intellectual education as an alternative in schools, we must draw not only on facts, but also on interpretation and imagination. In view of what has gone before and what is coming next, it seems a good moment to derive a few critical lessons from the forgoing arguments and facts:

1. American culture is a poor context for schooling that treats the mind with respect. (America does have stunning cultural achievements, and we ignore them.)

2. The purposes of American schooling have been narrowly instrumental for a long time. (Practical and vocational preparation is valuable for everyone, but Americans think it is for "losers.")

3. The instrumental purposes of schooling tolerate and propagate social injustice. (Getting ahead means leaving most Americans behind.)

4. Alternative plans for schooling must exhibit greater respect for talent. (Since everyone human has talent to develop, schooling provisions should honor that fact broadly.)

5. Most importantly, social justice is a prerequisite for excellence. (To put it more broadly, liberty depends on equality, and not vice versa.)

Chapter 8

Where Might an Intellectual Education Reside?

The narrative just concluded demonstrates three things: (1) that the good waits to be done, (2) that humans have continuing access to the means of the thoughtfulness needed to do good, and also (3) that they will be doing more of it in the future, the manifold difficulties notwithstanding. It has happened in the past, and we see in the legacy of good human works the evidence of an ongoing process. So we advise readers to place their bets on that potential, even if expecting the good is not "realistic"; and perhaps *especially* if it's not realistic.[55] Let us explain.

Realism seems limiting in this context, and perhaps the three-part logical chain in the list just given indicates what one might mean by "belief in human potential." What seems like "faith"—but is not faith *per se*—turns on material conditions (a kind of reality) that inform the logic: (1) enduring prospects for scaffolding thoughtfulness and (2) the resultant likelihood of doing additional good as a result.

Not everyone will be convinced (see Skovsmose, 2010, for a very different view), but we personally do believe in a human potential in pursuit

---

55 The argument given here is not for hope, but for imagination and planning. Hope sits and waits for things to improve, or not. It expects the good, and is usually, therefore, disappointed. So it is up to us to make things better. Maybe one cannot take action (but one often has, and so have others). Even so, one can always think and say (write) what one thinks. Such thinking, manifesting in written records of the imagination, can inform later action. But such records might be overlooked! Of course. So hope is irrelevant—a distraction from the work to be done.

of "the good." Again, good waits to be done, thoughtfulness supports the doing, and so one can—and should—think to do more of it. But how does one do it?

First, one develops a sense of sources—*the relevant stuff*. One may call it curriculum, but we have in mind sources much broader than usual. That's what this chapter does: It indicates the sources we have in mind. Second, one develops a sense of the schooling provisions that "scaffold thoughtfulness." That's what the final chapter does: It indicates those provisions, provisionally. These are not simple or easy matters, despite the simple language that frames them here.

The Relevant Stuff Lodges in the Mind

Essayist and novelist Marilynne Robinson (2010) believes that the potential for doing good already does prove actual. It is not just a "potentiality" (for a very different sort of agreement, see Norenzayan, 2013). Notably, though, Robinson argued her own position in a refreshing work that prizes the mind's capacity for thoughtfulness as the ability to look inward.

Her argument pushes intellectually against the modern insistence on looking outward (for instance, toward empirical data; see Bacon, 1620). Although much of our own intellectual work is empirical (e.g., Howley, Howley, & Dudek, 2016) and evidence is an essential feature of knowing and thinking, we have always clearly understood the limits of the ideology known as *empiricism* (the view that data are the foundation of knowledge and the standard for defining value and action). For instance, the previous chapter explained how an empirical approach proves momentously inadequate for ethical reasoning. Moreover, when an empirical approach dominates the interpretation of mind itself (e.g., Pinker, 1997), knowledge about brain activity enjoys a position of higher status than the meaningfulness that the "mind" seems to harbor.[56] Why is this insight so important? Empiricism holds what is most important hostage to what is inevitably less important.

For the cultivation of ethics, politics, literature, music, and art—not to mention domestic relationships—nothing else will do but meaningfulness, and certainly not an infatuation with the brain. The elusive mind actually "is" where the action is in this respect: the meaningful connections that humans make, the insights they develop, and the commitments they hold. All lodge in the mind. And from such "furnishing" of the mind come theories and astonishing works (with a supporting role from empirical descriptions in some works). The mind is also where humans determine courses of action, to whatever extent such determinations are thoughtfully possible (usually time is quite limited).

So what if the "mind" does not really exist as a palpable organ? One must *still* acknowledge the curious webs of meanings that somehow exist in the consciousness that the brain enables; that is, unless one chooses to deny the meanings themselves.[57] Something whole exists and is worth calling by a name other than "the brain." This view differs from what social psychologists (e.g., Norenzayan, 2013) call *mind-body dualism* because it does not take the distinction between mind and brain as real, but only as usefully apparent.

So, as do we, Robinson (2010) rejected any view that collapses the mind into brain functions, or that belittles as self-deception the inte-

---

56   We certainly understand that the brain harbors the mind. The brain is interesting, as interesting, perhaps, as the endocrine system. But knowing something about the brain (or the endocrine system, for that matter) is not actually very helpful for education or schooling, nor for grasping the work of Johann Sebastian Bach, Toni Morrison, Henry Ford, Nel Noddings, nor that of farmers and bakers, or the work of keeping house.

57   This choice might derive from a position on the "mind-body question"—for instance, from reductive materialism, in which—ultimately—all mental operations (including meanings, theories, and ideas) are reduced to functions of the brain (for a thoughtful treatment see Feigel, 1981). Our consideration, however, is not at all about *psychology*, nor would we claim that concepts (love, truth, justice) are "real"; that is, except when written or performed. Anyone who writes seriously knows how chaotic the mind can be as compared to the products that come from that chaos. It seems, though, that all such cultural production and meanings proceed from something that is strangely real, and differently real from an ensemble of hormonal and electrical connections.

rior workings of the mind. The perspective of this book—obviously—accords, in this respect, with Robinson's view. Moreover, works of intellect exhibit, with an existence separate from their authors' personal being, undeniable realities, albeit ones that require other minds to reanimate them. So the intellect exists as more than brain, and in works of intellect, as something quite other than body or brain.

With a properly intellectual education, moreover, those webs of meanings that exist in the mind and in works of intellect form the content—object and subject—of a decent education. In this light, educative purpose becomes to understand, or at least to engage, such webs, to make some of them one's own in one's own life, and probably to extend them oneself in some way, in some sort of good work and action. Legions of writers of all sorts have argued the related positions across the centuries (e.g., in chronological order: Komensky, 1657/1907; Rousseau, 1762; Emerson, 1841; Tolstoy, 1878, 1889; Dewey, 1916; Barzun, 1945; Goodman, 1962; Postman, 1996; Rose, 2009; Deresiewicz, 2014). Apparently, in America we have stopped listening closely enough (Robinson, 2010). Perhaps American educators are too fascinated with the brain to concern themselves any longer with the mind?

Nonetheless, the ways of doing all that actually needs doing are remarkably various. So various are the ways, in fact, that no reasonable person could expect that the industrial production methods of contemporary mass schooling (Saltman & Gabbard, 2003; Glass, 2016; White, 2011) could begin to address such content or purpose. Only a few very lucky students will benefit in the way just described (connecting to webs of meaning in luminous works) from contemporary schooling. Most will be stymied and stultified, if not crushed (see, e.g., Goodman, 1962; Deresiewicz, 2014; Tye, 2000). It's a long tradition with schooling, even before the industrial perversions of mass schooling, which now wreak the damage on so many.

Does the Relevant Stuff Reside in "the Standards"?

To interpret what "the standards" might be doing (and how well they might be doing it), we can consider them from three perspectives. First, we can think about them as an alternative to what teachers, if left to their own devices, would construct as the relevant stuff. Second, we can consider them as a tool for shaming teachers and dismantling public education, and third, we might see them as a kind of rhetoric about curricular content that falls short of what *ought* to guide an education for intellect, what we refer to here as a "true education."

From the first perspective, standards reflect something other (arguably, something more important and more rigorous) than the content that ordinary teachers and schools would identify if left to their own devices. Before there were standards, teachers and schools primarily identified curricular content from textbooks. In some cases, they also constructed lessons based on their own knowledge and interests. Efforts to develop, promulgate, and impose state and national standards worked to remove teachers' and schools' prerogative to select content because policy makers, state officials, and university faculty judged the task to be beyond the capabilities of ordinary K–12 educators.

In some cases, these groups positioned standards as a way to fix the problem of limited teacher competence—teachers who themselves *did not know* the relevant content. In other cases, they positioned standards as a way to fix the problem of teacher prejudice—teachers who knew the content but did not believe the students they served could learn it. In both cases, "the standards" are aptly named because they judge local teachers and principals (and perhaps even families and communities) as *already* failing to exhibit them (see, e.g., Schlechty, 2008).

From the second perspective, because "the standards" tell educators what to exhibit that they are *not* already exhibiting, they readily serve as an "objective" basis for judging teachers and schools. If teachers and schools don't exhibit what they are supposed to in the future, it will be their fault. They've been *told*. Of course, teachers and schools are quick to pass the blame on to families and communities, especially when those families and communities are already seen, in a general sense, to be substandard (e.g., impoverished, non-White, speaking a language other than English, and so on).

Whatever machinations they inspire in particular districts and communities, "the standards" serve as the authoritative core of a regimen of accountability argued to address a variety of serious ills apparent in American mass society and its schooling (Apple, 2001; Eppley, 2015). But, depending on the political perspective of the groups seeking accountability, the serious ills that "the standards" address differ. For example, from the neoliberal perspective, they address erosion of American global dominance (Zhao, 2009). From the traditionally liberal perspective, they address American racism and inequality (Martin, 2015), inequitable school funding (Wyckoff & Naples, 2000), and the sharp alienation of schools from communities (Eppley, 2015; Schlechty, 2008). These are momentous, real issues—durable ones. But "the standards" are the wrong tool (Ravitch, 2013), and they are, indeed, often used for the wrong reasons (Mathis, 2016).

So the accountability conception is weak, even when the critique is warranted: The means (school reform) are so insufficient to the ends, curricular or societal, that they are much more likely, according to astute observers (e.g., Ravitch, 2013; Zhao, 2009) to worsen the ills. Is such a scheme at least well intended?

Many have reached the contrary conclusion (e.g., Eppley, 2015; Ravitch, 2013; Schlechty, 2008; Stotsky, 2000; Zhao, 2009). Perhaps, such observers argue, the scheme is *designed* to make things worse, for instance, so that the poor can be relegated to a standardized public schooling "sector," whereas better informed and more moneyed consumers can profitably patronize the private schooling "sector" (Glass, 2016). Or perhaps the design will demonstrate the foolishness of providing any sort of free and appropriate public schooling (Blacker, 2013; Sturges, 2015).

From the third perspective, the scheme represented by "the standards" attempts to routinize and constrain exactly what education history and philosophy have shown cannot and should not be routinized and constrained: learning and teaching (Egan, 2002; Eppley, 2015; Jardine, Friesen, & Clifford, 2006; Meier, 2003; White, 2011; Zhao,

2009). Of course, mass schooling already suffers from a legacy of routinizing and constraining: factory schooling engineered since about 1915. Further efforts to routinize and constrain schooling are likely to exacerbate existing inequities and inadequacies, rather than to remedy them (Blacker, 2013; Emery & Ohanian, 2004; Glass, 2016; Ravitch, 2013; Stotsky, 2000; Sturges, 2015).

Contemporary corporate leaders have, in recent decades, found the system their corporate ancestors created (Callahan, 1962; Cremin, 1962; Schlechty, 2008; Theobald, 2009) unsuited to contemporary business processes. But more of the same will not get the factory running properly, in the view of some observers (e.g., Zhao, 2009). Indeed, to the contrary, as Meier (2003) suggested, good teaching and learning require an outlook based on equality and generosity and not on inequality (greed) and efficiency. The problem is not the inapt industrial model versus the up-to-date digital version, but the corporate model based on efficiencies and profitability—versus a model based on a public-minded extension, say, of the living intellectual commons.[58]

Seen in this way, from the outlook of those who learn and teach, fretting about how to "implement the standards" misdirects our attention. As Eppley (2015) noted, "the standards" provoke much larger issues, but their application as a mechanism for shaming educators and undoing public commitment to common purpose often obscures those issues, in part by trapping educators into ignoring them. In fact, professional development focused on "the standards" often leads educators off track into a wilderness of minutiae.

For these reasons, "the standards" are likely to contribute little to improvement (Blacker, 2013; Glass, 2016; Ravitch, 2013; Stotsky, 2000). As an ensemble and as a whole phenomenon, they *cannot*, in short, be the *authentic* source of what anyone might want to know or be able to do—much less what everyone *must* know and be able to do (see, e.g., White, 2011). Rather than codifying the important "stuff" of education, they serve the rhetorical purpose of galvanizing radically different

---

58   One might phrase it otherwise as a corporate versus a community model, or a corporate versus a family model, or a corporate versus an upbringing model. The point of all these contrasts, however, is private versus common purpose, with the common models based on generosity and the corporate models based on greed (see, e.g., Sturges, 2015).

perspectives about what schooling ought to do: serve corporate interests or mobilize communities on behalf of a better future. Thus far, from our vantage, corporate interests have prevailed—and mightily—and the common good continues to suffer. In fact, corporate interests work hard to convince individuals and communities that the human potential expressed in the idea and promise of a common good is outmoded and irrelevant.

Seeking and Finding Elsewhere

What we think of as a "true education" would do just the opposite: encourage both skepticism about corporate greed and thoughtfulness about what human potential might look like for individuals and communities. A true education, on this view, concerns learning to think more attentively—exercising increasingly critical engagement with the important issues of life (the practicalities of work and craft, relationships, family, community, and the concepts and realities of economics, politics, aesthetics, and ethics). Schooling that supported this sort of education would logically feature less imposition and more consideration, more dialogue, and more improvisation (see, e.g., Egan, 2002; Goodman, 1962; Jardine et al., 2006; Kincheloe & Steinberg, 1998; Rousseau, 1762; White, 2011; Whitehead, 1929). The details of schooling provisions that might better honor this purpose appear in the final chapter, but the present chapter indicates the *sources* of substance ("content," "curriculum") that, we argue, better respect the intellect. Recall, again, that intellect in our telling is the common human cultural artifact and, as argued in the previous chapter, that common artifact is necessarily tied up with the common good. What are these sources?

"Sources" are springs—they *flow*. This usage is metaphorical for a reason: to suggest the idea of wellspring. Educators may use or misuse the flow. But the flow continues nonetheless. Content as reified in textbooks and standards, however, does not flow, and cannot be made to flow because it exists as a time-bound and arbitrary product. The distinction between "real science" and "school science" illustrates the comparison between dynamic and static sources of knowledge in general:

> As art teachers would want their students to have experience of doing art; as music teachers would want their students to have experience of playing music; so science teachers would want students to have experience of doing science, and doing science of a form which is not dissimilar to that done by practicing scientists. (Woolnough, 2000, pp. 293–294)

In comparison to static sources of content, the sources characterized shortly already have full, legitimate lives of their own, lives with intellective features largely unremarked by contemporary factory schooling. The sources are inherently educative because they are human productions that humans engage, learn, and extend. Teachers can work with such engagement, learning, and extension, and good teachers always have done so (for similar views consult Bruner, 1996; Crawford, 2009; Dewey, 1897; Jardine et al., 2006; Rexroth, 1966; Rose, 2009; White, 2011). That is the proper pedagogical use of sources.

What are these organically flowing sources supposedly so readily accessible and widely ignored? We've already given one related list:
- the practicalities of work and craft,
- relationships and family,
- community, and
- the concepts and realities of economics, politics, aesthetics, and ethics.

Readers may be horrified. Is this all? This is surely not enough! What about geometry and algebra? Calculus? Reading? Penmanship? Chemistry, biology, band, and "foreign" languages? Art? Music? What about family and consumer science? Vocational and technical education? Physical education? Citizenship? Multicultural education? All of it is ruled in, but only *sort of,* because we are not considering vested curricular interests, but rather their antecedents in the real world. Perhaps any school may and should rule some in and some out—thoughtfully (see, e.g., Meier, 1995; Sizer, 2013).

Surprisingly perhaps, until about 1980, mention of such "alternative" sources was common, rather than rare, as is now the case (Howley et al., 2011; Mathis, 2016; Schlechty, 2008; Theobald, 2009). In that previous era, citizens were more routinely questioned about what *they* expected of *their* schools. In that earlier era, a reasonable and common-sensical[59] typology had emerged. Downey (1960) reported the following broad types of purpose prized by ordinary people (see also, Mathis, 2016; Taggart, 1980):

- ➢ intellectual or academic,
- ➢ instrumental or productive,
- ➢ social or political, and
- ➢ personal (spiritual or aesthetic).

Today, though, a corporate-controlled State and its professional allies arrogate such decisions and such conversations to themselves (Glass, 2016; Theobald, 2009). Purposes, though, are not sources—they are endpoints rather than wellsprings (sources). Still, as purposes, they are related to what we intend with "sources."[60]

Sources are origins rather than endpoints or even domains. They are active, and they flow toward (and from) such varied engagements as learning to read, becoming proficient in French, mastering the rebuilding of internal combustion engines, and, perhaps most important, struggling to conduct a fulfilling life (see Chapter 4).

So here are the sources that we believe engage intellect as the common project of humanity: (1) low culture, (2) high culture, (3) intimate culture, and (4) the public realm. We describe each at some length, though briefly overall, in sections devoted to each. One must keep in mind that these are educative sources, with education construed as a much broader idea than schooling. The chapter then concludes by synthesizing all the sources, as the transition to the description of our own imagined alternative in the final chapter.

---

59   That is, the consensus reflected the common sense of ordinary citizens (see Howley et al., 2011).

60   Our emphasis, always, is on works (reading and writing) more than on process, even if process (e.g., pedagogy) is clearly and subtly critical to teaching. The pedagogy serves the works. And the works serve the students, and they them (see also, Egan, 2002.)

Low Culture

By "low" we mean the sense of culture invented by anthropologists. Whereas the 19th and previous centuries constructed *culture* as the province of leisured cultivation (as Williams, 1958/2001, complained), the early 20th century saw anthropologists traveling the world to examine for the most part how non-Western people (remote tribes and small-scale societies inhabiting particular locales or practicing certain customs) conducted their lives (Davis, 2009). The anthropologists reached an important insight: *Ordinary life* constituted and sustained culture(s).

As Williams (1958/2001) later put it: "Culture is ordinary." Symphonies, philosophy, poetry, and architecture hardly defined all, or even most, of cultural production. Subsequently, anthropology turned its attention to the everyday cultural productions in the developed world, including in institutions such as schools (Spindler, 1988) and business organizations (Wright, 1994).

This way of looking at culture recognizes that institutions of all sorts cultivate certain practices and dispositions in their participants. And everyone participates in multiple collectives that sponsor such cultivation, as they have to some extent done for thousands of years (Renfrew, 2007). In this light, one might observe that almost the only way that people could possibly engage the literate intellectual legacy of "high" culture (symphonies, poetry, philosophy, mathematics, science) is indeed via some collectivity that ordinarily cultivates it!

In this sense, the anthropological, or low, culture is the ontologically prior one, and not the formal, high, culture (as many 19th-century thinkers treated it, perhaps attributing to it a sort of Platonic "higher" reality). That is, everyday life is prior to everything meaningful in life, unless one either doubts the existence of reality altogether, or believes, with Plato for instance, that ideas themselves constitute the true reality, a difficult reality accessible only to those who possess the capacity to apprehend it (e.g., well-tutored philosopher-kings, professional intellectuals, or perhaps only children of the well-schooled affluent).

Absent such a view—which seems increasingly dubious—the priority of low culture is incontestably true. Take for instance the preliterate, oral tradition in what we call *literature*. Originally (perhaps 3,000 years ago or more) an oral entertainment, *The Iliad* and *The Odyssey* only later became written texts taught in schools, where they may and often may not now provide entertainment to students.

That small-scale society, classical Athens, cultivated dramatists and tolerated philosophers whose works have enjoyed the fate of Homer's works. The formal (high) culture that now grounds works of intellect has emerged (and emerges still) under the press of a kind of ordinary, every-day cultivation, repeatedly and simultaneously—in China, in Islamic Africa, in India, in northern Europe. American Indian culture also sustained oral traditions, some of which have been preserved for us in writing, so that they, too, despite what we now recognize as genocide, have joined the intellectual legacy of all.

More to the point about low culture, in fact, would be the rise of farming about 10,000 years ago or more, and the related invention of the wheel about 7,000 years ago (Renfrew, 2007). According to Renfrew, the habit of this inventiveness has forever altered the way humans evolve—no longer by biology, but culturally. Farming itself, as Berry (1977, 1990, 2010) noted, is a devotion that requires remarkable thoughtfulness, no more so than in contemporary America. Hanson (1995), a classical scholar, also reminds us that high classical Greek culture (the dramatists and the philosophers) emerged from a low culture built by ordinary farmers.

In short, even the historically ancient practice of agriculture harbors much to teach about nature, character, family, and community. These matters go well beyond, say, the curricula of vocational agriculture or family and consumer science (a.k.a. home economics) to evoke wonder and innovation (see Berry, 1977, 1990, 2010). Crawford (2009) and Pirsig (1974) offered insights of this sort related to—of all things—motorcycles. Their books are very different, but each demonstrates in its own ways the operation of the intellect involved with these famous, and romantic, low-culture machines.

This source flows from and leads to remarkable profundities, typically overlooked by industrial schooling. Thoughtfulness lives where the "culture of schooling" assumes it not to reside. With the examples just given, a range of every ordinary activity must harbor similar, or parallel, connections to the life of the mind. One does not need to look very far to find relevant treatments—in writing—of working overall (e.g.,

Terkel, 1974), stonework (e.g., Jerome, 1989), weaving (e.g., Zolbrod & Willink, 1996), logging (e.g., Jones, 1993), waiting tables (e.g., Ginsberg, 2001), and factory labor (Rose, 2004). Writers have consistently cautioned educators that ignorance of this source imperils society itself (e.g., Berry, 1990; Crawford, 2009; Howley et al., 2015; Jardine et al., 2006; Lewicki, 2010; Rose, 2004; Shava, Krasny, Tidball, & Zazu, 2010; Theobald, 2009).

Why is this source so widely ignored by the institution of schooling? Nearly everyone already accepts (and therefore knows) the answer: Vocational and technical fields, and all species of manual work—not to mention domesticity itself—are disparaged across American schooling (Hubbard, 1988). In fact, educational improvement regimes, particularly in recent decades, have reinforced the mantra of college-for-all (Fletcher, 2006). And this mantra results from and reinforces the culture's exaggerated regard for professional credentials and its belittling of physical work.

In gifted education a common presumption is that bright students *deserve* the disparate rewards that professional status bestows (see, e.g., Renzulli, 2012; Subotnik et al., 2011; Subotnik & Rickoff, 2010). Such "knowledge" and such presumptions are difficult to get beyond, let alone replace with more appropriate cultural norms.

If one uses educational standards as a gauge, low culture is marginal to life. Arguably, efforts to marginalize low culture serve a purpose similar to that of the punitive accountability regime—they judge certain types of knowledge and ways of life as superior to others (e.g., De Lissovoy, 2013): Being an engineer is better than being a plumber; owning a house in an affluent, gated community is better than renting an apartment in a subsidized high-rise.

But, as argued previously, the cultural margins (such as those on offer from this source) are intellectually much more promising places to deploy one's talent and time on Earth than so many in education believe them to be. Despite the marginalization of this source by schooling, in our experience many ordinary Americans—and humans worldwide—do prize this source.

High Culture[61]

What we are calling "high culture" is to some extent the advertised most important subject matter of formal schooling, but in reality it achieves such importance only for the very few people with genuine access to this "content": whether in happy families[62], in unusual schools, or with rare good fortune elsewhere. Many people, however, experience schooling more as intellectual stultification than as a path toward enlarged agency and liberation (Deresiewicz, 2014; Montesquieu, 1899; Saltman & Gabbard, 2003; White, 2011). Of secondary education, Montesquieu (1899) long ago observed:

> The level is low and the worst I can say about it is that the best you take away from it is a bigoted mind. A hundred petty betrayals . . . [and] treacheries . . . maintain a certain external order . . . but they damn the hearts of everyone involved. (p. 218)

Montesquieu was writing about an institution in another country a long time ago, but some contemporary observers have dared to argue that the high school is a dysfunctional institutional feature of American schooling (e.g., Coleman, 1961; Raywid, 1997).[63] The concept of "early college high school" and "middle college" attest to considerable anxiety about the American high school (see, e.g., Lieberman, 2004; Pierce, 2001), as does the long-neglected (Stanley, 1976) practice of acceleration for the very talented. The common goal, improvement of "the high school experience," has proven a monumental task indeed (Jordan, Cavalluzzo, & Corallo, 2006, p. 731).

Despite the routine betrayals of this intellectual source by schooling, especially secondary schooling, the meaningful works within it nonethe-

---

61   This source harbors the necessarily written but not necessarily practiced record; the former harbors the necessarily practiced but largely unwritten record. Both sources can occupy the same cultural space simultaneously; the works of Wendell Berry are a good example, but so are many others.

62   Happy families are (as Tolstoy famously noted in the opening sentence of *Anna Karenina*) all happy in the same way, and in this aspect, too. In some ways, therefore, intellectually unhappy families are more interesting.

63   Far more common is the finding that some high schools exhibit dysfunctional organizational cultures (e.g., Johnson et al., 2012).

less persist as an *accumulating* wellspring of intellectually valuable *works* that anyone might learn to understand, consult, and love. They embody the intellect and, in league with readers' intentions, form it anew: their *raison d'être*.

High differs from low culture because in it writing more often makes visible the intellect and systematically (by the existence of the works) inspires its ongoing flow. Everyday life focuses on what is in front of one, and the force of that exigency sustains the flow, but written works move beyond immediate, and pressing, frames of reference. Indeed, some works motivated in the low culture wind up in the high culture, and some writers exploit the overlap (e.g., Berry, 1977; Robinson, 2010). Perhaps, as an accumulation, the high culture seems to invite a backward look? Surely it does (reading and writing take time), but engaging the legacy invites readers to imagine a different present and future—to characterize the present critically and to imagine, to conceptualize, and to willfully shape the future.

Exposure to a canonized high-culture curriculum, however, is a misstep. Exposure does not elicit engagement. Sometimes, in fact, a canonized high-culture curriculum is so uninviting as to be repulsive, suggesting, as Montesquieu noted, that its purpose is to be ineffective.

Instead of "exposing" a canon, authentic engagement requires teachers who, as their own *raison d'être*, invite students to explore ideas—the stuff of meaningfulness in whatever relevant works of "high culture" they find useful to the purpose. Thus, only teachers already intellectually engaged by such works can issue the invitation. This is what an authentic version of "highly qualified teachers" would actually look like. Can any sort of schooling, even a far more decent sort, ever rise to the challenge?

On one hand, we can understand why it might not. For instance, the confinement of elementary students to "the basics" and secondary students to preparation for college and career (see, e.g., Booker, 2007) routinely sidetracks the necessary invitation, perhaps even among those educators capable of practicing a more invitational pedagogy (Au, 2009). Even worse, a list of the right courses, good test scores, and a roster of leadership activities in high school is misunderstood as needed for college and career success (see, e.g., Deresiewicz, 2014).

Such an anti-intellectual pedagogy deflects students and teachers alike from the project of education most of the time (Deresiewicz, 2014; Mathis, 2016). The phoniness is intrinsic to forms of schooling that fixate on cultivating individual competition and greed, as American factory schooling now does (Blacker, 2013; De Lissovoy, 2013; Deresiewicz, 2014; Mathis, 2016; Ravitch, 2010).

On the other hand, one can also imagine schooling alternatives that might invite far more students, far more regularly, to play with ideas (see, e.g., Jardine et al., 2006). Again, such ideas come from all sources, and not only from the high culture, but the invitation is especially necessary to the works from this source. As a most affluent nation, with a comparatively open system of higher education, the invitation to engage this formally acknowledged pathway should, it would seem, appear stronger. Playing with ideas, however, is not an efficient way to mobilize students on behalf of corporate or nationalistic interests or to allocate them neatly according to their background characteristics to adult roles. What about living life well right now? What about making sense of life with ideas and pursuits that engage the mind?

In any case, the high culture, in addition to being a source of curious ideas, and ideas for the curious, is also the stuff of the varied canons of supposed good taste and approved meaningfulness. Academics have debated what ought to belong on approved lists of varied sorts for centuries, perhaps millennia. Which works make it onto any such list is a question of authority: an existential fact that makes the decision a sort of turf war about whose turf dominates others, whose authority counts to rule (e.g., Ward & Connolly, 2008).

Determining whose version of "the best" prevails is a debilitating feature of human pretense: It is the mortal enemy of the good on at least one account (Montesquieu, 1899).[64] Most lists, therefore, are adequate to the purposes of education in general and to schooling in particular—so long as, with this source, intellectually engaged teachers extend to students, every day, the invitation to engage for themselves the treasure

---

64 See *Mes Pensées*: "The best is the mortal enemy of the good" (No. 13 in General Maxims of Politics). For Montesquieu the famous aphorism—with its "mortal" inserted— seems to be a principle of good living and good judgment; "le mieux" in this context may also be translated as "perfection."

trove of ideas in good works. The forms and methods of the invitation will vary with teachers, with teachers' sense of their students, and with students' reactions. One must be clear: The authority of the works lies with the works themselves and not their supporters and promoters or even their teachers (e.g., Bloom, 2014). The ultimate authority of choice, though, lies with teachers. A teacher can, and perhaps should, exercise it in conversation with colleagues, students, and families.

Questions of whose authority counts brings the discussion to the connection between high culture and power. The "highness" of the entangled legacy (the *royal* highness of this legacy, in fact) comes via the association—even the definition—of these cultural canons with (or by) whatever elites prevail in whatever societies. For instance, the Nazi regime sanctioned a canon of its own, which seems to have included works by the composer Richard Wagner and the philosopher-visionary Friedrich Nietzsche. Much in those works lives on as wonderful, despite the foul association. So what? Although elites enjoy the power of misappropriation and can spread misapprehension via schooling, their claims and maneuvers cannot render the meaningfulness *theirs*. The works live independently on; the rulers shall pass, and the works will yet live on.[65]

The reason for the weakness of brute power is that real apprehension requires engagement of the subjects—ordinary people—whose reading and listening might apprehend and use meanings that the elite suppress—as well as those the elites approve. Alas, too often, States do suppress such meanings, writing them out of the official knowledge of State schooling (Apple, 2000; Scott, 2012; Williams, 2014). This move has been comparatively well-documented in American schooling (Fitzgerald, 1979; Howley, Eppley, & Dudek, 2016; Loewen, 1995; Zinn, 2003).

Here, with the possibility of ordinary people apprehending such meanings, one sees more clearly the reason that factory schooling leads *away from* authentic engagement in the literate ("high") culture. With factory schooling, elites use high culture more to intimidate most people, particularly those most likely to object to the way elites are organiz-

---

65 For instance, Tolstoy's tract, "What Then Must We Do?" (1889), was first published in western Europe because the Tsarist State would not permit publication: The work was an inherent criticism of State and Church. It's a very old story with such works; ideas are dangerous to established power.

ing the world (Blacker, 2013). So if one's mind is led away from struggle with such works—if it is so formed as to avoid the requisite effort—it *will* be ruled by others. Alas, such struggle is required for intellectual independence and for pushing back against efforts to intimidate.

The invitation to engage works from the high culture leads importantly to writing. Writing, by contrast to producing video clips, blocks of computer code, or anything else considered creative, handles stories, logic, extended reflection—and meaningfulness—as nothing else yet has (Bruner, 1996). The act of writing helps one stay skeptical: It is the domain in which one can consciously revise one's thinking (Barzun, 2001; Mitchell, 1979). So the act of habitual writing cultivates habits of thinking, observation, and reflection (Lamott, 1994) quite unlike other engagements. These same habits are found by many to be essential for a good life among humans (e.g., Bruner, 1996; White, 2011). Everyone can write better. But, vexingly, only adept writers can teach better writing (Barzun, 1945).

Apprehending the beauty and meaning in just some of the accumulated works from this source requires considerable effort, and decent schooling would surely help. No one need love it all or even much of it—but many startling things within this source await *everyone*. It seems that much in schooling might be rearranged to foil the widespread suppression of engagement by all but a very few students with sources from the "high culture."

Intimate Culture

The third source is the domestic realm, a cultural aspect that most conceptions consign to anthropological culture as a kind of footnote, where it still languishes most often as "women's work." It figures separately in our account because the domestic is where most (or a great many) humans center most of their existence, and most of the attributions of personal meaningfulness reside: family and home. Overall, the home itself may well have greater schooling capacity than does the factory school. One can hardly be certain, but limited empirical evidence on achievement and socialization suggests the hypothesis as reasonable (Medlin, 2013; Rudner, 1999).

Where Might an Intellectual Education Reside?

Of course, simple survival is a challenge for many families in contemporary America (see, e.g., Desmond, 2016), and a family under duress may not cultivate a consistent or rich source of meaning. Many fictional narratives, however, demonstrate not only that many families are under some sort of duress, but also that duress within the context of family is often a source of significant learning.

Factory schooling's efforts to separate education from the home notwithstanding (see the critiques of de Carvalho, 2001; Friedenberg, 1979; Gray, 2013; Holt, 1981; Lareau, 1989; Medlin, 2013; Ross, 1994; Saunders, 1995; Weber, 1976), the domestic realm has received considerable attention from some important thinkers. The home, for instance, is the classical private realm (Arendt, 1958). In this role, it has been far, far too long considered deficient simply because it was under the charge of women (Arendt, 1958; Lasch, 1977; Thompson, 2002). And yet the home was the center of both economic production and education across even much of 19th-century America and everywhere earlier, and the contemporary home surely retains something of these traditional functions because it is where families actually live (Berry, 1987). Though "besieged"[66], it remains the realm in which most humans understand themselves to be most themselves (Ross, 1994).

That fact underscores the importance of the domestic culture to human identity and to education. Many Americans, it is true, regard the home place as temporary, changeable; a few own many houses and a few live in hotels; some live in cars, on the street, or in the woods. But at a very deep level, the home place retains a force and a salience even for footloose Americans (Berry, 1977), and certainly it does for the homeless (Desmond, 2016).

Home connects humans to the Earth, to family, and to community in a rooted way (Berry, 1977, 1990; Confucius, 1938; Lasch, 1977; Thompson, 2002). Roots point to culture. Thus, Alex Haley's prominent use of the word (*Roots*; Haley, 1976) was cultural as well as politically progressive and, at the same time, deeply personal.

For education—even in its guise as factory schooling—the home must be (as an ontological necessity) a centerpiece of existence for all

---

66 *The Family Besieged* was sociologist Christopher Lasch's subtitle for his 1977 *Haven in a Heartless World*.

those humans whom educators call *students*. If they lack a real home—as do most foster children and all homeless children—the lack is manifest, and a manifestly wretched experience for most of them (Desmond, 2016); it should not be permitted in an affluent society. Students, after all, are children and youth who, in order to thrive, *must* be members of a domestic arrangement (the social institution known, down the ages, and in its evolving variations, as the family). The family produces and raises (educates) children (Ross, 1994). This reality appears to be forgotten in American educational practice and theory (see, e.g., de Carvalho, 2001; Holt, 1981; Leichter, 1974). In fact, parent engagement programs too often try to find ways for families to serve schools, rather than the reverse (Lareau, 2003).

But unlike large-scale and abstract entities known (in other aspects) as cultures, homes (and domestic cultures) are specific, individuated, particular, and the real and material site where all other aspects roost—and come home to roost. If evils beset other dimensions of culture, they will buffet, besiege, invade, and undo the home place (Jencks, 1995; Lasch, 1977). When homes fail, so does much else in people's lives. When many homes fail, so do communities and perhaps nations (Mathis, 2016).

Thus, one must ask: How might one make home a generative, thoughtful, good place to be? The home, arguably, is one site in which the formal and the anthropological cultures are mediated, synthesized, adapted, or repudiated. Finally, one would do well to recognize the home as the original locus of "culture": For at least 10,000 years, humans have been agriculturists, and the multigenerational home and kinship aggregates of such homes sponsored this most significant cultural evolution (Berry, 1977; Diamond, 1997; Hanson, 1995; Norenzayan, 2013; Renfrew, 2007).

How does one live well in the here-and-now, in each others' lives and faces? Educative features of home and family include (1) the raising of children, (2) intimacy, (3) sexuality, (4) home maintenance and production, and (5) health and well-being.

Raising children is not simply the work of fostering small children ("parents are the child's first teachers"), but in the contemporary world it includes raising, forming, advising, encouraging, and exercising concern for them into and throughout adulthood (Nelson, Padilla-Walker,

Christensen, & Evans, 2011). In this contemporary light, one might wonder if the home should not comprise multiple generations, because there is so much to be done and, of course, because the American social safety net is smaller and more frail than in other industrialized societies (see, e.g., Kenworthy, 2011).

Intimacy—for instance, being emotionally close with and committed to a partner—entails all sorts of difficulties and rewards that figure in literature and music and therapy, but seldom connect in any way with formal schooling (Deresiewicz, 2014). Sexuality is arguably the most intimate part of intimacy, but one that harbors its own gloriously educative and disastrously miseducative potentials. According to Orenstein (2016), compared to Europeans, Americans are handicapped and confused about what comes in conducting sexual relationships after "yes"— the silence, she claims, is a yawning void. And yet one feature of high school and of undergraduate life most prized by adolescents is the chance to explore one's sexuality (D'Emilio & Freedman, 2012). Americans can't talk about it, and American education can't do anything with it.

Across the globe, families remain a fundamental economic unit. And some sponsor a wide variety of work: gardening, house construction, cooking, cleaning, heating, and much else. The word *economy* itself means *household management*—although it is now applied mostly to the management of firms and nation-states (Berry, 1987): peculiar metaphorical "households." Differences in the character of the management of actual households are of course large. Little of the larger meaning of this work forms a part of any schooling. And yet, for many humans, this work—and its mindful part, too—looms large in life. Health and well-being indicate psychological and physiological realities that the home sponsors, for better and worse, and in part for how families conceptualize household management. How do people arrange their lives for wholeness or sickness? Why is the production of sickness a growth industry? What makes us fulfilled, happy? We all must grapple with the issues somehow in trying to form, to good purpose, a whole life.

All these realms of meaning animate this source. Educators may nonetheless be baffled by the claim that the home is a principal source for education that often honors the intellect much better than does factory schooling. The reason may be that American anti-intellectualism, and its schooling, misapprehend home and family as irrelevant to intellect—an assessment that many observers might approve but that some find to be a betrayal (e.g., Berry, 1987; Robinson, 2010; Ross, 1994; Thompson, 2002). Professional educators, embedded as they are in schooling that elites have designed to alienate family and community (see, e.g., Lareau, 2003; Schlechty, 2008; Spring, 1994), are at great risk of such misapprehension.

The Public Realm

This expression, "the public realm," may not be familiar to some readers. It is a classical expression that means "the public thing" (*res publica;* see, e.g., Arendt, 1958). As in Arendt's work, the public realm is often considered as the political realm; not "political" in the usual American sense of the warfare of Republicans and Democrats, but, rather, of the thing—the *public* thing, the common good—over which American politicians so typically pose and bluster (Lasch, 1995; Lofgren, 2013).

The public realm, then, is that feature of existence concerned with the management of society. An ancient idea of politics, certainly, but more particularly what was once, more recently (from the 17th through the 19th centuries), called *political-economy*: the inseparable interplay of politics, production, and trade, and most critically the implications for society, classes, and individuals (see, e.g., Heilbroner & Thurow, 1998). As a source for the intellect, then, the public realm—in contrast to the domestic realm—has accepted value for schooling (just as does high culture).

The corporate version of educational purpose, indeed, is preparation for college and careers, as enshrined in most sets of standards, whereas the once traditional political value was citizenship (Mathis, 2016). But with the decline of the individual citizen and the rise of the corporate citizen, this once-valued aspect of the public domain receives less and less billing in official standards, and for obvious reasons (Schlechty, 2008; Theobald, 2009).

So by the public realm we mean the rough-and-tumble domain of real adult life in large-scale society.[67] Because schooling is so often misunderstood as preparation for adult life, it is no wonder that political-economic aims (college, career, citizenship) have been so long promoted. In a sense, this source already dominates American schooling, not as a source for intellectual development, but as the entire *destination*.

The public realm, however, is much better applied educationally as an *origin*—as a source. Indeed, children need protection from the roughness of the public realm. Genuine action in the public realm is inherently dangerous and is not suitable for children according to one important observer (Arendt, 1954/1968).[68] We agree, but as a source of drama related to culture, intellect, ideas, debates, and concern for (or disregard of) the common good, the public realm has undeniable educative value—a value that is quite different from preparation for college and careers. The dramas of the public realm offer an unparalleled venue, moreover, about which students should ask questions, and to which students can apply principles and insights derived from other sources. Indeed, they can interrogate the public realm, intellectually, about its influence on the other sources.

In a sense, the public realm is not only a source, but also the real-world laboratory for whatever one is learning from the other sources. It is the here-and-now (rough-and-tumble) where ideas and principles about the public clash with self-interest and opportunism. The danger is clear, but so is the need for students, and for the mind, to engage the danger *intellectually*.

Arendt's (1954/1968) caveat applied only to children however—to statutory minors. The term *minor* is perhaps more relative than the age range 0–18 establishes. Humans tend to take on adult roles unpredictably; sometimes prematurely, sometimes belatedly. They do so by vol-

---

67   The Greeks invented the idea of the public realm in classical Athens, initially a small-scale society, but one evolving soon thereafter toward empire (Hanson, 1995). The American polity, though, is imperial already: continental and global (Williams, 1969). The rough-and-tumble public realm takes on immense scale, harbors immense dangers, and it colonizes home and heart much too readily (see, e.g., Tan, 2014; Theobald, 2009)

68   For instance, Arendt (1954/1968), like others, bemoaned the use of African-American children to "integrate" American society. American society, of course, remains fractured half a century later.

unteering for the associated roles: parent, soldier, activist, worker. They may sign up for dangers quite early and unadvisedly. So the danger of the public realm is both easily underestimated and appealingly avoided by children young and old. Parents are wise to regulate, facilitate, and guide entry into the public realm (adult life, the real world).

That expression—*the real world*—connotes the danger entailed: Adult life is differently challenging from life as a child. In particular, neither parents nor teachers can protect one in it. And, in America, the inadequate social safety net granted families with young children actually subjects children too often to the dangers of "the real world" (Giroux, 2000). The comparatively meager protections on offer in America are the result of ways accepted in America for management of the public realm (Kenworthy, 2011).

One particular feature of the public realm deserves consideration: digital media. Computers and software have feet in both low and high culture, but one can give the unusual argument (unusual in education, that is) that digital media are features of the public realm. The goods and services that large digital-age firms make popular are not at all what we have in mind as belonging to low culture—or to high culture, for that matter.

Digital media are manifestations of a largely economic phenomenon, with cultural implications for the long term as momentous as were those of the industrial (mechanical) revolution. But we cannot yet see where the implications will lead, although the imaginations of writers and thinkers and researchers actively pursue the fascinating questions.

Digital media might be useful in schooling, but they are not nearly so useful as advertised (Bowers, 2000; Cuban, 2001). Decades of digital revolution, and the vigorous marketing of computers to schools, have not touched the deep structure of schooling (Cuban, 2001; Tye, 2000). And there is no evidence that their presence in schools has systematically improved student achievement (e.g., Cuban, 2001; Norris, Hossain, & Soloway, 2012).[69]

Mass-market goods and services on average exhibit little thoughtfulness of the sort we mean, and harbor meager ties to intellect. They seem,

---

69   Certainly, digital media *can* be used for educative purposes: to access source material, help explore ideas, and to augment thinking powers somewhat.

overall, unlikely sources for a schooling that would be more friendly to intellect as the common project of humankind. Computers? Tablets? The Internet? Smartphones? They have surely introduced many changes to ordinary life. Do students need "media literacy"? Sure, children should track the evolving digital media. These developments may constitute a remarkable new source for human intellect, but they are more critically a momentous part of the public realm. Engagement with the intellectual work of making sense of digital media is more about what those media are up to than about what they convey (Gee, 2014).

Putting It Together:
The Four Sources as a Whole

Not surprisingly, the four sources sum to *life*. Dewey (1897) famously observed that education was not preparation for life, but life itself. The version of "life" just presented, especially via the emphasis on *low culture* and the *domestic realm*, rehabilitates ordinary life as a source for the cultivation of intellect. In other words, it seeks to animate the idea of education (chez Dewey) as life, and to animate educational aims as mindful of real life and real works about life, and not only of a phony reflection of high culture unhappily married to the rough-and-tumble outrages of the public realm.

One should, in short, foster a lively and lovely education (Egan, 2002; Gilham & Jardine, 2015; Tye, 2000; White, 2011), not impose, like so much of contemporary American factory schooling, a stultification (Deresiewicz, 2014; Goodman, 1962; Tye, 2000). One imagines the great educational practitioners and writers of the centuries in agreement (Socrates, Komensky, Rousseau, Alcott, Montessori, and others). Apparently, the factory cannot provide very well for such an experience.

Low and high culture sources put the stress on two varieties of culture, and both are, in this conception, ordinary. The intellect should grasp both as familiar, friendly, and (indeed) lovely; the high culture, educationally speaking, should not appear so strange and unfriendly as those attempting ownership would have it. Aristotle, Boethius, Shakespeare, and Samuel Barber are among the friends we love. So is the logic of mathematics, and so is the skepticism that animates science (and clear thinking in general).

The domestic realm puts the stress on the intellectual source-work of home and family: the private realm. This is the place where so many humans make meaning and, under the stress on the family created by a mismanaged public realm, where so many often lose it. But management of the home, whatever the state of the public realm, benefits from—and ought to enact—mindfulness in all it does, all it is, and in all it might become.

The public realm is the political economy. It is where adults obtain employment, where they labor, where they debate, and where they conduct struggle and warfare. Children will eventually enter it, but need protection from it, too, as minors.

The distinction among sources might be tricky, except that these sources are just pedagogical handles, here, for parts of the experience of life, which does not present itself in such neat packages. Low culture, here, has a populist flavor: what ordinary people do with meanings, symbols, and everyday practices (in neighborhoods, communities, and a range of ethnic groups of all colors). And, in this conception of culture, we view "high" culture as an outcropping of these more tribal practices: written up and down and preserved and cultivated beyond the ordinary practicalities of doing, observing, and talking among living beings. High culture miraculously accumulates dead voices, which nonetheless live, and the living can help the living, and even the dead themselves, live better. It's good work to be done.

The real mission of education, perhaps best understood as the project of cultivating thoughtfulness for the common good, now lies well outside the contemporary American State's version of schooling, and most of that schooling is, we have also concluded, *actively hostile* to intellectual development. This corrupted State schooling often teaches some things, but it seldom directs even what it teaches toward thoughtfulness and the common good. Worse still, most contemporary schooling "succeeds" by inuring children to boredom and repressing their curiosity and thoughtfulness; it remains stultifying in the name of preparing them for confinement to approved roles in the public realm of rough-and-tumble adult survival. It's offensive: We humans can do much better simply because, as humans, we can imagine alternatives and so enact them at least to some extent.

Intellect, Imagination, and Ordinary Schooling

We have argued as best we can for the value of a schooling that prizes and cultivates intellect rather broadly. At the same time, our particular concern has been the reading, writing, and reasoning (including all the disciplines) that support the disposition to think, to question, to doubt, to dialogue, and to debate, and to contribute to the production of works that represent such a disposition and such practices. From the vantage of the previous chapters, the American cultural and economic picture is bleak, and therefore so is the manifestation of schooling within that culture, sadly including public schooling in its present state.

So where might an intellectual education reside? This chapter has taken four sources from life itself; from, as one might otherwise say, the ridiculous (domestic life) to the sublime (high culture, so called). We find encouragement for a properly intellectual sort of education in egalitarian sources of things to learn, the appreciation of talent and talent development as endemic in all humans, intellectual practices that focus on the common good rather than private gain, and practical and technical purposes directed toward an enlarged view of life (not directly tied to "needs of employers"). Always, in this scheme, reading, writing, and reasoning appear essential: These practices access the intellect, but also constitute it as transmissible from the past to the future.

So we also need to describe schooling arrangements proper to the intellect. Just as individuals change their lives by imagining alternative future lives, educators—including parents, teachers, administrators, and students everywhere—ought to break out of their confinement to unlovely and dysfunctional professional norms. We ought to think larger, not for ourselves, but for everyone's schooling. This effort is what we make in the final chapter.

Chapter 9

Imagining a Decent Schooling for Intellect

Education, in one version, is the accumulated meaning and usefulness wrested from all experience, including schooling (e.g., Rousseau, 1762; Komensky, 1657/1907; Tiller, 2000). This version is nearly always what we ourselves mean by *education*. Schooling can help—decent schooling certainly helps—but schooling is only one part of a contemporary education, and much of American schooling, as the previous chapters argue, is systemically miseducative and anti-intellectual.

So this chapter imagines alternatives to such schooling for all Americans. It has two parts: One part, for everyone, imagines a schooling that better honors what we mean by *intellect*, and another part improvises a better sort of schooling for intellectually talented students (including the nurture of talented arts students and two options for able learners engaging the university). These ideas build on the evident opportunities of American schooling as it already exists. We offer them because the critique, which has tested the limits of key ideas about American schooling, suggests that Americans can do much better with schooling. This is how we think they might do so.

Education as the Measure of Schooling

Education belongs *inalienably* to each person as an agent and is increasingly acknowledged as a human right (Nicolau & Lupu, 2013). Schooling, by contrast, is typically something onerous to which one is compelled at a young age, and such subjection has become the characteristic status of being a minor (childhood through high school). American parents are justly wary of relinquishing their children to it (see, e.g., Druckerman, 2012), but we all accept the regime, and nearly all adults, too, find themselves compelled to accept their diminished agency as parents and grandparents.

Decent schooling would advance the human project of education: of agency, of competence, and of productive experience generally. A decent schooling would intersect with out-of-school experiences that move people robustly toward thinking for themselves and making (and doing) good works that occupy the full range of unique places in the real world.

Strategic Principles

It seems quite possible, does it not? What might it take? First, it has to be principled. So we highlight four strategic principles associated with the following concepts: (1) protection, (2) plurality, (3) experience, and (4) competence. They are familiar enough in educational discourse (see, e.g., Arendt, 1958; Dewey, 1897; Egan, 2002; Rousseau, 1762), but we use them here to help warrant the more educative provisions for American *schooling* that follow shortly. They are a link between educational high-mindedness and imagined schooling practicalities.

Protection. Education for children and youth requires the protection from the rough-and-tumble "public realm" of adult life that Arendt (1958) long ago insisted it did (see Chapter 8). She wrote, for instance, about the misuse (abuse) of children to redress the crimes of American racism (Arendt 1954/1968), but in the early 21st century, notable additional abuses require protections. In particular, education (and whatever system of schooling supports it) ought to protect children from exploitation by marketers and advertisers (see, e.g., Molnar, 1996; Schor, 2004), harsh discipline (see, e.g., Nguyen, 2013; Saltman & Gabbard, 2003; Skiba, 2014), inequitable funding (see, e.g., J. Johnson, 2014; Kozol, 1991), and public schooling conducted as a for-profit enterprise (see, e.g., Ravitch, 2013; Sturges, 2015).

Plurality. Plurality implies what American schooling and education theorizing (e.g., Tomlinson, 1999) treat under concepts such as *individualization* or *differentiation*. Plurality encompasses difference that is more clearly related to solidarity than to individuality. It renders as solidarity what the current individualist versions of this reality render as elitism: *E pluribus unum*, in fact.

For instance, in the light of plurality, the idea of an exceptionally talented child becoming a mechanic is admirable: What a good idea! Intellectually able students should go only to a 4-year college and win doctorates? Matthew Crawford's (2009) *Shop Class as Soulcraft*, often cited in previous chapters, illustrates the author's own embrace of the possibility that academically talented young people might pursue trades rather than professions. The relentless sorting of factory schooling, however, makes the choice seem perverse to nearly everyone. Plurality accommodates the sense of life's many possibilities and supports decent education and forms of schooling.

Experience. Education depends on authentic experiences (Komensky, 1657/1907; Rousseau, 1762). Critics since at least Komensky's and Rousseau's centuries have also often noted that schools have seldom been able to sponsor them consistently. Indeed, the experiences that contemporary students typically encounter in schools are relentlessly phony (Anyon, 1980; Brown, 1991; Egan, 2002; Friedenberg, 1979; Jardine, 1995). Bringing such experiences "to scale," one might well conclude, seems *impossible*. Our scheme accommodates the challenge by reducing the scale and arranging much better the accommodation to genuine sources.

Competence. Growth in competence actually has no limit except mortality, and it cannot be circumscribed by a schooling program of any sort (including the one proposed shortly). To master a craft (gardening, auto repair, welding, laboratory research, writing poetry, musical composition, mathematical proof) requires something like 10,000 hours (Gladwell, 2008) or 10 years (Bloom, 1985) of mostly real-world practice.

Besides making genuine experience part of schooling, what else does a high level of competence require—particularly an academic sort of intellectual competence? The answer is not obscure. As Kieran Egan (2002) suggested, growing competence with intellectual matters depends *mostly* on the engagement of content—and much less on decisions related to debates about process or pedagogical technique.

Teachers honoring the principles already. Some very clever and very stalwart teachers can exploit educational openings in the prevailing systemic arrangements of factory schooling (see, e.g., Gutstein, 2003; Jardine et al., 2006; Sturges, 2015), but such teaching remains comparatively rare because little cultivates or sustains it (see, e.g., Capps, Crawford, & Constas, 2012; Gatto, 2002; Orr, 1995). Indeed, the deep structure of schooling works against educative teaching. Little apart from a teacher's own exceptionally strong will and intellectual prescience can provide for it. What is to be done? It is a question we have often asked, and so we turn to an imagined system of State-sponsored schooling as an intellectual antithesis of the present one, or at least one that provides greater opening for intellect.

More Educative Schooling

Is our scheme practical? It diverges considerably from schooling as we know it, yet the provisions are still familiar *as* schooling and the scheme is *not* utopian. It builds on the strengths of the permeability of schooling arrangements across the lifespan, and on the famed American decentralization. It moves away from the standardization, massification, and credentialism that plague contemporary schooling, K–24. It makes sense to us, at least, in light of the critique given in preceding chapters.

A System of Schooling to Care for Intellect

Presentation of the scheme unfolds in seven parts: (1) design principles, (2) equitable school financing K–24, (3) small elementary schools of no more than 50 students, (4) retirement of high schools, (5) postelementary options, (6) postelementary financial support of living needs, and (7) provisions for access. The roster hints at the scale and scope we have in mind. We include, as well, a note on performance assessment, which we regard as essential—even as we find the current rash of punitive accountability measures so damaging and even as we understand that testing is far more often *utilized* than used.

The imagined system is free, universal, accessible across the life span, open to changes in the life plans of individuals, and humanly scaled. It honors both curiosity and practicality. It builds on key strengths of the existing system. It honors the educative principles of protection, plurality, experience, and competence. The imagined system derives not only from principles, of course, but also from actual practices in the real world. The main difference with what follows is the packaging of the system—the ensemble. Radical as these provisions may appear, they have established precedents in the real world, and we will consider some of these after presenting the scheme, as a kind of debriefing.

1. Design principles. We begin with a statement of five simple design concepts: (1) entitlement, (2) access, (3) the difference between schooling and training, (4) the relevance of efficiency, and (5) the relevance of effectiveness. The meaning of each proceeds from all of them together.

Entitlement. All residents (i.e., all those living within national borders) are equally entitled and funded to schooling at public expense and to training, the latter provided largely at industry expense.

Access. Residents can pursue training and schooling options (including efforts to qualify to pursue the options) *at any time they choose* and with stipends to meet basic living needs (provisions described subsequently).

Education and training. Education and training differ, although they both contribute to education. Education is a process of becoming; it can result from both evil and good experiences. *True education* is a thoughtful maturation through many, and differing, experiences. Training is prepared skill and related knowledge (which can also be done poorly or well). All people already experience both; all need both. Schooling accommodates both.

Efficiency. True education cannot be efficient, and it must be fostered in schools solely with public funds because thoughtful maturation through experience is a requirement for wise citizenship. Good training, though, *can* be efficient, and private enterprise (a chief beneficiary) must, as major beneficiary, provide most of the funding and most of the sites for apprenticeship training.

Effectiveness. The ultimate warrant of effectiveness is the quality of government and the fairness of economic life. The ultimate judge of effectiveness in this scheme is the person who, with guidance from his or her family, determines which postelementary options to pursue, and when, and how. The State's elementary testing regime (described subsequently) informs policy making relevant to fostering the *fairness* of the outcomes of elementary schooling.

2. Equitable school financing K–24. The state will provide *exactly the same per-pupil support* for all elementary schools and all postelementary enterprises. *All universities will be fully funded from public sources,* and they will be smaller. Private universities will exist no longer. The scheme will not encourage survival of universities larger than 10,000 students, and it will actively foster smaller ones, thus avoiding some of the famous diseconomies of academic scale in PK–24.

There will be *no tuition for any option at any level* (not elementary, not apprenticeship, not any level in the university). All postelementary students will also receive basic-support stipends (described subsequently).

3. Small elementary schools (PK–8). Such schools will have perhaps 10 teachers for 50 students: two professionals and eight people from the community. One expects the following from this arrangement: (1) far more care of and attention to students, (2) far better communication with and attention to families, (3) far better integration with communities and neighborhoods in general, (4) far less professional pretense to phony expertise, (5) far less use of content as an instrument to control misbehavior, (6) far more project-based learning, and (7) far more locally relevant instruction.

The typical claim about educational decisions that are "in the best interests of the child" rings hollow in view of the rank inequity endemic to factory schooling. The best interests of the child are hardly discernible by educators in that system. Determination, instead, requires long and open conversation with parents. The prevailing system of factory schooling is set up to frustrate and disable engagement with families.

4. Retirement of high schools. The high school is part of the industrial system of schooling; it accounted for nearly all of the proportional enrollment increases across the 20th century (see, e.g., Tyack, 1974). In league with the sorting of the housing market (Gingrich & Ansell, 2014), secondary schooling is the principal "sorting machine" of the industrial age (Orfield, 2001; Spring, 2013). Students in high schools routinely ask, "Why do we need to know this stuff?", and they have rarely received convincing answers. People deserve much better treatment on their path to adulthood—a more generous education and a more efficient training. The State will provide the former (across the life span), and industry and commerce the latter (across the life span).

5. Postelementary options. Postelementary schooling will devolve to three options: (1) the apprenticeship option, (2) the university option, and (3) the autodidact (self-instruction) option. These are ordered here by what we imagine to be their relative popularity. However, the *sine qua non* of completion for each option must be valid, reliable, and relevant examination: requiring, we believe, a national effort. Once qualified by apprenticeship, completers proceed to actual employment: Positions are *guaranteed*. If no employment ensues subsequent to apprenticeship because there is none on offer from businesses, students exercise a continuing option to qualify—with continuing State support—for some *other* employment via *any* of the three options. A separate section sketches the provisions related to access and support for the options, but descriptions of the options themselves follow, next.

Apprenticeship. The principal postelementary schooling arrangement will make use of ubiquitous apprenticeship options. Eligibility begins after completion of an elementary program but will continue for all citizens for life. For minors, apprenticeship choice is by election of the student's family (which includes the student). The State contributes funding for administration of the apprenticeship option, but large employers in the private sector must play a determining role in the operation and will provide all of the funding for instruction and the actual apprenticeship experiences.

The apprenticeship option is clearly a disturbing postelementary innovation for American schooling (see Crawford, 2009, for the particular inspiration). This major option is culturally discordant—not because of the connection with despised manual or technical labor—but because completing the option entitles everyone to employment *as the result* of preparation and qualification. One apprentices, one qualifies, and then one secures employment. Training leads inexorably to employment. Qualification at the journey or master level—subsequent to employment—will also occur by examination (with preparation largely a matter of work experience and in-service training).

Because the prospect of employment figures currently as a goad to continued schooling (especially a "college education"), the apprenticeship option that leads directly to adequately paid employment will have predictably wide appeal. It will exempt students from long, aversive, and ritualistic (phony) academic performances, and it will provide everyone (including intellectually talented students) with a much better pathway to reasonable employment, much of it locally obtainable. Again, anyone may, at *any* time, exercise *any* schooling option—including the university option. Observe that employment prepared for in this way provides the economic threshold of the decent life on which decent education (as the experiences in life itself) must depend (see previous discussion).

University. The university option is a "liberal learning" option that is explicitly intellective (requiring devotion to reading, writing, mathematics, and the arts and sciences generally). Notably, it includes teacher education. Access is contingent on evidence of intellectual devotion and capacity, but it will be open free of charge (through the dissertation or terminal project) to anyone who qualifies for admittance. More intellectually talented students will, we imagine, probably choose this option, rather than apprenticeship. But an exceptionally talented elementary "graduate" could well complete an apprenticeship and experience employment *before* undertaking the serious intellectual project that the university option will facilitate.

In any of the postelementary options, moreover, age does not restrict enrollment or engagement. Anyone may pursue a university program at any time, free of charge, and with a modest living stipend. Those who discover that intellectual work is not their métier can take up the apprenticeship option (again, at any time).

To qualify for the university option, instead of the common "high" school, a variety of preparatory sites will help anyone seeking university admittance to prepare and qualify, again provided free of charge. Qualification for admittance might well include legitimate writing and other performance assessments, although excellent (nationally prepared) multiple-choice testing would likely persist (good qualifying exams exist across all fields, and Americans have proven remarkably capable at creating them). One may, of course, take as long as necessary to qualify. There is no schedule and no toting up of Carnegie Units. The work itself is the criterion of entry, not one's age. University entry is not a rat race.

Unlike the apprenticeship option, however, completion of the university option will *not entail an employment guarantee.* Graduates (e.g., physicians, lawyers, and teachers, to use popular examples) are likely to be in demand, but will need to secure a position without the State's active authorization. For guaranteed employment, students need to undertake apprenticeship. One can, after all, pursue *both* university and apprenticeship, as the options seem advisable to an individual across the lifespan.

Autodidact option. Perhaps a small percentage of the population might *successfully* pursue both the apprenticeship and the university option, and perhaps a somewhat larger percentage might *experiment* with both. Some few will complete neither option. And "completion" itself under present circumstances, as we well know, cannot ensure competence, not even when the assessment schemes are valid and reliable. Examination schemes embed error—inevitably. Not everyone tests well, and not everyone is adaptable to schooling routines or "school knowledge." Apprenticeship programs, too, may not suit even some of those who can actually participate in the relevant trade.

The autodidact provision is simply the openness of qualifying exams for trades and academics that can be taken at any time, by anyone, anywhere. The autodidact option invites students to "mess around" to find what makes sense to them. If an option is not going smoothly, access to "completion" can be by examination. Again, examinations for varied fields will exhibit varied qualities—many will be by performance and not by completing test items on paper or on a computer.

Community college note. Community colleges will become centers to coordinate apprenticeships and may, in addition, offer preparation alternatives for university qualification and for autodidacts. Concepts of small scale and proximity apply, too, and the State would have a logical interest in sustaining most community colleges. (Note that in France, a *collège* is a middle school. The word "college" is just a word; postelementary students once went directly to "college," of the higher education sort, even in America, into the early 20th century. And at one time, both architecture and the law were apprenticeship arrangements.)

6. Postelementary financial support of living needs. People who are engaged in study beyond elementary school will receive living stipends so that they can be unencumbered by privation or the need to engage in other employment. This provision makes schooling accessible whenever needed, without encouraging routine exploitation of one's status as a subsidized student. Adults, of course, have usually created a balance between their practical need to return to paid employment and their appreciation for the learning offered through postsecondary schooling (trade schools, college, professional schools), and adolescents have longed for secondary education that demonstrates legitimate connections between what they are studying and the work they hope to undertake (Deresiewicz, 2014; Eliot, 1910; Etzioni, 1970). In fact, Etzioni (1970) believed, in this light, that doctoral programs (oddly) demonstrated the most powerful connections between a field of study and a field of work; they were, he found, the most instrumental of all preparations. Financial support sharpens awareness of the linkage and broadens the prospect for individuals deciding what pathway to follow. A small proportion of adults may choose to be lifelong students, but the choice comes with a student's life of penury. Most people will not find this sort of existence reasonable, but they will occupy an interesting margin, perhaps like William Sidis, though with less financial insecurity.

7. Provisions for access. Educational access means the entitlement to learn whatever makes sense: a moving target, always, for individuals and for society in general. What limits access overall? First are limitations resulting from bad economic systems, which squeeze families and individuals, neighborhoods and communities, rural villages and large cities toward collapse. Second—an ironically lesser set of limitations—

results from bad schooling, the sort that fails to foster meaningful and useful learning.

In this plan, *assessment policy serves as a way to open access rather than to restrict it* by (1) monitoring the progress of equity at the elementary level for the purpose of fostering more equitable outcomes, (2) allowing anyone at any time to take qualifying exams, and (3) providing for endless qualification effort as citizens determine their own schooling needs in response to their own development and to structural changes in "the economy."

Note that a small minority of people is likely to qualify *without* enrollment in the formal provisions for either trade or academic qualification, or even without attending elementary school (e.g., via home schooling). The system is thus designed to engage even the participation of those who would otherwise be its nonparticipants.

The system sponsors assessment for the benefit of students and for the fundamental equality on which competence itself depends. American experts know how to create and administer a wide range of reliable and valid examinations; the system proposed will redirect that effort to purposes useful to citizens (and to employers as well). The national elementary testing provision focuses on the behavior of the system with a goal of equity (rather than phony "excellence" and rather than punishing students, teachers, or families); this provision, too, will require major redirection of current testing regimes (and support systems for educators). But the system will use many other sorts of assessment to validate accomplishment in all useful bodies of skill and knowledge: Many will need to be individually administered; many will have a basis in performance.

Debriefing the scheme. Some of the provisions in the imagined system reflect American educational research: for instance, the requirement of a smaller scale for schooling (see, e.g., Friedkin & Necochea, 1988; Kuziemko, 2006). From the perspective of this work, K–12 and university schooling has been moving in the wrong direction for many decades. Specifics of the proposal for elementary schooling, as well, owe something to the thought of Paul Goodman (see Lee, 2008).

The need for apprenticeship programs in America has been evident for a very long time. Germany has provided them, and the German public strongly supports that model and its effectiveness (see, e.g., Eliot, 1910; Riphahn & Zibrowius, 2016). The need is well established and almost completely ignored in America; in fact, it's been ignored for a full century (see Wirth, 1970, for interesting explanations of this peculiar negligence).

The proposal to eliminate high schools (and private universities) will surely provoke derision, since the vested interests are, indeed, so solidly vested. But some observers and scholars have voiced skepticism in ways that resonate with the view of intellect given in this book (see, e.g., Deresiewicz, 2014; Gatto, 2002; Raywid, 1997). One must note, again, the odd contemporary insistence that nearly everyone needs a college degree, and the fact that dysfunctional high schools often stand as a notable barrier to university qualification. Full support for university participation, and qualification by examination rather than wasted seat-time seem sensible alternatives to both high schools and fabulously pricey elite schools.

Provisions for access, however, build more on the mainstream—on the remarkable openness of American higher education, inaugurated with the GI Bill (Servicemen's Readjustment Act of 1944, P.L. 78-346). Adult Americans have subsequently endorsed the notion of "lifelong learning" with their adult feet on American campuses for several generations now. That phrase—lifelong learning—rings hollow in significant ways, however. In particular, for adults with families, access to higher education is more difficult than it ought to be.[70]

Most notably, and perhaps most objectionably from the vantage of wealth and privilege, the proposal intertwines education with the social safety net. It ties a guaranteed income to schooling, as well as to work, as a human right. At present, Americans understand the connection between well-being and educational attainment, but policy making uses schooling and training as if they were both a bandage and a scapegoat for the economic problems of big business (see, e.g., Berliner & Biddle, 1995; Glass, 2007). The scheme given here, therefore, joins schooling

---

70   Lifelong access to higher education is a very different proposition from lifelong learning. Learning is something we all mostly do anyhow up to the moment of death because we can't avoid the demands of scrambling through a furiously changeable existence. Lifelong schooling access requires better State support.

and economics in a way that makes common sense for the common good, including even corporate health.[71]

Proposals for apprenticeship and postelementary university preparation clearly owe something to *Deschooling Society* (Illich, 1971). In this case, and very different from Illich, the imagined arrangements preserve a key schooling institution by building on the current community college mission and, indeed, by improving upon an already open university system (compared to the restricted entry provisions that prevail internationally).

Finally, the proposed scheme draws on Dewey's wider sense of the educational supports needed across the lifespan in a developed society (Dewey, 1913/1979). "Lifelong learning," by contrast, has been a rear-guard action to suggest to individuals that they accommodate structural changes in the economy by going back to school as adults (currently a difficult proposition). The proposed scheme takes the burden of adjustment out of the private realm, off the individual, and returns it to the public realm, where it very clearly belongs. The ensemble, in short, reflects Dewey's concerns for agency, thoughtful scope, and the common good. It defends a wider educational field for adults, both in terms of practicality and imagination.

Let's get real. Eighty years after Counts (1932) asked his famous question (*Dare the school build a new social order?*), the answer seems clear: "Yes!" Factory schooling is slanted and shaped to serve wealth and privilege; the evidence abounds. It hits one between the eyes, so long as one's eyes are open.

Social change is the work of politically active adults who, as citizens, find themselves obligated to fight for the common good. Schooling alone cannot build a new social order, although decent schooling would, we believe (as did Counts), contribute to social equality. The first task for educators, then, is to enact a schooling that better serves the common good, and one that engages the agency of individuals. A decent schooling, reflecting a true education, will do that. It's not happening widely.

Maybe the proposed scheme is utopian. Maybe it's impractical. We don't think so, but we also realize that no scheme for improvement survives its implementation and that unintended consequences are involved

---

71   It might make sense to a reincarnated Charles Eliot (1910).

in what one might call the "fog of improvement." The point here is not whether or not the scheme can be realized, but whether something of this sort can be imagined.

An ordinary example: Imani Laboy. One might, along these lines, imagine the education of an academically talented youngster—we'll call her Imani Laboy. She's of Puerto Rican descent, born in Perth Amboy, NJ. She reads early; she's outgoing and well organized. She enters her small elementary school at age 5, where the teachers and community helpers actually recognize her precocity. She receives instruction, in other words, at her level and is not subjected to the stultifying repetition of what she already knows. After 2 years of schooling, both her reading and her math levels are very advanced; she reads "chapter books" independently and is beginning, surprisingly, to work with ratios and proportions.

The school team realizes that her program will be so different from average that they will soon need to access uncommon options. Over the course of the year, they hold several meetings to line up these options. Another neighborhood school has a community helper who will supervise math instruction through elementary algebra, and that helper agrees to work with Imani 2 days a week. Imani simply walks to that school for part of the day.

By the end of her sixth year in the school, Imani is sufficiently well prepared to undertake serious studies in science—that is, at what used to be the "high school level." Henceforth, she studies at the Perth Amboy Center of Middlesex Community College. Imani has decided that she wants to pursue some kind of scientific work, and at the community college she has experiences, in addition to instruction, that help her explore the possibilities.

At age 13, Imani sits for qualifying exams for university entrance, but doesn't pass. She takes the exams again at 14, and does pass. She has decided, following a rewarding internship the previous year, that she wants to study astronomy. Cosmology intrigues her, and the thought of discovery and investigation enhances her wonder. She applies to Case Western Reserve University, in Cleveland. Cleveland has a large Puerto Rican community, and that's important to Imani. She understands that she'd have been unlikely to attend in previous decades. Her family couldn't have afforded it. Now she even has a stipend to cover living expenses: She doesn't have to work more than 10 hours a week, and that work will be in the observatory.

What happens next? Imani might fall in love, leave school, and start a family; she might return to school in a couple of years and complete an astronomy degree. She might have a manic-depressive episode and reorient her life, for instance, encountering the good fortune to become a full-time assistant in the astronomy department or a lab technician at the Cleveland Clinic. But she'll continue to be intellectually active, and perhaps continue the study of astronomy informally. At the age of 40, she might decide to sit for the astronomy exam and secure the astronomy bachelor's degree, but only as an entry point to pursuing a astrophysics doctorate, perhaps at (for instance) University of California, Santa Cruz?

Finally, after a late career studying exoplanets, at the age of 65, Imani might not be ready for retirement. Instead, she will become a community helper in the local elementary school in rural northern California, to which she has recently moved with her new girlfriend.

Maybe readers will get the point: Life has a lot of surprises for all of us. The provisions of schooling would, we think, do better by imagining and accommodating webs of meaning and action instead of those invalid straight-line assumptions that factory schooling prizes.

Rethinking Education for Exceptional Talent Under Prevailing Circumstances

We answered the demands of imagination above; here we answer the demands of realism. Intellectually talented students need more and better opportunities to engage intellectual substance. They rarely get it today, though children in more affluent communities get more of it, accompanied, most often, with a solid miseducation in privilege.

First there are the antecedents to the discussion: the importance of (1) stewardship of intellect among the young in difficult straits and (2) the requirements of generosity in such stewardship. After that, we suggest rules of thumb for working in K–12 schools with exceptionally rapid learners and, next, learners with pronounced artistic talents, followed by a discussion of two models for engagement with higher education (completing the consideration begun in Chapter 5).

Antecedents

Even if the radically practical scheme described above were realized exactly to plan, and all the devils cast out of the details, concern for the unusually apt within any line of endeavor would still persist. Why? The nature of the schooling that intellectually talented students experience (and the eventual work they will do) warrants the concern: Work wants—as one might personify it—to be done well. This compulsion includes the work of teaching. The fate of the work therefore requires, and always will require, concern for those who do it now and those who are to do it later.

Such a formulation seems remarkably simple, but experience suggests that the concern is by no means so commonly shared as one might expect. Credentialism, careerism, vanity, hubris, greed, the famed Peter principle, soldiering, schmoozing, and sad cluelessness continue to undo good work now and into the future. Remarkably, though, good work still gets done!

Stewardship of intellect among the young. Youngsters and junior colleagues who are unusually adept will continue to need championship. One cannot hazard more: the million coincidences needed to specify the devils and the details remain obscure to any grand scheme. We have seen how "elusive" (*destructive* is the better term) educational reform (*deformation* is the better term) has proven to be (e.g., Blacker, 2013; Tyack & Cuban, 1995) and how fads and distortions masquerade as "reform" (see, e.g., Howley, Howley, & Burgess, 2006). Under the prevailing scheme, certainly, the array of talents we prize and view as meaningful and useful in our imagined alternative to the system of factory schooling *will continue to be denigrated*.

So it seems that championship of talent requires stewardship of intellect—the intellectual legacy of remarkably good work that is everyone's birthright. The championship and stewardship can be practiced by anyone, including teachers of anything, wherever situated (prisons, hospitals, courts, the military, school, universities, workplaces). The focus here, though, is on talent that is already demonstrably exceptional and lodged in schools and universities.

Generosity in offering opportunities. This sort of intellectual stewardship requires a variety of *generosities*: personal, organizational, and financial. Personal generosity involves putting forth one's best intellectual effort and sharing one's own engagement with intellect. Organizational generosities implicate school and district leadership—the positions and persons who can stretch organizational boundaries (e.g., to rearrange schedules and requirements, to support acceleration, to transgress conventional wisdom, and so forth). Financial generosity moves beyond the school organization, because sustainable support requires various stripes of political action (creating agendas, holding meetings public and private, exerting influence on the organization).

This generosity is fundamental. For teachers, it requires reading, unconventional thinking, and actual engagement with intellectual production (of the great variety indicated, for instance, in Chapter 8). Teachers can also facilitate organizational generosity by learning how to think organizationally: whom to trust, whom to cultivate as allies, and when to bring the influence of allies to bear. Novice teachers rarely have a native sense of organizational dynamics, and many seasoned teachers feel betrayed by exactly those dynamics (see, e.g., Kushman, 1992). But using organizational dynamics strategically can alter organizational norms so that the intellectual generosity of teachers finds a more welcome organizational reception. Only a teacher who understands organizational dynamics (which vary from school to school and district to district) can organize public networks in the role of policy entrepreneur (Mintrom & Vergari, 1996) to secure the sort of funding and other support that alters district provisions from the outside.

It's a large scope of work, but all of it is founded on teachers' personal intellectual engagement. The work cannot be addressed without it. The point of this work is to expand the opportunities for genuine intellectual engagement inside and outside of schools. The same spirit that underlies our grand scheme underlies those that follow. We turn now to general principles for the schooling of K–12 students (rapid school learners and students talented in the arts) and, then, for postsecondary prospects (the rotated model and the accelerated model).

Pedagogy and Curriculum for Rapid School Learners

We have long believed that sensible practice for the education of rapid learners involves a set of strategic alternatives that make use of prevailing school arrangements. The specific way these alternatives might be used will vary from community to community, of course, but they are equally workable in any community (even though inequities in school resources inevitably limit what some communities are able to offer through the general education curriculum).

1. Rapid school learners should nearly always proceed rapidly through their K–12 schooling. Thirteen years in 10 ("radical acceleration") probably ought to be the rule of thumb (Stanley, 1976). Rapid school learners should ordinarily be schooled with other (but simply older) students rather than separated from them (VanTassel-Baska, 2009).

2. Many intellectually talented students can skip high school *completely* (Boles, 2009)—an arrangement currently ignored. The arrangement should become far more common, used by a much larger proportion of able students than is currently the case even in light of early college and dual-enrollment alternatives in many states.

3. Acceleration of this sort usually renders aspirations to attend elite schools inoperable: It in effect eliminates the academic redshirting that gives intellectually talented students the advantage within an age-grade cohort. This "sacrifice" is a *distinct benefit* (Deresiewicz, 2014).

4. Helping affluent parents appreciate the benefit of relinquishing the redshirting is very difficult work indeed. Championing acceleration in impoverished communities is difficult for other reasons—often because educators there view the lockstep as a salutary engagement with the sort of compliance that helps discipline and regulate the poor.

5. Students identified as intellectually talented are not entitled to special privileges. Instead, their talents demand habits of hard work with intellectual engagements that matter. This core mission is difficult to realize in an enrichment model in the general education program. But it can be approached. Teachers can start by replacing the focus on creativity, leadership, and affective needs with real content. Pull-out programs and other forms of segregation are elitist by definition.

6. Rapid school learners need to work hard at school knowledge that really matters (and not some imagined leadership role)—for instance, history, languages, literature, mathematics, sciences, art, music, dance, theater (see, e.g., Egan, 2002; Matthews, 2004; Sosniak & Gabelko, 2008; Whitty, 2010). This is work at which these students are fit to work (see, e.g., Olszewski-Kubilius, 2011), and teachers can help them discover the joy of such work. Their teachers need, of course, to know this joy themselves.

7. Students' academic progress (across the K–12 spectrum) must be regularly assessed with wide-range tests, individually administered (Feldhusen, Van Winkle, & Ehle, 1996). The implications of results of individually administered, wide-range tests should be obvious. Wide-range tests can demonstrate that a student dubbed "proficient" by state accountability tests is *also* proficient at much higher grade levels. Wide-range tests can show, for instance, that a student in second grade is performing at the eighth-grade level. This sort of evidence suggests the necessity of skipping grades. Teachers of the gifted need to make such implications obvious to colleagues who, as so often happens, want to sidestep, ignore, or deny both the facts and the implications.

Although each of these points is partially warranted by the concurring opinions of an odd assortment of "experts"—as indicated by citations—we frame them as rules of thumb so that teachers can help rapid school learners develop, discover, or invent an intellectual mission of their own. Doubtless, engaged teachers will generate additional rules of thumb as they pursue such a path (see also, Assouline et al., 2015, for additional counsel on acceleration in particular).

Helping Students in the Perilous Arts

We see the arts as serious intellectual work and repudiate a version of "arts" as mostly entertaining (Howley et al., 2015).[72] Works of art, and the process of creating artful works, engage the intellect and the heart jointly and at a high level of attention and understanding. No wonder they are difficult. Without understanding the arts, one's experience of the life of the mind is incomplete—a view that scientist C.P. Snow (1959/1993), who argued that humanists needed to understand science and scientists needed to understand literature, surely appreciated.

Aside from being difficult because it is a serious form of intellectual engagement, art is also perilous. It necessarily offers significant challenges to norms of all sorts—cultural, social, political, historical, and economic. This mission makes it impossible for "the arts" merely to be entertaining. As the philosopher Herbert Marcuse (1978; see Chapter 2) noted, the aesthetic dimension represents reality in a transformed way that has the potential to transform us personally; the transformation made possible through art also has the potential to transform the broad human apprehension of reality itself. Pianist and critic Charles Rosen (1998) observed that "almost all art is subversive" (p. 325). Understanding this intellectual power is what once led Heather Descollonges and Elliot Eisner (2003)—tongue in cheek and with justifiable bitterness—to advise policy makers on how to protect American children from art.

Predictably, then, schooling mostly sidelines genuine art as un-American. Art and music programs are the last added in good economic times and the first shed when economic crises lead to budget cuts (Descollonges & Eisner, 2003). The typical pattern is to cover the basics (band, chorus, an art teacher). Less than half of public secondary schools offer even so few as *five* "arts" courses in music, visual arts, dance, or

---

72   By *art* we mean fiction-related literature (novels, poetry, plays, and literary criticism); fine arts (painting, sculpture, conceptual art, and so forth); music (especially extended works, as in the classical and jazz traditions); dance; theater—and so forth. The "aesthetic dimension" (Marcuse, 1978) is more what we mean (see Chapter 2): Art is by definition both difficult and intrinsically connected to higher purpose.

theater, and just 15% require more than one "arts" course for graduation (Parsad, Spiegelman, & Coopersmith, 2012).[73]

A common explanation for this marginalization (e.g., Tutt, 2014) is that educators and the public do not appreciate how the arts are connected to daily life. Maybe, but precisely the same claim is made for all of school knowledge, especially mathematics (see, e.g., Stigler & Hiebert, 1999). So we have a different explanation: The aesthetic dimension embeds an intolerable critique of normalcy (Descollonges & Eisner, 2003; Marcuse, 1978; Rosen, 1998). What is to be done? Can schooling teach aesthetics, even to students talented in the arts?

Attending somewhat better to the perilous arts. Whereas public schools do not have the resources to provide the relevant instruction to students talented in the arts, they might still introduce students far better to art and music than they now do (Heilig, Cole, & Aguilar, 2010; Kohl & Oppenheim, 2012; Thomas, Singh, Klopfenstein, & Henry, 2013), and they could help the few artistically brilliant students and their families organize school experiences in ways that accommodate both academic and artistic studies.[74]

Despite the daunting barriers, a substantial program in art and music for everyone remains about as possible as a substantial program in science and mathematics for everyone (i.e., *very difficult*). So we simply advise teachers of the gifted who are intellectually positioned to do so to:

1. take a role as advocates for artistically talented students;
2. foster the talent and families' work on the talent;
3. expand options for the development of artistic talent in and out of school;
4. scaffold conceptions of what art is (i.e., intellectually exciting and socially relevant); and

---

73 An appreciative footnote on secondary art programs: Whereas high school music programs recruit students for ceremonial essentials (e.g., football intermissions), art programs seem to fly under the ceremonial radar, attracting odd assortments of disgruntled students who engage in painting and drawing (for instance) with often remarkable devotion. In many schools, students alienated from academics are fortunate to have the meager art program as an alternative.

74 We remain impressed by pianist-conductor-educator Lorin Hollander's (1978) grasp of this circumstance; the account of his own experience still merits reading and reflection.

5. conceptualize art broadly—a talent for bluegrass music-making is as wondrous as a talent for Mozart.

Students exceptionally talented in academics also need access to the concept of the arts explained in this section: difficult, transformative, intellectually essential. As a start, teachers might work to expand students' existing tastes in music and art. Or they might include engagement with music and art as part of units or other instructional episodes that touch on intellectual history.

As with all instruction that attempts to engage students seriously with intellectual methods and the issues those methods confront, it is difficult work. Arguably because it is so challenging, aesthetic education has rarely found any place in American schooling (Descollonges & Eisner, 2003). Sources exist, but one must invent the curriculum for oneself. Possible approaches might be drawn from art history and music courses in universities, but a great many additional sources also exist online. Both phases of this work—for the artistically talented and for the academically talented—are, nonetheless, within the reach of teachers with a developed aesthetic dimension, especially teachers with experience practicing their own art.

Imagination. Like Albert Einstein, we find that "imagination is more important than knowledge" (Viereck, 1929, p. 17). Einstein found that engagement with the aesthetic dimension was essential to the life of the mind and life in general. He observed, "If I were not a physicist, I would probably be a musician. I often think in music. I live my daydreams in music. I often see my life in terms of music" (Viereck, 1929, p. 113). Art merits attention for *its* purposes, not because it serves some *other* purpose.

Prospects for Intellectual Talent in Higher Learning Under Neoliberal Leadership

In higher education, even more than in K–12 schooling, contemporary purposes notably reflect neoliberal thinking (see Chapter 5 for the extended argument). Briefly, *neoliberalism* is the ideology of globalization—where the sovereignty of nation states encounters the competing authority of global capital, and where global capital pressures nation states (via neoliberal thinking and related maneuvers) to reduce the level of social services and to privatize many others, for instance public K–12 schooling (Bauman, 1998; De Blij, 2009; Glass, 2007; Harvey, 2005; Howley & Howley, 2015).

As Chapter 5 argued, American universities confront diminished public funding and so are rapidly shedding their public mission. It's no wonder that higher education is advertised for all as the pathway to economic security. Students and the intellect are the losers—that fear of this sort should have become the primary motive for university studies is truly appalling. Certainly insecurity, including economic insecurity, confronts human existence *de rigueur*: It is the human condition. But one needs more than much-admired degrees and grubby careerism for the inevitable confrontation with existence (Green, 2000).

What can one do with higher education, stuck in this "condition"? What should intellectually talented students do in this context? We see two options that honor intellect. They are time-honored paths, moreover, not radical proposals—even if their use is not so common. They are, however, seldom discussed as they are next: (1) the rotated model and (2) the accelerated model.

The rotated model. The conventional advice is to attend the "best" college possible right after high school to "get" an "excellent" education. Deresiewicz (2014) was clear-eyed about the very different reality that is expensively on offer in the "best" universities, as are we after a lifetime of observation and struggle.

The "rotation" involves this shift away from the traditional focus on immediate transition to 4 years of college after high school completion.[75] So instead of putting schooling first, the rotated pathway sets college or university attendance in the context of other plans (e.g., finding work, taking employment). Indeed, the expectation of an 18-year-old going immediately to college has become much less common, partly as the

---

75 Stopping out is interpreted in the research literature as a threat to degree completion. The "dropouts" of concern to university institutional research departments represent lost profit and lost critical mass. Intellectually gifted students who have accelerated in K–12 schooling represent an anomalous population from the vantage of such research (see, e.g., Kempner & Kinnick, 1990).

result of the infusion of adults matriculating as undergraduates in colleges and universities (see, e.g., Taniguchi & Kaufman, 2005).

One instructive study, for instance, is Beverly Burnell's (2003) investigation of college-capable students who did something else instead of going directly on to college. Burnell accepted the possibility that such students might have good reasons for making the choices they did. She discovered that the students wanted real-world experiences to inform their decisions about further studies, and most did plan to resume schooling later on in their adult lives. But the sad news from the study was that the teachers and school counselors with whom the students interacted made little effort to understand or support the students' thinking.

Indeed, most studies of student aspirations do not support adolescents' judgments about when (and whether or not) to attend college. The status-attainment model of education is too pervasive: It perpetuates the view that everyone *should* strive for status and ever more years of schooling. Exhortations that everyone must attend college conveniently extend the age-grade lockstep (and its disciplinary and regulatory implications) to the university.

Surely we have discovered, in compelling high school attendance, that one cannot compel learning? Having observed the fallout of compulsory secondary schooling, who would think to compel "higher education"? Compulsion (whether *de jure* or *de facto*) not only lowers the standard of engagement, but also, far more significantly, it rots away the higher purposes of higher education (see Chapter 5).

Notably, few 18-year-olds are prepared to make the most of the astonishing opportunity provided by college, an observation that applies *also* to many intellectually talented students (Mendaglio, 2013). The rapid school learner is perhaps more likely than others, all else equal, to use the opportunity. But all else is *un*equal—rapid school learners are defined by a narrow ability and a typical pattern of superficial engagement in high school (Barzun, 1945; Deresiewicz, 2014). An education is broader than this, and it cannot be had by more of the same. It's time for another model. So what does this "rotated model" look like?

A wiser choice is for high school completers (of any age) to find a job and work for up to several years before pursuing university studies. The educative potential of "stopping out" looms large (see, e.g., Burnell,

2003; Clery & Topper, 2009; Monaghan & Attewell, 2015). Our counsel differs in this way from that given by Julian Stanley, who was so concerned that bright youngsters enter "their careers" as soon as possible.[76]

So let us consider a high school graduate who has been appropriately accelerated, completing high school at the age of 15. Is stopping out appropriate? *Can* such a young person find a job? Of course. Paid employment is good, but volunteer work is still *work*, still *employment*, and still educative. The student can also simultaneously enroll in postsecondary coursework, perhaps at a community college.

As an educative program, on the edge of adulthood, the rotated pathway must fully occupy the student's time in much the way that adult employment does. Stopping out is not an excuse to play video games and vegetate. At first, in this pathway, employment (including volunteered, unpaid employment) is the essentially educative episode. Shortly, though, the generative tension between continued employment and further course-taking will emerge. Is the employment helping one to discover one's work? What contribution is part-time schooling making? Are they helping to focus plans for further postsecondary enrollment or for further life choices? In what way? This pathway potentially merges very different experiences to the benefit of personal and intellectual insight.

Moreover, subsequent engagement with postsecondary schooling (technical or university) need not be conducted on a fixed schedule (e.g., B.A. in 4 years). It can take place part-time, nearby, and partly online—as seems wise or opportune. We have seldom seen planning for intellectually talented students take this turn, but we have often seen life take it anyway. Part of the issue is the reputation of universities. Elite universities award degrees thought to be more valuable.

When the elite universities have succumbed to neoliberal domination, however, a better sort of experience is more likely, we have seen, at second- and third-rate schools. Deresiewicz (2014) agreed. The rota-

---

76   Recently we learned that Stanley had resented the delay that military service had imposed on him as a young man (Gene V Glass, personal communication, February 6, 2016). We do, however, appreciate the fact that mathematical talent usually produces accomplishments much earlier than is typical in other fields. If accelerated, however, a year or two of employment would not be a significant delay. The option needs to be surfaced in planning discussions, not dismissed.

tional approach is really *orthogonal* to the traditional model for intellectually talented students.

One should point out, too, that acceleration in K–12 schooling makes room in this pathway for the broadening experiences and insights that employment (paid and unpaid) provides. How strange it is, we think, for some young people—especially those from notably advantaged backgrounds—to achieve professional status with little experience of ordinary life and the struggles that are inevitably part of ordinary life. Such a sheltered upbringing is miseducative: an educational recipe for greed, hubris, and vanity.

Accelerated model. Some rapid school learners will arrive at high school completion already knowing what they want to be and to do with their lives, even at the age of 15 (Muratori, 2011). For these students, traditional or accelerated pursuit of a university degree probably makes sense. Because they are already sure of their avocational choices, these students are in a good position to exploit the university in the next 4 years (i.e., ages 15–19). These early college entrants can *also* complete their undergraduate tenure in fewer years if they push for the arrangement. In campus honors programs, for instance, they can often negotiate their curriculum in much the way that Ph.D. programs have doctoral students do. Some students will construct the work they love as narrowly focused, and completing a bachelor's degree in 2 or 3 years will seem helpful.

But acceleration through college is not essential. The options on offer for broadening the intellect are legion at most colleges and universities, compared to the options in high school. The principle underlying acceleration in K–12 does not apply so clearly, then, at the university level. Many intellectually advanced students have multiple talents that can be satisfied better, for instance, by pursuing multiple majors or by arranging an interdisciplinary honors program.

Caution and improvisation are still much needed, however. Running at breakneck speed through schooling entails recognizable hazards. Sending 15-year-olds to college campuses, for instance, will usually mean sending them to famously sexualized places (see, e.g., Caron & Ireland, 2013). These students will be attending college with nominal adults considered free (on most campuses) to explore sexuality, sexual relationships, and romance. It's one of the things "living away from home" means for university students.

Intellect, Elitism, and Ordinary Life

Since we published the first edition of this book in 1995, the prevailing circumstances have made a qualitative change, a momentously unfortunate one. Schooling as a K–24 enterprise has almost ceased existence as a public good; it is almost completely severed from the commonwealth, and the very idea of commonwealth itself now seems tinged with nostalgia. In revising the book, we have attempted to document and provide explanations for this qualitative change. But we can't prove it scientifically. If accused of "cherry picking" our sources, our reply to such an objection is that we have nonetheless gathered an awful lot of cherries.

This disturbing change bodes ill not simply for America, but for the entire planet, and across several aspects of existence: nature, politics, economy, and culture. Is it the culture we deserve? Perhaps. But the relevant decay, as other observers charge, is particularly widespread because of the global overreach of neoliberalism and its varied technologies (e.g., Harvey, 2005; Jacques, 2009; Orlov, 2011; Orr, 1995; Postman, 1985). Political theorist James Scott (1998, 2012) blamed high modernism, scientism, political centralization, and imperial aims for the disasters, and he shows that these ills are practiced equally by republicans, democrats, fascists, and communists—elites in many nations across the globe.

As conservationists, however, and as champions of thoughtfulness and judgment, we by no means argue that "the best education for the best is the best education for all."[77] Such prescriptions—often given implicitly or explicitly by broad-minded educators such as Ted Sizer and W. E. B. Dubois—are *dangerous* by our lights. The schooling that makes the elites what they are is the one needed by everyone? The education founded on greed, privilege, and hubris? It makes the wrong kind of sense altogether.

---

77 An epigraph attributed to "Great Books" founder Robert Hutchins and approvingly quoted by Berman, 2006, p. 13.

As we have argued several times in explaining the relevance of gifted education in rural places, humans inevitably make sense from local ways of living, knowing, working, and loving. *Culture is ordinary.* And this famed phrase of Raymond Williams (1958/2001) applies equally to the house of intellect and to the homes and communities in which we all live. They all need care, and they all benefit from thoughtfulness and from reasonable scrutiny. Many paths exist to such ends. Schooling might be one of them, eventually, but not now, and certainly not the "best" schooling. Such "best" schooling is clearly, to our minds, the enemy of good schooling.

Ultimately we cannot supply the education that the very privileged "best" supply to their very privileged "best" children because hardly any of us possess such resources. More to the point, what the "best" thus supplies is the continuation of privilege contrary to the common good. So, much as we admire the work of Sizer and Dubois, with respect to educational thinking, in the end (and as our proposal for restructured schooling suggests) we side more with Booker T. Washington than with Dubois, and more with Aristotle than with Plato. Ordinary life requires ordinary culture. The house of intellect is already a part of every household. It needs much better care in America.

References

Achinstein, B., Ogawa, R. T., & Speiglman, A. (2004). Are we creating separate and unequal tracks of teachers? The effects of state policy, local conditions, and teacher characteristics on new teacher socialization. *American Educational Research Journal, 41,* 557–603.

Adams, H. (1931). *The education of Henry Adams.* New York, NY: Random House. (Original work published 1918) Retrieved from http://www.bartleby.com/159/5.html

Adkins, T., & Castle, J. J. (2014). Moving pictures? Experimental evidence of cinematic influence on political attitudes. *Social Science Quarterly, 95,* 1230–1244.

Adler, M. J. (1990). *Intellect: Mind over matter.* New York, NY: Macmillan.

Aikin, S., & Talisse, R. (2011). *Reasonable atheism: A moral case for respectful disbelief.* Amherst, NY: Prometheus Books.

Albjerg-Graham, P. (2005). *Schooling in America: How the public schools meet the nation's changing needs.* New York, NY: Oxford University Press.

Algeo, K. (2003). Locals on local color: Imagining identity in Appalachia. *Southern Cultures, 9*(4), 27–54.

Allardyce, G. (1982). The rise and fall of the Western Civilization course. *American Historical Review, 87,* 695–725.

Aloe, A. M., & Becker, B. J. (2009). Teacher verbal ability and school outcomes: Where is the evidence? *Educational Researcher, 38,* 612–624. doi:10.3102/0013189X09353939

American Educational Research Association. (2006). Standards for reporting on empirical social science research in AERA publications. *Educational Researcher, 35*(6), 33–44.

Anderson, J. (1988). *The education of Blacks in the South, 1860–1935.* Chapel Hill, NC: University of North Carolina Press.

Anderson, L. (1981). *Student response to seatwork: Implications for the study of students' cognitive processing.* Lansing, MI: Michigan State University, Institute for Research on Teaching.

Anderson-Levitt, K. (2005). The schoolyard gate: Schooling and childhood in global perspective. *Journal of Social History, 38,* 987–1006.

Angus, D. L. (2001). *Professionalism and the public good: A brief history of teacher certification.* (J. Mirel, Ed.). Washington, DC: Thomas B. Fordham Foundation. Retrieved from http://files.eric.ed.gov/fulltext/ED449149.pdf

Anthony, E. K., King, B., & Austin, M. J. (2011). Reducing child poverty by promoting child well-being: Identifying best practices in a time of great need. *Children & Youth Services Review, 33,* 1999–2009. doi:10.1016/j.childyouth.2011.05.029

Anyon, J. (1980). Social class and the hidden curriculum of work. *Journal of Education, 162*(1), 67–92.

Anyon, J. (2005). *Radical possibilities: Public policy, urban education, and a new social movement.* New York, NY: Routledge.

Apple, M. W. (2000). *Official knowledge: Democratic education in a conservative age* (2nd ed.). New York, NY: Routledge.

Apple, M. W. (2001). Comparing neo-liberal projects and inequality in education. *Comparative Education, 37,* 409–23.

Apple, M. W. (2004). Creating difference: Neo-liberalism, neo-conservatism and the politics of educational reform. *Educational Policy, 18*(1), 12–44.

Applegate, A., & Applegate, M. (2004). The Peter effect: Reading habits and attitudes of preservice teachers. *The Reading Teacher, 57,* 554–563.

Applegate, A. J., DeKonty Applegate, M., Mercantini, M. A., McGeehan, C. M., Cobb, J. B., DeBoy, J. R., . . . Lewinski, K. E. (2014). The Peter effect revisited: Reading habits and attitudes of college students. *Literacy Research and Instruction, 53,* 188–204. doi:10.1080/19388071.2014.898719

Archambault, F. X., Jr., Westberg, K. L., Brown, S. W., Hallmark, B. W., Emmons, C. L., & Zhang, W. (1993). *Regular classroom practices with gifted students: Results of a national survey of classroom teachers.* Storrs: University of Connecticut, The National Research Center on the Gifted and Talented.

Archer, L., DeWitt, J., Osborne, J., Dillon, J., Willis, B., & Wong, B. (2013). "Not girly, not sexy, not glamorous": Primary school girls' and parents' construction of science aspirations. *Pedagogy, Culture, and Society, 21*(1), 173–194.

Arendale, D. R. (2011). Then and now: The early years of developmental education. *Research & Teaching in Developmental Education, 27*(2), 58–76.

Arendt, H. (1958). *The human condition.* Chicago, IL: University of Chicago Press.

Arendt, H. (1963). *Eichmann in Jerusalem: A report on the banality of evil.* New York, NY: Penguin Books.

Arendt, H. (1968). *The crisis in education. In between past and future: Eight exercises in political thought* (Rev. ed., pp. 173–196). New York, NY: Viking Press. (Original work published 1954)

References

Arendt, H. (1981). *The life of the mind.* New York, NY: Harcourt Brace Jovanovich.

Aristotle. (1812). *Treatise on poetry* (T. Twining & D. Twining, trans.). Retrieved from https://archive.org/stream/aristotlestreat01twingoog#page/n7/mode/2up (Original work composed ca. 335 BCE)

Aristotle. (1954). *Nichomachean ethics.* (D. Ross, Trans.). London, England: Oxford University Press. (Original work written 350 BC)

Aronowitz, S. (2000). *The knowledge factory: Dismantling the corporate university and creating true higher learning.* Boston, MA: Beacon Press.

Aronowitz, S. (2008). *Against schooling: And for an education that matters.* Boulder, CO: Paradigm Publishers.

Aronowitz, S., & DiFazio, W. (2010). *The jobless future.* Minneapolis, MN: University of Minnesota Press.

Arons, S. (1997). *Short route to chaos: Conscience, community, and the re-constitution of American schooling.* Amherst, MA: University of Massachusetts Press.

Arsen, D., & Ni, Y. (2012). *Is administration leaner in charter schools? Resource allocation in charter and traditional public schools.* New York, NY: Teachers College, Columbia University, National Center for the Study of Privatization in Education.

Assouline, S. G., Colangelo, N., VanTassel-Baska, J., & Lupkowski-Shoplik, A. (2015). *A nation empowered: Evidence trumps the excuses holding back America's brightest students* (Vol. 2). Iowa City: University of Iowa, The Connie Belin & Jacqueline N. Blank International Center for Gifted Education and Talent Development. Retrieved from http://www.accelerationinstitute.org/nation_empowered

Atkins, B. (2003). *More than a game: The computer game as fictional form.* Manchester, England: Manchester University Press.

Atkins, M. S., McKay, M. M., Frazier, S. L., Jakobsons, L. J., Arvanitis, P., Cunningham, T., . . . Lambrecht, L. (2002). Suspensions and detentions in an urban, low-income school: Punishment or reward? *Journal of Abnormal Child Psychology, 30,* 361–371.

Atwell, R. H. (1993). *An American imperative: Higher expectations for higher education* (Appendix D). Invited essay for Report of the Wingspread Group on Higher Education. Racine, WI: Johnson Foundation. Retrieved from http://eric.ed.gov/?id=ED364144

Au, W. (2009). Social studies, social justice: W(h)ither the social studies in high-stakes testing? *Teacher Education Quarterly, 36*(1), 43–58.

Austen, J. (1813). *Pride and prejudice.* London, England: T. Egerton. Retrieved from http://www.gutenberg.org/cache/epub/42671/pg42671.txt

Autor, D., Katz, L., & Kearney, M. (2006). *Polarization of the U.S. labor market.* (NBER Working Paper No. 11986). Cambridge, MA: National Bureau of Economic Research. Retrieved from http://www.nber.org/papers/w11986

Aviram, A., & Assor, A. (2010). In defence of personal autonomy as a fundamental educational aim in liberal democracies: A response to Hand. *Oxford Review of Education, 36*(1), 111–126.

Bacon, F. (1620). *Novum organum: Instauratio magna.* London, England: Apud Joannem Billium.

Baez, B., & Boyles, D. (2009). *The politics of inquiry: Education research and the "culture of science."* Albany: State University of New York Press.

Baker, V. L., Baldwin, R. G., & Makker, S. (2012). Where are they now? Revisiting Breneman's study of liberal arts colleges. *Liberal Education, 98*(3), 48–53.

Bankston, I. L. (2011). The mass production of credentials: Subsidies and the rise of the higher education industry. *Independent Review, 15,* 325–349.

Barlage, E. (1982). *The new math. An historical account of the reform of mathematics instruction in the United States of America.* (ED224703). Retrieved from http://eric.ed.gov/?id=ED224703

Barris, J. (2015). Metaphysics, deep pluralism, and paradoxes of informal logic. *International Journal of Philosophical Studies, 23*(1), 59–84.

Barrow, C. W. (1990). *Universities and the capitalist state: Corporate liberalism and the reconstruction of American higher education, 1894–1928.* Madison, WI: University of Wisconsin Press.

Barrow, L. H. (1989). Professional education reading patterns of presidential science honorees. *Journal of Research in Science Teaching, 26,* 519–532.

Bartlett, K. (1995). A democratic solution to literary tyranny. *English Journal, 84*(3), 39–41.

Barton, P. (2006). *High school reform and work: Facing labor market realities.* Princeton, NJ: Educational Testing Service. (ERIC Document ED492034)

Barzun, J. (1945). *Teacher in America.* Boston, MA: Little, Brown.

Barzun, J. (1959). *The house of intellect.* New York, NY: Harper & Row.

Barzun, J. (1968). *The American university: How it runs and where it is going.* New York, NY: Harper & Row.

Barzun, J. (1983). Preface. In *Teacher in America* (2nd ed.). Indianapolis, IN: Liberty Fund. Retrieved from http://www.the-rathouse.com/JacquesBarzunPreface.html

Barzun, J. (1989). *The culture we deserve.* Middletown, CT: Wesleyan University Press.

Barzun, J. (1991). *Begin here: The forgotten conditions of teaching and learning.* Chicago, IL: University of Chicago Press.

Barzun, J. (2000). *From dawn to decadence: 1500 to the present; 500 years of western cultural life.* New York, NY: HarperCollins.

References

Barzun, J. (2001). *Simple and direct: A rhetoric for writers*. New York, NY: Harper Perennial.

Bass, B. (2008). *The Bass handbook of leadership: Theory, research, and management applications*. New York, NY: Free Press.

Bauman, Z. (1998). *Globalization: The human consequences*. New York, NY: Columbia University Press.

Becker, G. S. (1964). *Human capital: A theoretical and empirical analysis, with special reference to education*. New York, NY: National Bureau of Economic Research and Columbia University Press.

Beghetto, R. A., Kaufman, J. C., & Baer, J. (2015). *Teaching for creativity in the common core classroom*. New York, NY: Teachers College Press.

Bell, D. (1973). *The coming of post-industrial society: A venture in social forecasting*. New York, NY: Basic Books.

Bell, D. (1976). *The cultural contradictions of capitalism*. New York, NY: Basic Books.

Bellah, R. N., Madsen, R., Sullivan, W. M., Swidler, A., & Tipton, S. M. (1985). *Habits of the heart: Individualism and commitment in American life*. Berkeley: University of California Press.

Beller, E., & Hout, M. (2006). Intergenerational social mobility: The United States in comparative perspective. *The Future of Children, 16*(2), 19–36.

Bénabou, R., & Tirole, J. (2006). Belief in a just world and redistributive politics. *Quarterly Journal of Economics, 121*, 699–746.

Benbow, C., & Stanley, J. (1980). Sex differences in mathematics ability: Fact or artifact? *Science, 210*, 1262–1264.

Benevides, T., & Stagg Peterson, S. (2010). Literacy attitudes, habits and achievements of future teachers. *Journal of Education for Teaching: International Research and Pedagogy, 36*, 291–302.

Bennett, E. W. (1988). Moral literacy and the formation of character. *NASSP Bulletin, 72*(512), 29–34.

Berliner, D. (1992, February). *Educational reform in an era of disinformation*. Paper presented at the annual meeting of the American Association of Colleges for Teacher Education, San Antonio, TX. Retrieved from http://files.eric.ed.gov/fulltext/ED348710.pdf

Berliner, D., & Glass, G. (2014). *Fifty myths and lies that threaten America's public schools: The real crisis in education*. New York, NY: Teachers College Press.

Berliner, D. C., & Biddle, B. J. (1995). *The manufactured crisis: Myths, fraud, and the attack on America's public schools*. Redding, MA: Addison-Wesley.

Berman, M. (2006). *The twilight of American culture*. New York, NY: W.W. Norton.

Berry, W. (1977). *The unsettling of America: Culture & agriculture*. San Francisco, CA: Sierra Club Books.

Berry, W. (1987). *Home economics*. Berkeley, CA: North Point Press.

Berry, W. (1990). *What are people for?* Berkeley, CA: Counterpoint.

Berry, W. (2010). *What matters most: Economics for a renewed commonwealth.* Berkeley, CA: Counterpoint.

Best, H. (2000a). Arts, words, intellect, emotion, Part 1: Cultural and intellectual contexts. *Arts Education Policy Review, 101*(6), 3–11.

Best, H. (2000b). Arts, words, intellect, emotion, Part 2: Toward artistic mindedness. *Arts Education Policy Review, 102*(1), 3–10.

Betts, J. R., & Tang, Y. E. (2011). *The effect of charter schools on student achievement: A meta-analysis of the literature.* Seattle, WA: Center on Reinventing Public Education. Retrieved from http://www.econ.ucsd.edu/~jbetts/Pub/A75%20pub_NCSRP_BettsTang_Oct11.pdf

Bianchi, A. J., & Lancianese, D. A. (2005). No child left behind? Role/identity development of the "good student." *International Journal of Educational Policy, Research, and Practice: Reconceptualizing Childhood Studies, 6*(1), 3–29.

Bicchieri, C. (2006). *The grammar of society: The nature and dynamics of social norms.* Cambridge, England: Cambridge University Press.

Bickel, R. (2013). *Classical social theory in use: Interpretation and application for educators and other non-specialists.* Charlotte, NC: Information Age Publishing.

Biddle, B. J., & Berliner, D. C. (May, 2002). A research synthesis: Unequal school funding in the United States. *Beyond Instructional Leadership, 59*(8), 48–59. Retrieved from http://www.ascd.org/publications/educational-leadership/may02/vol59/num08/Unequal-School-Funding-in-the-United-States.aspx

Bielick, S. (2008). *1.5 million homeschooled students in the United States in 2007.* Washington, DC: National Center for Education Statistics.

Biggers, J. (2006). *The United States of Appalachia: How southern mountaineers brought independence, culture, and enlightenment to America.* San Francisco, CA: Avalon.

Bishop, J., & Carter, S. (1991). The worsening shortage of college-graduate workers. *Educational Evaluation and Policy Analysis, 13,* 221–246.

Blacker, D. (2013). *The falling rate of learning and the neoliberal endgame.* Winchester, England: Zero Books.

Blair, M. M. (2015). Of corporations, courts, personhood, and morality. *Business Ethics Quarterly, 25,* 415–431. doi:10.1017/beq.2015.32

Blank, J. (2010). Early childhood teacher education: Historical themes and contemporary issues. *Journal of Early Childhood Teacher Education, 31,* 391–405.

Bledstein, B. J. (1976). *The culture of professionalism: The middle class and the development of higher education in America.* New York, NY: W.W. Norton.

References

Bloom, B. (Ed). (1956). *Taxonomy of educational objectives, Handbook 1: Cognitive domain.* New York, NY: David McKay

Bloom, B. (1985). *Talent development in young people.* New York, NY: Ballantine.

Bloom, B., & Sosniak, L. (1981). Talent development vs. schooling. *Educational Leadership, 39,* 86–94.

Bloom, H. (2014). *The western canon: The books and school of the ages.* New York, NY: Houghton Mifflin Harcourt.

Bok, D. (2004). *Universities in the marketplace: The commercialization of higher education.* Princeton, NJ: Princeton University Press.

Boles, B. (2009). *College without high school.* Gabriola Island, BC: New Society Publishers.

Booher-Jennings, J. (2005). Below the bubble: 'Educational triage' and the Texas accountability system. *American Educational Research Journal, 42,* 231–268.

Booker, M. (2007). A roof without walls: Benjamin Bloom's taxonomy and the misdirection of American education. *Academic Questions, 20,* 347–355.

Borland, J. H. (1997). The construct of giftedness. *Peabody Journal of Education, 72*(3&4), 6–20.

Borland, J. H. (2003a). The death of giftedness. In J. H. Borland (Ed.), *Rethinking gifted education* (pp. 105–124). New York, NY: Teachers College Press.

Borland, J. H. (2003b). *Rethinking gifted education.* New York, NY: Teachers College Press.

Borland, J. H. (2009). Myth 2: The gifted constitute 3% to 5% of the population. Moreover, giftedness equals high IQ, which is a stable measure of aptitude: Spinal Tap psychometrics in gifted education. *Gifted Child Quarterly, 53,* 236–238.

Bourdieu, P. (1997). Cultural reproduction and social reproduction. In R. Brown (Ed.), *Knowledge, education, and cultural change* (pp. 71–112). London, England: Tavistock.

Bourdieu, P., & Passeron, J.-C. (1977). *Reproduction in education, society and culture.* Beverly Hills, CA: Sage.

Bowers, C. A. (2000). *Let them eat data: How computers affect education, cultural diversity, and the prospects of ecological sustainability.* Athens, GA: University of Georgia Press.

Bowers, C. A. (2004). Revitalizing the commons or an individualized approach to planetary citizenship: The choice before us. *Educational Studies, 36*(1), 45–58.

Bowles, S., & Gintis, H. (1976). *Schooling in capitalist America: Educational reform and the contradictions of economic life.* New York, NY: Basic Books.

Bowles, S., Gintis, H., & Groves, M. O. (Eds). (2008). *Unequal chances: Family background and economic success.* Princeton, NJ: Princeton University Press.

Boynton, A., & Fischer, B. (2011). *The idea hunter: How to find the best ideas and make them happen*. San Francisco, CA: Jossey-Bass.

Brasington, D. (2003). Size and school district consolidation: Do opposites attract? *Economica, 70*, 673–690.

Brennan, C. M. (2006). On being human. *International Journal of the Humanities, 3*, 255–262.

Bridgeland, J. M., DiIulio, J. J., & Balfanz, R. (2009). The high school dropout problem: Perspectives of teachers and principals. *Education Digest, 75*(3), 20–26.

Brinkley, D. (2004). *Wheels for the world: Henry Ford, his company, and a century of progress*. New York, NY: Penguin.

Brown, D. K. (2001). The social sources of educational credentialism: Status cultures, labor markets, and organizations. *Sociology of Education, 74*, 19–34.

Brown, L. A., & Roloff, M. E. (2011). Extra-role time, burnout, and commitment: The power of promises kept. *Business Communication Quarterly, 74*, 450–474. doi:10.1177/1080569911424202

Brown, R. (1991). *Schools of thought: How the politics of literacy shape thinking in the classroom*. San Francisco, CA: Jossey-Bass.

Brown v. Board of Education of Topeka, 347 U.S. 483 (1954).

Bruce, J., & Calhoun, E. (Eds.). (1996). *Learning experiences in school renewal: An exploration of five successful programs*. Eugene, OR: ERIC Clearinghouse on Educational Management. Retrieved from http://www.eric.ed.gov/contentdelivery/servlet/ERICServlet?accno=ED401600

Bruner, J. (1960). *The process of education*. Cambridge, MA: Harvard University Press.

Bruner, J. (1996). *The culture of education*. Cambridge, MA: Harvard University Press.

Brunsting, N. C., Sreckovic, M. A., & Lane, K. L. (2014). Special education teacher burnout: A synthesis of research from 1979 to 2013. *Education & Treatment of Children, 37*, 681–711.

Brym, R. (1980). *Intellectuals and politics*. London, England: George Allen & Unwin.

Bull, B. L. (1985). Eminence and precocity: An examination of the justification of education for the gifted and talented. *Teachers College Record, 87*(1), 1–19.

Bullock, H. A. (1967). *A history of Negro education in the South*. Cambridge, MA: Harvard University Press.

Burgess, N. (2013). *The motherhood penalty: How gender and parental status influence judgments of job-related competence and organizational commitment*. Kingston: University of Rhode Island, Schmidt Labor Research

References

Center. Retrieved from http://web.uri.edu/lrc/files/Burgess_Motherhood_Penalty.pdf

Burgess, S. R., Sargent, S., Smith, M., Hill, N., & Morrison, S. (2011). Teachers' leisure reading habits and knowledge of children's books: Do they relate to the teaching practices of elementary school teachers? *Reading Improvement, 48,* 88–102.

Burnell, B. (2003). The real-world aspirations of work-bound rural students. *Journal of Research in Rural Education, 18,* 104–113.

Burney, V. H., & Beilke, J. (2008). The constraints of poverty on high achievement. *Journal for the Education of the Gifted, 31,* 171–197.

Burrell, G., & Morgan, G. (1979). *Sociological paradigms and organizational analysis.* London, England: Heinemann.

Burris, C. C., & Allison, K. E. (2013). *Review of "Does sorting students improve test scores?"* Boulder, CO: National Education Policy Center. Retrieved from http://nepc.colorado.edu/files/ttr-tracking-nber-burris_2.pdf

Bushaw, W., & Calderon, V. (2014). Try it again, Sam: The 46th annual PDK/Gallup poll of the public's attitudes toward the public schools. *Phi Delta Kappan, 96*(1), 9–20.

Busso, D. S., & Pollack, C. (2015). No brain left behind: Consequences of neuroscience discourse for education. *Learning, Media & Technology, 40,* 168–186. doi:10.1080/17439884.2014.908908

Butterfield, E. W. (1934). The new fifty per cent. *The Junior-Senior High School Clearing House, 8,* 265–272. Retrieved from http://www.jstor.org/stable/30174193

Byrd-Blake, M., Afolayan, M. O., Hunt, J. W., Fabunmi, M., Pryor, B. W., & Leander, R. (2010). Morale of teachers in high poverty schools: A post-NCLB mixed methods analysis. *Education and Urban Society, 42,* 450–472.

Calhoun, C. (2015). Geographies of meaningful living. *Journal of Applied Philosophy, 32*(1), 15–34.

Calhoun, D. H. (1973). *The intelligence of a people.* Princeton, NJ: Princeton University Press.

Callahan, R. (1962). *Education and the cult of efficiency.* Chicago, IL: University of Chicago Press.

Cameron, J. (2015). Give me a 3, tell me I'm effective, and leave me alone. In K. Sturges (Ed.), *Neoliberalizing education reform: America's quest for profitable market-colonies and the undoing of public good* (pp. 185–212). Rotterdam, Netherlands: Sense Publishers.

Cammarota, J., & Romero, A. (2006). A critically compassionate intellectualism for latina/o students: Raising voices above the silencing in our schools. *Multicultural Education, 14*(2), 16–23.

Capps, D. K., Crawford, B. A., & Constas, M. A. (2012). A review of empirical literature on inquiry professional development: Alignment with best practices and a critique of the findings. *Journal of Science Teacher Education, 23,* 291–318.

Caron, S., & Ireland, V. (2013). *The sex lives of college students: Two decades of attitudes and behaviors.* Orono, ME: Maine College Press.

Carper, A. (2002). Bright students in a wasteland: The at-risk gifted. A qualitative study of fourteen gifted dropouts. *Dissertation Abstracts International, 63*(11A), 118. (UMI No. 3071473)

Carr, D. (2014). Four perspectives on the value of literature for moral and character education. *Journal of Aesthetic Education, 48*(4), 1–16.

Carr, M. J., Gray, N. L., & Holley, M. J. (2007). Shortchanging disadvantaged students: An analysis of intra-district spending patterns in Ohio. *Journal of Educational Research & Policy Studies, 7*(1), 36–53.

Carrington, M. J., & Zwick, B. N. (2016). The ideology of the ethical consumption gap. *Marketing Theory, 16*(1), 21–38.

Chambliss, M. J. (1995). Text cues and strategies successful readers use to construct the gist of lengthy written arguments. *Reading Research Quarterly, 30,* 778–807.

Chen, G., & Weikart, L. A. (2008). Student background, school climate, school disorder, and student achievement: An empirical study of New York City's middle schools. *Journal of School Violence, 7*(4), 3–20.

Cherubini, L. (2009). Reconciling the tensions of new teachers' socialisation into school culture: A review of the research. *Issues in Educational Research, 19,* 83–99.

Chingos, M., & Whitehurst, G. (2012). *Choosing blindly: Instructional materials, teacher effectiveness, and the Common Core.* Washington, DC: Brookings Institution.

Chiu, M. M., & Khoo, L. (2005). Effects of resources, inequality, and privilege bias on achievement: Country, school, and student level analyses. *American Educational Research Journal, 42,* 575–603.

Christopherson, S. L. (1981). Developmental placement in the regular school program. *G/C/T, 19,* 40–41.

Chubb, J. E., & Moe, T. M. (1990). *Politics, markets, and America's schools.* Washington, DC: Brookings Institution.

Clark, E. M. (2014). Sociological theories of low-wage work. *Journal of Human Behavior in the Social Environment, 24*(1), 38–50. doi:10.1080/10911359.2014.844601

Clery, S., & Topper, A. (2009). Characteristics of students who stop-out. *Data Notes (Achieving the Dream), 4*(3), 1–4. Retrieved from http://files.eric.ed.gov/fulltext/ED521313.pdf

References

Clinkenbeard, P. R. (2012). Motivation and gifted students: Implications of theory and research. *Psychology in the Schools, 49,* 622–630.

Clotfelter, C., Ladd, H. F., & Vigdor, J. L. (2005). Who teaches whom? Race and the distribution of novice teachers. *Economics of Education Review, 24,* 377–392.

Clotfelter, C. T., Ladd, H. F., Vigdor, J. L., & Wheeler, J. (2007). High poverty schools and the distribution of teachers and principals. *North Carolina Law Review, 85,* 1345–1379.

Cobb, Jr., J. B. (2015). The anti-intellectualism of the American university. *Soundings, 98,* 218–232.

Cochran, B. (1978). *Labor and communism: The conflict that shaped American unions.* Princeton, NJ: Princeton University Press.

Cochran-Smith, M. (1991). Learning to teach against the grain. *Harvard Educational Review, 61,* 279–310.

Cogan, J. J., & Anderson, H. (1977). Teachers' professional reading habits. *Language Arts, 54,* 254–258.

Cohen, D. (1988). *Teaching practice: Plus ça change.* East Lansing, MI: National Center for Research on Teacher Education. Retrieved from http://www.eric.ed.gov/contentdelivery/servlet/ERICServlet?accno=ED299257

Cohen, D. (1990). A revolution in one classroom: The case of Mrs. Oublier. *Educational Evaluation and Policy Analysis, 12,* 327–345.

Cohen, M. D. (2012). *Reconstructing the campus: Higher education and the American civil war.* Charlottesville, VA: University of Virginia Press.

Cohn, S. J., George, W. C., & Stanley, J. C. (1979). *Educating the gifted: Acceleration and enrichment.* Baltimore, MD: Johns Hopkins University Press.

Colangelo, N., Assouline, S. G., & Gross, M. U. M. (2004). *A nation deceived: How schools hold back America's brightest students* (Vol. II). Iowa City: University of Iowa, The Connie Belin & Jacqueline N. Blank International Center for Gifted Education and Talent Development. Retrieved from http://files.eric.ed.gov/fulltext/ED535138.pdf

Colangelo, N., Assouline, S. G., & Lupkowski-Shoplik, A. E. (2004). Whole-grade acceleration. In N. Colangelo, S. Assouline, & M. Gross (Eds.), *A nation deceived: How schools hold back America's brightest students* (Vol. II, pp. 77–86). Iowa City: University of Iowa, The Connie Belin & Jacqueline N. Blank International Center for Gifted Education and Talent Development. Retrieved from http://files.eric.ed.gov/fulltext/ED535138.pdf

Cole, J. R. (2009). *The great American university: Its rise to preeminence; its indispensable national role; why it must be protected.* New York, NY: Public Affairs.

Coleman, J. (1961). *Adolescent society: The social life of the teenager and its impact on education.* New York, NY: Glencoe.

Collins, R. (1979). *The credential society: An historical sociology of education and stratification.* New York, NY: Academic Press.

Collins, R. (2002). Credential inflation and the future of universities. In S. Brint (Ed.), *The future of the city of intellect: The changing American university* (pp. 23–46). Palo Alto, CA: Stanford University Press.

Collinson, V. (2012). Exemplary teachers: Teaching for intellectual freedom. *Pedagogies, 7,* 101–114. doi:10.1080/1554480X.2012.655885

Committee for Economic Development. (1985). *Investing in our children: Business and the public schools.* New York, NY: Committee for Economic Development. (ED261117)

Common Core State Standards Initiative. (2015). *Read the standards.* Retrieved from http://www.corestandards.org/read-the-standards

Condron, D. (2011). Egalitarianism and educational excellence: Compatible goals for affluent societies? *Educational Researcher, 40*(2), 47–55.

Cone, J. H. (1992). *Martin and Malcolm and America: Dream or nightmare?* Maryknoll, NY: Orbis Books.

Confucius. (1938). *The analects of Confucius* (A. Waley, Trans.). New York, NY: Vintage.

Connell, R. (2013). The neoliberal cascade and education: An essay on the market agenda and its consequences. *Critical Studies in Education, 54,* 99–112. doi:10.1080/17508487.2013.776990

Cookson, P. W. (2015). Real education still matters: Exposing the limits and myths of educational instrumentalism. *Teachers College Record* (online publication). Retrieved from http://www.tcrecord.org/content. asp?contentid=18025

Corbett, C., Hill, C., & St. Rose, A. (2008). *Where the girls are: The facts about gender equity in education.* Washington, DC: American Association of University Women (AAUW) Educational Foundation. Retrieved from http://www.aauw.org/research/where-the-girls-are

Corcoran, S. P., Evans, W. N., & Schwab, R. M. (2004). Women, the labor market, and the declining relative quality of teachers. *Journal of Policy Analysis and Management, 23,* 449–470.

Corner, J. (2016). Passion and reason: Notes on a contested relationship. *European Journal of Cultural Studies, 19,* 209–217. doi:10.1177/1367549415609323

Correa, J., Martínez-Arbelaiz, A., & Gutierrez, L. P. (2014). Between the real school and the ideal school: Another step in building a teaching identity. *Educational Review, 66,* 447–464. doi:10.1080/00131911.2013.800956

Correll, S., Bernard, S., & Paik, I. (2007). Getting a job: Is there a motherhood penalty? *American Journal of Sociology, 112,* 1297–1338.

Cosner, S. (2011). Teacher learning, instructional considerations and principal communication: Lessons from a longitudinal study of collaborative data use by teachers. *Educational Management, Administration & Leadership, 39,* 568–589

Costa, A. L., Garmston, R. J., Zimmerman, D. P. (2013). *Cognitive capital: Investing in teacher quality.* New York, NY: Teachers College Press.

Counts, G. S. (1932). *Dare the school build a new social order?* New York, NY: The John Day Company.

Coutts, S. (2011, April 6). Charter schools outsource education to management firms, with mixed results. *ProPublica.* Retrieved from http://www.propublica.org/article/charter-schools-outsource-education-to-management-firms-with-mixed-results

Covaleskie, J. F. (2014). What good is college? The economics of college attendance. *Philosophical Studies in Education, 45,* 93–101.

Cox, J., Daniel, N., & Boston, B. (1985). *Educating able learners: Programs and promising practices.* Austin: University of Texas Press.

Craig, J., & Gunn, A. (2010). Higher skills and the knowledge economy: The challenge of offshoring. *Higher Education Management and Policy, 22*(3), 1–17.

Cranston, N., Mulford, B., & Keating, J. (2010). Primary school principals and the purposes of education in Australia: Results of a national survey. *Journal of Educational Administration, 48,* 517–539.

Crawford, M. B. (2009). *Shop class as soulcraft: An inquiry into the value of work.* New York, NY: Penguin.

Cremin, L. A. (1962). *The transformation of the school: Progressivism in American education, 1876–1957.* New York, NY: Knopf.

Cremin, L. A. (1970). *American education: The colonial experience 1607–1783.* New York, NY: Harper & Row.

Cremin, L. A. (1980). *American education: The national experience, 1783–1876.* New York, NY: Harper & Row.

Cremin, L. A. (1988). *American education: The metropolitan experience, 1876–1980.* New York, NY: Harper & Row.

Croft, L., & Wood., S. (2015). Professional development for teachers and school counselors: Empowering a change in perception and practice of acceleration. In S. G. Assouline, N. Colangelo, J. VanTassel-Baska, & A. Lupkowski-Shoplik (Eds.), *A nation empowered: Evidence trumps the excuses holding back America's brightest students* (pp. 87–98). Iowa City, IA: Iowa City: University of Iowa, The Connie Belin & Jacqueline N. Blank International Center for Gifted Education and Talent Development. Retrieved from http://www.accelerationinstitute.org/nation_empowered

Crookes, G. (1997). What influences what and how second and foreign language teachers teach? *Modern Language Journal, 81,* 67–79.

Cross, T. L., Andersen, L., & Mammadov, S. (2015). Effects of academic acceleration on the social and emotional lives of gifted students. In S. G.

Assouline, N. Colangelo, J. VanTassel-Baska, & A. Lupkowski-Shoplik (Eds.), *A nation empowered: Evidence trumps the excuses holding back America's brightest students* (pp. 31–42). Iowa City: University of Iowa, The Connie Belin & Jacqueline N. Blank International Center for Gifted Education and Talent Development. Retrieved from http://www.accelerationinstitute.org/nation_empowered

Cuban, L. (1982). Persistence of the inevitable: The teacher-centered classroom. *Education and Urban Society, 15*(1), 26–41.

Cuban, L. (2001). *Oversold and underused: Computers in the classroom.* Cambridge, MA: Harvard University Press.

Cuban, L. (2008). *Frogs into princes: Writings on school reform.* New York, NY: Teachers College Press.

Cullen, J. B., & Reback, R. (2006). *Tinkering toward accolades: School gaming under a performance accountability system.* Cambridge, MA: National Bureau of Economic Research. Retrieved from http://econweb.ucsd.edu/~jbcullen/research/Tinkering.pdf

Curti, M. (1943). *The growth of American thought.* New York, NY: Harper.

Cusick, P. A. (1983). *The egalitarian ideal and the American high school: Studies of three schools.* New York, NY: Longman.

Dade, K., Tartakov, C., Hargrave, C., & Leigh, P. (2015). Assessing the impact of racism on Black faculty in White academe: A collective case study of African American female faculty. *Western Journal of Black Studies, 39,* 134–146.

Dai, D. Y. (2010). *The nature and nurture of giftedness.* New York, NY: Teachers College Press.

Daly, A., Der-Martirosian, C., Ong-Dean, C., Park, V., & Wishard-Guerra, A. (2011). Leading under sanction: Principals' perceptions of threat rigidity, efficacy, and leadership in underperforming schools. *Leadership and Policy in Schools, 10,* 171–206.

Dana, N., Yendol-Hoppey, D., & Snow-Gerono, J. L. (2006). Deconstructing inquiry in the professional development school: Exploring the domains and contents of teachers' questions. *Action in Teacher Education, 27,* 59–71.

Darder, A. (2012). Neoliberalism in the academic borderlands: An on-going struggle for equality and human rights. *Educational Studies, 48,* 412–426.

Datnow, A., Park, V., & Kennedy, B. (2008). *Acting on data: How high schools use data for instructional improvement.* Los Angeles: University of Southern California Center on Educational Governance. Retrieved from http://www.newschools.org/files/ActingonData.pdf

David, J. L. (2011). High-stakes testing narrows the curriculum. *Educational Leadership, 66*(6), 78–80.

Davis, W. (2009). *The wayfinders: Why ancient wisdom matters in the modern world.* Toronto, Ontario, Canada: House of Anansi Press.

References

Day, C. (2012). New lives of teachers. *Teacher Education Quarterly, 39*(1), 7–26.

Daza, S. L. (2013). Putting Spivakian theorizing to work: Decolonizing neoliberal scientism in education. *Educational Theory, 63,* 601–620.

DeAngelo, L., Franke, R., Hurtado, S., Pryor, J. H. & Tran, S. (2011). *Completing college: Assessing graduation rates at four-year institutions.* Los Angeles, CA: Higher Education Research Institute. Retrieved from http://heri.ucla.edu/DARCU/CompletingCollege2011.pdf

Deaton, B., & McNamara, K. (1984). *Education in a changing rural environment: The impact of population and economic change on the demand for and costs of public education in rural America.* Starkville: Mississippi State University, Southern Rural Development Center. Retrieved from http://files.eric.ed.gov/fulltext/ED241210.pdf

De Blij, H. (2009). *The power of place: Geography, destiny, and globalization's rough landscape.* New York, NY: Oxford University Press.

de Carvalho, M. E. P. (2001). *Rethinking family-school relations: A critique of parental involvement in schooling.* Mahwah, NJ: Lawrence Erlbaum.

DeCastro-Ambrosetti, D., & Cho, G. (2011). A look at "lookism": A critical analysis of teachers' expectations based on students' appearance. *Multicultural Education, 18*(2), 51–54.

De Fruyt, F., Wille, B., & John, O. P. (2015). Employability in the 21st century: Complex (interactive) problem solving and other essential skills. *Industrial & Organizational Psychology, 8,* 276–281. doi:10.1017/iop.2015.33

Delisle, J., & Galbraith, J. (2002). *When gifted kids don't have all the answers: How to meet their social and emotional needs.* Minneapolis, MN: Free Spirit.

De Lissovoy, N. (2013). Pedagogy of the impossible: Neoliberalism and the ideology of accountability. *Policy Futures in Education, 11,* 423–435.

Delucci, M., & Korgen, K. (2002). We're the customer; we pay the tuition: Student consumerism among undergraduate sociology majors. *Teaching Sociology, 30*(1), 100–107.

Del Val, R. E., & Normore, A. H. (2008). Leadership for social justice: Bridging the digital divide. *International Journal of Urban Educational Leadership, 2,* 1–15.

deMarrais, K., & LeCompte, M. (1999). *The way schools work: A sociological analysis of education.* New York, NY: Longman.

Demerath, P., Lynch, J., & Davidson, M. (2008). Dimensions of psychological capital in a U.S. suburb and high school: Identities for neoliberal times. *Anthropology & Education Quarterly, 39,* 270–292. doi:10.1111/j.1548-1492.2008.00022.x

D'Emilio, J., & Freedman, E. (2012). *Intimate matters: A history of sexuality in America* (3rd ed.). Chicago, IL: University of Chicago Press.

Denton, S. (2014). The rural past-in-present and postwar sub/urban progress. *American Studies, 53,* 119–140.

DePalma, R., Matusov, E., & Smith, M. (2009). Smuggling authentic learning into the school context: Transitioning from an innovative elementary to a conventional high school. *Teachers College Record, 23,* 934–972.

Deresiewicz, W. (2014). *Excellent sheep: The miseducation of the American elite.* New York, NY: Simon & Schuster.

Descollonges, H., & Eisner, E. (2003). Protecting our children from the arts: Ten not-so-serious recommendations for policy makers. *American School Board Journal, 190*(10), 28–31.

Desmond, M. (2016). *Evicted: Poverty and profit in the American city.* New York, NY: Crown Publishers.

Devaney, K., & Sykes, G. (1988). Making the case for professionalism. In A. Lieberman (Ed.), *Building a professional culture in schools* (pp. 3–22). New York, NY: Teachers College Press.

DeVries, R., Zan, B., Hildebrandt, C., Edmiaston, R., & Sales, C. (2002). *Developing constructivist early childhood curriculum.* New York, NY: Teachers College Press.

Dewey, J. (1897). My pedagogic creed. *School Journal, 54*(3), 77–80. Retrieved from http://dewey.pragmatism.org/creed.htm

Dewey, J. (1916). *Democracy and education: An introduction to the philosophy of education.* New York, NY: Macmillan.

Dewey, J. (1979). Some dangers in the present movement for industrial education. In J. A. Boydston (Ed.), *The middle works: 1899–1924* (pp. 98–103). Carbondale, IL: Southern Illinois University Press. (Original work published 1913)

Dewey, J. (1997). *Experience and education.* New York, NY: Simon & Schuster. (Original work published 1938)

DeYoung, A. (1989). *Economics and American education: A historical and critical overview of the impact of economic theories on schooling in the United States.* New York, NY: Longman.

DeYoung, C. G., Quilty, L. C., Peterson, J. B., & Gray, J. R. (2014). Openness to experience, intellect, and cognitive ability. *Journal of Personality Assessment, 96*(1), 46–52.

Diamond, J. (1997). *Guns, germs, and steel: The fates of human societies.* New York, NY: W.W. Norton.

Di Paolantonio, M. (2016). The cruel optimism of education and education's implication with 'passing-on.' *Journal of Philosophy of Education, 50,* 147–159.

Doltot, F. (1994). *Les chemins de l'education* [The pathways of education]. Paris, France: Gallimard.

Dorling, D. (2010). The return to elitism in education. *Soundings, 44,* 35–46.

References

Dorn, S. (2014). Testing like William the Conqueror: Cultural and instrumental uses of examinations. *Education Policy Analysis Archives, 22*(119). http://dx.doi.org/10.14507/epaa.v22.1684

Dorrien, G. (2012). What kind of country: Economic crisis, the Obama presidency, the politics of loathing, and the common good. *Cross Currents, 62*(1), 110–142.

Douglas, S., & Walker, A. (2014). *Coal mining and the resource curse in the eastern United States.* Morgantown, WV: Social Sciences Resource Network. Retrieved from http://be.wvu.edu/phd_economics/pdf/14-01.pdf

Douthitt, V. L. (1992). A comparison of adaptive behavior in gifted and nongifted children. *Roeper Review, 14,* 149–151.

Downey, G. L. (2007). Low cost, mass use: American engineers and the metrics of progress. *History and Technology, 23,* 289–308. doi:10.1080/07341510701300387

Downey, L. (1960). *The task of public education.* Chicago, IL: Midwest Administration Center, University of Chicago.

Dresser, R. (2012). The impact of scripted literacy instruction on teachers and students. *Issues in Teacher Education, 21*(1), 71–87.

Dreyfus, H., & Rabinow, P. (1982). *Michel Foucault: Beyond structuralism and hermeneutics.* Chicago, IL: University of Chicago Press.

Druckerman, P. (2012). *Bringing up bébé: One American mother discovers the wisdom of French parenting.* New York, NY: Penguin.

Dryfoos, J., & McGuire, S. (2002). *Inside full-service community schools.* Thousand Oaks, CA: Corwin.

Duckworth, E. (1986). Teaching as research. *Harvard Educational Review, 56,* 481–495.

Duffey, R. V. (1974, October). *Elementary school teachers' reading.* Paper presented at the Annual Meeting of the College Reading Association, Bethesda, MD. Retrieved from http://files.eric.ed.gov/fulltext/ED098554.pdf

DuFour, R. (2004). What is a professional learning community? *Educational Leadership, 61*(8), 6–11.

Duncan, G. J., & Murnane, R. J. (2014). Meeting the educational challenges of income inequality. *Phi Delta Kappan, 95*(7), 50–54.

Dungan, R. A. (1970). Higher education: The effort to adjust. In S. R. Graubard & G.A. Ballotti (Eds.), *The embattled university* (pp. 141–153). New York, NY: George Braziller.

Dweck, C. S. (2008). *Mindset: The new psychology of success.* New York, NY: Ballantine Books.

Dweck, C. S. (2010). Even geniuses work hard. *Educational Leadership, 68*(1), 16–20.

Eagleton, T. (2003). *After theory.* New York, NY: Basic Books.

Easton, D. (1953). *The political system: An inquiry into the state of political science.* New York, NY: Knopf.

Eccles, J., Barber, B., Josefowicz, D., Malanchuk, O., & Vida, M. (1999). Self-evaluation of competence, task values, and self esteem. In N. G. Johnson, M. C. Roberts, & J. Morrell (Eds.), *Beyond appearance: A new look at adolescent girls* (pp. 53–84). Washington, DC: American Psychological Association. Retrieved from http://rcgd.isr.umich.edu/garp/articles/eccles99e.pdf

Edelstein, F., & Schoeffe, E. (1989). *A blueprint for business on restructuring education: Corporate action package.* Washington, DC: National Alliance of Business. (ED312486)

Egan, K. (1978). What is curriculum? *Curriculum Inquiry, 8*(1), 65–72.

Egan, K. (2001). Why education is so difficult and contentious. *Teachers College Record, 103,* 923–941.

Egan, K. (2002). *Getting it wrong from the beginning: Our progressivist inheritance from Herbert Spencer, John Dewey, and Jean Piaget.* New Haven, CT: Yale University Press.

Egan, K., & Madej, K. (2009). Learning in depth: Students as experts. *Education Canada, 49*(2), 18–23.

Ehren, M., & Hatch, T. (2013). Responses of schools to accountability systems using multiple measures: The case of New York City elementary schools. *Educational Assessment Evaluation and Accountability, 25,* 341–373.

Eigenberger, M. E., & Sealander, K. A. (2001). A scale for measuring students' anti-intellectualism. *Psychological Reports, 89,* 387–402.

Eisenbach, B. B. (2012). Teacher belief and practice in a scripted curriculum. *Clearing House: A Journal of Educational Strategies, Issues and Ideas, 85,* 153–156.

Eisner, E. W. (1983). The kind of schools we need. *Educational Leadership, 41*(2), 48–55.

Elias, R. Z. (2008). Anti-intellectual attitudes and academic self-efficacy among business students. *Journal of Education for Business, 84,* 110–117.

Eliot, C. W. (1908). Dr. Eliot on industrial education. *American Education, 12*(1), 35.

Eliot, C. W. (1910). The value during education of the life-career motive. *The National Education Association of the United States: Journal of Proceedings and Addresses, 48,* 133–141.

Eliot, T. S. (1948). *Notes towards the definition of culture.* London, England: Faber & Faber.

Emerson, R. W. (1841). *Essays: First series.* Boston, MA: James Munroe and Co.

Emery, K. (2002). *The business roundtable and systemic reform: How corporate-engineered high-stakes testing has eliminated community participation in developing educational goals and policies* (Unpublished doctoral

References

dissertation). University of California, Davis. Retrieved from http://www. educationanddemocracy.org/Emery_dissertation.html

Emery, K., & Ohanian, S. (2004). *Why is corporate America bashing our public schools?* Portsmouth, NH: Heinemann.

Engelen, E., Ertürk, I., Froud, J., Johal, S., Leaver, A., Moran, M., & Williams, K. (2012). Misrule of experts? The financial crisis as elite debacle. *Economy & Society, 41,* 360–382. doi:10.1080/03085147.2012.661634

Eppley, K. (2015). Seven traps of the Common Core State Standards. *Journal of Adolescent and Adult Literacy, 59,* 207–216.

Ericsson, K. A. (1996). *The road to excellence: The acquisition of expert performance in the arts and sciences, sports, and games.* Mahwah, NJ: Lawrence Erlbaum.

Esprivalo Harrell, P., & Eddy, C. M. (2012). Examining mathematics teacher content knowledge: Policy and practice. *Policy Futures in Education, 10*(1), 103–116.

Etzioni, A. (1970). *Towards higher education in an active society: Three policy guidelines.* New York, NY: Center for Policy Research. Retrieved from http://files.eric.ed.gov/fulltext/ED047618.pdf

Etzioni, A. (1985). *Self-discipline, schools, and the business community.* Washington, DC: Chamber of Commerce of the United States. (ED249335)

Etzioni, A. (2012). The privacy merchants: What is to be done? *Journal of Constitutional Law, 14,* 929–951.

Evers, C. W. (2007). Culture, cognitive pluralism and rationality. *Educational Philosophy & Theory, 39,* 364–382.

Facione, P. A., Sanchez, C. A., Facione, N. C., & Gainen, J. (1995). The disposition toward critical thinking. *Journal of General Education, 41*(1), 1–25.

Fancher, R. (1985). *The intelligence men: Makers of the IQ controversy.* New York, NY: W. W. Norton.

Farenga, P. (2015). *John Holt's GWS.* Retrieved from http://www.johnholtgws.com

Farkas, S., & Duffett, A. (2012). *How Americans would slim down public education.* Columbus, OH: Thomas B. Fordam Institute. Retrieved from https://edexcellence.net/publications/how-americans-would-slim-down-public-education.html

Fass, P. S., & Grossberg, M. (Eds.). (2012). *Reinventing childhood after World War II.* Philadelphia: University of Pennsylvania Press.

Federal Reserve Bank of St. Louis. (2014). *Shares of gross domestic income, Compensation of employees, paid; Wage and salary accruals, disbursements to persons.* Retrieved from http://research.stlouisfed.org/fred2/series/W270RE1A156NBEA

Feigel, H. (1981). *Inquiries and provocations: Selected writings 1929–1974.* Dordrecht, Netherlands: D. Reidel Publishing Company.

Feldhusen, J. F., Van Winkle, L., & Ehle, D. (1996). Is it acceleration or simply appropriate instruction for precocious youth? *Teaching Exceptional Children, 28*(3), 48–51.

Ferrero, D. J. (2011). The humanities: Why such a hard sell? *Educational Leadership, 68,* 22–26.

Fetterman, D. M. (1988). *Excellence and equality: A qualitatively different perspective on gifted education.* Albany: State University of New York Press.

Fields-Smith, C., & Williams, M. (2009). Motivations, sacrifices, and challenges: Black parents' decisions to home school. *Urban Review, 41,* 369–389.

Fine, M. (1991). *Framing dropouts: Notes on the politics of an urban high school.* Albany: State University of New York Press.

Fitzgerald, F. (1979). *America revised: History schoolbooks in the twentieth century.* Boston, MA: Little, Brown.

Fletcher, E. C. (2006). No curriculum left behind: The effects of the No Child Left Behind legislation on career and technical education. *Career & Technical Education Research, 31,* 157–174.

Flexner, A. (1939). The usefulness of useless knowledge. *Harpers, 179,* 544–552.

Florida Drivers Association. (2015). *Don't lose your driving privilege.* Retrieved from http://www.highschooldriver.com/truancy

Foner, E. (1984, Spring). Why is there no socialism in the United States? *History Workshop Journal,* 57–80. Retrieved from http://www.jstor.org/stable/4288545

Foner, E. (1991). *A short history of reconstruction.* New York, NY: Harper & Row.

Forester, J. (1993). *Critical theory, public policy, and planning practice: Toward a critical pragmatism.* Albany: State University of New York Press.

Forster, E. M. (1921). *Howards end.* New York, NY: Knopf. (Original work published 1910)

Foster, J. B., McChesney, R. W., & Jonna, J. (2011). The global reserve army of labor and the new imperialism. *Monthly Review, 63*(6), 1–31.

Foucault, M. (1975). *Surveiller et punir: Naissance de la prison* [Discipline and punish: Birth of the prison]. Paris, France: Gallimard.

Fox, L. H. (1976). Sex differences in mathematical precocity: Bridging the gap. In D. Keating (Ed.), *Intellectual talent research and development* (pp. 183–214). Baltimore, MD: Johns Hopkins University Press.

Frank, T. (2004). *What's the matter with Kansas?* New York, NY: Henry Holt.

Freeman, J. (2006). Giftedness in the long term. *Journal for the Education of the Gifted, 29,* 384–403.

Freire, P., & Macedo, D. (1987). *Literacy: Reading the word and the world.* South Hadley, MA: Bergin & Garvey.

References

Fried, J. (1993). Bridging emotion and intellect: Classroom diversity in process. *College Teaching, 41,* 123–128.

Friedenberg, E. Z. (1979). Children as objects of fear and loathing. *Educational Foundations, 10*(1), 63–75.

Friedkin, N., & Necochea, J. (1988). School system size and performance: A contingency perspective. *Educational Evaluation and Policy Analysis, 10,* 237–249.

Friedrich, C. (1972). *Tradition and authority.* New York, NY: Praeger.

Frontini, G. F., & Kennedy, S. L. (2003). *Manufacturing in real time: Managers, engineers and an age of smart machines.* London, England: Butterworth-Heinemann.

Fukuyama, F. (1992). *The end of history and the last man.* Toronto, Ontario, Canada: Maxwell Macmillan.

Fulmer, S. M., & Turner, J. C. (2014). The perception and implementation of challenging instruction by middle school teachers: Overcoming pressures from students. *The Elementary School Journal, 114,* 303–326.

Furman, J. (2016). The truth about American unemployment. *Foreign Affairs, 95,* 127–138.

Fuss, D. (1989). *Essentially speaking: Feminism, nature and difference.* New York, NY: Routledge.

Gabbard, D. A. (Ed.). (2000). *Knowledge and power in the global economy: Politics and the rhetoric of school reform.* Mahwah, NJ: Lawrence Erlbaum.

Gall, M. (1984). Synthesis of research on teachers' questioning. *Educational Leadership, 42*(3), 40–47.

Gallagher, J. (2003, June). Educational acceleration: Why or why not? *Parenting for High Potential,* 13.

Gallagher, J., & Gallagher, S. (1994). *Teaching the gifted child* (4th ed.). New York, NY: Allyn & Bacon.

Gallagher, J. J. (2004). Public policy and acceleration of gifted students. In N. Colangelo, S. Assouline, & M. Gross (Eds.), *A nation deceived: How schools hold back America's brightest students* (Vol. II, pp. 39–45). Iowa City: University of Iowa, The Connie Belin & Jacqueline N. Blank International Center for Gifted Education and Talent Development. Retrieved from http://files.eric.ed.gov/fulltext/ED535138.pdf

Gallup. (2013). *State of the American workplace: Insights for business leaders.* Washington, DC: Author.

Gamoran, A. (1992). The variable effects of high school tracking. *American Sociological Review, 57,* 812–828.

Gans, H. (1994). Positive functions of the undeserving poor: Uses of the underclass in America. *Politics and Society, 22,* 269–283.

Garcia, F. (2004). Developing sociopolitical literacy: Intellectual consciousness for urban middle school communities. *Clearing House, 78*(1), 34–40.

García Mancilla, C. D. (2012). Art and the passion of intellect. *At the Interface Probing the Boundaries, 78,* 129–140.

Gardner, H. (1983). *Frames of mind: The theory of multiple intelligences.* New York, NY: Basic Books.

Garrow, D. (1986). *Bearing the cross: Martin Luther King, Jr., and the Southern Christian Leadership Conference.* New York, NY: W. Morrow.

Gates, B. (2008). Strengthening American competitiveness for the 21st century. *Yearbook of the National Society for the Study of Education (Wiley-Blackwell), 107,* 95–98. doi:10.1111/j.1744-7984.2008.00173_1.x

Gates, H. L. (1992). *Loose canons: Notes on the culture wars.* New York, NY: Oxford University Press.

Gatto, J. T. (1995). Nine assumptions of schooling and twenty-one facts the institution would rather not discuss. *Skole: The Journal of Alternative Education, 12*(3), 19–30. Retrieved from http://files.eric.ed.gov/fulltext/ED399099.pdf

Gatto, J. T. (2002). *Dumbing us down: The hidden curriculum of compulsory schooling.* Gabriola Island, BC: New Society Publishers.

Gee, J. P. (2011). *How to do discourse analysis: A toolkit.* Milton Park, England: Routledge.

Gee, J. P. (2014). *An introduction to discourse analysis: Theory and method* (4th ed.). New York, NY: Routledge.

Gersten, R., Dimino, J., Jayanthi, M., Kim, J. S., & Santoro, L. (2010). Teacher study group: Impact of the professional development model on reading instruction and student outcomes in first grade classrooms. *American Educational Research Journal, 47,* 694–739.

Gibbs, P. (2014). Happiness and education: Recognising a fundamental attunement. In M. Papastephanou (Ed.), *Philosophical perspectives on compulsory education* (pp. 183–191). Dordrecht, Netherlands: Springer.

Gilead, T. (2009). Human capital, education and the promotion of social cooperation: a philosophical critique. *Studies in Philosophy and Education, 28,* 555–567.

Gilens, M., & Page, B. (2014). Testing theories of American politics: Elites, interest groups, and average citizens. *Perspectives on Politics, 12*(3), 564–581. https://doi.org/10.1017/S1537592714001595

Gilham, C., & Jardine, D. (2015). Review of *Social Efficiency and Instrumentalism in Education,* by James M. Magrini (Online publication). *Teachers College Record.* Retrieved from http://www.tcrecord.org/content.asp?contentid=17873

Gingrich, J., & Ansell, B. (2014). Sorting for schools: Housing, education, and inequality. *Socioeconomic Review, 12,* 329–351.

Ginsberg, D. (2001). *Waiting: The true confessions of a waitress.* New York, NY: Harper Perennial.

References

Giroux, H. (1988). *Teachers as intellectuals: Toward a critical pedagogy of learning.* Granby, MA: Bergin and Garvey.

Giroux, H. (2007). *The university in chains: Confronting the military-industrial-academic complex.* Boulder, CO: Paradigm Publishers.

Giroux, H. A. (1981). Hegemony, resistance, and the paradox of educational reform. *Interchange, 12*(2/3), 3–26.

Giroux, H. A. (2000). *Stealing innocence: Youth, corporate power, and the politics of culture.* New York, NY: St. Martin's Press.

Giroux, H. A. (2011). The disappearing intellectual in the age of economic Darwinism. Policy *Futures in Education, 9,* 163–171.

Giroux, H. A. (2013). *America's education deficit and the war on youth.* New York, NY: Monthly Review Press.

Giroux, H. A. (2014). *Neoliberalism's war on higher education.* Chicago, IL: Haymarket Books.

Gladwell, M. (2008). *Outliers: The story of success.* Boston, MA: Little, Brown.

Glass, G. (2007). *Fertilizers, pills, and magnetic strips: The fate of public education in America.* Charlotte, NC: Information Age Publishing.

Glass, G. V. (2016). *Advancing democratic education: Would Horace Mann tweet?* Presented at the Third Annual Deans Compact Conference, Dublin, OH. Retrieved from https://www.ohiodeanscompact.org/conference-presentation- materials/3-gene-glass-feb-4

Glass, G. V., & Berliner, D. C. (2014). Chipping away reforms that don't make a difference. *Educational Leadership, 71*(9), 28–33.

Glickman, C. D. (1990). *Supervision of instruction: A developmental approach* (2nd ed.). Boston, MA: Allyn & Bacon.

Goad, J. (1997). *The redneck manifesto: How hillbillies, hicks, and White trash became America's scapegoats.* New York, NY: Simon & Schuster.

Goldhaber, D., Lavery, L., & Theobald, R. (2015). Uneven playing field? Assessing the teacher quality gap between advantaged and disadvantaged students. *Educational Researcher, 44,* 293–307.

Good, C., Aronson, J., & Harder, J. A. (2008). Problems in the pipeline: Stereotype threat and women's achievement in high-level math courses. *Journal of Developmental Psychology, 29*(1), 17–28.

Good. T. (2014, October 31). Teachers matter (Letter to editor). *TIME Magazine.* Retrieved from http://cloakinginequity.com/2014/10/31/teachers-matter-the-letter-defending-educators-time-wouldnt-print-timeapologize-timefail

Goodlad, J. (1991). *Teachers for our nation's schools.* San Francisco, CA: Jossey-Bass.

Goodman, J. (1989). Education for critical democracy. *Journal of Education, 171,* 88–116.

Goodman, P. (1962). *Compulsory miseducation.* New York, NY: Horizon Press.

Goodwyn, A. (2014). Reading is now "cool": A study of English teachers' perspectives on e-reading devices as a challenge and an opportunity. *Educational Review, 66,* 263–275. doi:10.1080/00131911.2013.768960

Gordon, H. R. (2016). "We can't let them fail for one more day": School reform urgency and the politics of reformer-community alliances. *Race, Ethnicity and Education, 19*(1), 1–22.

Gorski, P. C. (2008). Peddling poverty for profit: Elements of oppression in Ruby Payne's framework. *Equity & Excellence In Education, 41*(1), 130–148. doi:10.1080/10665680701761854

Gould, S. (1981). *The mismeasure of man.* New York, NY: Norton.

Gouldner, A. W. (1982). *The future of intellectuals and the rise of the new class.* New York, NY: Oxford University Press.

Goyette, K. A., & Mullen, A. L. (2006). Who studies arts and sciences? Social background and the choice and consequences of undergraduate field of study. *The Journal of Higher Education, 7,* 497–538.

Gradin, C. (2014). Race and income distribution: Evidence from the USA, Brazil and South Africa. *Review of Development Economics, 18*(1), 73–92.

Grafton, A. J. (2015, Winter). Habits of mind: Why college students who do serious historical research become independent, analytical thinkers. *The American Scholar,* 31–37.

Grandin, T. (2006). *Thinking in pictures: My life with autism* (2nd ed.). New York, NY: Vintage Books.

Grant, A. M. (2015). Coaching the brain: Neuro-science or neuro-nonsense? *Coaching Psychologist, 11*(1), 21–27.

Gray, P. (2013, August 26). School is a prison, and damaging our kids. *Salon.* Retrieved from http://www.salon.com/2013/08/26/school_is_a_prison_and_damaging_our_kids

Green, E. (2000, March 17). A sociologist urges colleges to forget careers and foster intellectual growth. *Chronicle of Higher Education,* A20.

Gronostaj, A., Werner, E., Bochow, E., & Vrock, M. (2016). How to learn things at school you don't already know: Experiences of gifted grade-skippers in Germany. *Gifted Child Quarterly, 60*(1), 31–46.

Gross, M. U M. (1992). The use of radical acceleration in cases of extreme intellectual precocity. *Gifted Child Quarterly, 36,* 91–99.

Gross, M. U. M., & van Vliet, H. E. (2004). *Radical acceleration of highly gifted children: An annotated bibliography of international research on high gifted young people who graduate from high school three or more years early.* Sydney, Australia: University of New South Wales, Gifted Education Research, Resource, and Information Center.

Grubb, W. N., & Lazerson, M. (2005). Vocationalism in higher education: The triumph of the education gospel. *Journal of Higher Education, 76*(1), 1–25.

References

Gryphon, M. (2006). *Giving kids the chaff: How to find and keep the teachers we need* (Policy Analysis, No. 579). Washington, DC: Cato Institute. Retrieved from http://www.cato.org/sites/cato.org/files/pubs/pdf/pa579.pdf

Guilford, J. P. (1959). The three faces of intellect. *American Psychologist, 14,* 469–479.

Gutstein, E. (2003). Teaching and learning mathematics for social justice in an urban Latino school. *Journal of Research in Mathematics Education, 34*(1), 37–73.

Guttmann, A. (1987). *Democratic education.* Princeton, NJ: Princeton University Press.

Haberman, M. (1991). Pedagogy of poverty versus good teaching. *Phi Delta Kappan, 73*(4), 290–294.

Haberman, M. (2010a). 11 consequences of failing to address the "pedagogy of poverty." *Phi Delta Kappan, 92*(2), 45.

Haberman, M. (2010b). The pedagogy of poverty versus good teaching: It will be formidably difficult to institutionalize new forms of pedagogy for the children of poverty, but it is worthwhile to define and describe such alternatives. *Phi Delta Kappan, 92*(2), 81–87.

Habermas, J. (1984). *Reason and the rationalization of society* (Vol. 1; T. McCarthy, Trans). Boston, MA: Beacon Press.

Habermas, J. (1987). *Lifeworld and system: A critique of functionalist reason* (Vol. 2; T. McCarthy, Trans.). Boston, MA: Beacon Press.

Haley, A. (1976). *Roots: The saga of an American family.* Garden City, NY: Doubleday.

Hall, J. D. (1989). *Like a family: The making of a Southern cotton mill world.* New York, NY: W.W. Norton.

Hallahan, L. (2015). Disability policy in Australia: A triumph of the scriptio inferior on impotence and neediness? *Australian Journal of Social Issues, 50,* 191–208.

Hancock, R. (2013). The responsibility of reason: Tocqueville and the problem of modern transcendence. *Perspectives on Political Science, 42*(1), 27. doi:10 .1080/10457097.2013.741404

Haney, W. (1993). Testing and minorities. In L. Weis & M. Fine (Eds.), *Beyond silenced voices: Class, race, and gender in United States schools* (pp. 25–73). Albany: State University of New York Press.

Hanson, V. (1995). *The other Greeks: The family farm and the agrarian roots of Western civilization.* New York, NY: The Free Press.

Harkins, A. (2004). *Hillbilly: A cultural history of an American icon.* New York, NY: Oxford University Press.

Harland, T., McLean, A., Wass, R., & Sim, K. N. (2015). An assessment arms race and its fallout: High-stakes grading and the case for slow scholarship. *Assessment and Evaluation in Higher Education, 40,* 528–541.

Harvey, D. (2005). *A brief history of neoliberalism*. Oxford, England: Oxford University Press.

Hattie, J. (2008). *Visible learning: A synthesis of over 800 meta-analyses relating to achievement*. New York, NY: Routledge.

Hauser, M. H., Pager, D. I., & Simmons, S. J. (2000). *Race-ethnicity, social background, and grade retention*. Retrieved from http://www. russellsage.org/sites/all/files/u4/Hauser,%20Simmons,%20%26%20 Pager_Race-Ethnicity,%20Social%20Background,%20%26%20 Grade%20Retention.pdf

Hauser, R., Warren, J. R., Huang, M.-H., & Carter, W. (2000). Occupational status, education, and social mobility in the meritocracy. In J. Arrow, S. Bowles, & S. Durlauf (Eds.), *Meritocracy and economic inequality* (pp. 179–229). Princeton, NJ: Princeton University Press.

Hayek, F. (1988). *The fatal conceit: The errors of socialism*. Chicago, IL: University of Chicago Press.

Hayes, W. (2006). *The progressive education movement: Is it still a factor in today's schools?* Lanham, MD: Rowman & Littlefield.

Healy, M. (2007). School choice, brand loyalty and civic loyalty. *Journal of Philosophy of Education, 41*, 743–756.

Hedges, L., & Nowell, A. (1995). Sex differences in mental test scores, variability, and numbers of high-scoring individuals. *Science, 269*(5220), 41–45.

Hegewisch, A., & Ellis, E. (2015). *The gender wage gap by occupation 2014 and by race and ethnicity*. Washington, DC: George Washington University, Institute for Women's Policy Research. Retrieved from http:// www.iwpr.org/publications/pubs/the-gender-wage-gap-by-occupatio n-2014-and-by-race-and-ethnicity

Heibert, E. H., & Mesmer, H. A. (2013). Upping the ante of text complexity in the Common Core State Standards: Examining its potential impact on young readers. *Educational Researcher, 42*(1), 44–51. doi:10.3102/001 3189X12459802

Heilbroner, R. (1980). *Marxism: For and against*. New York, NY: Norton.

Heilbroner, R., & Thurow, L. (1998). *Economics explained: How the economy works and where it's going*. New York, NY: Touchstone Books.

Heilig, J., Cole, H., & Aguilar, A. (2010). From Dewey to No Child Left Behind: The evolution of and devolution of public arts education. *Arts Education Policy Review, 111*, 136–145.

Henry, T. S. (1920). *Classroom problems in the education of gifted children* (19th yearbook of the National Society for the Study of Education, Part 2). Bloomington, IL: Public School Publishing.

Herrnstein, R., & Murray, C. (1994). *The bell curve: Intelligence and class structure in American life*. New York, NY: Free Press.

References

Hertberg-Davis, H. (2009). Myth 7: Differentiation in the regular classroom is equivalent to gifted programs and is sufficient: Classroom teachers have the time, the skill, and the will to differentiate adequately. *Gifted Child Quarterly, 53,* 251–253.

Higgins, C. (2010). Human conditions for teaching: The place of pedagogy in Arendt's "Vita Activa." *Teachers College Record, 112,* 407–445.

Higgins, D. M. (2016). Dreams of accumulation: The economics of SF video games. *Science Fiction Studies, 43*(1), 51–66.

Híjar, A. (2014). Notes on utopia and the aesthetic dimension. *Third Text, 28,* 322–330.

Hirschfield, P. J. (2008). Preparing for prison? The criminalization of school discipline in the USA. *Theoretical Criminology, 12,* 79. doi:10.1177/1362480607085795

Hoadley, U. (2007). The reproduction of social class inequalities through mathematics pedagogies in South African primary schools. *Journal of Curriculum Studies, 39,* 679–706. doi:10.1080/00220270701261169

Hobbes, T. (1651). *Leviathan: Or the matter, forme, & power of a common-wealth ecclesiasticall and civill.* London, England: Printed for Andrew Ckooke [sic], at the Green Dragon in St. Paul's church yard. Retrieved from http://www.gutenberg.org/etext/3207

Hoffer, E. (1951). *The true believer.* New York, NY: Harper & Brothers.

Hoffman, D. (2009). How (not) to feel: Culture and the politics of emotion in the American parenting advice literature. *Studies in the Cultural Politics of Education, 30*(1), 15–31.

Hofstadter, R. (1961). *Academic freedom in the age of the college.* New York, NY: Columbia University Press.

Hofstadter, R. (1963). *Anti-intellectualism in American life.* New York, NY: Knopf.

Hollander, L. (1978). Extemporaneous speech presented at the National Forum on the Arts and Gifted. In E. Larsh (Ed.), *Someone's priority: The issues and recommendations on the state of the arts and gifted in America.* Denver, CO: Colorado State Department of Education. (ED181663)

Holloway, S. D. (1988). Concepts of ability and effort in Japan and the United States. *Review of Educational Research, 58,* 327–345.

Holmes, M. (2014). The psychologist and the bombardier: The Army Air Forces' aircrew classification program in WWII. *Endeavour, 38*(1), 43–54.

Holt, J. (1972). *Freedom and beyond.* New York, NY: E. P. Dutton and Company.

Holt, J. (1981). *Teach your own: A hopeful path for education.* New York, NY: Delacourte Press/Seymour Lawrence.

Hong, G., & Raudenbush, S. W. (2005). Effects of kindergarten retention policy on children's cognitive growth in reading and mathematics. *Education Evaluation and Policy Analysis, 27,* 205–224.

Hook, R. J. (2004). Students' anti-intellectual attitudes and adjustment to college. *Psychological Reports, 94,* 909–914.

Horkheimer, M., & Adorno, T. W. (1972). *Dialectic of enlightenment* (J. Cumming, Trans.). New York, NY: Herder and Herder.

Horvat, E., Weininger, E., & Lareau, A. (2003). From social ties to social capital: Class differences in the relations between schools and parent networks. *American Educational Research Journal, 40,* 319–351.

Hostetler, K. D. (2002). Responding to the technicist challenge to practical wisdom in teaching: The case of INTASC standards. *Educational Foundations, 16*(3), 45–64.

Houck, E. A. (2010). Teacher quality and school resegregation: A resource allocation case study. *Leadership and Policy in Schools, 9*(1), 49–77.

House, R. (1971). A path goal theory of leader effectiveness. *Administrative Science Quarterly, 16,* 321–338.

Howley, A. (1986). Gifted education and the spectre of elitism. *Journal of Education, 168*(1), 117–125.

Howley, A. (2002). The progress of gifted students in a rural district that emphasized acceleration strategies (Republished article). *Roeper Review, 24,* 158–160.

Howley, A., Eppley, K., & Dudek, M. H. (2016). From ingenious to ignorant, from idyllic to backwards: Representations of rural life in six U.S. textbooks over half a century. In J. H. Williams & W. D. Bokhorst-Heng (Eds.), *(Re) constructing memory: Textbooks, identity, nation, and state* (pp. 93–120). Rotterdam, Netherlands: Sense Publishers.

Howley, A., & Hartnett, R. (1994). Recalcitrance and the canon wars: A Foucaultian genealogical study. *Journal of Thought, 29*(1), 51–67.

Howley, A., & Howley, C. (2007). *Thinking about schools: New theories and innovative practices.* New York, NY: Routledge.

Howley, A., Howley, C., Burgess, L., & Pusateri, D. (2008). Social class, Amish culture, and an egalitarian ethos: Case study from a rural school serving Amish children. *Journal of Research in Rural Education, 23*(3), 1–12.

Howley, A., Howley, C., & Dudek, M. (2016). The ins and outs of rural teachers: Who are atheists, agnostics, and freethinkers. *Journal of Research in Rural Education, 31*(2), 1–22.

Howley, C. (1993). A territorial imperative: The authority of the state to reorganize public schools and districts. *Journal of Research in Rural Education, 9*(2), 74–83.

Howley, C. (2009). Critique and fiction: Doing science right in rural education research. *Journal of Research in Rural Education, 24,* 1–11. Retrieved from http://jrre.vmhost.psu.edu/wp-content/uploads/2014/02/24-15.pdf

Howley, C., & Howley, A. (1988). Gifted programs: Equal access in rural areas. *Rural Special Education Quarterly, 8*(4), 3–8.

References

Howley, C., & Howley, A. (2002). A personal record: Is acceleration worth the effort? (Republished article). *Roeper Review, 24,* 134–136.

Howley, C., Howley, A., & Burgess, L. (2006). Just say no to fads: Traditional rural pathways to success often bypass what some view as "best practice." *The School Administrator, 63*(3), 26–27, 29, 31–32, 33.

Howley, C., Howley, A., & Showalter, D. (2015). Staying or leaving home: Belief systems and paradigms. In T. Stambaugh & S. Wood (Eds.), *Serving gifted students in rural settings* (pp. 23–29). Waco, TX: Prufrock Press.

Howley, C. B., Howley, A., & Yahn, J. (2014). Motives for dissertation research at the intersection between rural education and curriculum and instruction. *Journal of Research in Rural Education, 29*(5), 1–12. Retrieved from http://jrre.vmhost.psu.edu/wp-content/uploads/2014/09/Howley.pdf

Howley, C., Pickett, D., Brown, P., & Kay, L. (2011). Loving and hating high school: Divided opinion among adults in a rural university town. *Critical Questions in Education, 2*(1), 28–43.

Howley, C. B., & Harmon, H. L. (2000). *Small high schools that flourish: Rural context, case studies, and resources.* Charleston, WV: AEL. Retrieved from http://files.eric.ed.gov/fulltext/ED447997.pdf

Howley, C. B., Johnson, J., & Petrie, J. (2010). *Consolidation: What the research says and what it means.* Boulder, CO: National Education Policy Center. Retrieved from http://nepc.colorado.edu/publication/consolidation-schools-districts

Howley, C. W., & Howley, C. B. (2015). Farming the poor: Cultivating profit at the schoolhouse door. In K. Sturges (Ed.), *Neoliberalizing education reform: America's quest for profitable market-colonies and the undoing of public good* (pp. 23–51). Rotterdam, Netherlands: Sense Publishers.

Howley, M., Howley, A., & Eppley, K. (2013). How agricultural science trumps rural community in the discourse of selected U.S. history textbooks. *Theory and Research in Social Education, 41,* 187–218.

Hrdy, S. B. (2009). *Mothers and others: The evolutionary origins of mutual understanding.* Cambridge, MA: Belknap Press.

Hubbard, R. (1988). Science, facts, and feminism. *Hypatia, 3*(1), 5–17.

Huddleston, A. P. (2014). Achievement at whose expense? A literature review of test-based rade retention policies in U.S. schools. *Education Policy Analysis Archives, 22*(18), 1–34.

Hudson-Ross, S. (1989). Student questions: Moving naturally into the student-centered classroom. *The Social Studies, 80,* 110–113.

Hursh, D. (2005). The growth of high-stakes testing in the USA: Accountability, markets and the decline in educational equality. *British Educational Research Journal, 31,* 605–622.

Illich, I. (1971). *Deschooling society.* New York, NY: Harper & Row.

Irwin, K., Davidson, J., & Hall-Sanchez, A. (2013). The race to punish in American schools: Class and race predictors of punitive school-crime control. *Critical Criminology, 21*(1), 47–71.

Isaacson, W. (2011). *Steve Jobs.* New York, NY: Simon & Schuster.

Isenberg, N. (2016). *White trash: The 400-year untold history of class in America.* New York, NY: Viking.

Jackendoff, R. (2012). *A user's guide to thought and meaning.* New York, NY: Oxford University Press.

Jackson, N., & Carter, P. (1991). In defence of paradigm incommensurability. *Organization Studies, 12*(1), 109–127.

Jacobs, J. (1994). *Systems of survival: A dialogue on the moral foundations of politics and commerce.* New York, NY: Vintage Books.

Jacques, M. (2009). *When China rules the world: The rise of the middle kingdom and the end of the western world.* London, England: Allen Lane.

Jardine, D. (1995). The stubborn particulars of grace. In B. Horwood (Ed.), *Experience and the curriculum* (pp. 261–275). Boulder, CO: Association for Experiential Education. Retrieved from http://files.eric.ed.gov/full text/ED398036.pdf

Jardine, D., Friesen, S., & Clifford, P. (2006). *Curriculum in abundance.* New York, NY: Routledge.

Jarrell, R. H., & Borland, J. H. (1990). The research base for Renzulli's Three-Ring Conception of Giftedness. *Journal for the Education of the Gifted, 13,* 288–308.

Jencks, C. (1979). *Who gets ahead? The determinants of economic success in America.* New York, NY: Basic Books.

Jencks, C. (1995). *The homeless.* Cambridge, MA: Harvard University Press.

Jerome, J. (1989). *Stone work: Reflections on serious play and other aspects of country life.* New York, NY: Viking.

Jimerson, S. (2001). Meta-analysis of grade retention research: Implications for practice in the twenty-first century, *School Psychology Review, 30,* 420–438.

Jimerson, S. (2004). Is grade retention educational malpractice? Empirical evidence from metaanalyses examining the efficacy of grade retention. In H. J. Walberg., A. J. Reynolds, & M. C. Wang (Eds), *Can unlike students learn together? Grade retention, tracking and grouping* (pp. 71–96). Greenwich, CT: Information Age.

Jobrack, B. (2011). *Tyranny of the textbook: An insider exposes how educational materials undermine reforms.* Lanham, MD: Rowman & Littlefield.

Johnson, H. B. (2014). *The American dream and the power of wealth: Choosing schools and inheriting inequality in the land of opportunity* (2nd ed.). New York, NY: Routledge.

References

Johnson, J. (2007). Critical theory and school leadership. In A. Howley & C. B. Howley (Eds.), *Thinking about schools: New theories and innovative practices* (pp. 233–265). Mahwah, NJ: Lawrence Erlbaum.

Johnson, J. (2014). School funding in Mississippi: A critical history and policy analysis. In C. Howley, A. Howley, & J. Johnson, (Eds.), *Dynamics of social class, race, and place in rural education* (pp. 165–192). Charlotte, NC: Information Age Press.

Johnson, K. (2001). Integrating an affective component in the curriculum for gifted and talented students. *Gifted Child Today, 24*(4), 14–18.

Johnson, S. M., Kardos, S. M., Kauffman, D., Liu, E., & Donaldson, M. L. (2004). The support gap: New teachers' early experiences in high-income and low-income schools. *Education Policy Analysis Archives, 12*(61). Retrieved from http://files.eric.ed.gov/fulltext/EJ853526.pdf

Johnson, S. M., Kraft, M. A., & Papay, J. P. (2012). How context matters in high-need schools: The effects of teachers' working conditions on their professional satisfaction and their students' achievement. *Teachers College Record, 114*(10), 1–39.

Jones, G. (1993). *A guide to logging aesthetics: Practical tips for loggers, foresters, and landowners.* Ithaca, NY: Northeast Regional Agricultural Engineering Service. Retrieved from http://www2.dnr.cornell.edu/ext/info/pubs/Harvesting/A%20Guide%20to%20Logging%20Aesthetics.pdf

Jordan, W. J., Cavalluzzo, L., & Corallo, C. (2006). Community college and high school reform: Lessons from five case studies. *Community College Journal of Research and Practice, 30,* 720–749.

Jung, J. Y., & Gross, M. U. M. (2015). Radical acceleration. In S. G. Assouline, N. Colangelo, J. VanTassel-Baska, & A. Lupkowski-Shoplik (Eds.), *A nation empowered: Evidence trumps the excuses holding back America's brightest students* (Vol. 2, pp. 199–208). Iowa City: University of Iowa, The Connie Belin & Jacqueline N. Blank International Center for Gifted Education and Talent Development. Retrieved from http://www.accelerationinstitute.org/nation_empowered

Kaiser Family Foundation. (2010). *Generation M2: Media in the lives of 8- to 18-year-olds.* Retrieved from https://kaiserfamilyfoundation.files.wordpress.com/2013/04/8010.pdf

Kalpakgian, M. (2013). Why read old books? *New Oxford Review, 80*(6), 36–42.

Kamali, M. (2009). *Racial discrimination: Institutional patterns and politics.* New York, NY: Taylor & Francis.

Kamin, L. (1977). *The science and politics of IQ.* Hammondsworth, England: Penguin Books.

Kanevsky, L. (2011). A survey of educational acceleration practices in Canada. *Canadian Journal of Education, 34,* 153–180. Retrieved from http://files.eric.ed.gov/fulltext/EJ946089.pdf

Kanevsky, L., & Keighley, T. (2003). To produce or not to produce? Understanding boredom and the honor in underachievement. *Roeper Review, 26*(1), 20–28.

Karabell, Z. (1998). *What's college for? The struggle to define American higher education.* Scranton, PA: Harper Collins.

Katz, M. B. (1968). *The irony of early school reform: Educational innovation in mid-nineteenth century Massachusetts.* Cambridge, MA: Harvard University Press.

Katz, M. B. (1989). *The undeserving poor: From the war on poverty to the war on welfare.* New York, NY: Pantheon Books.

Kauffman, J. M. (1993). How we might achieve the radical reform of special education. *Exceptional Children, 60*(1), 6–16.

Kavale, K., & Mattson, P. D. (1983). "One jumped off the balance beam:" Meta-analysis of perceptual-motor training. *Journal of Learning Disabilities, 16,* 165–73.

Keating, D. P. (1988). *Adolescents' ability to engage in critical thinking.* Madison: University of Wisconsin Center for Education Research. Retrieved from http://files.eric.ed.gov/fulltext/ED307508.pdf

Kempner, K., & Kinnick, M. (1990). Changing the window of opportunity: Being on time for higher education. *Journal of Higher Education, 61,* 535–547.

Kenworthy, L. (2011). *Progress for the poor.* New York, NY: Oxford University Press.

Kerr, C. (1963). *The uses of the university.* Cambridge, MA: Harvard University Press.

Kerr, C. (1991). International learning and national purposes in higher education. *American Behavioral Scientist, 35,* 17–42.

Khan, S. R. (2011). *Privilege: The making of an adolescent elite at St. Paul's School.* Princeton, NJ: Princeton University Press.

Kharem, H. (2006). *A curriculum of repression: A pedagogy of racial history in the United States.* New York, NY: Peter Lang.

Kim, M. (2016). A meta-analysis of the effects of enrichment programs on gifted students. *Gifted Child Quarterly, 60,* 102–116.

Kincheloe, J. L., & Steinberg, S. R. (1998). *Unauthorized methods: Strategies for critical teaching.* New York, NY: Routledge.

Kitano, M., & Kirby, D. (1986). *Gifted education: A comprehensive view.* Boston, MA: Little Brown.

Kliebard, H. (1995). *The struggle for the American curriculum, 1893–1958.* New York, NY: Routledge.

References

Kliebard, H. (2000). *Changing course: American curriculum reform in the 20th century.* New York, NY: Teachers College Press.

Kneller, G. (1994). *Educationists and their vanities: One-hundred missives to my colleagues.* San Francisco, CA: Caddo Gap Press. (Original work published 1957)

Knoeppel, R. C. (2007). Resource adequacy, equity, and the right to learn: Access to high-quality teachers in Kentucky. *Journal of Education Finance, 32,* 422–442.

Koballa, T. R. (1987). The professional reading patterns of Texas life science teachers. *School Science and Mathematics, 87,* 118–124.

Kohl, H. (1967). *Thirty-six children.* New York, NY: Signet Books.

Kohl, H., & Oppenheim, T. (2012). *The muses go to school: Inspiring stories about the importance of arts in education.* New York, NY: New Press.

Kohn, A. (1998). Only for my kid: How privileged parents undermine school reform. *Phi Delta Kappan, 79,* 568–577.

Kolander, C., & Chandler, C. (1990, March). *Spiritual health: A balance of all dimensions.* Paper presented at the annual meeting of the American Alliance for Health, Physical Education, Recreation, and Dance, New Orleans, LA. Retrieved from http://files.eric.ed.gov/fulltext/ED323172. pdf

Komensky, J. A. (1907). *The great didactic* [*Didactica magna* of Comenius.] (M. Keatinge, Trans.). London, England: Adam & Charles Black. Retrieved from https://archive.org/stream/cu31924031053709#page/n1/mode/2up (Original work published 1657)

Kompridis, N. (2000). So we need something else for reason to mean. *International Journal of Philosophical Studies, 8,* 271–295.

Konig, R. (2013). WIKIPEDIA: Between lay participation and elite knowledge representation. *Information Communication & Society, 16,* 160–177.

Koppl, R. (2010). The social construction of expertise. *Society, 47,* 220–226. doi:10.1007/s12115-010-9313-7

Kornhaber, M. L., Griffith, K., & Tyler, A. (2014). It's not education by zip code anymore but what is it? Conceptions of equity under the Common Core. *Education Policy Analysis Archives, 22*(4). http://dx.doi.org/10.14507/epaa.v22n4.2014

Koyama, J., & Kania, B. (2014). When transparency obscures: The political spectacle of accountability. *Journal for Critical Education Policy Studies, 12*(1), 143–169.

Kozol, J. (1967). *Death at an early age: The destruction of the hearts and minds of Negro children in the Boston public schools.* New York, NY: Houghton Mifflin.

Kozol, J. (1990). *The night is dark and I am far from home: Political indictment of US public schools* (rev). New York, NY: Simon & Schuster.

Kozol, J. (1991). *Savage inequalities: Children in America's schools.* New York, NY: Harper Perrenial.

Kozol, J. (1996). *Amazing grace: The lives of children and the conscience of a nation.* New York, NY: HarperPerennial.

Kozol, J. (2005). *The shame of the nation: The restoration of apartheid schooling in America.* New York, NY: Three Rivers Press.

Kozol, J. (2013). *Fire in the ashes: Twenty-five years among the poorest children in America.* New York, NY: Crown Publishers.

Krimsky, S. (2003). *Science in the private interest: Has the lure of profits corrupted biomedical research?* Lanham, MD: Rowman & Littlefield.

Kristal, T. (2013). The capitalist machine: Computerization, workers' power, and the decline in labor's share within U.S. industries. *American Sociological Review, 78,* 361–389. doi:10.1177/0003122413481351

Krueger, J. (2014). Musical manipulations and the emotionally extended mind. *Empirical Musicology Review, 9*(3–4), 208–212.

Krymkowski, D., & Krauze, T. (1992). Occupational mobility in the year 2000: Projections for American men and women. *Social Forces, 71*(1), 145–157. Retrieved from http://eric.ed.gov/?id=EJ453481

Kudrowitz, B. M., & Wallace, D. (2013). Assessing the quality of ideas from prolific, early-stage product ideation. *Journal of Engineering Design, 24,* 120–139. doi:10.1080/09544828.2012.676633

Kuhn, T. S. (1962). *The structure of scientific revolutions* (1st ed.). Chicago, IL: University of Chicago Press.

Kulik, J., & Kulik, C. (1984). Effects of accelerated instruction on students. *Review of Educational Research, 54,* 409–425.

Kunstler, J. H. (1993). *The geography of nowhere: The rise and decline of America's man-made landscape.* New York, NY: Simon & Schuster.

Kupchik, A. (2010). *Homeroom security: School discipline in an age of fear.* New York: New York University Press.

Kurtz, P. (1974). Excellence and irrelevance: Democracy and higher education. In S. Hook, P. Kurtz, & M. Todorovich (Eds.), *The idea of a modern university* (pp. 185–202). Buffalo, NY: Prometheus Books.

Kushman, J. W. (1992). The organizational dynamics of teacher workplace commitment: A study of urban elementary and middle schools. *Educational Administration Quarterly, 28*(1), 5–42.

Kuziemko, I. (2006). Using shocks to school enrollment to estimate the effect of school size on student achievement. *Economics of Education Review, 25*(1), 63–75.

Kvanvig, J. (2003). *The value of knowledge and the pursuit of understanding.* New York, NY: Cambridge University Press.

Labaree, D. (2005). Progressivism, schools and schools of education: An American romance. *Paedagogica Historica, 41*(1 & 2), 275–288.

References

Labaree, D. F. (1999). *How to succeed in school without really learning: The credentials race in American education.* New Haven, CT: Yale University Press.

Labaree, D. F. (2014). Let's measure what no one teaches: PISA, NCLB, and the shrinking aims of education. *Teachers College Record, 116*(9), 1–14.

Lagotte, B. W., & Wheeler-Bell, Q. (2015). Dominating educational policy: The normative harms of military recruiting under NCLB. In K. Sturges (Ed.), *Neoliberalizing educational reform: America's quest for profitable market-colonies and the undoing of public good* (pp. 79–100). Rotterdam, Netherlands: Sense Publishers.

Lakes, R. D. (2008). The neoliberal rhetoric of workforce readiness. *Journal for Critical Education Policy Studies, 6*(1), 335–351.

Lamott, A. (1994). *Bird by bird: Some instructions on writing and life.* New York, NY: Anchor Books.

Langer, E. (1989). *Mindfulness.* Reading, MA: Addison-Wesley.

Lareau, A. (1989). *Home advantage: Social class and parental intervention in elementary education.* Philadelphia, PA: The Falmer Press.

Lareau, A. (2003). *Unequal childhoods: Class, race, and family life.* Berkeley: University of California Press.

Larsen, M. T. (2011). The implications of academic enterprise for public science: An overview of the empirical evidence. *Research Policy, 40*, 6–19.

Lasch, C. (1977). *Haven in a heartless world: The family besieged.* New York, NY: Basic Books.

Lasch, C. (1979). *The culture of narcissism: American life in an age of diminishing expectations.* New York, NY: Norton.

Lasch, C. (1991). *The true and only heaven: Progress and its critics.* New York, NY: Norton.

Lasch, C. (1995). *The revolt of the elites and the betrayal of democracy.* New York, NY: W.W. Norton.

Lauermann, F., & Karabenick, S. A. (2013). The meaning and measure of teachers' sense of responsibility for educational outcomes. *Teaching and Teacher Education: An International Journal of Research and Studies, 30*, 13–26.

Lave, J., & Wenger, E. (1991). *Situated learning: Legitimate peripheral participation.* New York, NY: Cambridge University Press.

Lawrence, B., Abramson, P., Bergsagel, V., Bingler, S., Diamond, B., Greene, T., . . . Washor, E. (2005). *Dollars and sense II: Lessons from good, cost-effective small schools.* Cincinnati, OH: KnowledgeWorks Foundation.

Leafgren, S. (2009). The magnificence of getting in trouble: Finding hope in classroom disobedience and resistance. *International Journal of Social Education, 24*(1), 61–90.

Ledbetter, J. (2011). *Unwarranted influence: Dwight D. Eisenhower and the military-industrial complex.* New Haven, CT: Yale University Press.

Lederhouse, J. (2008). Four challenges of high-needs schools: Equipping teacher candidates to deal with less-than-ideal conditions. *AILACTE Journal, 5,* 61–74.

Lee, J. (2008). *Paul Goodman changed my life.* Documentary. Retrieved from http://www.paulgoodmanfilm.com

Lee, J. J. (2007). The shaping of the departmental culture: Measuring the relative influences of the institution and discipline. *Journal of Higher Education Policy & Management, 29*(1), 41–55. doi:10.1080/13600800601175771

Lee, V. E., & Ready, D. D. (2009). U.S. high school curriculum: Three phases of contemporary research and reform. *Future of Children, 19*(1), 135–156.

Leichter, H. J. (1974). *The family as educator.* New York, NY: Teachers College Press.

Leifer, R., & Udall, D. (2014). Support the Common Core with the right instructional materials. *Phi Delta Kappan, 96*(1), 21–26. doi:10.1177/0031721714547857

Lemann, N. (1995). The great sorting. *Atlantic, 276*(3), 84–100.

Lemley, M. (2004). *Property, intellectual property, and free riding* (Working Paper 291). Stanford, CA: Stanford University Law School. Retrieved from http://papers.ssrn.com/sol3/papers.cfm?abstract_id=582602

Leopold, A. (1949). *A Sand County almanac.* New York, NY: Oxford University Press.

Levine, D. O. (1986). *The American college and the culture of aspiration, 1915–1940.* Ithaca, NY: Cornell University Press.

Levine, T. H., & Marcus, A. S. (2007). Closing the achievement gap through teacher collaboration: facilitating multiple trajectories of teacher learning. *Journal of Advanced Academics, 19*(1), 116–138.

Lévy, B.-H. (2007). *American vertigo.* New York, NY: Random House.

Lewicki, J. (2010). *To know the joy of work well done: Place-based learning and sustaining school communities.* Westby, WI: coopecology.com.

Lewin, K. (1951). *Field theory in social science: Selected theoretical papers.* New York, NY: Harper & Row.

Lewis, C., Perry, R., & Murata, A. (2006). How should research contribute to instructional improvement? The case of lesson study. *Educational Researcher, 35*(3), 3–14.

Lewis, O. (1966). *La Vida: A Puerto Rican family in the culture of poverty.* New York, NY: Random House.

Leyva, R. (2009). No Child Left Behind: A neoliberal repackaging of social Darwinism. *Journal for Critical Education Policy Studies, 7*(1), 364–381.

Lieberman, J. (2004). *The early college concept: Requisites for success.* Boston, MA: Jobs for the Future.

References

Lindberg, S. M., Hyde, J. S., & Petersen, J. L. (2010). New trends in gender and mathematics performance: A meta-analysis. *Psychological Bulletin, 136,* 1123–1135.

Lleras, C. (2008). Hostile school climates: Explaining differential risk of student exposure to disruptive learning environments. *Journal of School Violence, 7,* 105–136.

Lleras, C., & Rangel, C. (February, 2009). Ability grouping practices in elementary school and African American/Hispanic achievement. *American Journal of Education, 115,* 279–304.

Loewen, J. (1995). *Lies my teacher told me: Everything your American history textbook got wrong.* New York, NY: Touchstone Books.

Lofgren, M. (2013). *The party is over: How Republicans went crazy, Democrats became useless, and the middle class got shafted.* New York, NY: Penguin.

Low, R. (2014). The genius of the generalist: Why environmental studies is essential to the workforce we need now. *Alternatives Journal, 40*(4), 18–22.

Lubinski, D., & Benbow, C. P. (2006). Study of Mathematically Precocious Youth after 35 years: Uncovering antecedents for the development of math-science expertise. *Perspectives on Psychological Science, 1,* 316–345.

Lucas, S., & Gamoran, A. (1993). *Race and track assignment: A reconsideration with course-based indicators of track locations.* Madison, WI: Center on Organization and Restructuring of Schools. Retrieved from http://eric.ed.gov/?id=ED357455

Lukes, S. (1974). *Power: A radical view.* London, England: Macmillan.

Luria, S. E., & Luria, Z. (1970). The role of the university: Ivory tower, service station, or frontier post. In S. R. Graubard & G. A. Ballotti (Eds.), *The embattled university* (pp. 75–83). New York, NY: George Braziller.

Lynam, E., & Fix, G. (2012). *How spending per pupil in New York State varies among districts.* Citizens Budget Commission Report. Retrieved from http://www.cbcny.org/cbc-blogs/blogs/how-spending-pupil-new-york-state-varies-among-districts

Lyotard, J. F. (1984). *The postmodern condition: A report on knowledge.* Minneapolis: University of Minnesota Press. (Original work published 1979)

Lyson, T. (2002). What does a school mean to a community? Assessing the social and economic benefits of schools to rural villages in New York. *Journal of Research in Rural Education, 17,* 131–137. Retrieved from http://jrre.vmhost.psu.edu/wp-content/uploads/2014/02/17-3_1.pdf

Magrini, J. (2014). *Social efficiency and instrumentalism in education: Critical essays in ontology, phenomenology, and philosophical hermeneutics.* New York, NY: Routledge.

Mandelbrot, B. (2012). *The fractalist: Memoir of a scientific maverick.* New York, NY: Pantheon Books

Marcuse, H. (1978). *The aesthetic dimension*. Boston, MA: Beacon Press.

Margolin, L. (1994). *Goodness personified: The emergence of gifted children*. New York, NY: Aldine de Gruyter.

Margolin, L. (1996). A pedagogy of privilege. *Journal for the Education of the Gifted, 19,* 164–180.

Martí, J. (1999). Wandering teachers. In D. Shnookal & M. Muñiz (Eds.), *José Martí reader: Writings on the Americas* (pp. 46–50). Melbourne, Australia: Ocean Press.

Martin, A. J. (2011). Holding back and holding behind: Grade retention and students' nonacademic and academic outcomes. *British Education Research Journal, 37,* 739–763.

Martin, D. B. (2015). The collective Black and "Principles to Actions." *Journal of Urban Mathematics Education, 8*(1), 17–23.

Martin, J. (1976). What should we do with a hidden curriculum when we find one? *Curriculum Inquiry, 6,* 135–151.

Marx, K. (1867). *Das kapital: Kritik der politischen oekenomie* [Capital: The critique of political economy]. Hamburg, Germany: Verlag Otto Meissner.

Mathis, W. J. (2016). *The purpose of education: Truing the balance wheel*. Boulder, CO: National Education Policy Center. Retrieved from http://nepc.colorado.edu/files/publications/Mathis%20RBOPM-7%20Balance%20Wheel.pdf

Matthews, J. (2010, September 22). Why grade-skipping should be back in fashion. *The Washington Post*. Retrieved from http://voices.washington-post.com/class-struggle/2010/09/why_grade-skipping_should_be_b.html

Matthews, M. S. (2004). Leadership education for gifted and talented youth: A review of the literature. *Journal for the Education of the Gifted, 28,* 77–113.

Mazama, A., & Lundy, G. (2013). African American homeschooling and the quest for a quality education. *Education and Urban Society, 47,* 160–181. http://doi.org/0.1177/0013124513495273

McCollum, S. (2005). Should schools court corporate sponsors? No, schools should reject corporate sponsorships in order to protect educational integrity. *Literary Cavalcade, 57*(5), 18–19.

McCullough, D. (2015). *The Wright brothers*. New York, NY: Simon & Schuster.

McDonnell, L. M., & Weatherford, M. S. (2013). Organized interests and the Common Core. *Educational Researcher, 42,* 488–497.

McGhee Hassrick, E. (2005, August). *The invisible hand: Middle class parent pressures in urban public schools*. Paper presented at the annual meeting of the American Sociological Society, Philadelphia, PA.

McGillivray, A. (2011). Children's rights, paternal power and fiduciary duty: From Roman law to the Supreme Court of Canada. *International Journal of Children's Rights, 19*(1), 21–54. doi:10.1163/157181810X527996

References

McKool, S. S., & Gespass, S. (2009). Does Johnny's reading teacher love to read? How teachers' personal reading habits affect instructional practices. *Literacy Research and Instruction, 48,* 264–276.

McNulty, B. A., & Besser, L. (2011). *Leaders make it happen! An administrator's guide to data teams.* Englewood, CO: Lead + Learn Press.

McPeck, J. E. (1986, October). *Teaching critical thinking through the disciplines: Content versus process.* Keynote address presented at the annual meeting of the South Atlantic Philosophy of Education Society, Baltimore, MD. Retrieved from http://www.eric.ed.gov/contentdelivery/servlet/ ERICServlet?accno=ED283823

Medlin, R. G. (2013). Homeschooling and the question of socialization revisited. *Peabody Journal of Education, 88,* 284–297.

Meier, D. (1995). *The power of their ideas: Lessons for America from a small school in Harlem.* Boston, MA: Beacon Press.

Meier, D. (2003). *In schools we trust: Creating communities of learning in an era of testing and standardization.* Boston, MA: Beacon Press.

Mendaglio, S. (2013). Gifted students' transition to university. *Gifted Education International, 29*(1), 3–12.

Meredith, C. C. (2009). Young, gifted, and female: A look at academic and social needs. *Gifted and Talented International, 24,* 109–120.

Merton, R. (1968). The Matthew effect in science. *Science, 159,* 1–8. Retrieved from http://www.garfield.library.upenn.edu/merton/matthew1.pdf

Metz, T. (2016). Meaning in life as the right metric. *Society, 53,* 294–296.

Meyer, J. W., Boli, J., Thomas, G., & Ramirez, F. O. (1997). World society and the nation state. *American Journal of Sociology, 27*(1), 144–181.

Miller, G. E. (1988). *The meaning of general education: The emergence of a curriculum paradigm.* New York, NY: Teachers College Press.

Mintrom, M., & Vergari, S. (1996). Adovcacy coalitions, policy entrepreneurs, and policy change. *Policy Studies Journal, 24,* 420–434.

Miron, G., & Urschel, J. L. (2010). *Equal or fair? A study of revenues and expenditure in American charter schools.* Retrieved from http://nepc.colorado. edu/files/EMO-RevExp.pdf

Mish, F. (Ed.). (2002). *Merriam-Webster's collegiate dictionary.* Springfield, MA: Merriam-Webster.

Misztal, B. (2012). Public intellectuals and think tanks: A free market in ideas?. *International Journal of Politics, Culture & Society, 25,* 127–141. doi:10.1007/s10767-012-9126-3

Mitchell, R. (1979). *Less than words can say.* Boston, MA: Little, Brown. Retrieved from http://www.sourcetext.com/sharetext/ug/less.pdf

Moir, J. (2012). The democratic intellect reconsidered. *At the Interface/Probing the Boundaries, 78,* 17–31.

Molnar, A. (1996). *Giving kids the business: The commercialization of America's schools.* Boulder, CO: Westview Press.

Molnar, A. (2005). *School commercialism: From democratic ideal to market commodity.* New York, NY: Routledge.

Molnar, A., & Garcia, D. R. (2007). The expanding role of privatization in education: Implications for teacher education and development. *Teacher Education Quarterly, 34*(2), 11–24.

Monaghan, D. B., & Attewell, P. (2015). The community college route to the bachelor's degree. *Educational Evaluation and Policy Analysis, 37*(1), 70–91.

Montesquieu, C. L. (1899). *Mes pensées.* Bordeaux, France: La Société des Bibliophiles de Guyenne. Retrieved from https://www.unicaen.fr/services/puc/sources/Montesquieu/index.php?texte=1007

Montour, K. M. (1977). William James Sidis: The broken twig. *American Psychologist, 32,* 265–279.

Moretti, F. A. (1993). Who controls the canon? A classicist in conversation with cultural conservatives. *Teachers College Record, 95*(1), 113–126.

Morison, S. E. (1935). *The founding of Harvard College.* Cambridge, MA: Harvard University Press.

Moro, M. (2014). Parenthood in migration: How to face vulnerability. *Culture, Medicine & Psychiatry, 38*(1), 13–27. doi:10.1007/s11013-014-9358-y

Mortenson, T. G. (2012). State funding: A race to the bottom. *Presidency, 15*(1), 26–29.

Moses, R. P., & Cobb, C. E. (2001). *Radical equations: Math literacy and civil rights.* Boston, MA: Beacon Press.

Muammar, O. M. (2015). The differences between intellectually gifted and average students on a set of leadership competencies. *Gifted Education International, 31,* 142–153.

Mukherjee, S. (2016). *The gene: An intimate history.* New York, NY: Scribner.

Müller, J., & Hernández, F. (2009). On the geography of accountability: Comparative analysis of teachers' experiences across seven European countries. *Journal of Educational Change, 11,* 307–322.

Muratori, M. (2011, March). Entering college early: It's all about the fit. *Parenting for High Potential,* 16–19.

Mussel, P. (2013). Intellect: A theoretical framework for personality traits related to intellectual achievements. *Journal of Personality & Social Psychology, 104,* 885–906. doi:10.1037/a0031918

Myers, D. G., & Ridl, J. (1981). Aren't all children gifted? *Today's Education, 70*(1), 30–33.

Nathanson, S., Pruslow, J., & Levitt, R. (2008). The reading habits and literacy attitudes of inservice and prospective teachers: Results of a questionnaire survey. *Journal of Teacher Education, 59,* 313–321.

References

National Association for Gifted Children, & Council of State Directors of Programs for the Gifted. (2015). *State of the states in gifted education: Policy and practice data*. Washington, DC: Authors.

National Center for Education Statistics. (2014). *Table 104.20, Percentage of persons 25 to 29 years old with selected levels of educational attainment by race/ethnicity and sex: Selected years, 1920 through 2013*. Washington, DC: Author. Retrieved from http://nces.ed.gov/programs/digest/d13/tables/dt13_104.20.asp

National Center on Education and the Economy. (1990). *America's choice: High skills or low wages*. Rochester, NY: National Center on Education and the Economy, Commission on the Skills of the American Workforce. Retrieved from http://files.eric.ed.gov/fulltext/ED323297.pdf

National Commission on Excellence in Education. (1983). *A nation at risk: The imperative for educational reform*. Washington, DC: United States Department of Education. Retrieved from http://www.ed.gov/pubs/NatAtRisk/index.html

National Education Access Network. (2015). *"Equity" and "adequacy"school funding liability court decisions*. New York, NY: Author. Retrieved from http://schoolfunding.info/wp-content/uploads/2015/01/Equity-and-Adequacy-School-Funding-Liability-Court-Decisions-July-20151.pdf

National Institute of Child Health and Human Development, Early Child Care Research Network (2005). A day in third grade: A large-scale study of classroom quality and teacher and student behavior. *Elementary School Journal, 105,* 305–323.

National Science Foundation. (2015). *Women, minorities, and persons with disabilities in science and engineering: 2015* (Special Report NSF 15-311). Arlington, VA. Retrieved from http://www.nsf.gov/statistics/wmpd

Navarro, V. (1991). Class and race: Life and death situations. *Monthly Review, 43*(4), 1–13.

Neill, A. S. (1960). *Summerhill: A radical approach to child rearing*. New York, NY: Hart Publishing Company.

Nelson, L. J., Padilla-Walker, L. M., Christensen, K. J., & Evans, C. (2011). Parenting in emerging adulthood: An examination of parenting clusters and correlates. *Journal of Youth and Adolescence, 40,* 730–743.

Nespor, J. (1997). *Tangled up in school: Politics, space, bodies, and signs in the educational process*. Mahwah, NJ: Lawrence Erlbaum.

Nguyen, N. (2013). Scripting "safe" schools: Mapping urban education and zero tolerance during the long war. *Review of Education, Pedagogy, and Cultural Studies, 35,* 277–297.

Nicolau, I., & Lupu, R. (2013). The child's right to education and culture in French legislation. *Contemporary Readings in Law and Social Justice, 5,* 255–260.

Niederle, M., & Vesterlund, L. (2010). Explaining the gender gap in math test scores: The role of competition. *The Journal of Economic Perspectives, 24,* 129–144.

Nieli, R. K. (2007). From Christian gentleman to bewildered seeker: The transformation of American higher education. *Academic Questions, 20,* 311–331.

Nieto, S. (2007). The color of innovative and sustainable leadership: Learning from teacher leaders. *Journal of Educational Change, 8,* 299–309.

Nisbet, R. (1971). *The degradation of the academic dogma: The university in America, 1945–1970.* New York, NY: Basic Books.

Nixon, G. M. (2012). You are not your brain: Against teaching to the brain. *Review of Higher Education & Self-Learning, 5*(15), 69–83.

Noddings, N. (2013). *Caring: A relational approach to ethics and moral education.* Berkeley: University of California Press.

Noltemeyer, A., & McLoughlin, C. S. (2010). Patterns of exclusionary discipline by school typology, ethnicity, and their interaction. *Penn GSE Perspectives on Urban Education, 7*(1), 27–40.

Norenzayan, A. (2013). *Big gods: How religion transformed cooperation and conflict.* Princeton, NJ: Princeton University Press.

Norris, C., Hossain, A., & Soloway, E. (2012). Under what conditions does computer use positively impact student achievement? Supplemental vs. essential use. In P. Resta (Ed.), *Proceedings of Society for Information Technology & Teacher Education International Conference 2012* (pp. 2021–2028). Chesapeake, VA: AACE.

Nunberg, G. (2011, October 4). Unlike most Marxist jargon, "class warfare" persists. *National Public Radio.* Retrieved from http://www.npr.org/templates/transcript /transcript.php?storyId=140874613

Nystrand, M., & Gamoran, A. (1989). *Instructional discourse and student engagement.* Madison, WI: National Center on Effective Secondary Schools. Retrieved from http://www.eric.ed.gov/contentdelivery/servlet/ERICServlet?accno=ED319780

Oakes, J. (1985). *Keeping track: How schools structure inequality.* New Haven, CT: Yale University Press.

Oakes, J., Ormseth, T., Bell, R., & Camp, P. (1990). *Multiplying inequalities: The effects of race, social inequality, and tracking on opportunities to learn mathematics and science.* Santa Monica, CA: RAND. Retrieved from http://eric.ed.gov/ERICWebPortal/contentdelivery/servlet/ERICServlet?accno=ED329615

Office for Civil Rights. (2011). *Guidance on the voluntary use of race to achieve diversity and to avoid racial isolation in elementary and secondary schools.* Washington, DC: Office of Justice and Department of Education. Retrieved from http://www2.ed.gov/about/offices/list/ocr/docs/guidance-ese-201111.html

Office for Civil Rights. (2012). *Revealing new truths about our nation's schools* (Civil Rights Data Collection Report.) Washington, DC: Author. Retrieved from http://www2.ed.gov/about/offices/list/ocr/docs/crdc-2012-data-summary.pdf

Ogbu, J. U. (2003). *Black American students in an affluent suburb: A study of academic disengagement.* Mahwah, NJ: Lawrence Erlbaum.

Olsen, B., & Sexton, D. (2009). Threat rigidity, school reform, and how teachers view their work inside current education policy contexts. *American Educational Research Journal, 46*(1), 9–44.

Olszewski-Kubilius, P. (2011, October). Playing the school game. *Parenting for High Potential,* 2–3.

Olthouse, J. M. (2015). Improving rural teachers' attitudes towards acceleration. *Gifted Education International, 31,* 154–161.

Ong-Dean, C. (2009). *Distinguishing disability: Parents, privilege, and special education.* Chicago, IL: University of Chicago Press.

Oral, S. (2013). Exploring the ideal of teaching as consummatory experience. *Education and Culture, 29,* 133–158.

Orenstein, P. (2016). *Girls and sex: Navigating the complicated new landscape.* New York, NY: Harper.

Oreskes, N., & Conway, E. (2010). *Merchants of doubt: How a handful of scientists obscured the truth on issues from tobacco smoke to global warming.* New York, NY: Bloomsbury Press.

Orfield, G. (2001). *Schools more separate: Consequences of a decade of resegregation.* Cambridge, MA: The Civil Rights Project, Harvard University. Retrieved from http://www.eric.ed.gov/contentdelivery/servlet/ERICServlet?accno=ED459217

Orfield, G., Kuscera, J., & Siegel-Hawley, G. (2012). *"E Pluribus" separation: Deepening double segregation for more students.* Los Angeles, CA: Civil Rights Project/Proyecto Derechos Civiles. Retrieved from http://www.files.eric.ed.gov/fulltext/ED535442.pdf

Orlov, D. (2011). *Reinventing collapse: The Soviet experience and American prospects.* Gabriola Island, BC: New Society Publishers.

Orne, D., & O'Connor, D. (2012, March). Gandhian truthfastness: A path to transcend willful thoughtlessness. *Conflict Resolution & Negotiation Journal, 2012*(1), 7–20.

Orr, D. (1995). *Earth in mind: On education, environment, and the human prospect.* Washington, DC: Island Press.

Orr, D. (2009). *Down to the wire: Confronting climate collapse.* New York, NY: Oxford University Press.

Orr, J., & Klein, F. (1991). Instruction in critical thinking as a form of character education. *Journal of Curriculum and Supervision, 6,* 130–144.

Ortiz, V. Z., & Gonzalez, A. (1989). Validation of the short form of the WISC-R with accelerated and gifted Hispanic students. *Gifted Child Quarterly, 33,* 152–156.

Owens, J. (2011). Enlightenment and education in eighteenth century America: A platform for further study in higher education and the colonial shift. *Educational Studies, 47,* 527–544.

Oxford English Dictionary (Compact edition). (1971). London, UK: Oxford University Press. (Original work published 1928)

Oxley, D. (2005). Small learning communities: Extending and improving practice. *Principal Leadership, 6*(3), 44–48.

Page, B., Bartels, L., & Seawright, J. (2013). Democracy and the policy preferences of wealthy Americans. *Perspectives on Politics, 11*(1), 51–73.

Papierno, P. B., Ceci, S. J., Makel, M. C., & Williams, W. M. (2005). The nature and nurture of talent: A bioecological perspective on the ontogeny of exceptional abilities. *Journal for the Education of the Gifted, 28,* 312–332.

Parish, S. L. (2013). Why dismantling the safety net for children with disabilities and their families is a poor idea. *Health & Social Work, 38,* 195–198.

Parker, D. (1928, February 4). A good novel, and a great story. *New Yorker,* 74–77.

Parks, A. N., & Bridges-Rhoads, S. (2012). Overly scripted: Exploring the impact of a scripted literacy curriculum on a preschool teacher's instructional practices in mathematics. *Journal of Research in Childhood Education, 26,* 308–324. doi:10.1080/02568543.2012.684422

Parsad, B., Spiegelman, M., & Coopersmith, J. (2012). *Arts education in public elementary and secondary schools: 1999-2000 and 2009-2010.* Washington DC: National Center for Education Statistics. Retrieved from http://files.eric.ed.gov/fulltext/ED530715.pdf

Pascarella, E., Pierson, C., Wolniak, G., & Terenzini, P. (2004). First-generation college students: Additional evidence on college experiences and outcomes. *The Journal of Higher Education, 75,* 249–284.

Pascoe, P. (1996). Miscegenation law, court cases, and ideologies of "race" in twentieth-century America. *The Journal of American History, 83*(1), 44–96.

Patriotta, G. (2003). Sensemaking on the shop floor: Narratives of knowledge in organizations. *Journal of Management Studies, 40,* 349–375. doi:10.1111/1467-6486.00343

Pecheone, R., & Vasudeva, A. (2006). *Review of "Giving students the chaff: How to find and keep the teachers we need."* Boulder, CO: Education and the Public Interest Center & Education Policy Research Unit. Retrieved from http://nepc.colorado.edu/thinktank/review-giving-students-chaff-how-find-and-keep-teachers-we-need

References

Pendarvis, E., Howley, A., & Howley, C. (1990). *The abilities of gifted children*. Englewood Cliffs, NJ: Prentice Hall.

Pendarvis, E., & Wood, E. W. (2009). Eligibility of historically underrepresented students referred for gifted education in a rural school district. *Journal for the Education of the Gifted, 32,* 495–514.

Perfetti, C. (1986). Cognitive and linguistic components of reading ability. In B. Foorman & A. Siegel (Eds.), *Acquisition of reading skills* (pp. 1–41). Hillsdale, NJ: Erlbaum.

Perkins, D., Tishman, S., Ritchhart, R., Donis, K., & Andrade, A. (2000). Intelligence in the wild: A dispositional view of intellectual traits. *Educational Psychology Review, 12,* 269–293.

Peters, S. J., Matthews, M. S., McBee, M. T., & McCoach, D. B. (2014). *Beyond gifted education: Designing and implementing advanced academic programs*. Waco, TX: Prufrock Press.

Pettit, B., & Ewert, S. (2009). Employment gains and wage declines: The erosion of Black women's relative wages since 1980. *Demography, 46,* 469–492.

Pierce, D. R. (2001). *Student pathways through high school to college: Preschool through postsecondary*. Denver, CO: Education Commission of the States. Retrieved from http://files.eric.ed.gov/fulltext/ED468538.pdf

Piketty, T. (2014). *Capital in the twenty-first century*. (A. Goldhammer, Trans.). Cambridge, MA: Belknap Press.

Pinker, S. (1997). *How the mind works*. New York, NY: Norton.

Pipho, C. (1986). States support academic rigor. *Phi Delta Kappan, 68,* 189–190.

Pirsig, R. (1974). *Zen and the art of motorcycle maintenance*. New York, NY: Morrow.

Plato. (1871). *The republic* (B. Jowett, Trans.). Oxford, UK: Clarendon Press. Retrieved from http://www.gutenberg.org/cache/epub/1497/pg1497.txt. (Original work composed ca. 370 BCE)

Plessy v. Ferguson, 163 U.S. 537 (1896).

Podgursky, M., Monroe, R., & Watson, D. (2004). The academic quality of public school teachers: An analysis of entry and exit behavior. *Economics of Education Review, 23,* 507–518.

Pollock, M. (2004). *Colormute: Race talk dilemmas in an American school*. Princeton, NJ: Princeton University Press.

Popkewitz, T. S. (1997). The production of reason and power: Curriculum history and intellectual traditions. *Journal of Curriculum Studies, 29,* 131–164. doi:10.1080/002202797184107

Porter, R. E., Fusarelli, L. D., & Fusarelli, B. C. (2015). Implementing the Common Core: How educators interpret curriculum reform. *Educational Policy, 29*(1), 111–139.

Postman, N. (1985). *Amusing ourselves to death: Public discourse in the age of show business*. New York, NY: Viking Penguin.

Postman, N. (1992). *Technopoly: The surrender of culture to technology*. New York, NY: Knopf.

Postman, N. (1996). *The end of education*. New York, NY: Knopf.

Postman, N. (2006). *Amusing ourselves to death: Public discourse in the age of show business* (2nd ed.). New York, NY: Penguin Books.

Prawat, R. (1991). Conversations with self and settings: A framework for thinking about teacher empowerment. *American Educational Research Journal, 28,* 737–757.

Puaca, G. (2014). Imperatives for 'right' educational choices in Swedish educational policy. *Journal for Critical Education Policy Studies, 12*(1), 262–291.

Pufal-Struzik, I. (1999). Self-actualization and other personality dimensions as predictors of mental health in intellectually gifted students. *Roeper Review, 22*(1), 44–47.

Purdy, D. H. (1997). An economical, thorough, and efficient school system: The West Virginia School Building Authority "economy of scale" numbers. *Journal of Research in Rural Education, 13,* 170–182.

Putnam, H. (1990). *Realism with a human face*. Cambridge, MA: Harvard University Press.

Rank, M. R. (2005). *One nation underprivileged: Why poverty affects us all*. New York, NY: Oxford University Press.

Rank, M. R., Yoon, H. S., & Hirschl, T. A. (2003). American poverty as a structural failing: Evidence and arguments. *Journal of Sociology & Social Welfare, 30*(4), 3–29.

Ransome, P. (2011). Qualitative pedagogy versus instrumentalism: The antinomies of higher education learning and teaching in the United Kingdom. *Higher Education Quarterly, 65,* 206–223.

Ravenscroft, A. (2007). Promoting thinking and conceptual change with digital dialogue games. *Journal of Computer Assisted Learning, 23,* 453–465. doi:10.1111/j.1365-2729.2007.00232.x

Ravitch, D. (1993). Launching a revolution in standards and assessments. *Phi Delta Kappan, 74,* 767–772.

Ravitch, D. (2010). *The death and life of the great American school system: How testing and choice are undermining education*. New York, NY: Basic Books.

Ravitch, D. (2013). *Reign of error: The hoax of the privatization movement and the danger to America's public schools*. New York, NY: Knopf.

Rawls, J. (1999). *A theory of justice*. Cambridge, MA: Belknap Press.

Ray, B. (1992). *Marching to the beat of their own drum! A profile of home education research*. Paeonian Springs, VA: Home School Legal Defense Association.

Raywid, M. A. (1997). About replacing the comprehensive high school. *Educational Administration Quarterly, 33,* 541–5.

Read, H. (1967). *Art and alienation: The role of the artist in society*. New York, NY: Horizon Press.

References

Readings, B. (1996). *The university in ruins.* Cambridge, MA: Harvard University Press.

Reardon, S. F. (2013). The widening income achievement gap. *Educational Leadership 70*(8), 10–16.

Reardon, S. F., & Galindo, C. (2002). *Do high-stakes tests affect students' decisions to drop out of school? Evidence from NELS.* University Park, PA: Population Research Institute. Retrieved from http://www.eric.ed.gov/contentdelivery/servlet/ERICServlet?accno=ED482665

Reilly, N. (2016). The gluten-free diet: Recognizing fact, fiction, and fad. *Journal of Pediatrics, 175,* 206–210. doi:10.1016/j.jpeds.2016.04.014

Reis, S. M., Gentry, M., & Sunghee, P. (1995). *Extending the pedagogy of gifted education to all students* (RM95118). Storrs: University of Connecticut, The National Research Center on the Gifted and Talented. Retrieved from http://nrcgt.uconn.edu/wp-content/uploads/sites/953/2015/04/rm95118.pdf

Reisman, D. (1981). *On higher education: The academic enterprise in an era of rising student consumerism.* San Francisco, CA: Jossey-Bass.

Renfrew, C. (2007). *Prehistory: The making of the human mind.* London, Endgland: Weidenfeld & Nicholson.

Renzulli, J. (1978). What makes giftedness? Re-examining a definition. *Phi Beta Kappan, 60,* 180–184, 261.

Renzulli, J. S. (2012). Reexamining the role of gifted education and talent development for the 21st century: A four-part theoretical approach. *Gifted Child Quarterly, 56,* 150–159.

Renzulli, J. S., & Richards, S. (2000). *Addressing the needs of gifted middle school students* (Practitioners' Guide A0023). Storrs: University of Connecticut, The National Research Center on the Gifted and Talented. Retrieved from http://files.eric.ed.gov/fulltext/ED456574.pdf

Rexroth, K. (1966). *An autobiographical novel.* New York, NY: New Directions.

Rhoads, R. A. (2011). The U.S. research university as a global model: Some fundamental problems to consider. *Interactions: UCLA Journal of Education & Information Studies, 7*(2), 1–27.

Ricardo, D. (1817). *On the principles of political economy and taxation.* London, England: John Murray.

Rice, J. M. (1913). *The scientific management in education.* New York, NY: Hines, Noble & Eldredge.

Richards, I. A. (1942). *How to read a page: A course in effective writing, with an introduction to a hundred great words.* New York, NY: W.W. Norton.

Richards, J. (2012). Teacher stress and coping strategies: A national snapshot. *Educational Forum, 76,* 299–316.

Rigakos, G., & Ergul, A. (2011). Policing the industrial reserve army: An international study. *Crime, Law & Social Change, 56,* 329–371. doi:10.1007/s10611-011-9327-0

Riphahn, R. T., & Zibrowius, M. (2016). Apprenticeship, vocational training, and early labor market outcomes: Evidence from East and West Germany. *Education Economics, 24*(1), 33–57.

Robertson, F. (2007). Economies of scale for large school districts: A national study with local implications. *Social Science Journal, 44,* 620–629.

Robinson, L., Maldonado, N., & Whaley, J. (2014). *Perceptions about implementation of differentiated instruction.* Presented at the Mid-South Educational Research Annual Conference, Knoxville, TN. Retrieved from http://files.eric.ed.gov/fulltext/ED554312.pdf

Robinson, M. (2010). *Absence of mind: The dispelling of inwardness from the modern myth of the self.* New Haven, CT: Yale University Press.

Robinson, V. (2011). *Student-centered leadership.* San Francisco, CA: John Wiley & Sons.

Rocques, M., & Paternoster, R. (2011). Understanding the antecedents of the "school-to-jail" link: The relationship between race and school discipline. *Journal of Criminal Law & Criminology, 101,* 633–665.

Rodriguez, A. (1999). *Making Latino news: Race, language, class.* Thousand Oaks, CA: Sage.

Rogers, K. (2007). Lessons learned about educating the gifted and talented. *Gifted Child Quarterly, 10,* 17–39.

Rorty, R. (1989). *Contingency, irony, and solidarity.* Cambridge, MA: Cambridge University Press.

Rorty, R. (1997). *Philosophy and social hope.* New York, NY: Penguin.

Rose, M. (2004). *The mind at work: Valuing the intelligence of the American worker.* New York, NY: Viking Penguin.

Rose, M. (2009). *Why school? Rethinking education for all of us.* New York, NY: New Press.

Rose, M. (2011, Summer). Making sparks fly: How occupational education can lead to a love of learning for its own sake. *The American Scholar,* 35–43.

Rosen, C. (1998). *The classical style: Haydn, Mozart, Beethoven.* New York, NY: W.W. Norton.

Rosenbaum, J., Stephan, J., & Rosenbaum, J. (2010). Beyond one-size-fits-all college dreams: Alternative pathways to desirable careers. *American Educator, 34*(3), 2–23.

Ross, J. J. (1994). *The virtues of the family.* New York, NY: Free Press.

Roth, P. L., Bevier, C. A., Bobko, P., Switzer, F. S., & Tyler, P. (2001). Ethnic group differences in cognitive ability in employment and educational settings: A meta-analysis. *Personnel Psychology, 54,* 297–330.

References

Rothblatt, S. (2003). *The living arts: Comparative and historical reflections on liberal education. The academy in transition.* Washington, DC: Association of American Colleges and Universities. Retrieved from http://files.eric. ed.gov/fulltext/ED478297.pdf

Rousseau, J.-J. (1762). *Emile, ou de l'education.* The Hague, Netherlands: Jean Neaulme.

Rubenstein, R. (2003). *Aristotle's children: How Christians, Muslims, and jews rediscovered ancient wisdom and illuminated the middle ages.* Orlando, FL: Harcourt.

Rudner, L. M. (1999). Achievement and demographics of home school students. *Education Policy Analysis Archives, 7*(8), 1–33.

Rudolph, F. (1977). *Curriculum: A history of the American undergraduate course of study since 1636.* San Francisco, CA: Jossey-Bass.

Rury, J. L., & Hill, S. (2011). *The African American struggle for secondary schooling, 1940–1980: Closing the graduation gap.* New York, NY: Teachers College Press.

Russett, C. E. (1976). *Darwin in America: The intellectual response, 1865–1912.* San Francisco, CA: W. H. Freeman.

Rytivaara, A., & Vehkakoski, T. (2015). What is individual in individualised instruction? Five storylines of meeting individual needs at school. *International Journal of Educational Research, 73,* 12–22. doi:10.1016/j. ijer.2015.09.002

Sachs, J. (2011). *The price of civilization: Reawakening American virtue and prosperity.* New York, NY: Random House.

Sahlberg, P. P. (2006). Education reform for raising economic competitiveness. *Journal of Educational Change, 7,* 259–287. doi:10.1007/s10833-005-4884-6

Saltman, K. J. (2014). Neoliberalism and corporate school reform: "Failure" and "creative destruction." *Review of Education, Pedagogy & Cultural Studies, 36,* 249–259.

Saltman, K. J., & Gabbard, D. (Eds.). (2003). *Education as enforcement: The militarization and corporatization of schools.* New York, NY: Routledge.

Salvia, J., Ysseldyke, J., & Witmer, S. (2012). *Assessment in special and inclusive education.* Independence, KY: Cengage Learning.

Samuel, L. R. (2014). *The American middle class: A cultural history.* New York, NY: Routledge.

Santayana, G. (1913). *The winds of doctrine.* New York, NY: Scribners.

Sapon-Shevin, M. (1994). *Playing favorites: Gifted education and the disruption of community.* Albany, NY: State University of New York Press.

Sapon-Shevin, M. (2003). Equity, excellence, and school reform: Why is finding common ground so hard? In J. H. Borland (Ed.), *Rethinking gifted education* (pp. 127–142). New York, NY: Teachers College Press.

Saul, J. R. (1993). *Voltaire's bastards: The dictatorship of reason in the West*. New York, NY: Vintage Books.

Saunders, D. J. (1995). Did your mom eat your homework? Schools shift the blame for academic failure to parents. *Policy Review, 72,* 68–71.

Schaefer, R. J. (1967). *The school as a center of inquiry*. New York, NY: Harper & Row.

Scheffler, I. (1985). *Of human potential: An essay in the philosophy of education*. Boston, MA: Routledge & Kegan Paul.

Schiff, J. (2013). The varieties of thoughtlessness and the limits of thinking. *European Journal of Political Theory, 12,* 99–115. doi:10.1177/1474885111430616

Schlechty, P. (2002). *Working on the work: An action plan for teachers, principals, and superintendents*. San Francisco, CA: Jossey-Bass.

Schlechty, P. C. (2008). No community left behind. *Phi Delta Kappan, 89,* 552–559.

Schlechty, P. C., & Vance, V. S. (1981). Do academically able teachers leave education? The North Carolina case. *Phi Delta Kappan, 63,* 106–112.

Schor, J. (1991). *The overworked American: The unexpected decline of leisure*. New York, NY: Basic Books.

Schor, J. (2004). *Born to buy: The commercialized child and the new consumer culture*. New York, NY: Scribner.

Schulz, R., & Mandzuk, D. (2005). Learning to teach, learning to inquire: A 3-year study of teacher candidates' experiences. *Teaching and Teacher Education, 21,* 315–331.

Schwartz, N. (2013, March 3). Recovery in U.S. is lifting profits, but not adding jobs. *The New York Times*, p. A1. Retrieved from http://www.nytimes.com/2013/03/04/business/economy/corporate-profits-soar-as-worker-income-limps.html

Scott, D. (2014). Knowledge and the curriculum. *Curriculum Journal, 25*(1), 14–28.

Scott, J. (1998). *Seeing like a state: How certain schemes to improve the human condition have failed*. New Haven, CT: Yale University Press.

Scott, J. (2012). *Two cheers for anarchism: Six easy pieces on autonomy, dignity, and meaningful work and play*. Princeton, NJ: Princeton University Press.

Scott, J. C. (2006). The mission of the university: Medieval to postmodern transformations. *Journal of Higher Education, 77*(1), 1–39.

Secretary's Commission on Achieving Necessary Skills. (1991). *What work requires of schools: A SCANS report for America 2000*. Washington, DC: United States Department of Labor. Retrieved from http://files.eric.ed.gov/fulltext/ED332054.pdf

References

Sedlak, M., Wheeler, C. W., Pullin, D. C., & Cusick, P. A. (1986). *Selling students short: Classroom bargains and academic reform in the American high school.* New York, NY: Teachers College Press.

Senge, P. M. (1994). *The fifth discipline: The art and practice of the learning organization.* New York, NY: Doubleday.

Servage, L. (2009). Alternative and professional doctoral programs: What is driving the demand? *Studies in Higher Education, 34,* 765–779.

Servicemen's Readjustment Act of 1944, P.L. 78-346, 58 Stat. 284m.

Shaunessy, E., & Karnes, F. A. (2004). Instruments for measuring leadership in children and youth. *Gifted Child Today, 27*(1), 42–47.

Shava, S., Krasny, M. E., Tidball, K. G., & Zazu, C. (2010). Agricultural knowledge in urban and resettled communities: Applications to social-ecological resilience and environmental education. *Environmental Education Research, 16,* 575–589.

Shavit, Y., Arum, R., & Gamoran, A. (2004, August). *Expansion, differentiation and stratification in higher education: A comparative study of 15 countries.* Paper presented at the annual conference of the American Sociological Association, San Francisco, CA.

Shea, C. (1989). Pentagon vs. multinational capitalism: The political economy of the 1980s school reform movement. In C. Shea, E. Kahane, & P. Sola (Eds.), *The new servants of power: A critique of the 1980s school reform movement* (Contributions to the Study of Education, No. 28). New York, NY: Greenwood.

Shepard, L. (2003). The hazards of high-stakes testing. *Issues in Science and Technology, 19*(2), 53–58.

Shernoff, D. J., & Schmidt, J. A. (2008). Further evidence of an engagement-achievement paradox among U.S. high school students. *Journal of Youth and Adolescence, 37,* 564–580.

Shore, B. M., Cornell, D. G., Robinson, A., & Ward, V. S. (1991). *Recommended practices in gifted education: A critical analysis.* New York, NY: Teachers College Press.

Siegle, D., Wilson, H. E., & Little, C. A. (2013). A sample of gifted and talented educators attitudes about academic acceleration. *Journal of Advanced Academics, 24*(1), 27–51.

Sigurdson, K. T. (2013). Clark Kerr's multiversity and technology transfer in the modern American research university. *College Quarterly, 16*(2). Retrieved from http://collegequarterly.ca/2013-vol16-num02-spring/sigurdson.html

Silzer, R. (2010). Critical research issues in talent management. In R. Silzer & B. E. Dowell (Eds.), *Strategy-driven talent management: A leadership imperative* (pp. 767–780). San Francisco, CA: Jossey-Bass.

Sismondi, J. C. L. de. (1819). *Nouveaux principes d'économie politique; ou, de la richesse dans ses rapports avec la population* [New principles of political economy, or about wealth in its relationship to population]. Paris, France: Delaunay.

Sizer, T. (2013). *The new American high school*. San Francisco, CA: Jossey-Bass.

Skiba, R. (2014). The failure of zero tolerance. *Reclaiming Children and Youth, 22*(4), 27–33.

Skiba, R. J. (2000). *Zero tolerance, zero evidence: An analysis of school disciplinary practice*. Bloomington, IN: Indiana University Education Policy Center.

Skovsmose, O. (2010). Mathematics: A critical rationality? *Philosophy of Mathematics Education Journal, 25*. Retrieved from http://people.exeter.ac.uk/PErnest

Slaughter, S., & Rhoades, G. (2000, Spring/Summer). The neo-liberal university. *New Labor Forum, 6,* 73–79.

Sleeter, C. (2008). Equity, democracy, and neoliberal assaults on teacher education. *Teaching and Teacher Education, 24,* 1947–1957.

Slekar, T. D. (2009). Democracy denied: Learning to teach history in elementary school. *Teacher Education Quarterly, 36*(1), 95–110.

Smilie, K. D. (2012). Humanitarian and humanistic ideals: Charles W. Eliot, Irving Babbitt, and the American curriculum at the turn of the 20th century. *Journal of Thought, 47,* 63–84.

Smith, A. (1776). *An inquiry into the nature and causes of the wealth of nations* (Vol. 1–2). London, England: W. Strahan & T. Cadell.

Snow, C. P. (1993). *The two cultures*. London, England: Cambridge University Press. (Original work published 1959)

Sohasky, K. E. (2016). Safeguarding the interests of the state from defective delinquent girls. *Journal of the History of the Behavioral Sciences, 52*(1), 20–40. doi:10.1002/jhbs.21765

Sosniak, L. A. (2006). Retrospective interviews in the study of expertise and expert performance. In K. A. Ericcson, N. Charness, P. J. Feltovich, & R. Hoffman (Eds.), *The Cambridge handbook of expertise and expert performance* (pp. 287–301). New York, NY: Cambridge University Press.

Sosniak, L. A., & Gabelko, N. H. (2008). *Every child's right: Academic talent development by choice, not chance*. New York, NY: Teachers College Press.

Southern, T. W., & Jones, E. D. (2015). Types of acceleration: Dimensions and issues. In S. G. Assouline, N. Colangelo, J. VanTassel-Baska, & A. Lupkowski-Shoplik (Eds.), *A nation empowered: Evidence trumps the excuses holding back America's brightest students* (pp. 9–18). Iowa City: University of Iowa, The Connie Belin & Jacqueline N. Blank International Center for Gifted Education and Talent Development. Retrieved from http://www.accelerationinstitute.org/nation_empowered

Spann, G., & Davison, B. (2004, August). *Anti-intellectualism in the new century*. Paper presented at the annual conference of the American Sociological Association, San Francisco, CA.

References

Speirs Neumeister, K. L., Williams, K. K., & Cross, T. L. (2007). Perfectionism in gifted high-school students: Responses to academic challenge. *Roeper Review, 29*(5), 11–18.

Speirs Neumeister, K. L., Williams, K. K., & Cross, T. L. (2009). Gifted high school students' perspectives on the development of perfectionism. *Roeper Review, 31,* 198–206. doi:10.1080/02783190903177564

Speirs Neumeister, K. L., Adams, C., Pierce, R., Cassady, J. C., & Dixon, F. A. (2007). Fourth-grade teachers' perceptions of giftedness: Implications for identifying and serving diverse gifted students. *Journal for the Education of the Gifted, 30,* 479–499.

Spillman, R. (2012, October 15). On William Faulkner's *As I Lay Dying* [Blog post]. Retrieved from http://www.pen.org/nonfiction/william-faulkner%E2%80%99s-i-lay-dying

Spindler, G. (1988). *Doing the ethnography of schooling.* Long Grove, IL: Waveland Press.

Sponsler, B. (2009). *The role and relevance of rankings in higher education policymaking.* Washington, DC: Institute for Higher Education Policy. Retrieved from http://www.ihep.org/sites/default/files/uploads/docs/pubs/issue_brief_the_role_and_relevance_of_rankings.pdf

Spring, J. (1986). *The American school 1642–1985.* New York, NY: Longman.

Spring, J. (1988). *The sorting machine: National educational policy since 1945.* White Plains, NY: Longman.

Spring, J. (1994). *Deculturalization and the struggle for equality: A brief history of the education of dominated cultures in the United States.* New York, NY: McGraw-Hill.

Spring, J. (2013). *American education* (16th ed.). New York, NY: McGraw-Hill.

Stanley, J. (1976). *Brilliant youth: Improving the quality and speed of their education.* Presented at the annual meeting of the American Psychological Association, Washington, DC. Retrieved from http://www.eric.ed.gov/ERICWebPortal/contentdelivery/servlet/ERICServlet?accno=ED136536

Stanley, J. (2004). Foreword. In M. Gross & H. Van Vliet, *Radical acceleration of highly gifted children.* Sydney, Australia: Gifted Education Research, Resource, and Information Center, University of New South Wales.

Stanley, J. C. (1978). Radical acceleration: Recent educational innovation at JHU. *The Gifted Child Quarterly, 22*(1), 62–67.

Stanley, J. C. (1986, April). *The urgent need for an academic focus.* Paper presented at the annual conference of the American Educational Research Association, San Francisco, CA. (ERIC Document Reproduction Service No. ED277205)

Stanovich, K. E., & West, R. F. (1997). Reasoning independently of prior belief and individual differences in actively open-minded thinking. *Journal of Educational Psychology, 89,* 342–357.

Stark, H. E. (2005). Philosophy as wonder. *Dialogue & Universalism, 15*(1/2), 133–140.

Stearns, R. M. (2009). Back to the future: For the job market, forget the predictions. *American Libraries, 40*(8–9), 44.

Steenbergen-Hu, S., & Moon, S. M. (2011). The effects of acceleration on high-ability learners: A meta-analysis. *Gifted Child Quarterly, 55*(1), 39–53.

Stehr, N., & Grundmann, R. (2011). *The knowledge and power of expertise.* New York, NY: Routledge.

Stehr, N., & Mast, J. (2011). The modern slaves: Specialized knowledge and democratic governance. *Society, 48*(1), 36–40.

Stern, W. (1912). *Die psychologischen methoden der intelligenzprüfung: Und deren anwendung an schulkindern.* Berlin, Germany: J.A. Barth.

Sternberg, R. (1995). *A triarchic approach to giftedness.* Storrs: University of Connecticut, The National Research Center on the Gifted and Talented.

Stewart, V. (2012). *A world class education: Learning from international models of excellence and innovation.* Alexandria, VA: ASCD.

Stigler, J., & Hiebert, J. (1999). *The teaching gap: Best ideas from the world's teachers for improving education in the classroom.* New York, NY: The Free Press.

Storr, A. (1988). *Solitude: A return to the self.* New York, NY: The Free Press.

Story, R. (1980). *Forging of an aristocracy: Harvard and the Boston upper class, 1800–1870.* Middletown, CT: Wesleyan University Press.

Stotsky, S. E. (2000). *What's at stake in the K–12 standards wars: A primer for educational policy makers.* New York, NY: Peter Lang.

Strang, D. (1987). The administrative transformation of American education: School district consolidation, 1938–1980. *Administrative Science Quarterly, 32,* 352–366.

Sturges, K. (Ed.). (2015). *Reforming schools in the age of neoliberalism.* Boston, MA: Sense Publishers.

Subotnik, R. F., Olszewski-Kubilius, P., & Worrell, F. C. (January, 2011). Rethinking giftedness and gifted education: A proposed direction forward based on psychological science. *Psychological Science in the Public Interest, 12*(1), 3–54.

Subotnik R. F., & Rickoff, R. (2010). Should eminence based on outstanding innovation be the goal of gifted education and talent development? Implications for policy and research. *Learning and Individual Differences, 20,* 358–364.

Surowiecki, J. (2004). *The wisdom of crowds: Why the many are smarter than the few and how collective wisdom shapes business, economies, societies and nations.* New York, NY: Doubleday.

References

Swisher, K., & Deyhle, D. (1987). Styles of learning and learning of styles: Educational conflicts for American Indian/Alaskan Native youth. *Journal of Multilingual and Multicultural Development, 8,* 345–360.

Taba, H. (1963). Learning by discovery: Psychological and educational rationale. *Elementary School Journal, 63,* 308–316.

Taggart, J. (1980). *Public perceptions of the importance of selected educational goals for elementary-secondary education in Idaho* (Unpublished doctoral dissertation). University of Idaho, Moscow. Retrieved from ProQuest Dissertations and Theses Database. (UMI No. 8100394)

Tam, H. (1998). *Communitarianism: A new agenda for politics and citizenship.* New York: New York University Press.

Tan, E. (2014). Human capital theory: A holistic criticism. *Review of Educational Research, 84,* 411–445.

Taniguchi, H., & Kaufman, G. (2005). Degree completion among nontraditional college students. *Social Science Quarterly, 86,* 913–927.

Tanner, L. N. (2000). Critical issues in curriculum revisited. *Educational Forum, 65*(1), 16–21.

Tarlau, R. (2014). From a language to a theory of resistance: Critical pedagogy, the limits of "framing," and social change. *Educational Theory, 64,* 369–392.

Tartaglia, J. (2016). Is philosophy all about the meaning of life? *Metaphilosophy, 47,* 283–303. doi:10.1111/meta.12176

Teixeira, R., & Rotta, T. (2012). Valueless knowledge-commodities and financialization: productive and financial dimensions of capital autonomization. *Review of Radical Political Economics, 44,* 448–467.

Terkel, S. (1974). *Working: People talk about what they do all day long and how they feel about what they do.* New York, NY: Pantheon Books.

Terman, L. (1925). *Mental and physical traits of a thousand gifted children: Genetic studies of genius* (Vol. 1). Stanford, CA: Stanford University Press.

Terman, L., & Oden, M. (1959). *The gifted child grows up: Genetic studies of genius* (Vol. 5). Stanford, CA: Stanford University Press.

Terras, M. M., & Ramsay, J. (2015). Massive Open Online Courses (MOOCs): Insights and challenges from a psychological perspective. *British Journal of Educational Technology, 46,* 472–487.

Terzian, S. G. (2008). "Adventures in science": Casting scientifically talented youth as national resources on American radio, 1942–1958. *Paedagogica Historica: International Journal of the History of Education, 44,* 309–325.

Thacker, L. (2008). Pulling rank: A plan to help students with college choice in an age of rankings. *New England Journal of Higher Education, 22*(4), 15–16.

Thadani, V., Cook, M. S., Griffis, K., Wise, J. A., & Blakey, A. (2010). The possibilities and limitations of curriculum-based science inquiry interventions for challenging the "pedagogy of poverty." *Equity and Excellence in Education, 43*(1), 21–37. doi:10.1080/10665680903408908

Thagard, P. (2010). *The brain and the meaning of life.* Princeton, NJ: Princeton University Press.

Thanksgiving Statement Group. (1984). *Developing character: Transmitting knowledge.* Posen, IL: Author. (ED251381)

Theobald, P. (2009). *Education now: How rethinking America's past can change its future.* Boulder, CO: Paradigm.

Theoharis, G. (2009). *The school leaders our children deserve: Seven keys to equity, social justice, and school reform.* New York, NY: Teachers College Press.

Thomas, K., Singh, P., Klopfenstein, K., & Henry, T. (2013). Access to high school arts education: Why student participation matters as much as course availability. *Education Policy Analysis Archives, 21*(83), 1–20. Retrieved from http://epaa.asu.edu/ojs/article/view/1224

Thompson, D. (2013, December 20). *The government is horrible at predictions (so is everybody else).* Retrieved from http://www.theatlantic.com/business/archive/2013/12/the-government-is-horrible-at-predictions-so-is-everybody-else/282558

Thompson, E. P. (1963). *The making of the English working class.* London, England: Gollancz.

Thompson, R. A., & Haskins, R. (2014). Early stress gets under the skin: Promising initiatives to help children facing chronic adversity. *Future of Children, 24*(1), 1–6.

Thompson, P. (2002). *The accidental theorist: The double helix of everyday life.* New York, NY: Peter Lang.

Thomson, D. L. (2010). Beyond the classroom walls: Teachers' and students' perspectives on how online learning can meet the needs of gifted students. *Journal of Advanced Academics, 21,* 662–712.

Tienken, C. (2012). Neoliberalism, Social Darwinism, and consumerism masquerading as school reform. *Interchange, 43,* 295–316.

Tierney, W. G., & Bensimon, E. M. (1996). *Promotion and tenure: Community and socialization in academe.* Albany: State University of New York Press.

Tiller, T. (2000). Keynote address: Every other day. In *Issues affecting rural communities 2* (pp. 218–224). Nanaimo, British Columbia, Canada: Malarpina University College, Rural Communities Research and Development Centre. (ERIC Document Reproduction Service No. ED455064) Retrieved from http://files.eric.ed.gov/fulltext/ED455064.pdf

Tobbell, D. A. (2014). "Coming to grips with the nursing question": The politics of nursing education reform in 1960s America. *Nursing History Review: Official Journal of The American Association for the History of Nursing, 22,* 37–60.

References

Tolstoy, L. (1878). Анна Каренина (Anna Karenina). Moscow, Russia: Tip. T. Ris.

Tolstoy, L. (1889). *Так что ж нам делать?* (What then must we do?). Geneva, Switzerland: M. K. Elpidin.

Tomasi, J. (2012). *Free market fairness*. Princeton, NJ: Princeton University Press.

Tomlinson, C. A. (1999). *The differentiated classroom: Responding to the needs of all learners*. Alexandria, VA: Association for Supervision and Curriculum Development.

Toossi, M. (2012). Labor force projections to 2020: A more slowly growing workforce. *Monthly Labor Review, 135*(1), 43–64.

Tough, P. (2014, May 15). Who gets to graduate? *The New York Times*. Retrieved from http://www.nytimes.com/2014/05/18/magazine/who-gets-to-graduate.html?_r=0

Towers, J. (2012). Administrative supports and curricular challenges: New teachers enacting and sustaining inquiry in schools. *Canadian Journal of Education, 35*(1), 259–278.

Traore, R. (2007). Implementing Afrocentricity: Connecting students of African descent to their cultural heritage. *Journal of Pan African Studies, 1*(10), 1–17.

Trumpbour, J. (1989). *How Harvard rules: Reason in the service of ideology*. Boston, MA: South End Press.

Truxaw, M. P., Casa, T. M., & Adelson, J. L. (2011). A stance toward inquiry: An investigation of preservice teachers' confidence regarding educational inquiry. *Teacher Education Quarterly, 38*, 69–95.

Tsuru, T. (1991). The reserve army effect, unions, and nominal wage growth. *Industrial Relations, 30*, 251–270.

Tutt, K. (2014). U.S. arts education requirements. *Arts Education Policy Review, 115*(3), 93–97.

Tuttle, F. B., & Brecker, L. A. (1980). *Characteristics and identification of gifted and talented students*. Washington, DC: National Education Association. Retrieved from http://files.eric.ed.gov/fulltext/ED197519.pdf

Tyack, D. (1974). *The one best system: A history of American urban education*. Cambridge, MA: Harvard University Press.

Tyack, D., & Cuban, L. (1995). *Tinkering toward utopia: A century of public school reform*. Cambridge, MA: Harvard University Press.

Tye, B. (2000). *Hard truths: Uncovering the deep structure of schooling*. New York, NY: Teachers College Press.

Tyson-Bernstein, H. (1988). *A conspiracy of good intentions: America's textbook fiasco*. Washington, DC: Council for Basic Education.

Urahn, S. K., Currier, E., Elliott, D., Wechsler, L., Wilson, D., & Colbert, D. (2012). *Pursuing the American dream: Economic mobility across generations*.

Washington, DC: Pew Charitable Trusts. Retrieved from http://www.pewtrusts.org/~/media/legacy/uploadedfiles/wwwpewtrustsorg/reports/economic_mobility/pursuingamericandreampdf.pdf

Urban, W. (2013). Anti-progressivism in education: Past and present. *International Journal of Progressive Education, 9*(1), 14–24.

U.S. Commission on Civil Rights. (1977). *Window dressing on the set: Women and minorities in television.* Washington, DC: Author. Retrieved from https://www.law.umaryland.edu/marshall/usccr/documents/cr12t23.pdf

Valli, L., & Buese, D. (2007). The changing roles of teachers in an era of high-stakes accountability. *American Educational Research Journal, 44,* 519–558.

Vance, V. S., & Schlechty, P. C. (1982). The distribution of academic ability in the teaching force: Policy implications. *Phi Delta Kappan, 64,* 22–27.

van der Merwe, L., & Habron, J. (2015). A conceptual model of spirituality in music education. *Journal of Research in Music Education, 63*(1), 47–69.

Van Maele, D., & Van Houtte, M. (2015). Trust in school: A pathway to inhibit teacher burnout? *Journal of Educational Administration, 53*(1), 93–115. doi:10.1108/JEA-02-2014-0018

Vann, A. (1988). Let's give values clarification another chance. A special report: Developing character. *Principal, 68*(2), 15–16, 18.

VanTassel-Baska, J. (2009). Myth 12: Gifted programs should stick out like a sore thumb. *Gifted Child Quarterly, 53,* 266–268.

VanTassel-Baska, J. (2015). Arguments for and against the Common Core State Standards. *Gifted Child Today, 38*(1), 60–62. doi:10.1177/1076217514556535

VanTassel-Baska, J., & Little, C. A. (2017). *Content-based curriculum for high-ability learners* (3rd ed.). Waco, TX: Prufrock.

Veblen, T. (2015). *The higher learning in America: A memorandum on the conduct of universities by business men.* Baltimore, MD: Johns Hopkins University Press. (Original work published 1918)

Vermeir, K. (2013). Scientific research: Commodities or commons? *Science & Education, 22,* 2485–2510. doi:10.1007/s11191-012-9524-y

Veysey, L. (1965). *The emergence of the American university.* Chicago, IL: University of Chicago Press.

Viereck, G. S. (1929, October 26). What life means to Einstein. *The Saturday Evening Post, 17,* 110, 113–114, 117.

Vigneault, M. (2012). Are you qualified? *Women's Studies, 41,* 891–903. doi:10.1080/00497878.2012.718622

Vitale, E. (2010). Philosophical reason and human rights in the thought of Norberto Bobbio. *Iris: European Journal of Philosophy & Public Debate, 2,* 385–400.

References

Volante, L. (2004). Teaching to the test: what every educator and policy-maker should know. *Canadian Journal of Educational Administration and Policy, 35,* 1–6.

Waitoller, F. R., & Kozleski, E. B. (2015). No stone left unturned: Exploring the convergence of New Capitalism in inclusive education in the U.S. *Education Policy Analysis Archives, 23*(37), 1–33.

Walker, B., & Mehr, M. (1992). *The courage to achieve: Why America's brightest women struggle to fulfill their promise.* New York, NY: Simon & Schuster.

Wallace, A. (1986). *The prodigy.* New York, NY: E. P. Dutton.

Walsh, D. (2015, May 18). Fake diplomas, real cash: Pakistani company Axact recaps millions. *The New York Times,* A1. Retrieved from http://www.ny times.com/2015/05/18/world/asia/fake-diplomas-real-cash-pakistani-company-axact-reaps-millions-columbiana-barkley.html?emc=eta1

Walsh, K. (2001). *Teacher certification reconsidered: Stumbling for quality.* Baltimore, MD: Abell Foundation.

Walters, P. B., & Lareau, A. (2009). Education research that matters: Influence, scientific rigor, and policymaking. In P. B. Walters, A. Lareau, & S. Ranis (Eds.), *Education research on trial: Policy reform and the call for scientific rigor* (pp. 197–220). New York, NY: Routledge.

Ward, S. C., & Connolly, R. (2008). Let them eat Shakespeare: Prescribed authors and the national curriculum. *Curriculum Journal, 19,* 293–307.

Warikoo, N., & Carter, P. (2009). Cultural explanations for racial and ethnic stratification in academic achievement: A call for a new and improved theory. *Review of Educational Research, 79*(1), 366–394.

Warnick, B. (2015). Against the "love of reading" as an educational aim. *Philosophical Studies in Education, 46,* 6–17.

Watanabe, M. (2007). Displaced teacher and state priorities in a high-stakes accountability context. *Educational Policy, 21,* 311–368.

Wayman, J. C., Cho, V., Jimerson, J. B., & Spikes, D. D. (2012). District-wide effects on data use in the classroom. *Education Policy Analysis Archives, 20*(25). Retrieved from http://epaa.asu.edu/ojs/article/view/979

Webb, C. (1993, March). *What is meant by the term, "thoughtfulness in schools"?* Paper presented at the Annual Conference on Creating the Quality School, Oklahoma City, OK. Retrieved from http://files.eric.ed.gov/full-text/ED358536.pdf

Weber, E. (1976). *Peasants into Frenchmen: The modernization of rural France, 1870–1914.* Stanford, CA: Stanford University Press.

Weiler, D. (1978). The alpha children: California's brave new world for the gifted. *Phi Delta Kappan, 60,* 185–187.

Weissglass, J. (2012). Listen first, then teach: Laying a foundation of respect in classrooms will enable teachers to learn from students even as the students learn from teachers. *Phi Delta Kappan, 93*(6), 29–33.

Weizenbaum, J. (1976). *Computer power and human reason: From judgment to calculation*. New York, NY: W. H. Freeman.

Westheimer, J. (2006). Politics and patriotism in education. *Phi Delta Kappan, 87,* 608–620.

What Students Want from Teachers. (2008). *Educational Leadership, 66*(3), 48–51.

Whitaker, S. (2015). Are millennials with student loans upwardly mobile? *Economic Commentary, 2015*(12), 1–5.

White, J. (2009). Education and a meaningful life. *Oxford Review of Education, 35,* 423–435.

White, J. (2011). *Exploring well-being in schools: A guide to making children's lives more fulfilling*. Abingdon, England: Routledge.

Whitehead, A. (1929). *The aims of education and other essays*. New York, NY: Macmillan.

Whitmore, J. (1980). *Giftedness, conflict, and underachievement*. Boston, MA: Allyn & Bacon.

Whitty, G. (2010). Revisiting school knowledge: Some sociological perspectives on new curricula. *European Journal of Education, 45*(1, Part 1), 28–45.

Wilcox, K. (1982). Differential socialization in the classroom: Implications for equal opportunity. In G. Spindler (Ed.), *Doing the ethnography of schooling* (pp. 268–309). New York, NY: CBS College Books.

Wilder, C. S. (2013). *Ebony and ivory: Race, slavery, and the troubled history of America's universities*. New York, NY: Bloomsbury Press.

Wiley, J., & Goldstein, D. (1991). Sex, handedness, and allergy: Are they related to academic giftedness? *Journal for the Education of the Gifted, 14,* 412–422.

Wiliam, D. (2010). Standardized testing and school accountability. *Educational Psychologist, 45,* 107–122.

Wilkerson, I. (2010). *The warmth of other suns: The epic story of America's great migration*. New York, NY: Random House.

Williams, J. H. (2005). Cross-national variations in rural mathematics achievement: A descriptive overview. *Journal of Research in Rural Education, 20*(5), 1–18.

Williams, J. H. (2014). *(Re)Constructing memory: School textbooks and the imagination of the nation*. Boston, MA: Sense Publishers.

Williams, R. (1973). *The country and the city*. London, England: Verso.

Williams, R. (1976). *Keywords: A vocabulary of culture and society*. New York, NY: Oxford University Press.

Williams, R. (1989). *The politics of modernism*. London, England: Verso.

Williams, R. (2001). Culture is ordinary. In J. Higgins (Ed.), *The Raymond Williams reader* (pp. 10–24). Oxford, England: Blackwell Publishers. (Original work published 1958)

References

Williams, W. A. (1969). *The roots of the modern American empire*. New York, NY: Vintage.

Willie, M. (2012). Taxing and tuition: A legislative solution to growing endowments and the rising costs of a college degree. *Brigham Young University Law Review, 2012,* 1665–1704.

Willis, P. (1977). *Learning to labor: How working class kids get working class jobs*. New York, NY: Columbia University Press.

Wilshire, B. (1990). *The moral collapse of the university: Professionalism, purity, and alienation*. Albany: State University of New York Press.

Winchester, I. (1987). Literacy and intellect. *Interchange, 18*(1), 23–31.

Wirth, A. (1970). *The vocational-liberal studies controversy between John Dewey and others: 1900–1917*. St Louis, MO: Washington University Institute of Education. Retrieved from http://files.eric.ed.gov/fulltext/ED051002.pdf

Wolf, M. K., Yuan, W., Blood, I., & Huang, B. H. (2014). Investigating the language demands in the Common Core State Standards for English language learners: A comparison study of standards. *Middle Grades Research Journal, 9*(1), 35–52.

Wolfe, P. (2010). *Brain matters: Translating research into classroom practice* (2nd ed.). Alexandria, VA: ASCD, 2010.

Wood, L., & Hendricks, M. (2009, May). *Media representations of Appalachian poverty: Culture or capital; corruption or coal?* Paper presented at the annual conference of the International Communication Association, Chicago, IL.

Wood, L., & Howley, A. (2012). Dividing at an early age: The hidden digital divide in Ohio elementary schools. *Learning, Media and Technology, 37*(1), 20–39.

Woodrum, A. (2004). State-mandated testing and cultural resistance in Appalachian schools: Competing values and expectations. *Journal of Research in Rural Education, 19*(1). Retrieved from http://jrre.vmhost.psu.edu/wp-content/uploads/2014/02/19-1.pdf

Woolnough, B. E. (2000). Authentic science in schools? An evidence-based rationale. *Physics Education, 35,* 293–300. doi:10.1088/0031-9120/35/4/14

Wright, E. O. (1985). *Classes*. London, England: Verso.

Wright, E. O. (1997). *Class counts: Comparative studies in class analysis*. Cambridge, England: Cambridge University Press.

Wright, S. (1994). *The anthropology of organizations*. London, England: Routledge.

Wuthrick, M. A. (1990). Blue jays win! Crows go down in defeat. *Phi Delta Kappan, 71*(7), 553–556.

Wyatt, I., & Hecker, D. (2006). Occupational changes during the 20th century. *Monthly Labor Review, 129*(3), 35–57.

Wyckoff, J., & Naples, M. (2000). Educational finance to support high learning standards: A synthesis. *Economics of Education Review, 19,* 305–318.

Wynne, E. (1988). Balancing character development and academics in the elementary school. *Phi Delta Kappan, 69,* 424–426.

Yogev, E., & Michaeli, N. (2011). Teachers as society-involved "organic intellectuals": Training teachers in a political context. *Journal of Teacher Education, 62,* 312–324.

Yoon, H. S. (2015). Assessing children in kindergarten: The narrowing of language, culture and identity in the testing era. *Journal of Early Childhood Literacy, 15,* 364–393.

Young, T. A. (1990). Alternatives to ability grouping in reading. *Reading Horizons, 30,* 169–183.

Young, T. A., & McCullough, D. (1992). Looking out for low-achieving readers. *Reading Horizons, 32,* 394–402.

Zeichner, K., & Gore, J. (1990). Teacher socialization. In W. R. Houston, M. Haberman, & J. Sikula (Eds.), *Handbook of research on teacher education* (pp. 329–348). New York, NY: Macmillan.

Zeidner, M., & Shani-Zinovitch, I. (2011). Do academically gifted and nongifted students differ on the big-five and adaptive status? Some recent data and conclusions. *Personality and Individual Differences, 51,* 566–570.

Zembylas, M. (2008). Trauma, justice and the politics of emotion: The violence of sentimentality in education. *Discourse: Studies in The Cultural Politics of Education, 29*(1), 1–17.

Zhao, Y. (2009). Comments on the Common Core standards initiative. *AASA Journal of Scholarship and Practice, 6*(3), 46–54.

Zinn, H. (2003). *A people's history of the United States.* New York, NY: HarperCollins.

Zolbrod, P. G., & Willink, R. S. (1996). *Weaving a world: Textiles and the Navajo way of seeing.* Albuquerque: Museum of New Mexico Press.

About the Authors

Craig Howley, Ed.D., has studied educational scale, rural education, intellect and talent development, mathematics education, and the relationship between culture, political economy, and schooling. Retired from Ohio University, he currently conducts evaluation and research for WordFarmers Associates (low-incidence sensory disabilities, paraprofessionals, and inclusive leadership). He is also part of a team analyzing transcripts of interviews with freethinking K–12 teachers (partly supported by a Spencer grant). Previously he directed an ERIC Clearinghouse and the research initiative of a National Science Foundation-funded center (ACCLAIM) that studied rural mathematics education. As an adjunct faculty member at the university, he taught courses on rural education, leadership, and policy, and directed dissertations. His undergraduate degree is in comparative literature, his master's degree in gifted education, and his Ed.D. in school administration (West Virginia University). He has authored or coauthored 27 books or book chapters and 60 peer-reviewed research articles. He lives with Aimee and Uncle Tristan (a gifted dachshund) on a small farm in rural Ohio. He visits rural France often, with his children and grandchildren.

Aimee Howley, Ph.D., founder and lead researcher for WordFarmers Associates, has a broad background in educational research, evaluation, and policy studies. She is also professor emerita at Ohio University, where she served as a faculty member in the Educational Studies Department and Senior Associate Dean of the Patton College of Education. Aimee Howley's research explores the intersection between social context and educational practice, and she has used both quantitative and qualitative methods to investigate a wide range of questions relating to education for diverse learners (including intellectually talented students), rural education, education reform, and school leadership. Dr. Howley has authored or coauthored five books, numerous book chapters, and more than

60 refereed journal articles. Prior to her work at Ohio University, Dr. Howley served as a faculty member and Associate Dean of the College of Education and Human Services at Marshall University. Her earlier work as a K–12 teacher and special education administrator provided opportunities for direct service to exceptional students, including those with intellectual talents.

Edwina D. Pendarvis, professor emeritus in the College of Education at Marshall University, coordinated Marshall's gifted education program from 1979 to 2004 and directed the university's Center for Academic Excellence from 2004 to 2006. She began her career in gifted education as a teacher of gifted students in Florida, from 1971 to 1974, after completing a master's degree in the field at the University of South Florida under the guidance of Dorothy Sisk, an early advocate for gifted education as special education. From 1974 to 1979, she directed the Professional Development Unit at the Kentucky Bureau of Education for Exceptional Children, while working toward a doctoral degree at the University of Kentucky. Gifted underachievers, how to identify them, and how to support development of their abilities have been the focus of her teaching, research, and advocacy. Since retirement from Marshall, she has worked on professional development projects with the West Virginia Department of Education, Ohio University, and the Ohio Center for Deafblind Education—usually in collaboration with her friends and colleagues, Aimee and Craig Howley.